Social Order through Contracts

Jian Qu

Social Order through Contracts

A Study of the Qingshui River Manuscripts

Springer

Jian Qu
Department of Law
College of Humanities and Development Studies
China Agricultural University
Beijing, China

ISBN 978-981-33-4946-9 ISBN 978-981-33-4947-6 (eBook)
https://doi.org/10.1007/978-981-33-4947-6

This Springer imprint is published by the registered company Springer Nature Singapore Pte Ltd.
The registered company address is: 152 Beach Road, #21-01/04 Gateway East, Singapore 189721, Singapore

Acknowledgments

The long story of this book started 10 years ago, when I entered the university library and came across a published collection of contracts from a remote village called Wendou. A few months after I put down the book, I arrived at the village: first by taking a train, then a long-distance bus, a motor tricycle, a truck, a boat, and finally after climbing up the mountain on foot. At that time, I would not have thought that, in the next few years, such a journey would become an almost annual event for me and the villagers' greetings would gradually change from "welcome" to "when will you come back?" I had also never thought that the starting point of these "journeys home" would change in the coming years from Chongqing to Beijing, then to Paris, and then, finally, to Heidelberg.

As the academic offspring of these journeys, this book was submitted to Heidelberg University as a doctoral dissertation supervised by Professor Enno Giele and Professor Joachim Kurtz. I am very fortunate to have had Professor Giele as my *Doktorvater*, and I am truly grateful for his insightful guidance, unstinting support, and consistent encouragement throughout my studies in this beautiful German town. I am also very indebted to my second advisor, Professor Kurtz, for his valuable help and suggestions to me and my dissertation. Likewise, I would like to sincerely thank Professor Michael Radich for chairing my *Disputation* on August 20, 2020.

In writing this book, I have also benefited enormously from many people and institutions. My profound thanks go, among others, to Thies Staack, Nick Vogt, Sun Hui, Tong Chun Fung, and Maxim Korolkov at Heidelberg University, Professor Hsing I-tien and Li Ren-Yuan at Academia Sinica, Professor Gao Hongjun, Professor Gao Qicai, Professor Lu Nan, and Chen Xixi at Tsinghua University, Professors Stefan Vogenauer, Thomas Duve, and Li Fupeng at the Max Planck Institute for European Legal History, Yoshiyuki Aihara at the Toyo Bunko Research Department, Joel Wing-Lun at Harvard University, Professor Jérôme Bourgon at the Lyon Institute of East Asian Studies, Professor Alain Arrault at the French School of the Far East (EFEO), Wang Zongxun, Wang Kui, and Zhang Jiyuan in the Jinping County Government, Professors Chen Jinquan, Xie Hui, Xu Xiaoguang, Pan Zhicheng, Miao Wenlong, Liu Li, Chen Wei, Zhao Jing, Li Bin, Wu Caimao, Long Zejiang, Jiang Ming, and Yang Yougeng at various universities and research institutes in China, as well as the Jinping County Archives, the National Science Library, Chinese Academy of

Sciences, the First Historical Archives of China, and the Max Planck Institute for Comparative Public Law and International Law, for their support in multiple ways. Special thanks also go to Huang Xiaoliu and Jiang Dabang and many other villagers in Wendou and its surrounding villages for hosting me generously as a member of their community.

I am grateful for the financial assistance from the China Scholarship Council, the Max Weber Foundation, the Max Planck Society, the EFEO, the Centre for Studies on Modern and Contemporary China (CECMC), and the German Academic Exchange Service (DAAD).

Finally and most significantly, I thank my parents. You have always been my strength.

About This Book

Contracts in the form of written and ritualized agreements played a conspicuous, albeit complicated, role in the daily lives of Chinese people during the eighteenth and nineteenth centuries. However, the extensive contract practices which are recorded from this time present a puzzle. In, and in many cases beyond, the fields of civil and commercial matters, written contracts were extremely widely used in a society with "shallow government" and, from a legal positivist perspective, largely in the absence of national statutory law. In other words, the society was well organized not because of a strong government and bureaucratic system or sophisticated statutory laws, but by means of the successful operation of numerous contracts, which, in many circumstances, merely had limited legal enforcement. This raises the question of how and why such a society with few laws but many contracts, i.e. the Hobbesian, "words without sword," could maintain a well-functioning social system.

The interaction between contracts and social order is particularly evident in the Qingshui River region, which was a frontier area with even less effective governmental and legal control than the norm, but which possessed a very prosperous economy in Southwest China during the Qing dynasty. By taking the Qingshui River Manuscripts, which refer to a large number of Ming-Qing manuscripts found in some remote Miao villages of the region, as the core source, three interrelated questions related to the contract, what it was and how and why it worked, are explained in this work at length. Firstly, an unambiguous definition, as well as a more theoretical tripartite structure, of the contract in the historical context is offered. Secondly, the workings of the two key figures in the drawing up and use of the contract, the middleman and the scribe, are thoroughly investigated. And thirdly, the functioning as well as the rightfulness mechanisms of contracts in the specific society are tentatively theorized. In this way, this study presents and analyzes an example for the existence of a non-stereotypical "society of contract" in Maine's conception, arguing that the social order which provides predictability and regularity for economic prosperity in this frontier area could be formed and maintained through contracts even in the condition of relatively weak influence on the part of the governmental and legal authorities.

Dates and Currency

The Qing Reign Periods

Shunzhi (1–18), 1644–1661
Kangxi (1–61), 1662–1722
Yongzheng (1–13), 1723–1735
Qianlong (1–60), 1736–1795
Jiaqing (1–25), 1796–1820
Daoguang (1–30), 1821–1850
Xianfeng (1–11), 1851–1861
Tongzhi (1–13), 1862–1874
Guangxu (1–33), 1875–1908
Xuantong (1–3), 1909–1911.

Dates and Dating Protocol

In the text of this work, lunar dates are rendered as they appear in the source manuscripts in their original order of (reign) year, month, and day and are followed in parentheses by the corresponding Gregorian date: for example, Qianlong, forty-fifth year, sixth month, twenty-second day (July 23, 1780).

Currency Equivalents

10 candareens, *fen* = 1 mace, *qian*
10 maces = 1 tael, *liang*, a Chinese ounce of silver
1,000 cash = 1 tael (approximately).

Contents

About the Author

Jian Qu is an Associate Professor of Law at the Department of Law, College of Humanities and Development Studies, China Agricultural University, Beijing, China. He has accomplished his doctorate from Heidelberg University, Germany, in 2020. Prior to that, he graduated from Tsinghua University with a Master of Law degree (2015). He also studied at Sciences Po, Paris, and obtained two bachelor's degrees from Southwest University of Political Science and Law (LL.B., 2012) and from Southwest University (B.A., 2012). His studies on legal theory and legal history were supported by the CSC, the Max Weber Foundation, and the DAAD. He was a visiting researcher with a scholarship at the Max Planck Institute for European Legal History, Frankfurt, in 2018, and the year after, he published his first book, *Yanchu fasui* ("Taking Promulgated Words as Law," in two volumes), for which he won the biennial Zeng Xianyi Prize for Outstanding Monographs on Legal History (2019).

About the Author

[illegible]

List of Figures

List of Tables

Manuscripts Cited and Translated

Chapter 1
Introduction

> There are few general propositions concerning the age to which we belong which seem at first sight likely to be received with readier concurrence than the assertion that the society of our day is mainly distinguished from that of preceding generations by the largeness of the sphere which is occupied in it by Contract.
> Maine [53].

1 The Story of the Wealthiest Man

A story is often told in Wendou Village about Jiang Shichao,[1] a man who made millions by plying timber on the Qingshui, or "Clear Water," River, which flows by the village and through the mountains of southwest China. In two short years, the man who started from scratch grew to become so wealthy that he was said to have turned the stream of clear water flowing downward into a channel of silver flowing up.[2] According to the story, Jiang was born into a poor family in the mid-eighteenth century[3] but exposed to silver at an early age. Jiang's father was a silversmith, but

[1]The following narrative of the story of Jiang Shichao is based on [26, 38, 40, 78, 79, 94]. A note is needed at the beginning to explain the style of references in this book. The references that appear for the first time in each chapter are cited in the form of "numbered citations," and their full information can be found correspondingly in the reference list at the end of the chapter. Repeated references are cited in the short form, i.e. as "author, (short) title, page number." For authors/editors of literature in East Asian languages, their names are given in the Western order ("given name – family name") in the reference list, while in the short form of references in the footnotes, their names appear as "family name – given name," following their own tradition of name order.

[2]The figure seems to be symbolic in the modern narrative of the local history, since his story has repeatedly appeared in numerous recent literature. See, e.g., [31, 69, 107].

[3]It is believed that Jiang Shichao was born in the twenty-fourth year of Qianlong reign (1759) and passed away in the fourteenth year of Jiangqing reign (1809). See Wang Zongxun, "Qingjiang jufu Jiang Shichao," 747–748; Jinping xian Hekou xiang renmin zhengfu, *Hekou xiang zhi*, 420–421; Wang Zongxun, *Maoping*, 108–109. According to Wang Zongxun, in an interview with the author, the basis for confirming the birth and death years of Jiang Shichao is the inscription on his tombstone in Wendou Village. For a record of the tombstone, see [80].

J. Qu, *Social Order through Contracts*,
https://doi.org/10.1007/978-981-33-4947-6_1

he died when the younger Jiang was only two years old, never knowing how much more silver his son would come to manage. The half-orphan was raised and educated by his mother and became a tenant planter, one of the most common occupations in the area.

When Jiang was planting trees with his mother up in the mountains, a business model of trading timber was gradually coming to be established.[4] Trees in the artificial forests of the upstream villages were continually felled and transported through the Qingshui River to the trading markets set up in the downstream villages, where timber sellers (so-called *shanke* or "guests from the mountains") and merchants who journeyed by river from the hinterland (*shuike* or "guests from the rivers") met.[5] It is conceivable that the brokerage business in these markets brought huge profits so that every village sought to monopolize it. As a result, there broke out a two-hundred-year battle over the control of the Qingshui River channel among downstream villages.[6]

The opportunity for Jiang Shichao to win his fortune finally came when he was in his mid-forties. In the tenth year of the Jiaqing reign (1805), the battle began to intensify when one of the downstream villages, Benchu, started to cut off the waterway abruptly, preventing traveling merchants from coming and therefore prohibiting the trade.[7] The impact of the disruption on the timber trade was devastating. As a time-consuming industry, the final realization of these efforts in the past two or three decades of tree growth was a vital step for all participants in the timber plantation. Yet on the other hand, the accumulated huge demand for timber in the hinterland could not be met. It was at this very time that Jiang, as a now experienced practitioner in the timber business, made his decision to gamble.

He bet all, or, in fact, more than all. One year before Benchu cut off the line, Jiang had started to buy both standing trees and timber rafts in large quantities.[8] During the two-year period of interrupted transactions, he spent up every coin he owned and started to borrow money from relatives to purchase timber. He even succeeded in persuading some despairing sellers to conclude the sale contract of timber with him in advance and promised to pay the price later.[9] In this way, his manipulation can actually be seen as an instance of high leverage trading in the eyes of modern financial authorities. By the spring of the eleventh year of Jiaqing (1806), the speculator had bought up half of the timber alongside the river by various means.[10]

When the autumn came, the harvesting season for Jiang Shichao came with it, and the interruption finally ended. Buyers from all over the country poured into the

[4]See [37].

[5]See [95]. Sometimes there were officials who came as buyers. For a detailed record of two times of imperial government procurements of timber in these village markets in 1777 and 1781, see [63].

[6]For a collection of related materials, see [57]. For a case study on one of these villages which served as a timber market, see [83].

[7]See Guizhou sheng bianjizu, *Dongzu shehui lishi diaocha*, 175.

[8]There were two different kinds of trading models concerning timber in the area at the time; one can either buy the standing trees in the mountains or the timber rafts that were anchored by the river. See [36, 62].

[9]See Wang Zongxun, "Qingjiang jufu Jiang Shichao," 747.

[10]See Jiang Zuoqing, "Shixi jilüe," 143.

re-opening market and soon found that Jiang was the one who was controlling the supply side. He then sold out all his timber that had been brought over the last two years in forty or fifty days, and of course at three times or an even more than three times price. A brand-new rich man was born at this time. Legend has it that Jiang once hired six ships to transport his silver up-river from the trading market to his home.[11] Seventy years later, in "a brief account of the lineage" written by his descendant in the second year of Guangxu (1876), it was written that "the gold and silver [he owned] rank first among a thousand families."[12]

2 A Contract Society? Research Question and State of the Field

2.1 Economic Success, Social Order, and Contracts

What was the reason behind Jiang Shichao's success? This may be a worthwhile discussion topic after presenting such a get-rich-quick story. Was it his keen sense of market changes, his accurate analysis of information, or his wise use of credit? Rather than discussing Jiang's personality, a more fruitful topic for investigation may be the examination of Jiang's means or the opportunities he took in achieving this success. In other words, what were the social or institutional facts which served as the grounds for this fantastic trading and financing operation?

From this perspective, it is obvious that such an economic success of an ordinary person without the use of brutal force could only happen in a generally orderly and organized society; this business operation required a series of basic social or institutional guarantees, such as the general recognition of property rights and effective dispute resolution. In brief, the most obvious precondition for a non-violent wealth miracle should be operational certainty or social order.

As "a core theoretical issue in the social sciences,"[13] social order has long been conceived as a sensitive term that theorists have rarely paused to try to explain and define.[14] This study does not intend to participate directly in the discussion of its definition. Instead, in this study, the term "social order," as the opposite of social disorder, principally refers to a relatively stable state of society. Its core lies

[11] See Wang Zongxun, "Qingjiang jufu Jiang Shichao," 748. It is also said that 24 gold bricks were found in the house of the fifth-generation grandson of Jiang Shichao in 1952, see Jinping xian Hekou xiang renmin zhengfu, *Hekou xiang zhi*, 421.

[12] Jiang Zuoqing, "Shixi jilüe," 143.

[13] Hechter and Horne [32].

[14] A short review regarding the discussion of the question "what is social order" from the perspectives of Max Weber, Friedrich A. Hayek, and Jon Elster can be found in Calvert [5]. For a longer and more thorough critique of existing definitions of "social order," see [70]. Also, see [68].

in the establishment of predictability or regularity in society.[15] Specifically, it is assumed that Jiang Shichao's wealth could not be maintained and secured in a state of social chaos, and his operation or manipulation in the timber market would not have occurred in a society that lacks predictability. "Social order" should be seen as precisely the cornerstone of his "gold and silver."

However, what was the cornerstone of social order in the villages along the Qingshui River? Traditionally, social order is provided by a government and a law, although this might not have been the case in the region at the time. Firstly, as it is generally believed, in late imperial China "the emperor's power never descends below the county."[16] Consequently, the national legal power appears to have been relatively weak at the village level.[17] Moreover, for various historical and cultural reasons, there existed many enclaves in the sense of administrative divisions in the region; for example, two adjacent villages could be under the jurisdiction of different counties.[18] This phenomenon further weakened the effective control of state power over the local society. Secondly, as a Miao frontier area, it was often too far and too difficult for the power of the central imperial court and national law to reach the level of local governance.[19] A typical manifestation of this is the delay in applying the dynasty calendar in some contracts of the region: one can find some "non-existent" dates in these contracts, such as "Jiaqing, twenty-sixth year, first month, fifth day,"[20] or "Tongzhi, fourteenth year, third month, twenty-eighth day."[21] In fact, there were only twenty-five years during the Jiaqing reign and thirteen years during the Tongzhi reign. This means that, in the region, it was possible that villagers were still not informed of the change of emperor until almost four months after the transfer of power. Thirdly, forest land and mountains account for most of the area of the region, and the governmental control over mountain land and wet-rice fields was entirely different; the former enjoyed a much looser policing due to the tax exemption which existed in the Qing dynasty.[22] Therefore, for most transactions concerning real estate in the region, government intervention was not as far-reaching as in the hinterland.

The above three points show that, in general, the supply of law from the imperial dynasty in this rural, remote, and mountainous region was relatively scarce. Finally, concrete proof which illustrates the weak influence of the governmental and legal

---

[15]"Social-political order," at the basic level, shall be defined as the "[p]redictability of things within a community or social system." See Shiping Tang, "Order," 34. The importance of "predictability," and along with it of "cooperation," to the concept of social order has also been stressed by classics, see [20].

[16]For a discussion of this controversial assertion, see [35, 106]. The exact extent of the influence of imperial power in grass-roots units is often considered open to question, but the weakening of the imperial power at the local level in traditional society is undeniable.

[17]A detailed record of this phenomenon in the region and a discussion on this issue can be found in Qu Jian, *Yanchu fasui*, 77–90.

[18]See [97].

[19]For a debate on this issue, see, e.g., [91, 49]. For another related debate, see [16, 75].

[20]Zhang and Wang [102].

[21]Zhang and Wang [103].

[22]See Chen and Long [9].

power concerning civil and commercial activities in the region can be found in the extremely low ratio of "red" or officially sealed contracts, in comparison to "white" or unofficial contracts.[23] It is widely believed that the obligation of people to register their original white contracts as tax-related red/sealed contracts is the most important way for the national power to intervene in contractual activities.[24] Though the "white (unsealed) contracts" were widely considered to be "unregistered, had not paid taxes, and had no validity in court,"[25] in practice they were still the preferred option in most situations. Put succinctly, it seems that the social order of the region, as the premise for the individual possession of wealth, was not fully backed by governmental and legal authorities. Jiang's wealth story was hence closely bound up with the orderly operation of the entire society which had little legal or political power to rely on.

The possibility of economic success based on a social order without law evidently invites a number of questions. Why would people in the region and at the time believe that Jiang Shichao truly owned the timber, including those trees which stood in the mountains as immovable properties and those logs which were anchored by the river as movable properties, after drawing up contracts? Why did Jiang Shichao, while estimating the end of the interruption of the markets, also assume that his property could be protected from being infringed upon by those contracts he concluded? In particular, regarding those credit-sale contracts for which the price had not yet been paid, why did people accept that the ownership of the property had already been transferred according to the contract? One might find that, in this story, although there was no government and law, there were contracts. It seems that the "Qingshui River's dream," which allowed ordinary people to transform their lives from rags to riches, was not primarily protected by governmental or legal institutions, but rather by private and legally non-enforceable contracts. It is in this sense that the relationship between contracts and social order can be considered: can social order, which generally offers protection for rightful property and predictability for social activities and business operation, be formed and maintained through contracts?[26]

2.2 *A General Puzzle of How and Why the Contract Worked*

Such a question concerning the interaction between contracts and social order (which is deemed the prerequisite of economic success) would not be unique to areas such as the Qingshui River Basin. Although it is not necessarily based on materials from the specific region, previous scholarship with a broader concern also takes it as a general puzzle in late imperial China.

---

[23]For studies on the ratio of "red" to "white" contracts in the Qingshui River region, see [47, 41]. For a comparative analysis of the similar effectiveness of red and white contracts, see [12].

[24]See Wang [74].

[25]Duff [18].

[26]For a preliminary discussion of the relationship between contract and society in the context of the Qingshui River region, see [6].

In his masterpiece *Ancient Law*, which is considered one of the most important books on legal history,[27] Sir Henry Sumner Maine defined "Contract" as a pivotal element which differentiates "the society of our day" from that of previous ages.[28] The jurist, who coined the proverbial formula "from status to contract" in one of the previous chapters of his work,[29] might have not included China, which has a long tradition of using contracts,[30] as a society of "our day" at that time.[31] However, in January 1861, at the very time when his book was first published in London,[32] at least five contracts—two tenancy contracts, two sales contracts, and one property division contract—were concluded as rather prevalent activities in a remote Miao village located among the rolling mountains of southwest China.[33] The concept of contract obviously played a conspicuous, albeit complicated, role in the society of China in the eighteenth and nineteenth centuries.[34]

However, the extensive contract practices present a puzzle. In, and in many cases beyond, fields of civil and commercial matters, written contracts and contract-like documents were extremely widely used[35] in a society with "shallow government"[36] and, from a legal positivist perspective,[37] largely in the absence of national statutory law.[38] Concerning Maine's characterization of the largeness of the sphere in a society occupied by contract, this society could be deemed "a society of contract."[39] In other words, the society was well organized, civilly and commercially, not because of a

---

[27]See [64].

[28]See, as cited at the beginning of this chapter, Henry Sumner Maine, *Ancient Law*, 304.

[29]Scholars have highlighted that Maine's sources are principally Western Europe and Northern India. See [65].

[30]See [28].

[31]In Maine's book, China is only directly mentioned once as an example of a stationary society (versus a progressive society): "In China this point has been past, but progress seems to have been there arrested, because the civil laws are coextensive with all the ideas of which the race is capable." See Henry Sumner Maine, *Ancient Law*, 23.

[32]See [22].

[33]For the five contracts, dated from "the twenty-first day of the eleventh month in the tenth year of Xianfeng [emperor's reign] (January 1, 1861)" to "the eighth day of the twelfth month (January 18, 1861)" of the same year according to the traditional Chinese calendar, see [11, 101].

[34]See [33].

[35]Written contracts at that time were used in a wide range of civil and commercial matters. Evidence can be found in widely circulated contract form-books or encyclopedias such as that by Li et al. [44]. Similar books, with introductions, are also noted in Hayes [29]. Professor Myron Cohen also observes the widespread use of contracts in social organization, see [13].

[36]The "shallowness" of the government was institutionally understood "not to impose order on the local community from the outside, but leave the community to do so through its own means" because of "economic and political reasons." For more discussion of the "shallow government" of Qing China, see Dan Fenno Henderson and Preston M. Torbert, "Contract in the Far East," 19, 29, 31.

[37]Relative discussion was noted in Scogin [67].

[38]For the study of the state law of Qing China, see [81].

[39]Following Maine's tradition, "society of contract/society of status" could refer to two antithetic "[relations] of the individual to the group." See [58]. However, it could also be understood as a society in which contract occupies a significant position. Professor Cohen argued that that "…all

strong government and bureaucratic system or sophisticated statutory laws, but by means of the successful operation of numerous contracts, which, in many circumstances, merely had limited legal enforcement.[40] This raises the question of how and why such a society with few laws but many contracts and with little possibility of actually enforcing them, i.e. the Hobbesian "words without sword,"[41] could maintain a well-functioning civil and commercial system. Although this puzzle concerning pre-modern Chinese contracts has been noticed by researchers to some degree, hardly any answers have been given to these various questions, especially in the context of the Qingshui River region, to this day.[42]

As an effort to tackle this puzzle which has been mentioned but not yet been thoroughly examined in a specific context, this study attempts to argue that, even without effective "social control through law,"[43] social order could be formed and maintained in various aspects by means of contracts.[44] For this purpose, the following investigation aims to target both why and how contracts functioned beyond their immediate context in the formation and maintenance of social order. Furthermore, since contracts in pre-modern China are certainly different from their Western or modern counterparts,[45] the following inquiries will bring the study back to the more fundamental question of what these contracts and contract laws, understood as the institution or functioning mechanism of contract,[46] genuinely are, or, rather, in what way they should be understood.

over China, men created, maintained, or severed relationships through contract," thus "the use of contract for instrumental purpose must therefore be seen as a fundamental feature of Chinese behavior in general." See Myron L. Cohen, "The Role of Contract in Traditional Chinese Social Organization," 132.

[40]These contracts were considered "probably not what would be called enforceable contracts in a modern court." See Dan Fenno Henderson and Preston M. Torbert, "Contract in the Far East," 20. Therefore, while in contemporary China, as in other places, it is well recognized that "weak legal enforcement is a major cause for contract failure," the obvious success of these contracts or at least their pervasiveness is puzzling. See [17].

[41]"Covenants, without the Sword, are but Words, and of no strength to secure a man at all." See [34].

[42]For one of the most-cited works that refers to this puzzle, see [72]. Also, see Dan Fenno Henderson and Preston M. Torbert, "Contract in the Far East," 19–20. Both these two studies raised the similar puzzle, but did not offer any explanation of it. Professor Terada Hiroaki believed that this puzzle ought to be solved by the study of legal history in the future. Meanwhile, the authors of the latter study indicated that the puzzles of Chinese contracts "pose engaging questions for students of comparative contract law".

[43]See [59].

[44]It needs to be stressed that, unlike the classic theory of the "social contract," which was mainly established by Hugo Grotius, Thomas Hobbes, John Locke, and Jean-Jacques Rousseau, this study focuses on realistic and practical contracts in a historical context rather than theoretical or fictional contracts. For a study which discusses classic contractarianism in its historical context, see [1].

[45]This point is broadly realized by comparative legal historians, see [2,14, 436673]. Contract in its Western sense has been divided into four categories by an observer from the east, namely contract as a concept of economy and law, contract as a concept of religious theology, contract as a concept of social politics (viz. social contract theory), and contract as a concept of moral philosophy. See [30]. Also, this point will be further discussed in Chap. 2.

[46]For a remark of the distinction between contract and contract law, see [3].

3 Sources: The Qingshui River Region and Beyond

As the society of Qing China was "large, linguistically and regionally diverse and complex,"[47] this study concentrates on the villages of the Qingshui River region. In this way, the examination of the puzzle concerning the relation between contracts and social order in late imperial times will be conducted with relatively specific and limited firsthand materials, namely the *Qingshui River Manuscripts.*

3.1 A Brief Introduction to the Qingshui River Manuscripts and Their Studies[48]

The Qingshui River manuscripts consist of a large number of Ming-Qing written contracts as well as various other kinds of documents that were found in the Qingshui River Basin of southwest China.[49] Over the last decade, these manuscripts have been enjoying increasing popularity among scholars. However, given the lack of widespread knowledge of them in English-language literature, this part intends to offer some basic information for understanding the Qingshui River manuscripts in their entirety (Fig. 1).[50]

3.1.1 The Discovery

Although there are a handful of discussions in Republican-era periodicals, mostly concerning the timber industry in the eastern Guizhou province,[51] these manuscripts only began to attract serious scholarly attention after the discovery of some 300 paper

---

[47] Buxbaum [4].

[48] An earlier version of a part of this subsection has been published following the requirement of the Max Weber Foundation—German Humanities Institutes Abroad (with the support of the Fritz Thyssen Foundation), which awarded a travel grant in support of the author's archival research and field research in 2018 to Beijing and Guizhou. See Qu [61]. The newer version in this subsection includes a number of further revisions as well as supplements.

[49] On the use of the terms *the Qingshui River region* and *the Qingshui River Basin*, there is no huge difference between the two, except that the latter is a geographical denotation. However, there are different nuances to each term, since contracts were not discovered in all or most places of the Qingshui River Basin, and, in general, not all contract manuscripts which are academically classified as the Qingshui River Manuscripts were found in the geographical-defined Qingshui River Basin. For this reason, the former term is used in this study to refer to the historical field of occurrence that is related, but not strictly restricted, to the geographical concept of the Basin. For an explanation of the *Qingshui River Basin* as an academic concept that is not limited to geography, see [100].

[50] Picture created by the author, with materials extracted from Zhang Yingqiang and Wang Zongxun, *Qingshuijiang wenshu*, vol. 1–3.

[51] See, for example, Hu Jingxiu, "Qiandong muye gaikuang," 41–42; [39].

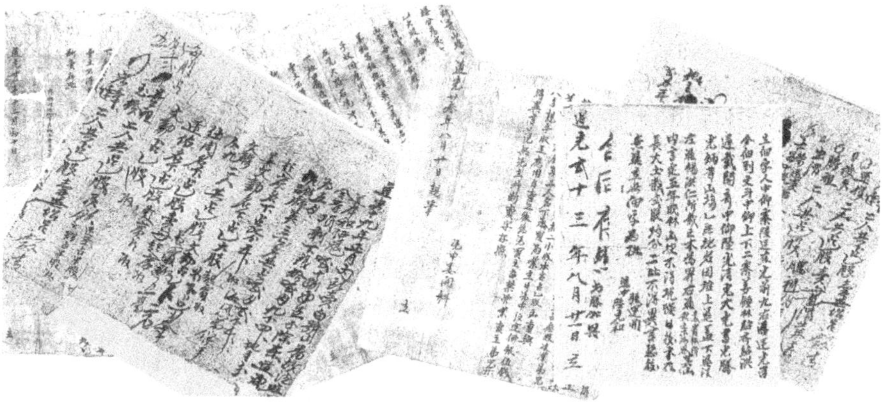

Fig. 1 Contracts from the Qingshui River region

contracts in Wendou Village in 1964.[52] Furthermore, these findings only became known to the public over two decades later in 1988 in the form of quotations in an investigation report.[53] After this discovery, more manuscripts were subsequently found and collected from villagers by researchers and local archives, and as a result, by the end of the second millennium, the number of discovered manuscripts in the region had exceeded 4,000.[54]

Systematic surveys were carried out at the beginning of the 2000s thanks to a collaboration between the local government and various academic institutions. At present, it is recognized that the total number of Qingshui River manuscripts, including those that have not yet been discovered or collected, is enormous. It is estimated by some to stand at more than 500,000,[55] while a more conservative estimate counts a total of ca. 300,000 manuscripts.[56]

3.1.2 Where and When?

These manuscripts have been named "Qingshui River Manuscripts" by academics, after the region in which they were found.[57] The middle and lower reaches of the river

[52] See Guizhou sheng bianjizu, *Dongzu shehui lishi diaocha*, 222–223; Wu [86]. According to one statistic, research papers in the field may now be counted by the thousand. See [93].

[53] See Guizhou sheng bianjizu, *Dongzu shehui lishi diaocha*, 11–19. For the story of these contracts during the time between discovery and publication, see Wang Zongxun, *Xunshi yiluo de jiyi*, 3.

[54] See Wu Caimao, *Minjian wenshu yu Qingshuijiang diqu de shehui bianqian*, 2.

[55] See [104].

[56] See [99].

[57] See [98]. These manuscripts could perhaps also be, and are sometimes, called "Jinping (Forestry) Manuscripts.".

flow through several counties, such as Jinping, Jianhe, and Tianzhu of the Southeast Qian Autonomous Prefecture of Miao and Dong, Guizhou province.[58]

A popular old saying, which is regarded as a stereotypical reflection of Guizhou, is that here "[n]o three days are clear, no three feet of land are level, and no one has three ounces of silver."[59] The Qingshui River region, although it is located in one of the least developed provinces of China, is rich in timber resources even up to the present day. As noted, a pre-eminent geographic feature of the region is that it is a very hilly and mountainous place. Consequently, it is not very suitable for agriculture, but, since people of the region could not make a living from agricultural planting, it has given birth to large-scale plantations of forests. Many of the contracts discussed in this study were related to the forestry industry.

Although, from the perspective of the Chinese hinterland, the Qingshui River region was not exceedingly remote since it still borders some of the major hinterland provinces, such as Hunan, and even though there have been several waves of Han Chinese migration leading to the establishment of military stations since the Ming dynasty,[60] for much of its history the area was not really well-controlled by the central government, with the so-called Miao "rebellions" or "uprisings" in the early eighteenth century irregularly but persistently flaring up well into the late nineteenth century.[61] These facts seem to suggest that ethnicity played an important role in forming the particularity of this frontier area. Although many studies on the Qingshui River manuscripts take ethnicity as a starting point for their discussion, after cautiously examining the ancestral legends of the local people through field and documentary research, this study has chosen not to focus on the significance of ethnicity in the following discussion, since ethnic identity is a complicated issue—inhabitants of the Qingshui River region claimed that their ancestors were Han people, but after their voluntary immigration to the region, due to geomantic reasons, they became Miao.[62] However, whether it is due to geographical or ethnic reasons, the fact is that this area was relatively peripheral under the central control system of the Qing dynasty.

The summary provided above of the geographical and ethnic make-up of the local society in question presents a basic impression of the region in southwest China that was considered to be the central part of the *Miao Jiang* (or Miao frontier area) during the Qing dynasty,[63] although the period of the manuscripts found there is not limited to the Qing era. In fact, the manuscripts were collected from remote villages along

[58]Guizhou was translated by the China Inland Mission as the "Noble-Land" during the Qing time. See [71].

[59]Weinstein [84].

[60]See Gao and Tan [25].

[61]It has to be noted that there existed several versions of the narrative of the event, from both positive and negative sides. For the so-called "uprisings" or "rebellions," see Zhongguo diyi lishi dang'an guan et al. [105]; Robert Darrah Jenks, *Insurgency and Social Disorder in Guizhou: The "Miao" Rebellion, 1854–1873.*

[62]For the ancestral legends of the local people, see, e.g., Zhang Yingqiang, *Mucai zhi liudong*, 200–203. For a study of their transition from Han to Miao in the 1980s, see [82].

[63]See Lin et al. [46].

the river date from the middle and late Ming dynasty to the Republican period, although it is reported that in fact only 13 Ming manuscripts have been published until recently.[64] Even at the present time, as the findings from the author's field research suggest, people in this area are still producing manuscripts following the continued tradition of earlier times.

3.1.3 The Content

As far as one can see, all of these manuscripts are written in Chinese, with Suzhou numerals being used as shorthand in number-intensive cases.[65] These manuscripts contain a broad spectrum of subjects, including worship, funeral activities, litigation, marriage, genealogy, taxes, succession, the division of families, and so on. While covering a range of genres related to everyday life, contracts account for the majority of these manuscripts.

As stated above, the most unique feature of these contracts stems from the fact that the overwhelming majority of them are white (unsealed) contracts. It has been shown in one study that only 6.65% (424/6,378) of the examined contracts are "red (sealed) contracts."[66] Compared to the respective number of the renowned Huizhou manuscripts,[67] the portion of white contracts in the Qingshui River manuscripts is considerably higher,[68] which suggests weaker governmental and legal control in this region.

3.1.4 Major Collections, Publications, and Studies of the Manuscripts

In addition to limited university and private holdings, the major collections of these manuscripts, which numbered 103,556 by 2012,[69] are stored in six county archives in the region, including originals and copies (in both paper and digital forms). It has recently been reported that the archive in Jinping County might possess the largest collection with over 60,000 manuscripts, most of which have already been

---

[64] Lin [45].

[65] For the Suzhou numerals, see [7]. For a list of them and their comparisons with Arabic numerals, see Qu Jian, *Yanchu fasui*, 319.

[66] See Liu Yanan and Wu Caimao, "Cong qiyue wenshu kan Qing dai Qingshuijiang xiayou diqu de lunli jingji," 38–39.

[67] Huizhou manuscripts constitute a large number of historical materials found in and around Huizhou area in former Anhui Province. For a thorough English-language introduction to the these sources, see "Appendix. From private records to national treasures: A brief history of the Huizhou sources," [55].

[68] See [42].

[69] It should be noted that by now the number is undoubtedly much higher, standing at perhaps around 240,000, according to a government official of Jinping County. See [51].

digitized but are only accessible from the archive's intranet.[70] This archive also owns a purpose-built museum which houses a special collection of manuscripts from the county.

The publication of the Qingshui River manuscripts was mainly promoted by universities and research institutes. The first compilation of these manuscripts was published in Japan in 2001 by the Research Institute for Languages and Cultures of Asia and Africa, Tokyo University of Foreign Studies.[71] Since then, large-scale publication programs were launched by (in chronological order) the Sun Yat-sen University, Southwest University of Political Science and Law, Guizhou University, and Kaili University. Until now, at least 50,000 manuscripts have been published. A long list including 142 volumes of publications of the Qingshui River manuscripts from 2001 to 2019 is provided in the appendix offered in this study. These volumes also form a major part of the basic materials that this study relies on.

Along with the process of the massive publication of the materials, the studies of the manuscripts developed rapidly, and copious reviews of the studies in different stages have emerged. Two noticeable features among these reviews are noteworthy. The first is that these studies have continued to mine more deeply as the manuscripts were gradually published. It is suggested that the research of the Qingshui River manuscripts can be divided into three phases, i.e. 1964–1988, 1989–1999, and 2000–2014, according to the degree of the depth of the study and the level of manuscripts publication.[72] Although pioneering research appeared earlier, plentiful introductory articles only emerged at the beginning of this century.[73] As for the period after these phases, newer reviews of the studies,[74] including those concerning the recent conferences on the manuscripts,[75] also show the importance of accessibility of the materials to researchers.

The second feature is the multi-disciplinary nature of the studies which is owed to the extreme diversity of the manuscripts themselves. This aspect gives rise to a great number of controversial issues, such as the origin of the manuscripts, the property rights of the forest land, the mechanism of diverse dispute resolutions, etc., and the scholarly debates on them have established a foundation stone for further studies.[76] In particular, legal studies of the manuscripts,[77] and especially those from the perspective of legal history, have proven significant since a large proportion of the manuscripts could be described as legal documents. The international dimension

---

[70] See Long [48].

[71] Daniels et al. [15].

[72] See Wu Caimao, *Minjian wenshu yu Qingshuijiang diqu de shehui bianqian*, 7–19; [85]. For another earlier literature review, see Ma Guojun and Li Hongxiang, "Jin liushinian lai Qingshuijiang linye qiyue de shouji zhengli yu yanjiu zongshu," 74–81.

[73] See Wu Caimao, *Minjian wenshu yu Qingshuijiang diqu de shehui bianqian*, 9.

[74] See [52].

[75] See [8, 89].

[76] See [92].

[77] See [50].

of the study of the Qingshui River manuscripts has also distinguished itself from the outset, since many overseas scholars have become engaged in both the research and the investigation and publication of the manuscripts.[78]

In general, the research of the Qingshui River manuscripts today is maturing thanks to the continuous publication of original documents. However, even though the contracts account for the vast majority of the manuscripts, the research on them has not yet reached a theoretical level and the logic behind the workings of the contract system in the society has not yet been thoroughly revealed. These objectives are exactly what this study hopes to bring to light. A more comprehensive study of the contracts of the Qingshui River manuscripts will thereby reveal the existence of a non-stereotypical "society of contract," in Maine's terminology, in the region. For even though the villages are remote, they are far from peripheral, and at any rate it is believed that "events in a remote corner of the world can illuminate central questions about the organization of social life."[79]

3.2 Sources in and Beyond the Region

3.2.1 Taking the Qingshui River Manuscripts as the Core Source

This study focuses on the Qingshui River region and the manuscripts from the area are selected as the core source. Among many reasons for this decision, two need to be especially emphasized in explaining why the source is ideal for this study. Firstly, in a relatively small area, the large number and chronological density of these well-preserved contracts allow for meaningful statistical analysis. For example, 2,931 contracts which are dated from 1743 to 1911 were collected from one single village named *Wendou*.[80] This indicates that, throughout a period of 169 years, at least one contract was concluded in approximately every 3 weeks in a community of around 1,000 residents.[81] This provides this study with the opportunity to conduct not only descriptive but also statistical studies and quantitative analyses, all of which help to explore more fully and precisely the social life and its contractual order in this particular area of pre-modern China.

Secondly, as noted, the "white contracts" account for the overwhelming majority of the contracts found in the region. In fact, the wider application of white contracts did not prevent this region from enjoying a high level of commercial engagement

[78] See [96].

[79] Ellickson [19].

[80] Wendou Village will be discussed as a major case in this study. However, it has to be noted here that non-contract manuscripts are not included. A list of publications of the manuscripts from Wendou Village can be found in Qu [60]. For some information of the village of Wendou in English, see [24, 21]. For a Chinese introduction, see [77].

[81] The latest census numbers show that the village's population today is 1,385. See [27]. The estimated number of households in the village throughout its history is noted in Wang Zongxun, *Wendou*, 61.

in the timber industry,[82] and the vigor and prosperity of its economy inevitably required a complex contractual system to be (self-)generated. Accordingly, it benefits our investigation to seek to understand how people used the contracts to conduct transactions and form relations autonomously, with only minimal government intervention.

In addition, the method of material processing in this study needs to be explained. First, although the contractual tradition of the Qingshui River region can be distinguished by its strong continuity, the time-span of this study and the materials used in the following discussion are limited to the Qing dynasty only (1644–1912). Only a few manuscripts during the period of the following early Republican period are selectively used as secondary references when necessary, and in general the lower limit of the time of the materials is defined as 1912.

Second, it should also be noted that this study may appear synchronic from a historical perspective. Minor changes or any process of evolution concerning reginal contracts in different periods of the Qing dynasty, if they can be attested at all, are not the central focus of this research. Still, discussions around this area are mentioned in Chap. 3 in connection with the role that scribes have played in the evolution and localization of contract forms and the contractual tradition. In general, the following investigation is more inclined to treat the Qing contracts in the Qingshui River area as a whole. Although this approach will obviously "flatten" some historical details, it is undoubtedly beneficial to the construction of a more general theoretical framework.

3.2.2 Wendou, a Cluster of Villages, the Region, and Beyond

The sources which are the object of this study sketchily form a structure of four concentric circles; the inclusion and concerns of these four levels of research materials are as follows.

(1) The innermost circle covers all presently accessible contract manuscripts from the village of Wendou.[83] It includes 2,944 pieces of contracts in total, of which 2,109 are complete contracts (Group A), while the remaining 835 cases are records or copies of the content of the original contracts. The quantitative analyses in this study will take Wendou as an example for discussion, especially in Chaps. 3 and 4, as the contract data in this village is relatively complete and relevant studies, as well as supplementary materials of the village environment, seem to be sufficient to complement the story behind the data. It should also be noted that, although it is believed that in many places in China "many villages consisted of single lineages,"[84] this was not the case in Wendou Village. The residents of this village are composed of more than ten main surnames,

[82] See Zhang Yingqiang, *Mucai zhi liudong*, esp. 39–47.

[83] For a list of published and collected (by the author) contracts of the village, see Qu Jian, "Yikou daibi," 184–185. In addition, a later published volume of contracts of the village is added to the dataset in this study, see [10].

[84] Freedman [23].

including Jiang, Yi, Li, Long, etc., of which Jiang is the most prominent one.[85] However, there have been large-scale alteration of family surnames in the history of the village, such as the famous event of changing Long to Jiang.[86] Therefore, although there were many people with the surname Jiang who were later residents in Wendou Village, they in fact belonged to four divided branches, "each of which had its own origin, and did not marry members of each other."[87] Thus, they did not actually belong to the same clan. To a certain extent, this family composition of Wendou Village shows the diversity of the sources of its contracts. The contracts are, then, not internal documents of one big clan, but come from many different families in a village society. In addition, it should be especially stressed that the term village, *cun*, is different from *zhai*, which is "in fact a term used widely by ethnic communities in southwest China."[88] This difference in designation has already been noticed and recorded by people of that time.[89] A *zhai* normally includes more than one hundred households or sometimes up to two or three hundred households,[90] and implies a more defensive meaning—to prevent outsiders from entering at will—compared to *cun*.

(2) However, this does not mean that there was no communication between villages; on the contrary, within a certain area, such exchanges were commonplace. Thus, the second circle incorporates manuscripts from a nucleated cluster of villages that are not only geographically adjacent to Wendou, but also economically and culturally affiliated to it,[91] primarily including the villages of Jiachi, Ping'ao, and Yanwan.[92] As Wendou was considered the central village of the regional society and these villages shared similar, if not identical, customs and traditions concerning contracts and beyond, this study intends to center the village cluster on Wendou as a whole,[93] which constitutes the basic spatial field studied in this study.

(3) Furthermore, the third circle is comprised of the whole Qingshui River manuscripts collected from different places of the region, which includes but is not limited to Jinping County, Tianzhu County, and Liping County. Various nuances of contractual customs and social conditions appear to exist among

[85] See [76].

[86] See Zhang Yingqiang, *Mucai zhi liudong*, 228–235.

[87] Wang Zongxun, *Wendou*, 23.

[88] Wu [88].

[89] See Xu [90].

[90] See ibid.

[91] For the relations and interactions between Wendou and its circumjacent villages, especially Yanwan, see Zhang Yingqiang, *Mucai zhi liudong*, 245–263.

[92] For the geographical locations of the village cluster, see Wang Zongxun, *Wendou*, 3.

[93] For the relations and the historical development of the relations between Wendou Village and other villages around it, see Zhang Yingqiang, *Mucai zhi liudong*, 245–263.

these places,[94] but as noted, based on their geographical and cultural connections, they have self-narrated and were narrated both historically and academically as a whole region. The above-mentioned village cluster serves as an illustrative example for the examination of the entire region.

(4) The outermost circle includes contracts and other manuscripts from all over China, such as sources from Huizhou, Guangdong, Hainan, Taiwan, Hongkong, Jiangnan area, Beijing, and Dunhuang. These sources produce the effect of conveying the culture of Chinese contract as a consistent and integrated tradition. In addition, the study tries to discuss the differences in the details of the contract and its customs between the hinterland and the frontier areas.[95] Comparable materials, and especially contract laws and theoretical sources from other civilizations in both ancient and modern times, will also be considered.

In sum, the main concern of this study is the Qingshui River region, with a special focus on a cluster of villages centered on Wendou, while taking contracts and other materials from other places in and beyond China into account for comparative purposes.

4 Analytical Framework and Synopsis

This introduction shall be concluded by a brief explanation of the analytical framework and an outline of the chapters that follow.

As noted, this study attempts to solve the puzzle concerning contracts in the specific context of the Qingshui River region by proposing that contracts constitute the key to the formation and maintenance of social order in a region without strong governmental and legal power. "Contracts" are therefore the central focus of this study. Based on the understanding that a contract can be deemed a specific device rooted in its social context, a comprehensive investigation of contracts in the Qingshui River region requires two analytical perspectives in particular. Specifically, such a study should not only be conducted socio-historically but also textually/materially, as the contract was, after all, a written document. Thus, the approach chosen in this research is first to clarify the basic socio-historical facts about the contract, and then to try to construct an explanatory theoretical framework of the contract and its interaction with the social order in the given specific context.

Accordingly, on the one hand, this study will first examine the contract within its own scope, treating it as a probably non-legal (in terms of the absence of contract law) but practical device applicable for all social members who intended to re-arrange

[94] Differences seem to exist between mountain-based areas and field-based areas, as well as between areas of natural villages and areas of *tunpu*. For *tunpu* in Guizhou, see [56].

[95] The term "hinterland" has a complex meaning in the context of China. For the convenience of narrative, in this study the term is used mainly to refer to those provinces included in the customs survey conducted in the late Qing and Republican periods, e.g. Hunan, Anhui, Jiangxi, Henan, see [87]. The frontier areas in this study mostly refers to the Guizhou province.

their properties or interpersonal rights and obligations and were willing to bear the intermediate cost, whether monetary or not. On the other hand, having clarified the basic elements of a contract, this study then endeavors to situate it in its social context. For a contextualized understanding of a contract is necessary to investigate its functioning mechanism towards the formation of social order. In particular, after inviting middlemen and scribes and so many other social factors into the functioning mechanism of contracts, one can come to realize that the device of the contract should also be deemed a social system which was able to mobilize and incorporate diverse elements of the whole society into a "seamless web"[96] of contracts.

Contracts cannot be separated from their social environment, but this does not mean that contracts themselves did not have a relatively independent internal structure. Also, the effectiveness of the contract certainly does not come from within, but additionally stems from the external society in which it is situated. A complete understanding of this issue needs to consider both the contract and its social context. Thus, this study tends to analyze the contract from both its decontextualized and (re)contextualized perspectives.

Based on the above two perspectives of analysis, three interrelated questions regarding contracts will be answered in context, namely what they were, how they were formed and worked, and why they worked. The main part of the study, besides the "Introduction" and "Conclusion," is arranged as follows. After this Introduction, Chap. 2 will be devoted to the first question. The following two chapters explain how contracts were formed and worked in the Qingshui River region by scrutinizing two fundamental types of actors involved in their negotiation and drafting: respectively, middlemen (Chap. 3) and scribes (Chap. 4). Chapter 5 will then mainly answer the third question of why contracts were broadly honored in the region and thus how they generated the perceived social order.

Specifically, Chap. 2 seeks to rediscover the familiar concept of contract in the unfamiliar context of the Qingshui River region. It presents a general description and an unambiguous definition of what could be taken into account as a "contract" in this particular context. A new understanding of contract within the specified context is proposed from a comparative perspective. Differently from a Western or modern perception of a contract as a *legal agreement*, the combination of substantiality, formality, and materiality marks its complexity in the practice of the region. Also, the often-forgotten material aspect of the contract is especially stressed. Based on the examination of the above-mentioned three aspects of contracts, a tripartite structure of contracts is brought forward in order to distinguish contracts from non-contract documents clearly. This chapter tries to reveal the difference and the sameness between the contracts in context and their modern counterparts and shows that it is the seemingly slight differences at the margin that shape and highlight the nature of the contract in context and mark it off as a relatively unique notion which should be re-understood.

The proposed re-definition of the contract in Chap. 2 is followed by Chaps. 3 and 4, which each address one key structural element of the contract, i.e. the middleman and the scribe. These two elements in fact constitute the determinant factors in explaining

[96] Maitland [54].

the effectiveness and rightfulness of a contract as well as the dispute settlement mechanism through contracts. For a long time, the fundamental role of these two figures (and especially the scribe, considered in Chap. 4) in the contract system has not been properly noticed, for the theory of contract law tends to believe that a contract is in essence merely a matter between the two contracting parties. This study singles these two figures out and argues that the comprehensive perception of the uniqueness of the contract system in context lies in the systematic analyses of them, for they act not merely as helpers in concluding a contract but also as the decisive third parties. Chapter 3 examines the four roles of middlemen at the primary and secondary levels, focusing on their long-ignored technical contribution and suggesting that a middleman could become a constructional element of the contract mechanism. This chapter also brings forth a partly open system of middlemen to incorporate other atypical middleman-like contractual figures and to elucidate the social source of middlemen. Chapter 4 presents a rare systematic study of the often-ignored contractual scribes and provides a thorough account of the institution of scribes and its operation. In contrast to the impression of being a "printer," this chapter argues that a scribe might not be as "powerful" as the middleman in the negotiation, but possesses the "power" of writing and therefore should be deemed one of the two underpinnings of a contract. While clarifying the historical facts, Chaps. 3 and 4 also shed some light on the basic workings of middlemen and scribes in the context of the region. This will help readers to understand the further explanatory narrative in the following chapter.

After gaining a clear understanding of what these contracts were, Chap. 5 will try to unveil the functioning mechanism of contracts in the society of the region during the Qing period, interpreting and rationalizing why contracts *should* be observed. This chapter aims to present a tentative answer of the long-lasting question of why people honor the contract in the region, by investigating the mechanism which guarantees the contract to be a container of *tamper-resistant provable recognition*. Specifically, the contract is firstly a symbol of *recognition* since it is willingly offered and follows the norm of estoppel; secondly, the *recognition* is *provable*, spatially and temporally, due to the help from the middleman and the scribe; and, finally, it is *tamper-resistant* since it is protected by a blockchain-like noncentral trust network. This trust network is constructed by the effective operation of the broadcasting and chaining mechanism of contracts as well as the technical barrier of literacy. This chapter further discusses how contracts function in the restoration of social order when facing challenges from breaches and forgeries. Finally, special attention is paid to contracts that created social relationships in public respects, and a possible limitation of the theorization of the findings will be discussed in a larger context.

In sum, this study seeks to provide a new understanding of the Chinese contract within a specific context in the Qingshui River region during the Qing dynasty in both institutional and normative terms. Accordingly, the long-existing puzzle of how and why the social order within the Qingshui River societies was formed and maintained can be resolved through a centralized focus on contracts.

References

1. Baumgold, Deborah. 2010. *Contract theory in historical context: Essays on Grotius, Hobbes, and Locke*. Leiden and Boston: Brill.
2. Bourgon, Jérôme. 2009. Ditan shang de tu'an: Shilun Qing dai falü wenhua zhong de 'xiguan' yu 'qiyue' [Figures in the carpet: 'Customs' and 'contracts' in Qing legal culture]. (trans. Shijie Huang). In *Ming Qing falü yunzuo zhong de quanli yu wenhua* [Power and legal culture in legal activities under the Ming and Qing dynasties], ed. Pengsheng Qiu and Xiyuan Chen, 238–246. Taipei: Lianjing chuban gongsi.
3. Brockman, Rosser H. 1980. Commercial Contract Law in Late Nineteenth-Century Taiwan. In *Essays on China's Legal Tradition*, ed. Jerome Alan Cohen, R. Randle Edwards, and Fu-Mei Chang Chen, 79–80. Princeton: Princeton University Press.
4. Buxbaum, David C. 1993. Contracts in China During the Qing Dynasty: Key to the Civil Law. *Journal of Oriental Studies XXXI* (2): 201.
5. Calvert, R.L. 1998. Explaining Social Order: Internalization, External Enforcement, or Equilibrium? In *Institutions and Social Order*, ed. Karol Sołtan, Eric M. Uslaner, and Virginia Haufler, 131–132. Ann Arbor: The University of Michigan Press.
6. Chang, Wejen. 2008. Xu er [The second preface]. In *Guizhou Wendouzhai Miaozu qiyue falü wenshu huibian—Jiang Yuanze jiacang qiyue wenshu* [The compilation of contractual and legal manuscripts of the Miao from Wendou Village, Guizhou—Manuscripts from Jiang Yuanze's family collection], ed. Jinquan Chen and Wanhua Du, 7–8. Beijing: Renmin chubanshe.
7. Changzhou shi mucai gongsi ed. 1986. *Changzhou shi mucai zhi (1800–1985)* [Changzhou timber gazetteer (1800–1985)], 213. Changzhou: Changzhou shi mucai gongsi.
8. Chen, Hanfei. 2018. Wenshu, shengtai yu wenhua: Jinping wenshu yanjiu de xin jinzhan—2017 nian disijie Jinping wenshu xueshu yantaohui zongshu [Documents, ecology, and culture: New breakthroughs in the study on Jinping documents: Review of the 4th Jinping documents seminar]. *Guizhou daxue xuebao (shehui kexue ban)* 36 (1): 54–62.
9. Chen, Hongbo, and Zejiang Long. 2014. Xin faxian Guizhou Qingshuijiang Dongzu yulin ce pingjie [A study of the newly discovered Dong's *Yulince* in Tianzhu County on the Qingshui River in Guizhou Province]. *Yunnan minzu daxue xuebao (zhexue shehui kexue ban)* 31 (4): 107.
10. Chen, Jinquan, and Liang Guo, eds. 2017. *Guizhou Wendouzhai Miaozu qiyue falü wenshu huibian—Yi Zunfa Jiang Qicheng deng jiacang susong wenshu* [The compilation of contractual and legal manuscripts of the Miao from Wendou Village, Guizhou—Litigation manuscripts from family collections of Yi Zunfa, Jiang Qicheng, etc.]. Beijing: Renmin chubanshe.
11. Chen, Jinquan, and Wanhua Du, eds. 2015. *Guizhou Wendouzhai Miaozu qiyue falü wenshu huibian—Jiang Qigui jiacang qiyue wenshu* [The compilation of contractual and legal manuscripts of the Miao from Wendou Village, Guizhou—Manuscripts from Jiang Qigui's family collection], 366, 367, 368, 369. Beijing: Renmin chubanshe.
12. Cheng, Zeshi. 2017. *Hudong yu gongxiang: Qing dai Miao Jiang shehui zhuanxing zhi lisong tiaoshi* [Trial adjustment and social transition in Qing Miao areas], 315–318. Beijing: Zhongguo fazhi chubanshe.
13. Cohen, Myron L. 1969. The role of contract in traditional Chinese social organization. In *Proceedings: VIIIth international congress of anthropological and ethnological sciences, Tokyo and Kyoto, 1968, Vol. 2, Ethnology*, 130–132. Tokyo: Science Council of Japan.
14. Cohen, Myron L. 2004. Writs of passage in late imperial China: The documentation of practical understandings in Minong, Taiwan. In *Contract and property in early modern China*, ed. Madeleine Zelin, Jonathan K. Ocko, and Robert Gardella, 88. Stanford: Stanford University Press.
15. Daniels, Christian, Yougeng Yang, and Fusaji Takeuchi, eds. 2001. *Kishū Myaozoku ringyō keiyaku monjo kaihen (1736–1950-nen)* [Old forestry contracts of the Miao in Guizhou, 1736–1950], vol. 1. Tokyo: Tōkyō gaikokugo daigaku Ajia Afurika gengo bunka kenkyūjo.

16. Deng, Jianpeng, and Kai Qiu. 2013. Cong heyi dao qiangzhi: Qing zhi Minguo Qingshuijiang jiufen wenshu yanjiu [From consensus to enforcement: A study on disputes manuscripts in the Qing and Republican periods]. *Gansu zhengfa xueyuan xuebao* 126 (1): 32–33.
17. Duan, Mingming. 2012. The role of formal contracts with weak legal enforcement: A study in the chinese context. *Strategic oganization* 10 (2): 158.
18. Duff, J. Arthur. 2017. The history of Kuling, China. In *Grace: A China Ddary, 1910–16*, ed. Judy Hogan, 145. Eugene, Oregon: Resource Publications.
19. Ellickson, Robert C. 1991. *Order without law: How neighbors settle disputes*, 1. Cambridge and London: Harvard University Press.
20. Elster, Jon. 2003. *The cement of society: A survey of social order*, reprinted ed., 1–3. Cambridge: Cambridge University Press.
21. Faure, David, and Helen F. Siu. 2006. The original translocal society and its modern fate: Historical and post-reform South China. In *Translocal China: linkages, identities and the reimagining of space*, ed. Tim Oakes and Louisa Schein, 39, 51. London and New York: Routledge.
22. Feaver, George. 1969. *From status to contract: A biography of Sir Henry Maine 1822–1888*, 43. London and Harlow: Longmans, Green & Co Ltd.
23. Freedman, Maurice. 1965. *Lineage organization in Southeastern China*, reprinted ed., 1. London: University of London, Athlone Press.
24. Gao, Qicai. 2019. Role of rural regulations in environmental protection and green development: Findings from Wendou village in qiandongnan miao and dong minority autonomous prefecture Pinghe County Hekou township in Guizhou Province. In *The right to development: Sustainable development and the practice of good governance*, ed. Wei Zhang, 94–104. Leiden, Boston: Brill.
25. Gao, Cong, and Hongpei Tan, eds. 2013. *Guizhou Qingshuijiang liuyu Ming Qing tusi qiyue wenshu, Jiunan pian* [Tusi contract manuscripts in the Qingshui River Basin of Guizhou during the Ming-Qing eras, Jiunan volume], 8–10. Beijing: Minzu chubanshe.
26. Guizhou sheng bianjizu, ed. 1988. *Dongzu shehui lishi diaocha* [Investigation into the society and history of the Dong people], 31–32. Guiyang: Guizhou minzu chubanshe.
27. Guizhou sheng Jinping xian minzhengju, ed. 2010. *Jinping xian minzhengzhi (1915–2007)* [Chronicle of civil affairs in Jinping County (1915–2007)], 227. Jinping: Guizhou sheng Jinping xian minzhengju.
28. Hansen, Valerie. 1995. *Negotiating daily life in traditional China: How ordinary people used contracts, 600–1400*. New Haven and London: Yale University Press.
29. Hayes, James. 1985. Specialists and written materials in the village world. In *Popular culture in late imperial China*, ed. David Johnson, Andrew J. Nathan, and Evelyn S. Rawski, 86–87. Berkeley, Los Angeles, London: University of California Press.
30. He, Huaihong. 1993. *Qiyue lunli yu shehui zhengyi—Luo'ersi zhengyilun zhong de lishi yu lixing* [Contract ethic and social justice—History and rationality in the theory of justice of Rawls], 10–12. Beijing: Zhongguo renmin daxue chubanshe.
31. He, Guangyu, and Xin He. 2013. *Guizhou shehui liubai nian* [Six hundred years of Guizhou society], 80. Guiyang: Guizhou renmin chubanshe.
32. Hechter, Michael, and Christine Horne, eds. 2009. *Theories of Social Order: A Reader*, 2nd ed., 1. Stanford, California: Stanford University Press.
33. Henderson, Dan Fenno, and Preston M. Torbert. 1992. Contract in the Far East—China and Japan. In *International encyclopedia of comparative law: Volume VII: contracts in General*, ed. Arthur von Mehren, 3 ff. Tübingen: J. C. B. Mohr.
34. Hobbes, Thomas. 1651. *Leviathan, Or, the matter, forme, & power of a common-wealth ecclesiasticall and civill*, 85. London: Andrew Crooke.
35. Hu, Heng. 2015. 'Huangquan bu xia xian' de youlai jiqi fansi [Origin and reflection of 'the emperor's power never descends below the county']. *Zhonghua dushu bao*, November 4.
36. Hu, Jingxiu. 1941. Qiandong muye gaikuang [The general situation of the timber industry in east Guizhou province]. *Qiguang yuekan* 2 (3): 41.

37. Jenks, Robert Darrah. 1994. *Insurgency and social disorder in Guizhou: The "Miao" rebellion, 1854–1873*, 22. Honolulu: University of Hawaii Press.
38. Jiang, Zuoqing. 2011. Shixi jilüe [A brief account of the lineage]. In *Tudi guanxi ji qita shiwu wenshu* [Manuscripts on land relationship and other issues], ed. Zhicheng Pan and Dahua Wu, 143, 145. Guiyang: Guizhou minzu chubanshe.
39. Jing, Cheng. 1940. Fuxing Qiandong muye de chujian [Suggestions on reviving the timber industry in east Guizhou province]. *Qiguang yuekan* 1 (3): 55–57.
40. Jinping xian Hekou xiang renmin zhengfu, ed. 2010. *Hekou xiang zhi* [Hekou Sub-county gazetteer], 420–421. Jinping: Jinping xian Hekou xiang renmin zhengfu.
41. Kim, Hanbark. 2015. Yinhe qianqu guanya: Qingshuijiang wenshu zhong de hongqi fenxi [The reason to go to yamen: An analysis of red contracts in the Qingshui River manuscripts]. *Yuanshengtai minzu wenhua xuekan* 7 (4): 75–81.
42. Kishimoto, Mio. Kishū no sanrin keiyaku monjo to Kishū no sanrin keiyaku monjo [A comparative study of the mountain forestry contractual manuscripts in Guizhou and Huizhou]. In *Kishū Myaozoku ringyō keiyaku monjo kaihen (1736–1950-nen)* [Old forestry contracts of the Miao in Guizhou, 1736–1950], ed. Christian Daniels, Yougeng Yang, and Fusaji Takeuchi, 182. Tokyo: Tōkyō gaikokugo daigaku Ajia Afurika gengo bunka kenkyūjo.
43. Lee, Tahirih V. 1997. Volume introduction. In *Chinese law: Contract, Guanxi, and dispute resolution in China*, ed. Tahirih V. Lee, xiv–xvi. New York & London: Garland Publishing, Ing.
44. Li, Zhi, Meigong Chen, and Baigu Wang, eds. 1669. *Zengbu Suweng zhizhang zazhu quanji* [An enlarged edition of Suweng encyclopedia for daily-use contracts and documents]. Shulin qianfu tang.
45. Lin, Qian. 2015. Guonei chengshu wenshu zai shaoshu minzu diqu de yunyong: Ming dai Qingshuijiang wenshu qizhi yangshi jianlun—Ming dai Qingshuijiang wenshu yanjiu zhiyi [The application of domestic mature documents in the ethnic minority regions: Historical information from Qingshuijiang documents in the Ming Dynasty—A study of Qingshuijiang documents in the Ming Dynasty I]. *Guizhou daxue xuebao (shehui kexue ban)* 33 (4): 54.
46. Lin, Qian, et al. 2012. *Ming Qing shiqi Guizhou minzu diqu shehui lishi fazhan yanjiu: Yi Qingshuijiang wei zhongxin lishi dili de shijiao* [Studies of the social and historical development in the minorities area of Guizhou during the Ming and Qing dynasties: From a perspective of historical geography centering on the Qingshui River], 5–11. Beijing: Zhishi chanquan chubanshe.
47. Liu, Yanan, and Caimao Wu. 2012. Cong qiyue wenshu kan Qing dai Qingshuijiang xiayou diqu de lunli jingji [Morality economy reflected in the contracts of the Qing dynasty in the lower reaches of the Qingshui River valley]. *Yuanshengtai minzu wenhua xuekan* 4 (2): 36–45.
48. Long, Linglie. 2018. Guizhou shengwei lingdao diaoyan Jinping wenshu tecangguan [Leaders of Guizhou investigated the special collection of Jinping manuscripts]. *Zhongguo dang'an* (5): 10.
49. Luo, Hongyang. 2005. Qing dai Qiandongnan Jinping Miaozu linye qiyue de jiufen jiejue jizhi [The solution mechanism of the dissension concerning the forestry contract in Jinping located in the south-east of the Guizhou province in the Qing dynasty]. *Minzu yanjiu* (1): 88–96.
50. Ma, Jing. 2017. Guifan chuancheng, zhixu weichi he fazhi jianshe de tansuo—Jinping wenshu faxue yanjiu zongshu [Inheriting norms, maintaining order, and establishing the rule of law—A review of legal studies on the Jinping documents]. In *Jinping wenshu yu fawenhua yanjiu* [Jinping manuscripts and the studies of legal culture], ed. Qicai Gao and Kui Wang, 486–516. Beijing: Zhongguo zhengfa daxue chubanshe.
51. Ma, Guojun, and Hongxiang Li. 2012. Jin liushinian lai Qingshuijiang linye qiyue de shouji zhengli yu yanjiu zongshu [The collecting, sorting, and research on the forestry contracts in the Qingshui River region in the past 60 years]. *Guizhou daxue xuebao (shehui kexue ban)* 30 (4): 75.
52. Ma, Guojun, and Ziyue Wang. 2019. Guizhou Qingshuijiang liuyu linye qiyue wenshu zhengli he yanjiu zongshu [The forestry contract documents arangement and research review in the Qingshui River Basin of Guizhou]. *Gujin nongye* (4): 109–120.

53. Maine, Henry Sumner. 1861. *Ancient law: Its connection with the early history of society, and its relation to modern ideas*, 304. London: John Murray.
54. Maitland, Frederic William. 1989. Prologue to a history of english law. *Law Quarterly Review* 14 (1): 13.
55. McDermott, Joseph P. 2013. *The making of a new rural order in South China: I. village, land, and lineage in Huizhou, 900–1600*, 2 vols., vol. 1, 16–38. Cambridge: Cambridge University Press.
56. Oakes, Tim. 2007. Land of living fossils: Scaling cultural prestige in China's periphery. In *Locating China: Space, place, and popular culture*, ed. Jing Wang, 39–42. London and New York: Routledge.
57. Pan, Zhicheng, Dahua Wu, and Cong Liang, eds. 2014. *Qingjiang si an yanjiu* [Studies on the four cases in the Qingshui River region], vol. 3, 29–50. Guiyang: Guizhou minzu chubanshe.
58. Paterson, Isabel. 1943. *The God of the machine*, 41–52. New York: G. P. Putnam's Sons.
59. Pound, Roscoe. 1997. *Social control through law*. New Haven: Transaction Publishers.
60. Qu, Jian. 2017. Yikou daibi: Qing dai Wendou zhai falü shuxie de xianchang yu biaoda [The scribe: The scenario and expression of legal writing practice in Wendou Village in the Qing dynasty]. In *Jinping wenshu yu fawenhua yanjiu* [Jinping manuscripts and the studies of legal culture], ed. Qicai Gao and Kui Wang, 183–185. Beijing: Zhongguo zhengfa daxue chubanshe.
61. Qu, Jian. 2018. A brief introduction to the Qingshui river manuscripts. *ERCCS–Research Notes* (2): 1–6.
62. Qu, Jian. 2019. *Yanchu fasui: Caiyun huangmu andu jiaojian yu yanjiu (shang)* [Taking promulgated words as law: Collation, annotation, and study of 'Records of the procurement of imperial timber'], 2 vols., vol. 1, 98, 103. New Taipei City: Hua Mulan wenhua shiye youxian gongsi.
63. Qu, Jian. 2019. *Yanchu fasui: Caiyun huangmu andu jiaojian yu yanjiu (xia)* [Taking promulgated words as law: Collation, annotation, and study of 'Records of the procurement of imperial timber'], 2 vols., vol. 2, 160–213. New Taipei City: Hua Mulan wenhua shiye youxian gongsi.
64. Rabban, David M. 2009. From Maine to Maitland via America. *The Cambridge Law Journal* 68 (2): 410.
65. Redfield, Robert. 1950. Maine's ancient law in the light of primitive societies. *Western Political Quarterly* 3 (4): 576.
66. Scogin, Hugh T. 1990. Between heaven and man: Contract and the state in Han Dynasty China. *Southern California Law Review* 63 (5): esp. 1370–1402.
67. Scogin, Hugh T. 1994. Civil 'Law' in traditional China: History and theory. In *Civil law in Qing and Republican China*, ed. Kathryn Bernhardt and Philip C. C. Huang, 19–23. Standford: Standford University Press.
68. Scott, John, and Gordon Marshall, eds. 2009. *A dictionary of sociology*, 3rd ed., 706–707. Oxford: Oxford University Press.
69. Sun, Hua, and Hongguang Wang, eds. 2016. *Guizhou Miaozu cunzhai diaocha jianbao* [Investigation report of Miao villages in Guizhou], vol. 4, 70, 92. Chengdu: Bashu shushe.
70. Tang, Shiping. 2016. Order: A conceptual analysis. *Chinese Political Science Review* 1 (1): 31–33.
71. Taylor, J. Husdon, ed. 1875. *China's millions, and our work among them*, 42, 159. London: Morgan & Scott.
72. Terada, Hiroaki. 1989. Shindai tochihō chitsujo ni okeru 'kanko' no kōzō [The role of custom in the real estate legal system of the Qing period]. *Tōyō shi kenkyū* 48 (2): 347.
73. Terada, Hiroaki. 2004. Gōi to keiyaku–Chūgoku kinsei ni okeru 'keiyaku' o tegakari ni [Agreements and contracts: An examination of 'contracts' in early modern China]. In *Hikakushi no Ajia: Shoyū, keiyaku, shijō, kōsei* [Asia in comprative perspective: Ownership, contracts, markets, fairness and justice], ed. Toru Miura, Mio Kishimoto, and Teruo Sekimoto, 89–112. Tokyo: Tōkyō Daigaku Shuppankai.
74. Wang, Shuaiyi. 2012. Ming Qing shidai guanfang duiyu qiyue de ganyu: Tongguo 'shuiqi' fangshi de jieru [The official intervention to the contracts in the Ming-Qing eras: The intervention through 'tax deed']. *Zhongwai faxue* 24 (6): 1278–1291.

75. Wang, Zongxun. 2002. Wendou xingshuai shilue [A brief history of the rise and fall of Wendou Village]. *Guizhou dang'an shiliao* (1): 52–57.
76. Wang, Zongxun, ed. 2008. *Xiangtu Jinping* [Rural Jinping County], 179. Guiyang: Guizhou daxue chubanshe.
77. Wang, Zongxun. 2009. *Wendou: Kan de jian lishi de cunzhai* [Wendou: A village with visible history]. Guiyang: Guizhou renmin chubanshe.
78. Wang, Zongxun. 2017. *Qingshuijiang mushang guzhen—Maoping* [The old town of timber merchants along the Qingshui River—Maoping], 108–109. Guiyang: Guizhou minzu chubanshe.
79. Wang, Zongxun. 2013. Qingjiang jufu Jiang Shichao [The tycoon of the Qingshui River region: Jiang Shichao]. In *Qiandongnan renwu zhi, Ming Qing juan* [Qiandongnan gazetteer of personages, the volume of the Ming and Qing dynasties], ed. Zhengxie Qiandongnan zhou weiyuanhui, 747–748. Kunming: Yunnan minzu chubanshe.
80. Wang, Zongxun. 2015. *Xunshi yiluo de jiyi: Jinping wenshu zhengji shouji* [Finding the lost memories: A diary of collecting the Jinping manuscripts], 150. Guangzhou: Shijie tushu chuban Guangdong youxian gongsi.
81. Wang, Zhiqiang. 2017. *Qing dai guojiafa: Duoyuan chayi yu jiquan tongyi* [State law in the Qing dynasty: Heterogeneous plurality and power centralization]. Beijing: Shehui kexue wenxian chubanshe.
82. Wang, Qinmei, and Yingqiang Zhang. 2016. Wenzi shuxie yu xingdong celüe—Yi Guizhou Miao ren tusi jiapu *Longshi diguang lu* wei zhongxin de tantao [Text writing and action strategies: A discussion centered on the genealogy of the Miao people's *Longshi diguang lu*]. *Beifang minzu daxue xuebao (zhexue shehui kexue ban)* (2): 12–17.
83. Wei, Li, and Yingqiang Zhang. 2018. Impacts of timber trade on social economic life during the 'Ming & Qing' dynasty in South-western China—The evidence from Qingshui river basin. *Journal of Applied Business and Economics* 20 (3): 58–60.
84. Weinstein, Jodi L. 2013. *Empire and identity in Guizhou: Local resistance to Qing expansion*, 11. Seattle and London: University of Washington Press.
85. Wu, Caimao. 2014. Jin wushinian lai Qingshuijiang wenshu de faxian yu yanjiu [The discovery and studies on the Qingshui River manuscripts in 50 years]. *Zhongguoshi yanjiu dongtai* (1): 39–52.
86. Wu, Caimao. 2016. *Minjian wenshu yu Qingshuijiang diqu de shehui bianqian* [Folk documents and the social change in the Qingshui River region], 2. Beijing: Minzu chubanshe.
87. Wu, Xiangxiang, ed. [1923] 1962. *Zhongguo minshi xiguan daquan* [A compendium of Chinese popular customs], 25–26. Taipei: Wenxing shudian.
88. Wu, Yi. 2016. *Negotiating rural land ownership in Southwest China: State, village, family*, 23. Honolulu: University of Hawai'i Press.
89. Xie, Jinglian. 2019. Diwujie Jinping wenshu xueshu yantaohui zongshu [A review of the fifth Jinping documents symposium]. *Yuanshengtai minzu wenhua xuekan* 11 (5): 32–36.
90. Xu, Jiagan. [1878] 1997. *Miao jiang wen jian lu* [Record of things seen and heard on the Miao frontier], ed. Yiwen Wu, 162. Guiyang: Guizhou renmin chubanshe.
91. Xu, Xiaoguang. 2006. *Qingshuijiang liuyu linye jingji fazhi de lishi huisu* [A historical study on the forestry economic legal system in the Qingshui River Basin], 221 ff. Guiyang: Guizhou renmin chubanshe.
92. Xu, Xiaoguang, and Zeshi Cheng. 2015. Qingshuijiang wenshu yanjiu zhengyi wenti pingshu [A review of controversial issues in the studies of the Qingshui River manuscripts]. *Yuanshengtai minzu wenhua xuekan* 7 (1): 45–62.
93. Yang, Junchang. 2017. Zhangxian diyu wenhua, zhutui xueshu fazhan: 'Qingshuijiangxue yanjiu' tese lanmu jianshe shijiantan [Discussion on the experiences of setting out the distinctive column 'Qingshui River Studies']. *Jiaoyu wenhua luntan* (5): 134.
94. Yang, Yougeng. 1988. Jiangshi zupu fanying de Ming Qing shiqi Wendou Miaozu diqu jingji wenhua zhuangkuang [Economic and cultural conditions in the Miao area of Wendou in the Ming and Qing dynasties reflected in the *Genealogy of the Jiang Clan*]. In *Guizhou minzu diaocha* [Guizhou Ethnic Investigation], ed. Guizhou minzu yanjiu xuehui and Guizhou sheng minzu yanjiusuo, 346–353. Guiyang: Guizhou sheng minzu yanjiusuo.

95. Zhang, Meng. 2017. Timber trade along the Yangzi river: Market, institutions, and environment, 1750–1911. Doctoral dissertation, University of California, Los Angeles, 204.
96. Zhang, Jiyuan. 2017. Jin sanshinian lai haiwai ji Gang Tai diqu Qingshuijiang wenshu yanjiu de huigu yu sikao [A review of overseas (including Hongkong and Taiwan) studies on the Qingshui River manuscripts in 30 years], 555–567. Paper presented at the 4th Conference of Jinping Documents, Jinping, Guizhou.
97. Zhang, Yingqiang. 2006. *Mucai zhi liudong: Qing dai Qingshuijiang xiayou diqu de shichang, quanli yu shehui* [The wood flow: Market, power, and society in the downstream sections of Qingshui River in the Qing dynasty], 205. Beijing: Shenghuo, dushu, xinzhi sanlianshudian.
98. Zhang, Yingqiang. 2013. Qingshuijiang wenshu de shouji zhengli yu yanjiu chuyi [On the collection, classification, and research of the Qingshui River manuscripts]. *Yuanshengtai minzu wenhua xuekan* 5 (3): 33.
99. Zhang, Yingqiang. 2015. Wenxian yu tianye: 'Qingshuijiang wenshu' zhengli yanjiu de fangfalun [Literature and field: Methodology of the collation and study on the 'Qingshui River manuscripts']. *Guangming ribao* (Beijing), October 15.
100. Zhang, Yingqiang. 2019. Zong xu [Preface]. In *Ren shen zhi jian: Xiang Qian Gui jielin diqu Feishangong xinyang yanjiu* [Between god and man: A study on the belief of Feishangong in the bordering areas of Hunan, Guizhou, and Guangxi], ed. Zhaojun Luo, 1–4. Beijing: Shehui kexue wenxian chubanshe.
101. Zhang, Yingqiang, and Zongxun Wang, eds. 2007. *Qingshuijiang wenshu* [Qingshui River manuscripts], vol. 1(12), 119. Guilin: Guangxi shifan daxue chubanshe.
102. Zhang, Yingqiang, and Zongxun Wang, eds. 2007. *Qingshuijiang wenshu* [Qingshui River manuscripts], vol. 1(13), 105. Guilin: Guangxi shifan daxue chubanshe.
103. Zhang, Yingqiang, and Zongxun Wang, eds. 2011. *Qingshuijiang wenshu* [Qingshui River manuscripts], vol. 3(7), 421. Guilin: Guangxi shifan daxue chubanshe.
104. Zhang, Ming, Zejun Dai, and Zhengping Ding. 2016. Qingshuijiang wenshu de lishi zhenshixing kaozheng [Research on the facticity of the Qingshui River manuscripts]. *Guizhou daxue xuebao(shehui kexue ban)* 34 (1): 111.
105. Zhongguo diyi lishi dang'an guang, Zhongguo renmin daxue Qing shi yanjiusuo, and Guizhou sheng dang'an guang, eds. 1987. *Qing dai qianqi Miaomin qiyi dang'an shiliao huibian* [Collected archival materials on Miao uprising in the early Qing], 3 vols. Beijing: Guangming ribao chubanshe.
106. Zhou, Dongtao. 2010. *Reforming China: Experiences and lessons,* (trans. Xin Zhou and Qinhua Shao), 70–71. Hong Kong: Enrich Professional Publishing.
107. Zhu, Hanqin, ed. 2009. *Jinping renwu, wenshi ziliao* [Jinping personages, cultural, and historical materials], 29. Guangzhou: Nanfang wenshi chubanshe.

Chapter 2
Rediscovering Contracts in the Qingshui River Region

> [I]t is not a peculiarity of complex terms like 'law' and 'legal system' that we are forced to recognize both clear standard cases and challengeable borderline cases. It is now a familiar fact (though once too little stressed) that this distinction must be made in the case of almost every general term which we use in classifying features of human life and of the world in which we live.... Is a flying boat a 'vessel'? Is it still 'chess' if the game is played without a queen?
> Hart [70].

1 Introduction: Standard and Borderline Contracts

1.1 A General and Complex Term

The contract is a familiar fact for both professionals and laypeople, although this may not be the case when referring to the traditional Chinese contract, especially in the context of the Qingshui River region during the Qing dynasty. A focused study of these contract manuscripts therefore needs to investigate the notion of a contract in the eyes of the people at the time and the region, thereby defining its research object within its historical and social context. For this provides one with a chance of rediscovering the familiar concept of a contract in an unfamiliar context.

It may seem ironic that, despite the immense amount of related literature, studies on traditional Chinese contracts may not be able to provide any direct help to the endeavor of trying to define the contract in context. Although "contract," especially in traditional China, is not just a "general" but also a "complex" term, it is still not

The basic idea of this chapter was presented at the "Max Planck Legal History Quarterly Forum: History of Privat Law in East Asia" on 3 September 2018 at Max Planck Institute for European Legal History in Frankfurt, under the title "What is A Contract? Definition and Designation in the Context of Late Imperial China." In addition, a rather concise version was presented at conferences at the School of Law, Sun Yat-sen University in Guangzhou, and the School of Law, Hainan University in Haikou, respectively on 29 December 2019 and 5 January 2020. All the participants are appreciated.

J. Qu, *Social Order through Contracts*,
https://doi.org/10.1007/978-981-33-4947-6_2

Fig. 1 Undigested paper manuscripts found in fieldwork in Wendou Village

"a familiar fact" that the distinction between a contract and a non-contract must be made in the first instance for a historical analysis of Chinese contracts.

The reason for this is quite clear: the overwhelming majority of contracts that one may encounter, such as those from published collections or selected references in second-hand materials, can be regarded as the "clear standard cases" in Hart's sense.[1] Alternatively, for the "challengeable borderline cases," one may only realize their existence when, for instance, conducting field research in a remote village as a legal sociologist or anthropologist, in which one faces a whole array of undigested paper manuscripts which have not been labeled as contracts, and one is attempting to tell which piece of them is a contract and which is not (see Fig. 1).[2] Obviously, there is always a selection process, consciously or unconsciously, and so, while processing these raw materials, an unambiguous borderline, which has too long been disregarded, is inevitable.

Thanks to the continuous discovery of manuscripts and documents in Ming-Qing China, studies on traditional contracts have emerged with increasing frequency over recent years.[3] However, only a few of them have shown their intention to investigate

[1] As to the "standard cases and borderline cases," see H. L. A. Hart, *The Concept of Law*, 278.

[2] Courtesy of Prof. Xie Hui, Wendou, Guizhou, August 2002.

[3] See Wu [209], Luan [127].

contracts in a general sense,[4] and even fewer have tried to offer a clear-cut definition. Among these attempts, Valerie Hansen has proposed "a working definition" of traditional Chinese contracts, albeit one based on materials from a much earlier period (600–1400), at the beginning of her book:

> Chinese contracts, then, were written agreements between two or more parties to buy, sell, rent, or borrow a given commodity.[5]

This definition evidently reveals several key ingredients of a Chinese contract. Yet, as the author stresses, "[m]ost of the contracts in this book are about straightforward, sometimes poignant, transactions," such as "the purchase, sale, or rental of a house, a plot of land, a draft animal, a slave, a concubine, even a child."[6] From this perspective, it is easy to tell that the definition is mainly derived from civil and commercial contracts, which are the most typical kinds of contracts not only in ancient China but also in the modern world. However, for the "borderline cases" which have not been included, this way of defining contracts might be far from enough.

1.2 *The Chinese Terminology of Contracts*

Before formally entering into the discussion of the contract as an English term, some issues of cross-lingual terminology require clarification. This study, which deals with a Chinese phenomenon of using contracts, is written in English. However, the practice of contracts in the Qingshui River region during the Qing dynasty was in no way based on an English context; on the contrary, the practice of using contracts, to a large extent as well as the rural society in which the practice took place, operated in the Chinese language and, inasmuch as its participants were literate, with Chinese writing. Hence, the protagonists in this study surely did not hold a perception of "contract," but its Chinese counterpart. In this case, as with many previous works in

---

[4]For attempts to inspect Chinese contracts at a conceptual level, see Henderson and Torbert [76], Cohen [33–35], Hansen [69], Bourgon [15], Brockman [17], Buxbaum [19], Zelin [227], Kishimoto [107], Terada [171, 172], Trombert [177]. For Chinese scholars, see He [74], Yu [223, 224].

[5]Valerie Hansen, *Negotiating Daily Life in Traditional China*, 10.

[6]See ibid., 1. A comment on this definition from Professor Cohen is that "[a]lthough this definition is based squarely on Chinese documents, it would exclude those which, while not agreements, can be placed together with these in particular spheres of document production." See Myron L. Cohen, "Writs of Passage in Late Imperial China," 89. He also appears to offer a description of Chinese contracts at the beginning of his discussion, namely as a "signed and witnessed written product of China's late imperial culture when many basic arrangements of social life were fixed through the use of documents." See ibid., 37.

a similar bilingual context,[7] the key term employed in the following discussion, i.e. "contract," needs to be explained.

In this study, the English term "contract,"[8] when used in a context related to China and especially the Qingshui River region, translates the term *qiyue* or *ziyue*.[9] This term refers to four Chinese words that were prevalent in the contract practice of the region: *qi*, *yue*, *zi*, and *hetong*. Also, when the last word is especially mentioned, this study uses either the term *hetong* or the English "indenture." The literal differences, if any, between the first three Chinese words *qi*, *yue*, and *zi* have been discussed within the larger context of late imperial China,[10] but, at least in the Qingshui River region, there was no significant difference between the three in writing practice, apart from the fact that, according to statistical evidence, the latter two appear to be more popular.[11] Thus, this study does not plan to treat the three words differently as there was barely any distinction in practice, but it will collectively refer to them as "contract." The *hetong* was slightly different from the first three, since, unlike those contracts that have only one copy, it was often written in duplicate or even triplicate on several pieces of paper.[12] Beyond that, *hetong* can still be covered by the more general concept of *qiyue* or *ziyue*.

In short, all four Chinese words listed above fall under the English umbrella-term "contract" in this study, while sometimes *hetong* is singled out when discussing its material aspect. This study agrees with the statement in another study that, while conducting a scholarly investigation of Ming-Qing contracts, the term "contracts" shall be understood as "the Chinese style of contracts," namely "the notion held by officials and common people concerning *qi* and *yue* at Ming-Qing period."[13] In addition, it should also be noted that, although there are unavoidable gaps between

[7]For a noteworthy discussion on terms that were used by an English-language study on issues of Chinese legal history, see Hase [71]. In this regard, see also Myron L. Cohen, "Writs of Passage in Late Imperial China," 37 ff.

[8]It has also to be noted that, English (and Latin) has a rich vocabulary which bears a similar meaning of contract, e.g. *contractus*, compact, pact, *pacta*, agreement, indenture, deed, charter, covenant, bargain, treaty, consensus, engagement, and stipulation. However, many of these seem ill-suited to the context of this study. Although there are some terms that are frequently used in studies of Chinese contracts, such as "deed," this study opts to keep to the term "contract" for the purpose of conciseness and consistency.

[9]For the difference between the two, see Qu [147]. The latter is considered more appropriate in the context of the Qingshui River region. In addtion, some have noticed that there might be a problem when using *qiyue* as a term to include both *qi* and *yue* in Ming-Qing China. See Kishimoto [107].

[10]Kishimoto Mio, "Ming Qing qiyu wenshu," 181–182; Terada Hiroaki, "Ming Qing shiqi fazhixu zhong 'yue' de xingzhi," 136–181.

[11]See Qu Jian, "Yikou daibi," 185.

[12]The characteristics of this kind of contract will be discussed in the later chapter of scribes. For discussions about the term *hetong*, see He Weifang, "'Qiyue' yu 'hetong' de bianxi," 36–40; Yu Jiang, "'Qiyue' yu 'hetong' zhibian—Yi Qing dai qiyue wenshu wei chufadian," 134–148; Liu [119], Yu and Chen [225].

[13]Kishimoto Mio, "Lijiao, qiyue, shengcun," 42.

the use of terms in different lingual contexts, these differences are believed to be largely "immaterial in the context of discussions of broad principles."[14]

1.3 "Standard Cases" and "Borderline Cases"

It is a familiar fact that, although contractual materials from the Ming-Qing period have notably increased, scholars still tend to place more attention on the "standard cases," as they are the most visible ones. While some pioneering research had precisely limited their objects of study to "land-related contracts"[15] instead of "contracts" as a whole, people might still be inclined to believe that, implicitly or explicitly, "civil and commercial contracts" are approximately equal to "contracts" in the context of late imperial China. The extreme diversity of traditional Chinese contracts was therefore neglected to a large extent.[16]

Nevertheless, any study that seeks to define "contract" must face, or rather largely rely on, this diversity, for an applicable definition will not be easily derived from the summary of only central cases; the dividing line can only be found through a thorough analysis of multiple cases at the margin.

Before turning to these challenging cases, however, it might be helpful to offer some account of the undisputed ones. It is not difficult to find a clear standard contract in the Qinghshui River manuscripts corpus—most contracts can be considered standard in terms of quantity. The following is a contract from the region given as an example of a standard case[17]:

> Manuscript 1: A standard contract (July 23, 1780)
>
> The establisher of the contract of irrevocable sale of wet-rice fields, Jiang Yingyou,[18] because of the lack of money [to pay for] living expenses and having no other way [to raise money], personally asked the middleman to sell his two parcels of wet-rice fields, named Dangyi, with willingness, to [his] younger male patrilineal cousin, Jiang Yinghui. With this sale [the land is to be] under [Jiang Yinghui's] name as [his] property. On that day, through the middleman, [both parties] discussed the price of the irrevocable sale and agreed on one tael, eight maces, and two candareens exactly, [and Jiang Yingyou] received the money with his own hands. Since the sale of the fields, the vendee can farm and manage this property at will, and the vendor shall not raise any dissenting voices afterward. If there are any dissenting voices [raised by others], the vendor shall be in charge of them. Fearing that a verbal agreement might not suffice as proof, the contract of irrevocable sale is hereby established for retention and reference.

---

[14]Patrick H. Hase, *Custom, Land and Livelihood in Rural South China*, 1.

[15]See, e.g., Yang [218]. This book claims in its introduction that its research object "is confined to one category of contract documents in Ming-Qing eras". See ibid., 3. For a newer version of this groundbreaking monograph, see Yang [219].

[16]For the widespread use of contracts especially in social organizations, see Myron L. Cohen, "The Role of Contract in Traditional Chinese Social Organization," 132.

[17]Chen and Du [26].

[18]The editor of the contract wrongly transcribed the name as "Jiang Yingjiao".

Four characters were added to this contract.[19]

Middleman: Lu Honggui

Scribe: Jiang Tingjun

Qianlong, forty-fifth year, sixth month, twenty-second day (July 23, 1780), established.

In this contract, Jiang Yingyou sold two parcels of his fields to his cousin for a price of 1.82 taels of silver. Although relatively brief, it is no doubt a wholly typical contract of sale and seems to contain all familiar elements required, such as an offer, an acceptance, a consideration or *cause*,[20] leading to the formation of a contract.[21]

These elements, however, might be difficult to find in some other manuscripts, and this makes these manuscripts questionable in the sense of "contract." Here is an excerpt of a "contract" that would be described as a borderline case[22]:

Manuscript 2: A non-standard contract (July 17, 1908)

On Guangxu, thirty-fourth year, sixth month, nineteenth day (July 17, 1908), all [who own the mountain] harvested [the timber on] the Jingdu mountain by themselves. Under Dengxiang's wet-rice field, and above Xuezheng's wet-rice field, is the place where this one mountain is located. The timber has been sold to Jiang Haishun, who lives in this village, and [after] discussion the timber price [was agreed to be] eighteen taels, eight maces, and eight candareens. Apart from the cost of the feast [and] the wages for the lumberers, two taels, three maces, and eight candareens, there are still sixteen taels, five maces, and four candareens remaining. There are five shares to be divided between the landowners and the forestry workers: the landowners hold three shares, namely nine taels, five maces, and four candareens shall be allocated [to them]; the forestry workers hold two shares, namely six taels, six maces, one candareen, and six cashes shall be allocated [to them]. Weibang holds one share from the forestry workers, therefore three taels, three maces, and eight cashes [shall] be allocated [to him]. Weiguang,[23] Weiming, Weichen, and Xuanshu and his nephew hold one share together, and [this share] is further divided into six small shares. Weiming and Weichen hold three small shares, therefore one tael, six maces, five candareens, and three cashes [shall] be allocated [to them]; Weiguang holds one small share, therefore five maces, five candareens, and one cash [shall] be allocated [to him]; Xuanshu [and his nephew] hold two small shares, therefore one tael, one mace, two candereens, and six cashes [shall] be allocated [to them].

...

Scribe: Weiming

Kept by Weibang

[This] contract list [has] two copies.[24]

The story that this manuscript tells is quite straightforward: a group of people sold the timber on their mountain, and after deducting the costs (meal fee and workers'

[19] This line is a postscript and the four characters it mentioned refer to "if there is any dissenting voice" (*ruyou yiyan*) according to the image of the contract, and they were written in small characters.

[20] See Walton [183].

[21] See Smits [158].

[22] Daniels et al. [40].

[23] The editor of the manuscript wrongly transcribed the name as "Weixian".

[24] This sentence was written at the junction of the edges of two sheets of paper, so only the left part was written on this manuscript.

wages) the remaining sum (net earnings) was distributed to all shareholders accordingly. This manuscript records at length the number of shares that everyone held and the amount of money that shall be allocated. The omitted parts are similar paragraphs concerning the timber on another mountain.

Apparently, this transcription has nothing to do with a contract of sale but instead with a list of profit allocation. Interestingly, although neither the substance nor the form of the manuscript resembles the standard contract shown above, at the end of the paper it describes itself as a "*hetong* (indenture)," which, as mentioned, is a typical type of contract in traditional China. This word is also most commonly used to translate "contract" in modern Chinese. Despite the possibility of a transcription error,[25] evidence from the ways of writing—the most prominent way being to write at the joining of two sheets of paper—clearly show that the manuscript was deliberately produced as a "*hetong*." Moreover, other manuscripts which deal with the same subject of profit allocation and bear identical, or at least similar, text forms as those standard contracts can also be found.[26] Although there may still be some doubts concerning the uncommon form of the manuscript, these manuscripts have shown that the same content can also be presented in a way that more closely resembles a "contract."

This comparison now poses the question: can manuscripts like the second example, with its various points of dissimilarity, be considered as contracts? Or can only those that look like the first one be called contracts? Ultimately, for the distinction between contract and non-contract to be maintained, where is the exact demarcation line to be drawn?[27]

This chapter intends to figure out, practically, how contracts can be identified in numerous raw manuscripts, and if a set of criteria of contracts can be found or given, either within the Qingshui River manuscripts or more broadly in the context of late imperial China.[28] In addition, since the lack of a clear definition also reveals that a thorough and integrated understanding of Chinese contracts in late imperial times is still missing, this chapter further attempts to offer a new understanding of the contract in its context in relation to its conception in modern times, by investigating the substantiality, formality, and materiality of the contract as well as its various definitions in different legal jurisdictions.

---

[25]If one takes a close look at the image of the manuscript, the transcription of the left half given by the editors might not be fully convincing, since only half of the writings remain. See Christian Daniels, Yang Yougeng, and Takeuchi Fusaji, *Kishū Myaozoku ringyō keiyaku monjo kaihen (1736–1950-nen)*, vol. 3, E-0050.

[26]For example, see Zhang and Wang [243]. For similar manuscripts with a middleman, see Zhang and Wang [241].

[27]Recent scholars are still trying to establish the distinction of contract and non-contract in terms of the modern contract law in order to adapt to the development of the times. See, e.g., Kar and Radin [102].

[28]This chapter will chiefly deal with materials from the Qingshui River region in the Qing dynasty, while manuscripts from other areas are also taken into account, in order to offer the proposed definition the possibility of greater application in late imperial China as a whole.

2 Contracts: Legal Definitions and Chinese Practice

2.1 Contracts in Contract Laws

2.1.1 Defining Contract in Laws: A Comparative Approach

The term "contract" is commonly understood as "a *legal* agreement between people, companies, etc.,"[29] and it is believed that "[i]n searching for definitions, we need to look at legislation," and "where appropriate, at case law and academic legal literature."[30] Given the tight connection between contract and law, it seems that the precise definition of the contract could, and should, be found in corresponding contract laws.

As an English legal term,[31] a contract firstly denotes "an agreement between two or more parties creating obligations that are enforceable or otherwise recognizable at law."[32] Although lacking the tradition of written law, similar descriptions of contract can also be seen in the doctrines of English and American laws. One classical definition from an eighteenth-century English jurist, William Blackstone, asserts that "[a] contract is an agreement, upon sufficient consideration, to do or not to do a particular thing."[33] In a leading and frequently updated textbook on the English contract law, *Treitel on the Law of Contract*, a contract is defined as "an agreement giving rise to obligations which are enforced or recognized by law."[34] As for American contract law, one of its best-recognized legal treatises, the *Second Restatement on Contracts*, defines "a contract" as "a promise or a set of promises for the breach of which the law gives a remedy or the performance of which the law in some way recognizes as a duty."[35] In the "Definitions" of American legal literature, which is not formally a law but has crucial influence on contract law globally, namely the *Uniformed Commercial Code (UCC)*, "contract" is understood as "the total legal obligation that results from the parties' agreement as determined by this act as supplemented by any other applicable laws."[36]

In legal systems outside the common law tradition, definitions of the contract are often clearly provided in written laws.[37] In France, "a contract is an agreement (*convention*) by which one or several persons bind themselves, towards one or several others, to transfer, to do or not to do something" (*Code civil 1804*, Article

---

[29] See "contract," Perrault [142].

[30] Beale et al. [11].

[31] A thorough discussion on "contract" as a legal term and word, as well as its difference from "engagement" and "accord," can be found in Fauvarque-Cosson and Mazeaud [51].

[32] See "contract," Garner [61].

[33] Blackstone [12].

[34] Peel [141].

[35] "Contract Defined," see American Law Institute [4].

[36] See "Uniform Commercial Code," (2001), Section 1-201 (11).

[37] For the English translations of the articles mentioned below in this paragraph, see Hugh Beale et al., *Cases, Materials and Text on Contract Law*, Sect. 5.1.A.

1101).[38] In the German Civil Code, "contract" (*Vertrag*) is mentioned under the title of "Obligations created by legal transaction and similar obligations," as "unless otherwise provided by statute, a contract between the parties is necessary in order to create an obligation by legal transaction or to alter the content of an obligation" (BGB, Section 311: 1). The provision of Italian law is that "[a] contract is an agreement between two or more parties for the purpose of creating, providing for or extinguishing amongst themselves a legal patrimonial relation" (*Codice civile*, Article 1321), while Dutch law considers a contract as "a multi-lateral juridical act whereby one or more parties assume an obligation towards one or more other parties" (*Burgerlijk Wetboek*, Article 6: 213).

In a significant effort to harmonize private law in the European Union, the *Draft Common Frame of Reference (DCFR)* has sought to unify the definitions of contract from various European laws, including the aforementioned ones. It suggests that "[a] contract is an agreement which is intended to give rise to a binding legal relationship or to have some other legal effect" and thus "[i]t is a bilateral or multi-lateral juridical act" (*DCFR*, II-1: 101).[39] In addition, it is remarkable that, concerning contract law at the international level, seemingly neither of the two most important legal documents in this field, i.e. the *United Nations Convention on Contracts for the International Sale of Goods (CISG)* and the *UNIDROIT Principles of International Commercial Contracts (PICC)*, offer a clear general definition of the contract.[40]

Although Islamic contract law[41] has its own point of view on the validity of a contract—it specially prescribes that "contracts should be permitted by religion"[42]—there is not any significant difference in the "main principles of contract law" between the sharia contract law and secular contract laws.[43] The contract of sale acts as the foundation of its system of contract and obligation law,[44] and offer (*īĝāb*), acceptance (*qabūl*) and the "free consent of parties" or "mutual consent" (*tarāḍin*) are the keywords in defining a contract in laws here too.[45]

Contract law might represent one of the most universal legal branches[46] and has long been the classical subject matter of comparative law,[47] so it is possible

---

[38] A revision in 2016 states that "[a] contract is a concordance of wills of two or more persons intended to create, modify, transfer or extinguish obligations" (*Code civil 1804*, Article 1101). See ibid.

[39] Further, "[a] juridical act is any statement or agreement, whether express or implied from conduct, which is intended to have legal effect as such. It may be unilateral, bilateral, or multilateral." See "Meaning of 'contract' and 'juridical act'," von Bar et al. [181].

[40] See United Nations [180], UNIDROIT [179].

[41] For the formation of Islamic contract law as a distinct discipline and the codification of the law of contracts in the Islamic world, see Mallat [132].

[42] Jan M. Smits, *Contract Law*, 35.

[43] See ibid.

[44] See Gao [58].

[45] See Mohammed [136], Oberauer [138].

[46] See Han [68].

[47] See Farnsworth [48].

to single out something in common from among the numerous differences.[48] After reviewing the definitions of contract in the above-mentioned major legal systems, the most concise description of a contract may be that it is a "legal agreement." This expression effectively reveals the two elements that underlie the concept of contract: (1) *Legal* means that a contract has to be somehow associated with the Law, mostly in the way that the Law recognizes the contract and, where appropriate, offers remedies or makes the contract enforceable[49]; and (2) *agreement* denotes that the elementary issue in forming a contract involves the consent of the parties[50] (or *der Konsens, consensus ad idem*, a meeting of minds, or mutual assent) or promise.[51] These two elements can be explained in this way: since the contract is legally binding, it needs to be ascertained by the Law,[52] and, among all other requirements, the consent of the parties may mark a point of departure in identifying a contract.

Putting aside the question whether the standard of "consent of the parties" was suitable for the contracts in question, or if they were even "agreements," the immediate question might be whether a contract in late imperial China was "legal" or not. If so, a contract should be one that can be recognized by its (positive) Law, and a definition or description should appear in the text of relevant laws. This leads this study to the legal context of contracts in Qing China, and, especially in terms of positive law, the *Great Qing Code*.

2.1.2 Contracts and the *Great Qing Code*

Although its de facto effectiveness was frequently challenged by customs or rituals, Qing China enjoyed a strong tradition of positive law that can be traced back a long time.[53] A series of relevant legal instruments formed the main legal basis of contractual activities in the Qing dynasty, including the *Great Qing Code*, the *Da Qing Huidian* (considered as the Administrative Code of the Qing dynasty),[54] the

---

[48] For a comparative legal study of contract laws both inside and outside the European Union, see Benedicte Fauvarque-Cosson and Denis Mazeaud, *European Contract Law—Materials for a Common Frame of Reference*, 21–24.

[49] For the purpose of enforcing the contract, the Law shall ascertain what the contract is and provide "a suitable remedy against its non-fulfillment." For the relation of law and contract, see Spear [161].

[50] See Kötz [104].

[51] Traditionally, it is considered that the common law system tends to view the contract as a promise, while the civil law system holds it as mutual consent. See Han Shiyuan, *Hetongfa zonglun*, 8–9; Wang and Wang [189], Hogg [83].

[52] The content of the parties' agreement needs to "lie within the scope of legal recognition." See Samuel Thayer Spear, *The Legal-tender Acts*, 55; Jan M. Smits, *Contract Law*, 3.

[53] As to the positive laws in the Ming and Qing eras, see Liang [113]. As to the written laws and customs as legal sources in Ming-Qing China, see Su [165]. In addition, for the early Chinese legal transition from "legal practice based upon oral and customary law" to written (positive) law, see Caldwell [20].

[54] See Chen [24], Keliher [106], Liu [120].

zeli (considered as regulations),[55] the *cheng'an* (considered as leading cases),[56] and so on. Out of all these normative texts, whether in terms of the scope of application or the legal hierarchy, the most important one was undoubtedly the *Great Qing Code*.[57]

The *Great Qing Code* has a long history of evolving from one version to another,[58] but the main body of the statutes (*lü*) remained unchanged since it was completed in the fifth year of Qianlong (1740),[59]which was perceived as the indication of "the maturity of dynastic legislation."[60] Therefore, the Code 1740, at least for the purposes of this study, can be regarded as a standard version out of many alternatives.[61] This version of the Code contained 436 statutes and 1049 sub-statutes (*li*) in total,[62] but the number of sub-statutes increased considerably in later times. As an example, it had grown to 1892 in the ninth year of Tongzhi (1870) according to one of the most famous jurists and lawmakers in the late Qing period, Shen Jiaben's calculation.[63] In this case, a much later version of the Code recorded in the *Duli cunyi* (*Doubts remaining after perusing the substatutes*),[64] which was published in the thirty-second year of Guangxu (1906), was also included for analysis as a supplementary source.[65]

Can any contract laws be found in the text of the *Great Qing Code*? Among all 436 statutes, only 7 of them, i.e. no. 93, 95, 101, 102, 125, 146, and 149, mentioned the contract in certain ways. Out of nearly two thousand sub-statutes, the term "contract" appeared in 36 of them; the Code 1740 accounts for 15 sub-statutes and the other 21 were added in the version of 1906.

Within all these statutes and sub-statutes, none can be deemed a definitional clause of the contract, and not even one directly and integrally describes what a contract should be like in terms of the law. These articles refer to "contract" as a matter of course. For example, the no. 93 statute, titled "The Theft and Sale of Fields and Houses", stated:

---

[55]See Su Yigong, *Ming Qing lüdian yu tiaoli*, 70–73.

[56]See Wang [194, 195].

[57]It is seen as "the most important book of the Qing legal world." See Zhang [230].

[58]For both imperial and commercial editions of the Code printed in the Qing dynasty, see the chart in ibid., 236. For a more comprehensive study, see Zhang [231].

[59]See Sun [167]. Some studies have argued that the Code was actually promulgated in 1743, see Chen [22]. For an earlier version of the Code, see Shen [154].

[60]Zheng and Zhou [246].

[61]See "Editors' notes," Tian and Zheng [174].

[62]See Zheng Qin and Guangyuan Zhou, "Formation of the Qing Code," 332.

[63]See "Shen Jiaben's Preface," Xue [214].

[64]See ibid.

[65]The database of this analysis was based on the work of the "Legalizing Space in China" project, see Bourgon et al. [16]. The digitalized 1740 version of the Code "has been established according to the modern punctuated edition by Zheng Qin and Tian Tao" (see Tian Tao and Zheng Qin, *Da Qing lüli*), and "under close scrutiny" of Sun Jiahong and Luca Gabbiani in Beijing, with a double check by two other project members (Lee Ju-ling and Wu Chun-huei) during its transcription. The digitalization of the Code 1906 was done by Sun Jiahong, basing on the original text of Xue Yunsheng, *Duli cunyi*, with referenced works by Terada Hiroaki and Huang Jingjia. See Terada [173], Xue [215].

> Whoever steals (another's fields and houses and) sells them, or (takes his unusable fields, and houses and exchanges them [for another's good fields and houses], or falsely declares (another person's fields and houses to be his own), or who falsely (writes the price) in money (in a written) contract of dian,[66] or who wrongfully takes possession of the field and houses of another, will, for a field of 1 mou or one room or below, be punished with 50 strokes of the light bamboo.[67]

The term "contract" appeared in this text as a common word that did not need any further explanation. It is true that "contract" was not an uncommon word, but the absence of characterization was an uncommon phenomenon in the context of the Qing law. For instance, the Code devoted at least three articles to defining the tutor (*shi*), which might be an even more popular word, from different perspectives,[68] and then presented a sophisticated description of the *shi* in law.[69]

With regard to the contract, it was used in various contexts with reference to different kinds of contracts, such as the white contracts and the red contracts/sealed contracts/tax contracts as shown in Table 1. In fact, this pair of keywords (white/red contracts) explains 40.63% (39/96) of all the appearance of *qi* and *yue* in the Code.[70]

The varied usages of the term also indicated the lawmaker's insights into the classification of contracts, but still did not offer any delimitation between contracts and non-contracts. However, this does not mean that no regulations concerning contracts were provided by the law. On the contrary, a limited number of articles still formulated requirements in writing a contract.

For example, the Code presented certain instructions about the phrases that should or should not be used in a contract. If a written contract of irrevocable sale does not give a clear indication of *zhaotie*, "a closing payment that transferred the rights of the land permanently to the buyers,"[71] then the seller will not be allowed to acquire the "closing payment" or ask to be in the future.[72] Similar regulations for contracts of *dian* can also be found in relevant sub-statutes.[73] Also, for contracts of sale of a

---

[66]For a thorough introduction to *dian*, considered as the "conditional sales of land," and its economic analysis, see Huang [91], Long et al. [125].

[67]See Tian Tao and Zheng Qin, *Da Qing lüli*, 195. For the translation, see Jones [101]. For an earlier, and perhaps the first version of the translation of the Code, see Staunton [163]. For a study of Staunton's translation of the Code, see Chen [23]. An introduction to the later 1812 Italian version, which took Staunton's translation as the basis, is also provided in Abbattista [1].

[68]For example, statute no. 42 and 311, and sub-statute no. 365.01, see Tian Tao and Zheng Qin, *Da Qing lüli*, 126, 452, 519–20.

[69]For discussion of this point, see Qu [146].

[70]The distinction between white and red contracts is largely related to the dynastic taxation system. It is believed that the tax contracts, as listed in Table 1, were the important instruments for the official to intervene or control the activities of contracts in Qing China, see Wang [201], Liang [114].

[71]Isett [96].

[72]See Article 95.03, Tian Tao and Zheng Qin, *Da Qing lüli*, 199–200.

[73]See e.g. Article 95.07, Xue Yunsheng, *Duli cunyi*, vol. 10, 32.

Table 1 The word frequency of Qi & Yue in the Great Qing Code (1740 & 1906)

Keywords		Number of cases	Articles
Baiqi	White contracts	19	76.02/76.06/76.08/76.11/76.12/76.16/314.03/314.03 (1906)/314.04/314.05/314.07/314.14/314.15
Yinqi	Sealed contracts	12	76.06/76.08/93.06/95.08/95.11/275.06/314.04/314.07
Wenqi	Written contracts	7	93.00/93.01/95.03/314.03 (1906)/314.04/314.07
Qimai	Purchase by contracts	7	76.10/76.10 (1906)/76.11/76.12/314.03 (1906)/314.05/314.06
Hongqi	Red contracts	5	76.16/314.03/314.15
Wenyue	Written contracts	4	95.01/125.00/125.04/274.05
Liyue	Establishing contracts	4	102.00/274.04/274.05/275.18
Liqi	Establishing contracts	4	220.06/220.08/275.06
Maiqi	Contracts of sale	4	95.07/95.09
Shuiqi	Tax contracts	3	95.00/95.08/146.00
Qimai	Sale by contracts	2	314.03 (1906)/314/06
Qizhi	Contract paper	2	95.03/220.08
Dianqi	Contract of *dian*	2	95.07/95.09
Weiyue	Breach of contract	2	149.00
Jiaqi	Fake contracts	1	9.05
Qiquan	Contractual bonds	1	24.09
Jiuqi	Old contracts	1	93.06
Huoqi	Revocable contracts	1	95.09
Siyue	Private agreements	1	101.00
Jieyue	Due bills	1	273.04
Yuanqi	Original contracts	1	314.06
Tiaoyue	Treaties	1	376.01
Qi	Contracts	11	75.10/95.00/95.03/95.07/95.08/275.06

person, it was required by the law that the contract should record the name, address, gender, and age of the person for sale, and the contract should be sent to and sealed by the government.[74]

These provisions, along with the analysis of all other "contractual" articles, illustrate that the *Great Qing Code* did have specific perceptions with regard to how certain contracts in practice should meet the requirements of the law. As such, they did not entirely ignore the contract as a matter of a civil nature,[75] even though this does not amount to a general concept about contracts.

2.1.3 Contracts Without Contract Law?

It seems that no conception of contract law, in a relatively strict sense, can be found in the context of Qing China.[76] The positive laws of the dynasty cannot provide a legal definition of contracts as examples of what was discussed in the previous section. In this case, if the question cannot be answered at the legislative or administrative level, then perhaps one should turn to seek a solution from a more practical or social perspective.

It has been noted that, rather than being a legal term, contracts can be envisioned as having a more social function:

> These [contracts and written agreements] documents, then, are far more social than they are legal insofar as they are basic instrumentalities in the regulation of social, economic, and even religious affairs in daily life.[77]

Thus, it appears that, if a contract is not explicitly defined by the law, then it should be defined within the society. As a society that was occupied by contracts to a large extent, the vacancies of contract law, if any, should be filled by other unnoticed rules. Following this path with regard to contracts without contract law, the implicit criteria might be revealed in the way that people used contracts in everyday life.

---

[74] See Article 275.06, Tian Tao and Zheng Qin, *Da Qing lüli*, 407.

[75] It is considered that, given "[t]he penal emphasis of such law," "contract" was exactly the example that "matters of a civil nature" ignored by the law entirely. See Bodde [13].

[76] It has been noticed that no contract law, understood as the rules on what type of contractual agreements can be enforced with the help of state authorities, was developed by the state. See Foerste [56].

[77] Myron L. Cohen, "Writs of Passage in Late Imperial China," 88. The term "contracts and other written agreements" was used by Myron L. Cohen in the footnote of this quotation, which drew a distinction between "contracts" and "written agreements," and they together might be what "these documents" referred to.

2.2 *Categorization of Contracts in Everyday Life*

2.2.1 Contractual Manuals

At a general level, what kind of documents or manuscripts were perceived as contracts by the common people in late imperial China? And how did the people of that time define contracts in the absence of any clear legal or judicial instructions about them?

The phenomenon that one needs to pay attention to at the outset is that, as it is believed, "by the Qing, customs relating to contract already had a national character."[78] An observer of the folk society[79] at that time will easily discover that, based on some inherent unity of form and content that they possess, contracts can be distinctly recognized not only by experts with special legal training but also by ordinary people. Records have shown that even some contemporary authors, although writing in western languages, were able to become more aware of this point. For example, Pierre Hoang,[80] a Jesuit scholar, wrote down the following lines on Chinese contracts in around 1889, or the fifteenth year of Guangxu:

> Though there is no legally prescribed form for Deeds, yet the differences which exist in different localities give rise to no trouble, since the technical expressions for the conditions of the contract are everywhere the same; if one knows well the ordinary forms of one district, it will be easy for him to ascertain the special usages and customs of other districts, if any there be, and to conform to them as may be required.[81]

It is now well established among modern scholars that "a common contract culture existed in China across regional boundaries."[82] As someone of an "insider" of his time, Pierre Hoang's observation further suggests that the geographical universality of contracts might be upheld thanks to their inherent unity, which was formed, at least to a large extent, by numerous and widespread manuals of contract forms instead of the law.[83]

As a matter of fact, this aspect relates to the long and solid tradition of a specific emphasis on the format of formal instruments, including contracts, by means of some sorts of form documents or manuals. Written materials which were considered as samples illustrating some forms of administrative documents, for example, can easily be found in excavated bamboo slips of early China.[84] Another type of writing later

---

[78] Madeleine Zelin, "A Critique of Rights of Property in Prewar China," 24.

[79] In regard to the term "folk society," see Redfield [149].

[80] See Cordier [38].

[81] Hoang [77]. For a reprinted version, see Hoang [78]. For its original version, see Hoang [81]. The French version directly mentions the Chinese code and states that it does not prescribe any form for the validity of contracts (*Le code chinois ne prescrit aucune formule qui soit de rigueur pour la validité des contrats*).

[82] Zelin et al. [228]. Also see Wang [191].

[83] See Feng [53]; Qu Jian, "Yikou daibi," 197–202.

[84] See, e.g., Zhang [238]. The no. 18 material of this article recorded an unspecified day in the second year of Shenjue (60 BC) of the Han dynasty. For introductions to the form bamboo and wooden slips documents, see Hsing [88], Zhang [240, 242].

called *yangwen*,[85] meaning model texts or model contracts in particular, appeared in the medieval period.[86] At a later time, it is considered that, rather than the officially issued "standard contracts,"[87] privately edited contract forms started to come into vogue in the Ming-Qing eras.[88]

In the encyclopedias for daily use that were widely popular at the time, such as the "complete book of myriad treasures" (*Wanbao quanshu*), or the "do-it-yourself manuals" (*Wanshi buqiuren*, or "no seeking help in ten thousand matters"),[89] one can find various chapters on "geography, fengshui, fortune-telling, observations on security in travel, etc.," as well as "a section on written contracts."[90]

To some extent, these daily-use compendia can be regarded as categorized summaries of the knowledge of social life of the time[91] and, in no small part, the knowledge about contracts, which mainly refers to the forms of contracts, has not been left behind in most of these mushrooming manuals.[92] At the latest in the late Qing period, the content of contractual knowledge gradually began to separate from the overall encyclopedias,[93] as manuals that were solely or mainly[94] focused on contract forms started to emerge.[95] Some of the most widely discussed Qing contractual

[85]For a discussion of this type of writings as templates based on manuscripts from Turfan and Dunhuang, see Fu [57], Feng [54].

[86]See, e.g., manuscript S.1897 in Dunhuang yanjiuyuan [44]. Also, for contract forms in the Yuan dynasty, see Niwa [137].

[87]See Tang [169], Zhang [230].

[88]See Tang Honglin, "Zhongguo chuantong minshi qiyue geshi yanjiu," 32. For a summary of contract forms in the Ming dynasty, see Yang Guozhen, *Ming Qing tudi qiyue wenshu yanjiu (xiudingban)*, 12. Some suggested that an ancient painting might show the popularity of contract forms in at least the Southern Song dynasty. See Feng Xuewei, *Ming Qing qiyue de jiegou gongneng ji yiyi*, 69–70.

[89]For a thorough discussion of these books, see Doleželová-Velingerová and Wagner [43].

[90]Faure and Pang [50].

[91]See Elman [46].

[92]For an overview of the contract part in these manuals, see Wu [208].

[93]Some realized that in the encyclopedias the content of contracts was greatly reduced in the Qing dynasty. See ibid., 257. Others argued that contractual content was only cut down in "general encyclopedias," but the same situation did not happen in other kinds of encyclopedias. Thus, in total, the contract knowledge was still easy to access in daily-use encyclopedias of the mid and late Qing dynasty. See You [222].

[94]It should be noted that some of these manuals consist of forms for both contracts and letters and, in this case, only the former part is considered in this chapter. An overview of letter writing guides, see Hayes [72].

[95]See Feng Xuewei, "Zhongguo chuantong qishi chutan," 468–469. The social context for this phenomenon has not been systematically discussed.

manuals are,[96] for instance, *Shuqi bianmeng* (1895)[97] and *Qiquan huishi* (1881)[98] in Shanghai,[99] and the recently republished and edited *Xieyue buqiuren* (1882)[100] in Sichuan province; another known manual published in the early Republican era is *Shuqi chengshi* (1919).[101] In addition to these block-printed editions of contractual manuals, countless manuscripts of contract forms proliferated among cities and (especially) villages at the same time.[102] It is not difficult to discover that, in accordance with the diversity of contracts in practice,[103] these manuals and handbooks contain a prodigiously wide range of different contract forms, including coverage of almost every aspect of Chinese social life, "from the cradle to the grave."[104]

2.2.2 A Necessary Assumption

These copybooks played a pivotal role in the production process of contracts[105]; each exemplar in the manual represented one certain type, or one variation thereof, of the commonly used contract in practice. As it was stated by the author in the preface of *Shuqi bianmeng*, these contract forms were collected, selected, and classified to serve as easily retrievable models for drafting genuine contracts.[106] In general, their functions can be concluded as:

[96] For a very brief overview and studies using these materials, see, e.g., James Hayes, "Specialists and Written Materials in the Village World," 86–87; Liu [122].

[97] Jiang [98]. The name was also transcribed as *Shu-ch'i pien-meng*, with no less than 84 different forms, see James Hayes, "Specialists and Written Materials in the Village World," 86–87. While Robert Gardella thought this is an "anonymously compiled" work, it is considered that the author is Jiang Yixu, using the name of *Nanchuang shizhe*, the attendant by the southern window. See Gardella [59]. For research on the author, see Ye and Zhang [221].

[98] See Hoang [77]. An introduction to its publication, which claims the publication year as 1881, see Gu [65].

[99] However, some believe that the *Shuqi bianmeng* was "apparently from the Canton delta." See Gardella [60].

[100] See Feng [52].

[101] Zhou [248].

[102] The author personally collected several anonymous manuscripts (although sometimes indicating the scribe's name) about framing contracts that can be dated, partly by the era name that was used, at least to the late Qing dynasty. See, e.g., Anonymous [6]. For a general study on the villatic daily-use encyclopedia, see Wang [196].

[103] See Madeleine Zelin, "A Critique of Rights of Property in Prewar China," 23–24.

[104] It seems that the well-known and widely cited metaphor in respect of the relation between the trust and the Anglo-Saxon can be borrowed to illustrate the relation between the contract and the Chinese, that "[t]he trust is the guardian angel of the Anglo-Saxon, accompanying him everywhere, impassively, from the cradle to the grave." See Lepaulle [109].

[105] See Qu Jian, "Yikou daibi," 202–208.

[106] Jiang Yixu, *Shuqi bianmeng*, 2.

> [T]he model documents in these manuals may legitimately be taken in two ways. They were intended as ideal types that represented patterns found in actual contracts. Manuals and handbooks might also act as transmission belts for textual conventions, serving to shape as well as reflect genuine documentary usages.[107]

These documents have shown a close connection between varied genuine contracts and themselves as categorized examples. For researchers today, these handbooks might offer a great opportunity, and indeed a shortcut, to investigate how a contract was perceived and recognized in the eyes of the people at that time. To some extent, they can be seen as an exhibition of contracts as they were popularly conceived. In other words, through the enumerated contract classifications in these manuals, one is able to explore where the boundaries of the contract lay. For those types of contract that were explicitly listed can be taken as contracts with no doubt, while those which were not included in most manuals or even any manuals at all should be considered as undetermined.

Accordingly, this study could propound an unsurprising but necessary assumption: a manuscript that conforms to the requirements of contractual manuals is a contract. If contracts can be identified through their "inherent unity," then this "inherent unity" should largely be formed through the extensive application of contractual manuals.

The basic logic of taking contract manuals as the starting point is that it might be reasonable to explore something's definition according to the way it describes or designates itself.[108] Not all contract manuscripts will explicitly indicate their status as contracts by bearing the characters of "*qi*" or "*yue*" on the paper, but authors of all contract manuals will clearly express their intention to guide the drafting of contracts. Therefore, manuscripts which conform to contract manuals could be regarded as implying that they have self-claimed their status as contracts.

However, not all kinds of contracts were gathered in these manuals.[109] Though it is conceivable that most contracts can find their samples in these manuals, there may still be many exceptions. Thus, the assumption is actually that a contract is a manuscript in line with an "inherent unity" that was shaped and represented by contractual manuals, and both explicit and implicit principles shall be included. In addition to the most obvious aspects of these manuals, namely the contract forms and their classification, an even more valuable feature might be that they explain, through enumeration, which subject matter can be handled by a contract and what kind of content can be included in it.

In brief, as models for making genuine contracts, what contract manuals can provide can predominantly be divided into two aspects: the content and the form,

---

[107] Robert Gardella, "Contracting Business Partnerships in Late Qing and Republican China: Paradigms and Patterns," 331.

[108] The philosophy of the relationship between names and reality can be found in Confucius' words, that "[i]f names are not rectified, speech will not accord with reality; when speech does not accord with reality, things will not be successfully accomplished." For the translation, see Slingerland [157].

[109] See Jiang Yixu, *Shuqi bianmeng*, 2.

just as the two sides of a coin.[110] Therefore, conforming to the requirements of contract manuals can mainly be understood as conforming to the "inherent unity" in these two aspects. The former signifies various contract categories, each of which represents one type of subject matter that were offered in the manuals, while the latter mostly plays a role in the process of writing. In other words, a contract should not deal with any ill-suited matter, nor should it be written in an inefficient way. In this case, based upon the assumption that this study propounded, the next step shall be to explore the specific meaning of the "inherent unity" of contract in these two aspects individually.

3 Contents of a Contract: Beyond Agreement

3.1 The Tense of a Contract: Future or Past?

Are there, and is there a need for, specific restrictions concerning the content of a contract? In modern contract law, it seems that such restrictions do not exist, or at least not in an obvious way.[111] Rather, as long as there is an agreement or "consent" among parties, a contract can generally be established.[112] On this view there is no need to further question the content of the agreement.

It is apparent, however, that "not every kind of consent can be relevant."[113] The content of a contract needs to be meaningful, or, more specifically, meaningful in law.[114] An agreement is to be binding. Reaching a consent means that the parties are willing to be bound by, and act in accordance with, the "consent" that they reached.[115] Otherwise, the "consent" will be enforced by law or a legal remedy shall be offered accordingly. The implicit premise of obtaining a legal remedy is that the content of an agreement is remediable in terms of the law. Therefore, in most cases, a "consent" is an agreement on what and/or how to perform, i.e. the consent "has to relate to

[110]It is believed that the contract is the combination of content and form. See Han Shiyuan, *Hetongfa zonglun*, 107.

[111]This may be deemed part of the principle of freedom of contract. See, e.g., PICC, Article 1.1 (Freedom of contract): "The parties are free to enter into a contract and to determine its content." See UNIDROIT, *Principles of International Commercial Contracts*, 7.

[112]See Kötz [103], Wolf and Neuner [204], Zimmermann [250].

[113]Reinhard Zimmermann, *The Law of Obligations*, 559.

[114]The definition of private documents, surely including contracts, in the Draft Criminal Code of the Great Qing Dynasty of 1907 states that they must have some relations with the power or right or obligation in law or can be regarded as evidence in fact. See Shangwu yinshuguan bianyisuo [153]. A similar opinion was expressed by one of the main drafters of this Code, who is Japanese, in his lecture notes, who said that private documents refer to documents that can be used to prove legal rights and obligations or facts. See Okada [139].

[115]It is a requirement that "the 'parties' should have intended to create binding effects," or, "to be legally bound." See Benedicte Fauvarque-Cosson and Denis Mazeaud, *European Contract Law—Materials for a Common Frame of Reference*, 22.

performance."[116] Agreements that do not contain such content seem to have no legal significance, and therefore the law cannot offer enforcement or remedy to them.

For instance, two parties surely can make an agreement that yesterday the sun rose in the east. The minds of the two parties are *ad idem* with no doubts, but such consent does not include matters that require any further performance and therefore will not receive any legal remedy or enforcement. A contract is not created in this case. This type of "consent" is evidently not a topic of concern to the law—whether the consent was reached or not, yesterday's sun has already risen above the eastern horizon.[117]

According to this reasoning, one may realize that the content of an agreement seems to be more concerned about the "future" in terms of the signing of a contract. This means that contracting parties shall do whatever is in accordance with the content of the contract after it is signed. This is also the normal situation of the contract one generally thinks of. Take the well-known contract, or bond, in William Shakespeare's *The Merchant of Venice* as an example[118]:

> *Shy.* This kindness will I show
> Go with me to a notary, seal me there
> Your single bond; and, in a merry sport,
> If you repay me not on such a day,
> In such a place, such sum or sums as are
> Express'd in the condition, let the forfeit
> Be nominated for an equal pound
> Of your fair flesh, to be cut off and taken
> In what part of your body pleaseth me.

In this scene Shylock and Antonio agreed that the Venetian merchant should repay the moneylender in full "on such a day," that is in the future, while the non-performance of the contract would lead to a forfeit, in a possible future, of "an equal pound" of the borrower's flesh.

This point is also reflected in the grammatical tense used in the contract text. Choosing a verb tense correctly is quite an important technique in drafting a contract and it has been emphasized repeatedly in many modern legal writing manuals.[119] The most frequently suggested tense is the future, since "contracts are to be performed but still have not," and therefore "'shall or should or to do' are used to express future tense."[120] Likewise, "[a]lthough clause is stipulated in the contract after signing," the present tense is still frequently applied in subordinate clauses,[121] for "you assume

---

116 Reinhard Zimmermann, *The Law of Obligations*, 559–560.

117 Similar examples in this case raised by Azo and Petrus Placentinus were quoted by Reinhard Zimmermann: "A and B agree that Socrates is a stone, or that Socrates is Socrates." See ibid., 559.

118 Staunton [162].

119 See, e.g., Barber [10], Wang [187], Ge [62].

120 Yang [217].

121 Ibid.

that it is being read when it is applied, not when it is written," and "[u]sing present tense will aid readability."[122] This indicates the "difference between contract writing and basic English usages."[123] In contrast, the past or perfect tense is rarely seen in the main body of a contract text. This presents an impression that what has been done in the past does not matter much, or at least is not as important as what shall be done in the future.

Such a discovery, if it can be called this, seems to be rather bland and completely unnecessary to raise specifically. However, if one tries to analyze the verbal tense that was used in late imperial Chinese contracts, one might find that they were mostly not formulated in the future tense, but the past. Besides many other reasons,[124] this might simply be the case because these contracts focus more on the past than the future. The difference in the tense might indicate a different emphasis on the content of contracts in late imperial China.

3.2 *The Performance of Contracts*

A contract denotes a performance, and, whether willingly or not, it needs to be performed. In this case, is a "contract" that is written in the past tense, and with no further need to be specifically performed, still a contract?

3.2.1 Contracts Need No Performance

One special type of contract, "the contract of apology," can be taken as an example of a contract that needs no performance. On the one hand, it is special concerning its non-conformity to the modern and normal understanding of a contract,[125] but on the other hand it is far from special in terms of its pervasiveness in the Qingshui River region and beyond.[126] It was recognized as a contract not only because it self-designates a contract (*zi*), but also because its form could be found in contractual

[122]Steve Barber, *Resource Manual for Legal Writing for Paralegals*, 147.

[123]Yang Jing, *International Business Contracts Bilingual Course*, 58–59.

[124]The meaning of the use of tense in contracts has been noticed in other ancient jurisdictions. For example, it is believed that the use of the past tense in a contract of sale is motivated not only by the need for formalism but also by what makes the transaction more secure and determined, see Mallat [131]. For discussions on other regions, see also McSheffrey [134].

[125]It is believed that this type of contract cannot be seen as a contract in a strict sense of the theory of modern civil law. See, along with three other examples, Feng Xuewei, "Zhongguo chuantong qishi chutan," 474–476.

[126]It is considered an important category in the classification of the Qingshui River manuscripts made by modern scholars. See Luo et al. [128].

manuals at the time,[127] which signifies that it was a familiar contract category which was widely used.

A genuine contract of apology is given as follows[128]:

Manuscript 3: A contract of apology (December 13, 1848)

The establishers of the contract (*zi*) of apology, Jiang Chaowang, [Jiang] Chaoji, [Jiang] Guangyu, [Jiang] Guangzhao, [Jiang] Guangzong, [Jiang] Guangdian, [Jiang] Guangzhen, [Jiang] Dazhen, [Jiang] Jiaosheng, [Jiang] Guangxian, [Jiang] Zhongying, [Jiang] Laosong, and [Jiang] Guang…, [established this contract] because of the wrong sale of the [timber of] the mountain, named Jiashitang, alias Randi, of Jiang Xiangrong, [Jiang] Xiangkui, [Jiang] Xiangkai, [Jiang] Zongkui, [Jiang] Guangwen, [Jiang] Guangben, [Jiang] Guangzu, and [Jiang] Tianxiang, to guest Peng Taihe for harvesting. The [Jiang] Xiangrong brothers found [this situation] out, stopped [the transaction of] the timber, and asked the *xiangbao*[129] to settle the dispute. We knew we were in the wrong. Thanks to [the intermediation] of the village head and the *xiangbao* [between us and] Xiangrong etc., and since [we] sincerely know we were wrong, Chaowang, Guangzhao, etc., called at [Xiangrong's] house and apologized willingly, established this contract of apology for reference and to stop us from making troubles on this pretext in the future. If we still [arouse disputes on this issue], then it will be our own troubles. This contract of apology is then established for reference.

Middlemen: Fan Xishou, Jiang Yongfa, [Jiang] Shaoqi, [Jiang] Dehong

Baozhang[130]: Luo Laolong

Scribe: Li Tiancai

Daoguang, twenty-eighth year, eleventh month, eighteenth day (December 13, 1848], established.

The story of this contract is uncomplicated: one group of people, who later acted as the establishers of the contract, intended to sell the timber owned by other people, and those who made a mistake apologized and asked for forgiveness with the help of an intermediators. The text of the contract chiefly describes, or records, what had happened in the past—the mistake and apology they made before the contract was signed—and therefore most parts of it are written in the past tense.[131] Unsurprisingly, it seems that nothing needs to be performed—the unauthorized disposal has been stopped, the apology has been made, and those sorry people have been forgiven. In a word, the matter was over before the contract was written.

---

[127] See, e.g., "*Cuo jianli yinji zi gao*"(The draft of the contract of wrongly built the foundation of a basement), see Anonymous, Huang Kechuo chao qishi ji, 43b–44a.

[128] Pan and Wu [140]. The same manuscript was also collected in Chen and Guo [25].

[129] The *xiangbao* were usually "unsalaried quasi-officials who were nominated by and drawn from local society, and then confirmed by the state," and they are believed to serve "as the main liaison between the county magistrate's yamen and their community." For more remarks on the matter, see Huang [93].

[130] Similarly to *xiangbao* in this context, *baozhang* were those selected as the head or leader of a *bao* and were "expected to assist the local magistrate in maintaining population registries, tracking local residents, and noting the appearance of newcomers, as well as policing and reporting crimes." For more discussions on this issue, see Isett [95], Huang [89].

[131] An observant reader will soon notice that, still, some limited parts of the text are about the future. This point will be discussed and explained in the later sections.

Another example, a contract of innocence, may be more explicit[132]:

Manuscript 4: A contract of innocence (May 20, 1829)

The establishers of the contract of innocence, Jiang Qihu [and Jiang] Qiming, [established this contract] because [they improperly,] orally claimed [their] ownership over the wasteland named Chongjiwang. The middlemen were invited for arbitration. Thanks to the intermediation by the middlemen, a feast was catered as compensation. The dispute was then clearly settled. Fearing that a verbal agreement might not suffice as proof, the contract of innocence is hereby established for reference.

Middlemen: Chen Zongyu, Jiang Han, Jiang Qiwei

Daoguang, ninth year, fourth month, eighteenth day (May 20, 1829), written by [Jiang] Qican.

In this case middlemen have done their job and the compensation has been paid in the form of a feast. No future affairs were discussed. The contract directly stated that "[t]he dispute was then clearly settled," which implies that no further move need be taken. In this case, if the fact contracts need no performance could also be deemed contracts in context, is the performance part still needed?

3.2.2 Producing Contracts as the Performance

A contract of apology or innocence may still be exotic for a modern legal researcher. In terms of quantity, such kinds of contracts were far from common, which may lead to a questionable conclusion. Hence, a prevailing type of contract should be taken into account. The land contract might denote the quantitatively dominant and most academically popular contract category in late imperial China.[133] As shown in the aforementioned example of the "standard case," a contract of the irrevocable sale of wet-rice fields, the main body of the text of such a contract was often formulated in the past tense as well. Thus, in these standard contracts, was the content of future performance still not of crucial importance as it is in those exotic non-standard contracts?

The answer may not be a straightforward yes. This is not because the issue of the contract has already been solved beforehand, as pointed out above, but because the process of producing the contract itself can be seen as the performance of the contract, or at least as a crucial part of it.

Take the previously quoted contract of irrevocable sale as an example. Jiang Yingyou and Jiang Yinghui agreed that the former should sell his wet-rice fields to the latter. The agreement created duties for both parties, the most important of which were that, respectively, the vendee should pay the price of the fields and the vendor should then convey the fields to the vendee. The vendee's duty has been exactly performed before the contract was drafted, for the contract recorded that "[Jiang

[132] Zhang Yingqiang and Wang Zongxun, *Qingshuijiang wenshu*, vol. 2 (1), 60. A transcription of this manuscript, while with mistaken citation information, is provided in Cheng [28].

[133] See Zhang [232].

Yingyou] received the money with his own hands".[134] Then the vendor needed to complete his performance. Surely the transferor cannot physically hand his fields, or mountains, forest land, or houses in other cases, over to the transferee. The way for him to fulfill the duty of conveyance was to draw up a contract with the help of many others and hand the paper, as the representative of the fields, over to the vendor.

In a noted collection of provincial regulations from the Qing period, *Zhi Zhe chenggui*, the custom about folk transactions was recorded as stipulating that, "once the money was paid, the contract shall then be delivered."[135] In other words, right after the contract was produced and delivered, which should theoretically be a continuous and uninterrupted process in an extremely short time, both parties of the contract were discharged from their obligations since there has been a substantial performance.[136] Therefore, it seems that the chronological distinction of the obligatory act (*Verpflichtungsgeschäft*) and disposition act (*Verfügungsgeschäft*) in the sense of the principles of separation (*Trennungsprinzip*) and abstraction (*Abstraktionsprinzip*)[137] did not exist in such situations. Since related obligations can be fulfilled before or at the time when the contract was produced, the provision of performance was not likely to be an essential part of the contract.

In brief, the transaction was to a large extent concluded with the conclusion of the contract. It is in this sense that the past tense of the main body of the contract text can be explained. Concerning the finality of a contract that has been shown by the examples above, unlike its modern notion, a contract in the context of late imperial China might be seen as more backward-looking than forward-looking.

3.3 *Championing the Past in the Future*

3.3.1 Negative Obligations in the Future Tense

A relatively backward-looking contract does not mean that it has no care about the future. It has to be noted that future performance surely can be involved in a contract under certain circumstances. The point is not that the clause of performance does not exist in these contracts, but the fact that the non-existence of performance was entirely possible, which may largely alter one's understanding of the contract in context.

---

[134] Chen Jinquan and Du Wanhua, *Jiang Yuanze jiacang qiyue wenshu*, 27.

[135] Anonymous [5].

[136] Obviously, only a simple but widely existing situation is discussed here. Transactions involving, for instance, *gouge*, "the substitution of the name of a new proprietor for that of his predecessor," are not included. *Guoge* "is the act by which a public official at the request of the new proprietor inscribes his name, or that of a community which he represents, in the public records, adding the quantity of land, in what prefecture and district, and under what number situated, and by whom sold to him. Then the name will be inscribed in the authentic schedules or certificates of payment of taxes." See Hoang [79].

[137] See Markesini et al. [133], Faber and Lurger [47].

Nonetheless, even in these mostly past-tense contracts, one may still have an inkling of the tense of the future.[138] Take the foregoing contract of apology, again, as the example. It specifies that "[the contract was established] to stop us from making troubles on this pretext in the future," and "[i]f we still [arouse disputes on this issue], then it will be our own troubles."[139] Also, in the contract of irrevocable sale of wet-rice fields, it stated that "[s]ince the sale of the fields, the vendee can farm and manage this property at will, and the vendor shall not raise any dissenting voices afterward."[140]

However, these terms that are variously related to the future seems to be more secondary. The principal obligations of the contract establishers, namely to apologize and to convey the fields, have been completed. One can tell that these subordinated obligations are de facto about to protect what has been performed. These clauses were stipulated to make sure that no further relevant disputes would be aroused by either of the contracting parties and to shield the transaction from any future objections of the predecessor. The contract establishers were therefore obliged to these provisions.

Obligations can be both positive and negative depending on whether one is bound "to do or not to do a particular thing."[141] In light of this distinction, it was the negative obligations that these terms of the future have created. That is to say, a contract can be primarily about the past, and can champion the past when speaking about the future.

3.3.2 The Established and Confirmed

As noted, a contract is more backward-looking in terms of its non-necessity of performance and its negativity towards subordinate obligations in the future. Therefore, the description of the content as the "meeting of wills"[142] might need to be altered accordingly from "what the parties agree to do" to "what the parties have done and agree to maintain thereafter." Ultimately, they are not the paper version of promises, which act as an instruction for future fulfillment, but rather the documentation of past events which demand a continuous effect by means of recording. If there is a promise, it will be the promise that both parties shall not deny what has been done or try to reverse it. Thus, on the basis of the shift of understanding from forward-looking to backward-looking, the content of the contract can then be concluded as "the established" or "the confirmed."

[138]The above-mentioned contract of innocence may represent an unusual contract with hardly any clear sign of the future. See Zhang Yingqiang and Wang Zongxun, *Qingshuijiang wenshu*, vol. 2 (1), 60.

[139]Pan Zhicheng and Wu Dahua, *Tudi guanxi ji qita shiwu wenshu*, vol. 1, 221–222.

[140]Chen Jinquan and Du Wanhua, *Jiang Yuanze jiacang qiyue wenshu*, 27.

[141]William Blackstone, *Commentaries on the Laws of England: in four books*, 446.

[142]See Benedicte Fauvarque-Cosson and Denis Mazeaud, *European Contract Law—Materials for a Common Frame of Reference*, 22.

The difference between these two possibilities is that the former refers to the development out of nothing, while the latter signifies the intention to ensure something that has been done previously, focusing on the process from informal to formal. More specifically, the example of the contract of apology is about "to confirm," for the apology has already been made and the contract was concluded to determine the past apology. In contrast, the contract of irrevocable sale is the example of "the established," since the finishing of contract writing, and the delivery of it right after it, marked the initiation of the possession of the fields by a new proprietor, which has not been an established fact before.

The conclusion of a contract shall mark the end, or at least a temporary but significant end, of the whole matter. The image that the representatives of both parties shaking hands and announcing the start of a new chapter may not quite fit in the context of late imperial China. For no new chapter would be needed if former chapters that have been written down were not erased.

3.4 Transcending as an Agreement

3.4.1 Contract Without Agreement?

If the content of a contract is about the established or the confirmed, then the question that immediately springs to mind is: what specifically has been established or confirmed in or by the contract? Since "consent" plays a vital role in modern contract law,[143] it is believed that agreement among parties is what shall be investigated in searching and interpreting the content of a contract.[144] Is, then, the contract in question an establishment or confirmation of consensus?

The aspect of consent can be seen in most Chinese contracts of late imperial times if an analytical method of modern contract law is properly applied. At first sight, it is a sound argument that traditional Chinese contracts were also based on mutual consent.[145] But the aforementioned cases of borderline contracts[146] might make this questionable.

There is a popular contract category in the Qingshui River region called "contract of allocating interests in the mountain" (*fenshan hetong*). The name was designated by the people of that time and was then followed by recent scholars,[147] which shows its clear identity as a contract. However, as mentioned, it appears more to be "a list of profit allocation" than a contract with conscious consent—the text merely records the

---

[143] See Reinhard Zimmermann, *The Law of Obligations*, 559.

[144] See Han Shiyuan, *Hetongfa zonglun*, 338.

[145] See Kishimoto Mio, "Ming Qing qiyu wenshu," 282; He [75].

[146] Christian Daniels, Yang Yougeng, and Takeuchi Fusaji, *Kishū Myaozoku ringyō keiyaku monjo kaihen (1736–1950-nen)*, vol. 3, E-0050.

[147] See Jinping xian linye zhi bianzuan weiyuanhui [100].

facts. Neither the intention of the parties nor its declaration is shown in the contract.[148] The allocation did not need any agreement as the amount had been settled, regardless of the shareholders' will. In a rather broad sense, however, a consensus base might be found if one traces back to the original stage of the contract. The allocation should be in accordance with the proportion that was agreed on beforehand. But this agreement was reflected in another previous contract of share allocation—can the consent, once reached, keep generating different contracts?

It is hard to acknowledge that there might be a contract without agreement according to the theory of contract law. As a matter of fact, the undetermined status of this statement, namely that a contract in the Qingshui River region might not necessarily need consent,[149] already invites the need to demonstrate the content of a contract through another approach, for it is arguable that the consent is inadequate in explaining the whole picture of contracts in the Qingshui River region.

3.4.2 Jural Relations: An External Observation

There should be two approaches in examining a contract: the internal and the external. The first and traditional approach has been interpreted above. It contends that "the prime purpose of interpretation is to seek to identify the true, subjective and shared intentions of the parties,"[150] and even the professed approach in the courts may be "to try to determine the intentions of the parties."[151]

In contrast, instead of pursuing the subjective and sometimes elusory intentions of contracting parties, the external approach may be able to provide a clearer, more objective, and more applicable way to identify a contract. Sometimes the appearance is more realistic than what lies within. This observation from an outside perspective means not looking at contracting parties' minds but viewing what concrete and apparent changes, both physically and non-physically, have been made through the process of contracting.[152]

The conclusion of a new contract as an interpersonal activity will result in profound changes in mutual relations among the people engaged.[153] For instance, producing a contract of sale can lead to a transfer of property rights and ultimately be reflected in the shifting relational positions of the vendor and vendee. Nevertheless, as legal

---

[148] See Reinhard Zimmermann, *The Law of Obligations*, 561.

[149] Similar opinions can be found in Xu [213].

[150] Sir Basil Markesinis, Hannes Unberath, and Angus Johnston, *The German Law of Contract*, 133.

[151] Stone and Devenney [164].

[152] A similar approach was taken by scholars, for example, in analyzing the concept of "rights" in Chinese society around the eighteenth century. See Liang Zhiping, *Qing dai xiguanfa: Shehui yu guojia*, 51.

[153] The possibility of applying the theory of relational contract provided by Ian R. Macneil may be indicated here. See Macneil [129], Campbell [21]. For its use in English contract law and court decisions, see Richard Stone and James Devenney, *The Modern Law of Contract*, 13–15, 190.

meaningfulness is required for the content of a contract in modern contract law, not all kinds of changing relations shall be taken into account. Accordingly, a conceptual expression as the answer to what has been established or confirmed could be the "jural relations."[154]

Here, the term "jural relations" is used in the sense proposed by Wesley Newcomb Hohfeld, who provided it as a systematic, essential, and fundamental concept for further analysis and description.[155] The concept advanced by the American jurist was considered "simplicity, precision, and universality" when it was applied in primitive jurisprudence,[156] which suggests its suitability in a pre- or early modern context.[157]

Initially, the meaning of the word "jural" is "[o]f or relating to rights and obligations."[158] In Hohfeld's eyes, however, "one of the greatest hindrances to the clear understanding, the incisive statement, and the true solution of legal problems frequently arises from the express or tacit assumption that all legal relations may be reduced to 'rights' and 'duties'." Thus, his significant contribution is that the single reciprocal relation of rights and duties was elaborated and developed into four fundamental pairs with eight basic concepts, namely "demand-right/duty," "privilege-right/no-demand-right," "power/liability," and "immunity/no-power."[159]

It is not in doubt that precision is of high importance in the Hohfeldian system[160]; rights and obligations are simply far too ambiguous. Nonetheless, a sophisticated system can still find its roots in the fundamental relation of the two indeterminate concepts, which can be understood most easily as the principle that "one can demand the other to do or refrain from doing something."

In sum, as the content of the contract in context has been found to have a more backward-looking nature, and the two fundamental elements in contract definitions, namely "finding the intention of the parties" and "the concrete legal obligations to perform,"[161] seem to be insufficient, the proposition of this study is as follows: a key statement for describing and so identifying contracts is that the content of a contract shall be about to establish or to confirm certain kinds of jural relations among parties.

---

[154] The term of "legal relations" has not been selected since both the notion and the practice of the contract in context tend not to be "legal" in most aspects, especially considering the positive law as it is argued above. On the contrary, the word "jural" can be used to imply a relation to the administration of justice, which exactly fits the situation that a traditional contract could face: there may not be any contractual regulations, but this does not affect the fact that contracts can commonly be judged in the courts. The difficulty of using the term "legal" in analyzing a society which does not fall under our prevailing legal system was discussed in Hoebel [82].

[155] See Hohfeld [85, 84, 86, 87], Radin [148].

[156] E. Adamson Hoebel, *The Law of Primitive Man*, 46–47.

[157] A test of the usefulness of applying Hohfeldian concepts can be found in ibid., 51 ff.

[158] See "jural," Bryan A. Garner, *Black's Law Dictionary*, 926.

[159] See Wesley Newcomb Hohfeld, "Some fundamental legal conceptions as applied in judicial reasoning," 30; Corbin [37]; E. Adamson Hoebel, *The Law of Primitive Man*, 48–49; Simmonds [156].

[160] See Westen [203].

[161] Cheng and Rosett [31].

4 Identifying Contracts by Form: The Internal and External

As for the other side of the coin, the form of contracts is discussed in this section concerning both its internal and external aspects. The former relates to the form of the text of a contract that is usually mentioned, and the latter refers to the ritual or ceremony of contracting, which played a customarily important role in forming a contract. In addition, a formulaic expression is singled out and explained at length as a shortcut in identifying contracts while integrating the contract form with content.

4.1 The Textual Form

4.1.1 Essential Elements? The Changing and Unchanged

"Contracts all had a similar format."[162] If this was the case, the form should be the most dominant feature in distinguishing contracts from other documents. But how can one describe the form of a contract?[163] At the textual level, is it possible to discover some factors that can summarize the multitudinous forms which contracts have?

This task involves defining the irreducible core content of contract forms,[164] which, if any, must consist of a few essential elements, presuming that all contracts, at least for the same category, shall include every single one of these elements, otherwise the contract cannot be considered as complete. This "irreducible core content" seems to be akin to the *essentialia negotii* (core components without which the agreement would be seen as unreached),[165] although the latter focuses more on the content of a contract while the former counts as the *essentialia* of the aspect of forms.

In fact, scholars have made great efforts in this regard. Table 2 illustrates six representative opinions on the elements that a contract should contain.[166] It should be clarified that some relevant elements raised by one or more scholars might be combined into one for the sake of simplicity. For instance, "name of the owner

---

[162] Madeleine Zelin, "A Critique of Rights of Property in Prewar China," 24.

[163] A valuable attempt in this regard is an illustration of a contract with annotations on its writing format and highlights of the elements it used, which can be found in Wang [192]. For another study on contracts with annotations of its elements, see Mindai shi kenkyu shi hen [135].

[164] The concept of "irreducible core content" derives from Hayton [73].

[165] See Hein Kötz, *Vertragsrecht*, 56. For the discussion of the essential elements of contracts in modern law, see Wang [186], Deng [41].

[166] As for opinions, written as Zhang, Trombert, Terada, W. X., W. & F., and Jiang in Table 2, see, successively, Zhang [229]; Trombert [178]; Terada [170]; Wang Xu, *Qizhi qiannian*, 166–171; Feng Xuewei, *Ming Qing qiyue de jiegou gongneng ji yiyi*, 30–32; Jiang [97]. The standpoint of Feng Xuewei, as stated in his book, is originated from Wang [184].

Table 2 Studies on contract elements

	Contract elements	Zhang	Trombert	Terada	W. X.	W. & F.	Jiang
1	Date	*	*	*			*
2	Names of parties	*	*	*			*
3	Reasons for contracting		*		*	*	*
4	Object description	*	*	*	*	*	*
5	Price or the total amount	*	*	*			*
6	Guarantee terms	*	*	*	*	*	
7	Signature of parties	*	*	*	*		
8	Middlemen	*	*	*		*	*
9	Due date		*			*	
10	Terms in case of debtor's death		*				
11	Formulaic words for ending		*			*	
12	Purity of silver			*			
13	Confirmation of payment			*	*	*	
14	Statement of irrevocability			*		*	
15	The origin of the object				*		*
16	The type of transaction				*	*	*
17	Persons with joint liability					*	
18	Procedure of transaction						*
19	Confirmation of conveyance						*
20	Rights and obligations						*
21	Postscript						*

of the property/vendor"[167] and "name of the owner of the money/vendee" raised by Zhang[168] as well as "identity of the debtor" and "identity of the creditor" by Trombert,[169] were all merged into "names of parties" in Table 2.

Two phenomena may be noteworthy concerning the viewpoints listed in the table. First, all of the mentioned scholars only summarized one type of contract (and sometimes from one region), such as land contracts,[170] contracts of loan,[171] or, most commonly, contracts of sale.[172] It is quite clear that taking all different kinds of contracts into account will not be easy.[173] Second, even by merely focusing on limited contract types, the concluded elements appear to display an extremely diverse picture.

167 Zhang Chuanxi, *Qin Han wenti yanjiu*, 191–194.

168 Ibid., 197–198.

169 Éric Trombert, *Dunhuang de jiedai*, 4.

170 See Wang Xu, *Qizhi qiannian*, 167.

171 See Éric Trombert, *Dunhuang de jiedai*, 4.

172 See Terada Hiroaki, "Zhongguo jinshi tudi suoyouzhi yanjiu," 429.

173 This point was also noted in Feng Xuewei, *Ming Qing qiyue de jiegou gongneng ji yiyi*, 31.

It is hard to find certain elements that are agreed by all—the only one in Table 2 is the "object description," which, as mentioned, also merges several elements with different points of focus. In this case, establishing the "irreducible core content" of the contract form seems to be out of the question.

It was believed by a contract manual's author of the day that "the forms of contracts shall follow the prevailing fashion or style, and there are normally no determined rules."[174] The reasons for this are simple. On the one hand, the range of the application of contract was not only extremely wide but also kept changing and expanding, which makes it hardly possible to have every facet examined. On the other hand, contract forms themselves changed from time to time,[175] with the result that no fixed template ever existed in the long term.

In this circumstance, are there any unchanged elements whereby contracts can be discovered out of the many changing ones? Generally speaking, the answer is yes, for there are several specific factors that must be included even if one just wants to narrate a story. For example, the date and the names of contracting parties ought at any rate to be mentioned. However, the only unexceptional aspect in this respect is that exceptions always exist. Contracts which do not indicate the date[176] or each contracting party's name[177] can easily be found—these were unusual but actually existed.[178]

Furthermore, even if these logically indispensable elements can be confirmed by genuine contracts in practice, are these elements sufficient to form a contract? The combination of names, dates, or object descriptions might be far from enough for even the simplest contract. They would result in an over-reduced version of a contract rather than an irreducible one. Hence, it has to be confessed that, while facing the complexity and variability of contract forms, the essential elements are barely possible to summarize thoroughly and are thus difficult to be taken as indicators in identifying contracts.

4.1.2 Specialized Language and Formulaic Expressions

What do we talk about when we talk about contract forms? In what way shall a contract conform to the form if contract elements are not definite in general? These questions can be answered by examining what a contract form can provide. By and large, apart from providing the subjects or types of relationship that can be managed

---

174 "Notes on the use," Jiang Yixu, *Shuqi bianmeng*, 2.

175 See Qu Jian, "Yikou daibi," 208–209; Wu [205].

176 See, e.g., Zhang and Wang [242, 244].

177 See, e.g., Chen Jinquan and Du Wanhua, *Jiang Yuanze jiacang qiyue wenshu*, 418. Also, in some places, it was a custom not to record the creditor's name in contracts. See Wu [210]. It should also be specifically noted that, unlike the general impression, not only the signatures of the parties involved are not indispensable to the contract, even in most contracts there is no signature, as the names of all parties are written by a single scribe. A detailed discussion on this point is provided in the section concerning postscripts and signatures in Chap. 4.

178 Explanations and examples on exceptions can be found in Qu [145].

through the device of "contract," contract forms play a role of directly offering a variety of formulaic expressions which are de facto standard and widely adopted contract terms from a legal or customary perspective.[179]

As legal practitioners widely believe nowadays, all formal documents of law, including (ancient) contracts, shall be written in a special type of "complex" language described as legal, and legal rights and obligations are "created, modified, and terminated by the language" contained in contracts and other documents.[180]

Similar attitudes may also be applied in analyzing contracts in late imperial times. In a conventional way, the specialized language of contracts should be employed by drafters in expressing the contract content. An example of this would be the "*sizhi*"—literally, "the four boundaries or ends,"—which was the way to describe the location and area of a piece of land or a construction site. Normally, the eastern, the western, the northern, and the southern boundaries of the land should be indicated in the contract,[181] and, in certain cases,[182] the upper and lower boundaries might be more useful if the contract was about a parcel of mountain or forest land.[183] The name of the owner of the adjacent land or characteristics of the natural topography, such as the mountain ridge and valley, should be given as a simple but precise means to limit the area. In some rarely seen documents, a more specific map might be provided as an illustration (see Fig. 2).[184]

As one important feature of specialized expression, formulaic phrases frequently appear in contract texts.[185] Many examples can be given here. The famous "*kongkou wupin, lizi weizheng*" (fearing that a verbal agreement might not suffice as proof, this contract is hereby established for reference) was an extremely popular formulaic expression in most kinds of contracts.[186] For contracts of sale, the phrase "*yi mai yi liao*" (it is sold this time and it is sold forever) signifies the irrevocability of the transaction.[187] As for the reason for contracting, "*weiyin wuyin yongdu*" (because

[179]Examples of "formulaic expressions" in contracts can be found in Liang Zhiping, *Qing dai xiguanfa: Shehui yu guojia*, 41–42. It is believed that these "formulaic expressions" can be seen as the model clauses of the "contract law" in the Qing.

[180]See Tiersma [175].

[181]This was frequently recorded in contractual manuals, see Jiang Yixu, *Shuqi bianmeng*, 9–14; Feng Xuewei, "Qing keben 'Xieyue bu qiuren'," 125.

[182]It is said that using "the upper, the lower, the right, and the left boundaries" rather than "the eastern, the western, the northern, and the southern boundaries" might mark a difference between contracts in the Qingshui River region and contracts in other places, such as Huizhou and Guangzhong. See Wu [206].

[183]See, e.g., Zhang Yingqiang and Wang Zongxun, *Qingshuijiang wenshu*, vol. 2 (2), 162.

[184]Courtesy of the Jinping County Archives, JPWS-JP 123-Ping'ao, 1143.

[185]The use of formulaic phrases in contracts has been noticed by many scholars, see, e.g., Kwan [105]. The functions of formulaic expressions have also been discussed in the context of the Han dynasty. See Tomiya [176].

[186]It can be seen in the previously cited contracts. This expression was also noted, for example, in contracts from Hong Kong's New Territories, see Patrick H. Hase, *Custom, Land and Livelihood in Rural South China*, 148.

[187]See, e.g., Chen Jinquan and Du Wanhua, *Jiang Yuanze jiacang qiyue wenshu*, 24, 48, 63, 67, 77, 78, 123. For a discussion especially on this term, see Wu [207].

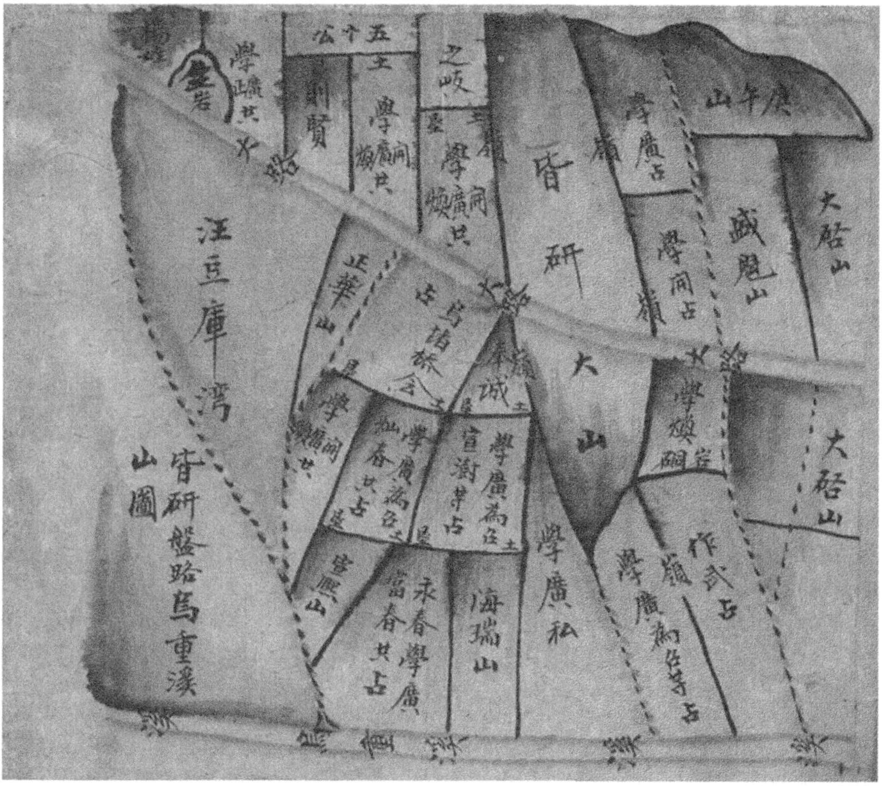

Fig. 2 A map of land and mountain parcels around Jieyanpan Road and Wuzhong Rivulet

of the lack of money [to pay for] living expenses) was often chosen as either a real or actually meaningless excuse.[188]

What is noteworthy is that the use of formulaic expressions should be considered legally (or customarily in most cases) significant, rather than optional, for contract disputes "often arose over the interpretation of specific clauses"[189] and these expressions as well-recognized terms can be of great help in avoiding vagueness. For instance, the choice of including or not including the statement of irrevocability made a huge difference—"only contracts designated as *juemai* ('final sale') were unredeemable."[190] Another matter needing attention on this issue is that the phrase

[188]Whether it was just a polite formula or it sometimes expressed the real situation remains to be seen. A discussion of this issue can be found in Qu Jian, "Qing zhonghouqi Qiandongnan Wendou zhai Miaozu dianzhi yanjiu," 205.

[189]Zelin [226].

[190]Zhang [229].

"*jikai*" (list)[191] should not be used in a contract of irrevocable sale, and, if it was used, according to a guidebook for scribes, the contract would be changed to a revocable one.[192]

In short, as prominent contributions of contract forms to the contract drafting, the question whether a contract was written in the specialized language or whether formulaic expressions were applied can be deemed a usable means in examining the conformity of documents to contract forms at the textual level.

4.2 The Ritual Form[193]

4.2.1 Customs of Contracting

The form of a contract was primarily understood at the textual level, as discussed above; a contract's form with regard to an external aspect has rarely been considered. Forming a contract was not only about how to draw it up in accordance with contract forms, but also implied that it had to meet its ritual requirements, which can be deemed the external form of a contract.

Rituals of contracting have long been a part of customs, and therefore the details were recorded in the results of many customs surveys.[194] In a most formal way, "the signing of a contract was often the occasion for a flamboyant feast or theatricals,"[195] although this would not be the situation for simple contracts. In the Qingshui River region, a meal would normally be provided by the initiator of the transaction.[196]

Nonetheless, the normal and formal requirement was to hold the event with "all four persons present," namely both sides of the contract, the middleman, and the scribe.[197] Moreover, a formal event and those who attended were undoubtedly seen as endorsements to the contract. The "more practical purpose" of the ritual has also been noticed: in simple terms, by means of organizing the event, people "announced to the larger community" the ongoing transaction over the property rights,[198] thereby legitimizing the ownership of the assignee.[199]

---

191 For the translation and its usage in context, see Allee [3].

192 Feng Xuewei, *Ming Qing qiyue de jiegou gongneng ji yiyi*, 29.

193 Issues related to this section will be explained at length in the following chapters.

194 See Wu Xiangxiang, *Zhongguo minshi xiguan daquan*, esp. 25–38; Committee for the Publication of the Rural Customs and Practices of China [36]; Qian Nanjing guomin zhengfu sifa xingzheng bu [144]; Linshi Taiwan tudi diaochaju [117].

195 Madeleine Zelin, "A Critique of Rights of Property in Prewar China," 25.

196 See *Zhongguo shaoshu minzu shehui lishi diaocha ziliao congkan* xiuding bianji weiyuanhui [247].

197 See Zhou [249].

198 See Madeleine Zelin, "A Critique of Rights of Property in Prewar China," 25–26.

199 This point will be elaborated later.

4.2.2 Textual Reflections

Through the study of historical and ethnographic materials, it is evident that rituals were customarily used in the circumstances of signing contracts. However, while facing an isolated contract without its original context and the facts that underlay it, which is the most common situation for researchers, one's inquiry into whether an event was truly held for this contract as required can only be answered by looking to its textual reflections.

In some contracts, the process of the whole event is written down directly, so that modern readers can learn its contracting ritual from the text. For most contracts, however, special attention should be paid to the ending part, which normally includes the names of middlemen, scribes, or other witnesses and guests. This can be treated as convincing evidence in examining the situation of the past event. Moreover, other specific information recorded in a contract, such as signatures, marks, seals, or the trace of revisions, can be used to investigate the ritual form of the contract.

It should additionally be stressed that, though its textual reflections might be the easiest way for understanding the content, the ritual form refers to the activities that actually occurred regarding the examined contract, and also needs to be distinguished from the internal form at the textual level.

4.3 The Formulaic Beginning of a Contract: Indicating and Integrating

4.3.1 The Formula of the Beginning

Among all the textual features of a contract, such as the above-mentioned essential elements, specialized language, formulaic expressions, and textual reflections of its ritual form, what this study called the "formula of the beginning" is unique. Specifically, in the Qing dynasty, the beginning of a contract normally follows a formula of "*li xx zi*," such as "*li duanmai tian zi*."[200]

This formula can be divided into three parts: (1) The verb *li* means to establish [the contract]; (2) *xx* in the middle summarizes the basic content and signifies the type of the contract; (3) *zi* can be replaced by *qi*, *yue* or other similar words that can express the meaning of "contract."[201] Taken altogether, these three parts mean "to establish the contract of [sale/apology/lease, etc.]" and the previous example "*li duanmai tian zi*" thus means "to establish the contract of irrevocable sale of wet-rice fields."[202]

[200] Chen Jinquan and Du Wanhua, *Jiang Yuanze jiacang qiyue wenshu*, 19.

[201] For the designations of contracts in Chinese, such as *zi*, *qi*, and *yue*, see Qu Jian, "Yikou daibi," 185. According to the statistics in footnote five, over 85% of contracts used *zi* and *yue* as there designation in Wendou Village.

[202] Chen Jinquan and Du Wanhua, *Jiang Yuanze jiacang qiyue wenshu*, 27.

Normally, the word "*ren*" (people) follows the formula and makes its meaning slightly change to "the establisher(s) of the contract of [sale/apology/lease, etc.]."[203] In addition, under limited circumstances, the type name (*xx*) or the last part (*zi/qi/yue*) is omitted,[204] while the *li* is taken as the cornerstone of the formula.[205] Generally, the character *li* was also used at the ending of the whole contract as the very last word after stating the date, to indicate when the contract was "established" (*li*).[206] Thus, a typical contract should at the same time be started and ended with the symbolic *li*.

Apart from the standard formula, there were also a few variants of it, such as *zaili* (re-establish)[207] or *tongli* (to establish together).[208] It should also be noted that, occasionally, the *li* or the whole formula will only appear at the ending part of the main body when concluding and restating the main points of the contract.[209]

4.3.2 Integrating the Form and Content

As a somewhat necessary sentence pattern or opening phrase, as well as an ending phrase in most cases, the formula manifests its importance. The reason why it can be seen as a must-use formula might be found in the lexical meaning of the symbolic verb *li*.

Within the context of the contract, *li* should be understood to denote the actions formulating the contract itself. These actions include the writing down of the text as well as certain rituals that the drafting process should follow. At a slightly more conceptual level, the Chinese character *li* can mean to establish (*chengli*) or to confirm (*queli*) in the context, which has been discussed above as core notions of the content of a contract.

---

203 See, e.g., ibid., 5.

204 See, e.g., ibid., 4, 131.

205 Only a few scholars have noticed the importance of the "*li*" or the whole formula at the beginning of contracts. For a study that has discussed this character in contracts, though from a completely different perspective, see, e.g., Wu Caimao, *Minjian wenshu yu Qingshuijiang diqu de shehui bianqian*, 33. In a collection of contracts in Tianjin, the editor chose the bold formatting for the beginning of every contract which, in another way, laid stress on the formula that is discussed here. See Song [159].

206 For example, the ending of the previous contract of irrevocable sale of wet-rice fields is "Qianlong, forty-fifth year, sixth month, twenty-second day (July 23, 1780), established." See Chen Jinquan and Du Wanhua, *Jiang Yuanze jiacang qiyue wenshu*, 27.

207 See, e.g., Mindai shi kenkyu shi hen, *Chūgoku tochi keiyaku bunsho shiryō shū (Kin–Shin)*, 65–66.

208 See, e.g., ibid., 63–64.

209 See, e.g., ibid., 67, 152–153. For the latter example (pp.152–153), no *li* appears at the beginning of the contract, but in the concluding part it states that "the contract is hereby established (*li*) for retention and reference" and mentions that "since the establishment (*li*) of the contract" what terms should be applied. It actually somehow followed the formula of *li* in another way. However, more often the formula is written twice at the beginning and at the end, or three times if the last one after the date is counted. The *li* in the ending part seems to be a restatement.

The *li* was certainly not written down in such an important place in a contract for no reason, but was used not only to describe the parties' action in formulating a contract (the form) but also to indicate their intention to establish or confirm certain relations (the content) by the contract. It is in this sense that this verb serves as the junction of the form and content of a contract. Its inner logic can be elucidated as follows. Since contracts are (defined) to establish or confirm certain relations with certainty, appropriate verbs should be selected and used in the contract text to express this intention. Therefore, as a conventional and formulaic phrase, the *li* and the whole formula were chosen to demonstrate the content and gradually became a symbolic feature in contract form.

Moreover, the second (*xx*, type of contract) and especially the third part of the formula (*zi/qi/yue*, contract) themselves present an explicit "self-awareness" of being a contract. Therefore, according to the above-discussed basic logic of seeing things from the way that they see themselves, if a manuscript starts, and under many circumstances closes, by drawing attention to its own status as a "contract," it shows that the text was deliberately made and initially identified as a contract.

In this case, those documents that bear the content of a contract were likely to use the formula of *li*; conversely, those documents that, in form, used the formula were in all probability recording the content of a contract. The formula which begins with *li* can then be considered as an indicator that integrates both the form and the content.

4.3.3 The Indicator as a Shortcut

In order to examine the popularity of the formula among genuine contracts (rather than contract forms) and, therefore, test its feasibility as a significative indicator, several contract collections from various areas in the Qing dynasty can be taken into account.

First and foremost, the two above-mentioned contractual manuals were reviewed since numerous other contracts were generated from these basic texts. In *Xieyue buqiuren*, all contract forms (21/21) contain the word *li*.[210] As for *Shuqi bianmeng*, 92.68% of all 82 contract forms use this formula, while one of only six exceptional cases resemble a list form and the other two are similar to receipt forms.[211]

Apart from contractual manuals, 326 genuine Qing contracts from an important contract collection published in Japan were examined. An overwhelming 98.77% of them applied the formula of *li*, with only four exceptions that did not.[212] Also, in the Qingshui River region, similar statistical evidence shows that, among 2096 contracts that were found in Wendou Village in southwest China, only 2.56% (54/2109) of them did not have this indicator.[213]

210 See Feng Xuewei, "Qing keben 'Xieyue bu qiuren'," 122–129. Three forms of letters in the manual were unexamined.

211 See Jiang Yixu, *Shuqi bianmeng*.

212 See Mindai shi kenkyu shi hen, *Chūgoku tochi keiyaku bunsho shiryō shū (Kin–Shin)*.

213 Group A of Wendou contracts is used for examination here.

In this case, since the popularity of the formula in contracts in the Qing dynasty can be proven in diverse regions,[214] this study suggests that this formula can be used at least as a shortcut to identify the contracts in context. Being a shortcut means that it stands a good chance of being a contract if this indicator can be seen in a manuscript. However, it does not imply that the documents that lack this formula should not be considered as contracts; they merely need a second review.

In sum, both the internal and external forms should be considered carefully when identifying contracts, especially concerning their non-textual and often overlooked ritual forms. As to the textual forms, rather than the changeable essential elements, the specialized language and formulaic expressions might be better symbols. Further, among these features, the formula of *li* at the beginning of a contract can be seen as a short-cut indicator as it represents the integration of the contract form and content and its feasibility is supported by statistics.

5 Paper Matters: The Materiality of Contracts

There is no doubt that the form and content are the two decisive aspects in forming the "inherent unity" of the contracts in context. However, apart from these frequently mentioned two sides, a factor which is most visible but often ignored—the piece of paper that we are holding when reading a contract—should be highlighted. Within the context that this study is discussing, the materiality also plays a unique role in defining contracts.[215]

5.1 The Burning of Contracts

Was the piece of paper that the contract was written on something important in people's eyes? How did they perceive its meaning at that time? Two piles of burning contracts might be the best answer.[216]

---

[214] It should be especially noted that the formula might be a distinctive feature for contracts in the Qing dynasty or later in the Republican period, while it can hardly be found in contracts of the Ming dynasty.

[215] Although the materiality can also be seen as an aspect of "formality," as the "material form," it is deliberately singled out as parallel to "formality" and "substantiality" for its fundamentality, which has been long neglected.

[216] Fires frequently occurred in the Qingshui River region in the Qing dynasty, and many of them were due to human factors. For a summary, see Dai and Wei [39].

5.1.1 The Story of Yao the Millionaire

A well-known true folk story about a millionaire in the Qingshui River region might be inspiring at this point.[217] The protagonist of the story was called Yao the Millionaire (*Yao Baiwan*), who, along with two other well-to-do men and their families, named Li and Jiang, were considered as the three richest families in the area during the eras of Jiaqing and Daoguang.[218] It is generally acknowledged that the Millionaire's real name was Yao Yukui[219] (1778–1830),[220] while some believe that the autonym was actually Yao Jizhou (1750–1821),[221] who was Yao Yukui's father, or that the name *Yao Baiwan* in fact simply referred to the whole family of Yao.[222] In any case, Yao the Millionaire became rich through timber trade, and therefore held an enormous number of properties, including the mountains, fields, and forests along both sides of the Wuxia River.[223] Thus, the contracts he owned could fill up dozens of chests.[224] It was said that the land of the whole village of Shao'ai had been bought by the Yao, and even the well of the village was exclusively owned by the family.[225]

In the folk story, Yao the Millionaire was rich but extremely heartless and cruel so that all villagers hated him.[226] Hence, the commoners covertly launched a plan to take revenge on him. A young and beautiful village girl, Jingui, was selected and hired by those villagers and was then sent to Yao's family to be a maidservant of the Millionaire.

As expected, in the following months the girl gradually earned Yao's trust.[227] The sixth day of the sixth month of the next summer was a key date, for this was an important festival date for the Miao people of the Qingshui River region. On that day, all people were expected to bring their genealogy books and contracts outdoors and dry them under the blazing sun, which was believed to be an effective and necessary means to protect paper manuscripts and books from all manner or mold or injury by

---

[217] The story was widely circulated and recorded and studied in various literature. See, e.g., Long [123], Guizhou sheng bianjizu [67], Wang [198, 190, 202, 200], Xu [212], Cheng [29, 30], Zhang [239], Shan [151].

[218] See Guizhou sheng bianjizu, *Dongzu shehui lishi diaocha*, 30; Zhang Yingqiang, *Mucai zhi liudong*, 159.

[219] See, e.g., Guizhou sheng bianjizu, *Dongzu shehui lishi diaocha*, 30; Cheng Zeshi, "'Yao Baiwan' wugao moufan an yu jiaoyi gongping," 46.

[220] Wang Zongxun, "Yao Baiwan de xingshuai," 224.

[221] See Zhang Yingqiang, *Mucai zhi liudong*, 160.

[222] See Wang Zongxun, "Yao Baiwan de xingshuai," 224; Xu Xiaoguang, *Qingshuijiang liuyu linye jingji fazhi de lishi huisu*, 189.

[223] See Guizhou sheng bianjizu, *Dongzu shehui lishi diaocha*, 30.

[224] See Wang Zongxun, "Yao Baiwan de xingshuai," 227.

[225] See Guizhou sheng bianjizu, *Dongzu shehui lishi diaocha*, 30.

[226] See Long Jialiang, "Jingui tang," 77; Wang Zongxun, *Xunshi yiluo de jiyi*, 71.

[227] See Long Jialiang, "Jingui tang," 77–78; Wang Zongxun, *Xunshi yiluo de jiyi*, 71; Zhang Yingqiang, *Mucai zhi liudong*, 164.

damp.[228] In fact, similar customs existed in not only the Miao region but also other areas of China.[229]

According to the plan, this was a perfect date for revenge. On that day, Jingui took the chance and secretly collected all the contracts that were taken outside because of the festival event and burned them all immediately. Afterward, the village girl ran away and committed suicide by jumping into a deep pond. In the end, the Millionaire was punished, according to the tale, by losing all his properties. Thereafter the pond was named "Jingui Pond" in memory of her sacrifice.[230]

The most eye-catching part of this story is that it is believed by the villagers that, without those contracts, the Millionaire would then have no evidence to claim his properties,[231] and will, therefore, lose his rights. Further, in their minds, burning the paper was an effective way to invalidate the contracts and extinguish the properties they recorded.[232] At the end of the folk story, after the contracts were burned to ashes, villagers started to retake the land and mountains that used to be "deforced" by the Millionaire.[233]

5.1.2 A Contract of Dispute Settlement

The story of Yao the Millionaire was not an individual case. As a matter of fact, the strong emphasis on the contract paper can be proven in many ways. A contract of dispute settlement stands as an excellent illustration of this point[234]:

> Manuscript 5: A contract of dispute settlement (April 29, 1911)
>
> The establishers of the contract of dispute settlement, Jiang Shichang, [Jiang] Yongwang, [Jiang] Yonglong, [Jiang] Yongxiang, [and] Jiang Xueguang, Jiang Birong, etc., [established this contract] because [they] argued about the [ownership over] the Sifang Mountain in Yuangupo. The two parties came to the city and intended to file a lawsuit. Fortunately, Huang Futing mediated between the two and persuaded them that, since they are members of the same clan, it is not a good choice to file a lawsuit. [Thus], all the contracts held by Jiang Shichang were burned in the middlemen's presence, and thereafter this mountain will still be in the possession of Jiang Guangxue and his son. Either party shall not follow others' abetment and harm his kindred. A feast was held in the middlemen's presence and the dispute was satisfactorily settled. [Both parties] shall continuously improve their family affection in days to come. The contract of dispute settlement ought to be established for reference.

---

[228] See Zhang and Hu [235], Wang [197].

[229] "On the sixth day [of the sixth month], the custom is that people shall take their books and paintings out to the courtyard and put them under the blazing sun, and it is said that this will help to prevent a moth infestation." See Gu [66].

[230] Details of the story can be seen in Long Jialiang, "Jingui tang," 77–80; Wang Zongxun, *Xunshi yiluo de jiyi*, 71.

[231] See Wang Zongxun, *Xunshi yiluo de jiyi*, 71.

[232] The connection between losing contracts and the fall of the family of Yao has been noticed by other interpreters. See Zhang Yingqiang, *Mucai zhi liudong*, 164.

[233] See Long Jialiang, "Jingui tang," 80.

[234] Zhang Yingqiang and Wang Zongxun, *Qingshuijiang wenshu*, vol. 2 (2), 244. A transcription of this contract can be found in Deng and Qiu [42].

[This contract of] dispute settlement [has] two copies.[235]

Middlemen: Huang Futing, Chen Mu'an, Chen Yutian

Scribe: Ma Fuxiang

Xuantong, third year, fourth month, first day (April 29, 1911), established.

According to this manuscript, two groups of people both claimed their ownership to one mountain at the same time, and the problem was later solved by the middlemen, who by some means eventually found out the lawful proprietor. More worthy of study is the next move that the middlemen took—burning all contracts of the losing party publicly in the middlemen's presence, perhaps not as a punishment for the losing side but as an insurance for the winning side.

Although not explicitly expressed, it seems that both parties revealed some contracts, probably as evidence of ownership, concerning the mountain at issue. Burning the possibly defective contracts presented by the losing party, in the end, showed the finality of the settlement, for they then lost the possibility of starting a further argument. Even if the intermediation had made the decision, the contract paper was still seen as a potential threat to the property.

Normally, a contract of dispute settlement was enough for the winning party to confirm their ownership of the property, but sometimes burning one's opponent's contracts may ultimately invalidate their claim for rights. The inadequacy of conceptual modification (the intermediation) and the practice of physical elimination (the action of burning) of the contract in this example once again illustrate the importance of the materiality to the contract.

The logic behind these two piles of burning contracts is rather simple: no contracts, no properties, and no contract paper, then no contracts. In the eyes of a modern lawyer, the loss of contract paper will only cause a limited and insubstantial impact on the performance of the contract—the possible trouble is that, for those contracts that required a written form, the parties might need to print and sign the contract again, and the contract would not directly disappear if they do not do so. However, in the eyes of those villagers, the ownership of properties relied not only on contracts but also on the contract paper. To some extent, the paper itself can be seen as the property, and this also explains why contracts were found well preserved.

[235]This sentence was written at the junction of the edges of two sheets of paper, and only the right part was left on this manuscript.

5.2 *The Non-conceptual Contract: The Contract and Its Material Carriers*

5.2.1 The Abstract and Concrete Contract

A well-known story in *Liezi* can also explain the significance of possessing the physical material of a contract[236]:

> There was a man of Sung who was strolling in the street and picked up a half tally [(contract)][237] someone had lost. He took it home and stored it away, and secretly counted the indentations of the broken edge. He told a neighbor: 'I shall be rich any day now.'

Though this story is from a much earlier time and can be seen as a satire against the Sung people, it still signifies to some degree that holding the physical material of a contract can refer to the possession of properties.

In the context, contracts can be understood as, to some extent, banknotes—one surely can dispossess others' money by burning the paper currency.[238] Conversely, destroying a bank card will not result in any loss of your money in the bank account, for it is digitalized and therefore more abstract than the paper money. One of the things that has often been overlooked is that, without doubt, contracts at that time have not been abstracted to such a high level that one experiences nowadays. The existence of a contract largely relied on its flesh body—the material carriers.

For this reason, the proper preservation of contract paper was a significant issue.[239] In fact, so long as it was a piece of paper with characters written or printed on it, it would be deemed special. China has a strong tradition of *jingxi zizhi* (showing reverence for lettered paper).[240] Specifically, in Wendou Village, it is said that "as long as it is a piece of paper with writing, whether it is useful or not, it shall not be thrown away easily," and there used to be places specially built for burning lettered wastepaper to prevent them from being trampled on and soiled.[241] As collateral evidence, a similar "special institution" could be found in the schools of Jinping County in the early Republican period: on the first and fifteenth day of every lunar month, every student was obliged to carry a bag tagged "*jing xi zi zhi*" and collect lettered paper all over the city, and then take them back to the place for burning.[242]

As for the contract paper, there is no need to mention its high value in ordinary people's eyes. The old saying in villages was: "Burning houses is like wounding the

---

[236] Yang [220]. The English translation can be found in Graham [64].

[237] It was translated as "half tally" in Graham's work, but the Chinese character used here is *qi*, which can also be translated as "contract" in the context.

[238] For the legal status of money and the important principle of "possession that is all" concerning money, see Sun [166].

[239] Sometimes there were even thefts of contracts reported. See Zhang [238].

[240] See Liu [121], Zhao and Baldauf [245].

[241] See Wang Zongxun, *Wendou*, 105.

[242] See Chen et al. [27].

flesh, but burning contracts is like breaking the bone;"[243] "Even if my house was burned, do not burn my contracts;" "When fire burns eyebrows and water floods the bed, do not coax my son even if he is crying, do not hold my daughter even if she is crying, but hold the chest of contracts tight."[244] Both the public discourse and the official discourse hence confirm the importance of the concrete contract. In the *Zhi Zhe chenggui*, the most-cited sentence is that "only holding the contract means owning the property, and losing the contract means losing the property."[245] This sentence explicitly expresses the official opinion and the fact that the material carriers of contracts were and ought to be of primary importance.

On the other hand, the reason why a lawyer in modern times would not value the contract paper as much as it was worth in the past is that contracts are deemed more abstract or conceptual than practical or physical nowadays. It has been noted that "[i]n the minds of most people, the term contract refers to a document, but in the minds of lawyers, it has a broader meaning that includes the totality of an agreement," which denotes "the entire relationship between two parties."[246] In other words, "contract" represents the formation of certain relations instead of several documents. Once a contract is validated, it is valid even if the documents are lost. Thus, the performance or enforcement of a contract does not rely on the material form of the contract and the contract paper is just not a farthing's matter.

The special attention paid to the material aspect of the contract offers a new way of understanding the contract itself. It suggests that "contract" in the context of late imperial China was not likely to be a general notion but more directly referred to an object—they were not abstract but concrete contracts. The non-conceptual nature of contracts indicates that they might be more practical and physical than one is used to thinking today.

5.2.2 Material Carriers Other Than Paper

Although paper had been the dominant contractual material in late imperial China from earlier times,[247] various other materials were used in the long history of Chinese contracts, such as metal, stone (including jade and stele), bamboo, wood, silk, etc.[248]

In the Qingshui River area, stone contracts, wooden contracts, cloth contracts, and paper contracts were the four main types of contracts, the last of which surely

243 Wang Zongxun, *Wendou*, 102.

244 Li and Liang [112].

245 Anonymous, *Zhi Zhe chenggui*, 277–278. A further discussion specifically on this sentence can be seen in Ren and Fang [150]. For the application of contracts as physical evidences in the judicial field, see Liang Zhiping, *Qing dai xiguanfa: Shehui yu guojia*, 129.

246 Lucie Cheng and Arthur Rosett, "Contract with a Chinese Face: Socially Embedded Factors in the Transformation from Hierarchy to Market, 1978–1989," 152.

247 See Wang Xu, *Qizhi qiannian*, 19.

248 See ibid., 6–21.

accounted for the vast majority.[249] The cloth contract was written on undyed cloth and rarely seen.[250] It is said that people used cloth because at that time paper might be hard to find,[251] but one existing example, a cloth contract of adoption,[252] shows that it might be as formal as a paper contract, if not more formal. Examples of stone contracts can also be found and were mostly about significant changes in the ownership among villages or families or had some relation to public interests.[253] Hence, this type of contract was sometimes called a "public contract."[254]

As for the wooden contract, this might be the traditional way of using contracts among the Miao people; or, more specifically, it may have been the predecessor of paper contracts in the area.[255] It is said that "the Miao people have been illiterate for a long time, and there were no written contracts. Even when purchasing fields or houses, they then saw a carved wood off and both parties hold one half of it as reference."[256] This situation was later changed completely; the wood was replaced by paper when contracting.[257] It is hard to find any wooden contract in the Qingshui River region today,[258] but its existence can be proved by the evidence in a criminal case which took place in the area during the Qing dynasty, in which the culprit claimed that he had the wooden contract for his field and the court further recognized it as a legitimate certificate.[259]

To put it in a nutshell, a contract firstly refers to the piece(s) of paper, or other material carriers such as wood, stone, or cloth. In this case, "the text must be embodied in a document,"[260] and a contract without any type of material carrier then is not seen as a contract.

---

[249] See Xu Xiaoguang, *Qingshuijiang liuyu linye jingji fazhi de lishi huisu*, 166; Wang [199].

[250] See Jinping xian difangzhi bianzuan weiyuanhui [100].

[251] See Xu Xiaoguang, *Qingshuijiang liuyu linye jingji fazhi de lishi huisu*, 166.

[252] See Wang [188].

[253] See Jinping xian difangzhi bianzuan weiyuanhui, *Jinping xianzhi, 1991–2009*, vol. 2, 1261–1263; Xu Xiaoguang, *Qingshuijiang liuyu linye jingji fazhi de lishi huisu*, 166; Li and Liang Mingwu, "Qiandongnan diqu linye wenhua chutan," 7; Liping xian linye ju [118].

[254] See Yan [216].

[255] See Cheng Zeshi, *Qingshuijiang wenshu zhi fayi chutan*, 32–35; Cheng Zeshi, *Hudong yu gongxiang*, 303–309.

[256] Lin [116]. The book was written in the Jiaqing era when the author was the sub-prefect of Guizhou. More relevant materials were cited in Li [110].

[257] See Cheng Zeshi, *Qingshuijiang wenshu zhi fayi chutan*, 35–37.

[258] See Aihara [2].

[259] See No. 02-01-07-06751-002 (FHAC), 1772, 1329–1352, The First Historical Archives of China, Beijing. For further details about the case, see Yoshiyuki Aihara, "Jinping wenshu yu xingke tiben," 289–291.

[260] Hein Kötz, *European Contract Law*, 76.

5.3 *The Validity of the Material: Oral and Non-original*

Since the material carrier was essential in defining contracts, two issues should be discussed concerning the validity of the material of contracts. First, was an oral contract a contract? Second, how did one deal with the many non-original versions of contracts?

5.3.1 Oral Contracts

Oral contracts have a long history that can be traced back to Roman law; for example, the famous *stipulatio*, which was made in the form of question and answer, was considered "the most important."[261] In general, however, in modern laws,[262] unless an agreement is required to be stated in writing,[263] "an oral contract is as valid as a written contract."[264] For the context in question, verbal agreements certainly existed extensively in all kinds of situations, but should they be seen as contracts according to the proposed definition?

Roughly speaking, verbal agreements fall into two main types in the light of whether the agreement would finally lead to a written contract or not. It is conceivable that there would be a preliminary and mostly oral agreement before a contract was finally written down in the contracting event. Sometimes the scribe of the contract would add "*yikou daibi*" or "to write according to the verbal [expressions]" at the end of the text, indicating a prepositive procedure of oral negotiation.[265] Obviously, this kind of verbal agreement was not fixed at the moment and should not be seen as a contract.

The second type of verbal agreements can be further categorized into two according to the necessity to draw up a document. For the simplest, most direct, and immediate transactions on personal properties, written contracts might not be needed. One villager could just pay the price and take his bottle of oil back home without writing anything. The two parties have formed a contract, according to the theory of modern contract law, but this type of "invisible" contract employed another set of much looser rules and applied to transactions of much lower value, which made it a de facto different concept from the visible one. As for those transactions that

---

[261]For verbal contracts in Roman law, see du Plessis and Borkowski [45]. It should still be noted that, as reminded by Maine, "[i]n the Verbal Contract, as soon as the Convention was effected, a form of words had to be gone through before the vinculum juris was attached to it." See Maine [130].

[262]See Han Shiyuan, *Hetongfa zonglun*, 110, 113–114.

[263]The treatment of laws applies to a contract if it "for which writing is required is made verbally," see Hein Kötz, *European Contract Law*, 78 ff.

[264]Sweet [168].

[265]See Qu Jian, "Yikou daibi," 186–190.

require written contracts, mostly concerning immovable properties or other important issues, exceptions still existed.[266] Why significant transactions such as trading real estates or even marriage might not have a written document could be explained by the illiteracy in earlier times.[267]

Differently from the "principle of informality" in modern laws,[268] the contract in context required a clear and probably strict formality, along with a special emphasis on the material aspect. The "material carriers" of bodiless verbal agreements can only be the memories of contracting parties,[269] which were undoubtedly highly "problematic"[270] and unreliable[271] and were wholly unable to meet the standard of formality. Therefore, the criterion of embodying in certain material carriers marks the exclusion of oral contracts from contracts, based on the proposed definition.

5.3.2 Copies of the Contract

Not only the nature of the material carriers but also that of the documents as a whole should also be considered—was it an "original," a "copy," a mere "draft" or even a "sample"[272] or "writing practice"?[273]

Chronologically speaking, all of these except the "original" can be sorted into two kinds: the pre-contract documents and the post-contract documents. The former includes "drafts" and "samples" or "writing practices," while the latter is mainly "copies," including "*chaobai*" (single piece of contract copy) and "account books" (collection of contract copies) in the Qingshui River region.[274] It has been noted that "[s]ometimes account books for certain properties carry the text of the purchase document for ease of reference."[275] This situation widely existed in the Qingshui River region. However, these familiar copies were surely not contracts, for burning

---

[266] See He Xiaoping, *Qing dai xiguanfa: Zudian guanxi yanjiu*, 60–63. Also, for verbal agreements of land rentals, see Huang [90]. For a later Chinese translation of the book, see Huang [92]. A revised and enlarged version, see Huang [94].

[267] According to a survey conducted in the 1930s, the start of using written contracts was based on the emerging intellectuals in the recent few decades in the Miao area of Hunan province. See Shi [155]. It is also believed, in another study based on evidence from the Pearl River Delta, that the popularization of land contracts might have arisen through a process from "oral transmission" to written land contracts. See Faure [49].

[268] See Han Shiyuan, *Hetongfa zonglun*, 107; Edwin Peel, *Treitel The Law of Contract*, 5-003.

[269] See He Xiaoping, *Qing dai xiguanfa: Zudian guanxi yanjiu*, 53.

[270] See Patrick H. Hase, *Custom, Land and Livelihood in Rural South China*, 148.

[271] In medieval China, even Judge Bao, who was prefect of Kaifeng and "thought to have superman powers," "was unable to make people fulfill unrecorded agreements," and "all evidence suggests that earlier officials also had to rely on written agreements when verbal accounts conflicted." See Valerie Hansen, *Negotiating Daily Life in Traditional China*, 82.

[272] See Qu Jian, "Yikou daibi," 202 ff; James Hayes, "Specialists and Written Materials in the Village World," 87.

[273] See Giele [63].

[274] See Qu Jian, "Yikou daibi," 208.

[275] James Hayes, "Specialists and Written Materials in the Village World," 87.

contract copies or drafts[276] could never cause effects equal to burning the original. That was also why the village girl in the story told above waited until the special day, namely the sixth day of the sixth month when all original contracts were finally taken out. Lost copies could be reproduced easily while the original could not. In this case, the copy of a contract was not a contract.

Though it is "not always identifiable with a sufficient degree of certainty,"[277] in theory a valid contract can only be the original in the context. All other copies or drafts might be able to provide certain content or even the whole and exact text of the contract, which is of great value for researchers but should still be labeled as invalid.

In short, attaching importance to the materiality of contracts draws attention to the valid material carriers for contracts, which therefore excludes human memories and any copies or drafts that are not the original.

6 The Tripartite Structure of Contracts: A Theory

6.1 Three Stages and the Sequence of Examination

Three aspects of the contract, i.e. the material carrier, the form, and the content, have been set forth in the previous sections. Descriptions of each of these aspects have been discussed thoroughly and the criteria corresponding to each aspect have been clearly provided; in the following section they will be organized together logically. Here a tentative theory of the tripartite structure of contracts, that can be applied in defining and identifying contracts in context, is propounded, with an explanatory verification of the structure.

The idea of the tripartite structure of contracts derives directly from the classic "tripartite structure of criminal offenses" (*dreistufiger Verbrechensaufbau*) in German criminal law and other jurisdictions influenced by it.[278] The structure of criminal offenses consists of three dimensions, or (more exactly) stages, as procedurally there is an examination sequence[279] within the structure. These three stages can be concluded as the offense description (*Tatbestand*), general unlawfulness/wrongdoing (*Rechtswidrigkeit*), and culpability (*Schuld*).[280]

[276] In fact, "[u]sually, the draft deed would then be destroyed and only the final version would survive." See Patrick H. Hase, *Custom, Land and Livelihood in Rural South China*, 155.

[277] See Enno Giele, "Signatures of 'Scribes' in Early Imperial China," 381.

[278] See "The Tripartite Structure of Offences—an Overview," in Bohlander [14]; Vormbaum [182], Christopher [32], Fletcher [55].

[279] A schematic overview of the structure in graphic form can be seen in Michael Bohlander, *Principles of German Criminal Law*, 17.

[280] See ibid., 16; Russell L. Christopher, "Tripartite Structures of Criminal Law in Germany and Other Civil Law Jurisdictions," 2676.

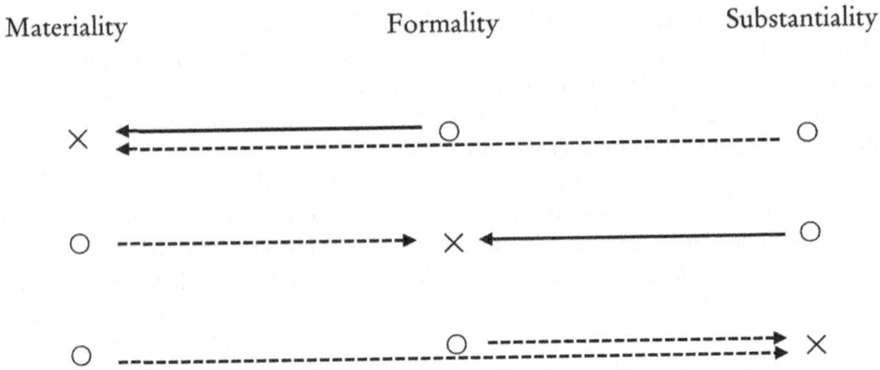

Fig. 3 The rule of "healing" in the tripartite structure of contracts

Accordingly, the three stages of the proposed tripartite structure of contracts are materiality, formality, and substantiality. Thus, ideally and generally, a contract is a document that perfectly meets the aforementioned requirements of the three aspects of the structure; falling short of the expectation of any aspect marks a failure to be regarded as a contract. The tripartite structure, including all the criteria within it, not only can define a contract in context but also serves as a device to distinguish contracts from non-contracts. Each contract in the context should be subject to these three stages of examination by the tripartite structure of contracts, just as each offense is subject to its counterpart in German criminal law.[281]

Further, these three aspects of the structure are deemed as stages, rather than merely as dimensions, since they are chronologically organized by an important and fixed examination sequence, i.e. one which progresses from materiality to formality to substantiality, which plays a pivotal role in the application of the structure. In practice, not all contracts can fulfill all parts of these requirements perfectly. The test of whether one meets each level of criteria can be carefully divided into three types: satisfied, unsatisfied, and defective. The first and second results refer to perfect fulfillment or nonfulfillment of the requirements, while the last stands for the imperfect situation in-between. At this point the importance of the examination sequence becomes more evident: within the tripartite structure, the defects of contracts might somehow be able to be "cured" (*geheilt*)[282] by the result of the next stage according to the sequence of examination.

The rule of "healing" (see Fig. 3)[283] states that the defects of a manuscript in the previous stage can be cured by its perfect or enhanced performance in the next stage,

[281] See Michael Bohlander, *Principles of German Criminal Law*, 16.

[282] The term "healing" or "cure" (*Heilung*) refers to a legally recognized means to remedy contractual defects in German law. See, e.g., BGB, Section 518: (2): "A defect of form is cured by rendering the performance promised." (*Der Mangel der Form wird durch die Bewirkung der versprochenen Leistung geheilt*). See also Wang [185].

[283] The full lines denote that the defects (X) are curable by the enhanced performance (O) in the direction signified, while the dash lines denote that the defects are incurable in the given direction.

but, most importantly and interestingly, not the other way around. In other words, a manuscript which is defective with respect to its materiality can still be healed through its efforts with respect to its formality, and defects in form can be cured by the satisfaction of its substantiality. Conversely, deficiency in substantiality cannot be complemented by a better form, and problems in formality can seek no remedy from materiality. In addition, skipping over the middle stage will not be possible, i.e. substantiality is unable to help fix the trouble of materiality.

This non-reversing principle in dealing with commonly seen imperfect contract manuscripts highlights the crucial importance of the sequence of examination. This sequence, along with the three clusters of criteria in different dimensions, acts as the cornerstone of the tripartite structure of contracts.

6.2 Application and Verification

A potential theory or structure of criteria needs to show its applicability and to be verified in practice. Several examples are therefore raised to help further explain the tripartite structure in terms of its application.

6.2.1 Materiality: The Re-made Contracts

Materiality is ranked first in the tripartite structure. What can one do if the requirements of materiality were not fulfilled properly? The third pile of burning contracts (the other two of which have been shown in previous parts), which is locally high-profile, is referred to here to answer the question.

The document relating to the fire is deemed the key exemplar and most precious treasure of the collections of Jinping County Archives, for it is the largest document in size and contains the most characters in number among all collected contract documents.[284] It was found by the Archives in 2004 and was called "the contract king" at the time.[285] According to the record in the manuscript, it was made, or more precisely re-made, due to the loss of a great number of original contracts.[286] On the dawn of the fifth day of the sixth month of the fourteenth year of Guangxu (July 13,

[284] It is 2080 cm long and 528 cm wide, with 2888 Chinese characters written on it. A relatively high-resolution image of the document is recorded in Wang Kui, *Jinping wenshu jiyi duben*, 102–103.

[285] See Anonymous [7]. For the picture, see Anonymous [8].

[286] For a specific introduction to the manuscript, see Long [124]. In fact, it might not merely be a contract but also a "license" issued by the government. The license was stuck to the right end of the manuscript and the left part is a list of properties, summarizing the basic information of the contract accordingly. In this case, the left part can be seen as a de facto contract with the right part as the official document relating to it, as was the common practice in the Qing dynasty. See Yang Guozhen, *Ming Qing tudi qiyue wenshu yanjiu (xiudingban)*, 54–69. A transcription of this license, though riddled with errors, can be found in Xu [211].

1988), a fire broke out in Peiliang Village, and all the contracts of Fan Guorui and Fan Guofan were burned to ashes.[287] The Fan brothers experienced a similar situation to Yao the Millionaire, but only this time the fire might not have been deliberate. In order to save their properties, they went to the county yamen and asked the official to seal the document which listed every land and field they "used to own" before the fire. This explains the unusual length of the manuscript, since it has to be long enough to include all items.[288]

The items on the manuscript were transcribed from a private collection of contract copies preserved by the Fans.[289] In this case, "the contract king" is definitely not an original contract. Nonetheless, the official procedures which the manuscript has gone through, the explicit recognition it received from Fans' neighbors and fellow villagers,[290] and finally the red seal on the paper, which served as a powerful guarantee of its content, all enhanced the formality of the document from different perspectives, curing thereby the defects of its materiality. Although, compared to the normal experience of a contract, this was obviously a more complicated, costly, and formal process, it was nevertheless sufficient and effective as a remedial measure regarding the previous stage of materiality.

Another example is related to a situation commonly seen in contract practice. Regarding the contract paper, there is another status between existence and non-existence: disappearance. Sometimes the contract cannot be found at the moment of contracting[291] but might reappear later. The pendent status of one contract's materiality can be solved by another properly made contract. In this circumstance, the new contract takes over what was established or confirmed by the old one, and the missing paper would be declared void thereafter at the same time. The phrase "*rihou qingchu, yiwei guzhi*" (if [the contract] is found out later in the future, [it] is to be seen as an annulled paper) was frequently used in such situations.[292]

No matter what kind of flaws exist in the materiality of a contract, whether burned or lost, they can be cured by the proper formality within another re-made contract. In this way, going through the formal procedure anew could somehow re-endow the contract with the nature of being an original. Whether one piece of paper has been through the process of formality or not corresponds exactly to the distinction between the original and its copies.

287 See Jinping xian difangzhi bianzuan weiyuanhui, *Jinping xianzhi, 1991–2009*, vol. 2, 1261.

288 See also Shan [152].

289 See Long Linglie, "Minjian xiguan yu guanfu guifan hutong huren de fanben," 134–135.

290 The officials have asked the neighbors of the Fan brothers, other villagers, and the head of the village if what was stated in the manuscript was true or not. See the manuscript in Wang Kui, *Jinping wenshu jiyi duben*, 103.

291 This situation happened so frequently in contracting practice that it had been enumerated in contract forms, see Jiang Yixu, *Shuqi bianmeng*, 15, 16.

292 See, e.g., Chen Jinquan and Du Wanhua, *Jiang Yuanze jiacang qiyue wenshu*, 573.

6.2.2 Formality: The Contract of Mountain Allocation

The special emphasis on the formality of the contract[293] in this context suggests the belief that the conclusion of the contract is not only a private act but also a public one, for the appearance of the content is of similar, if not greater, importance than the content itself. The focus in this case lies not on the parties' intentions but the declaration of their intentions—the way that they are presented determines how they are perceived by the public. For this reason, the lack of formality makes it harder for a contract to be accepted by the community.

The contract of mountain allocation cited at the beginning of this chapter as an example of borderline contracts is also an appropriate instance of a contract with deficient formality.[294] The manuscript firstly meets the requirements of materiality without doubt. Regarding its formality, however, it might be considered defective. As mentioned, since the vast majority of contracts in the Qing dynasty start with the formula of *li*, a contract without this significant part could be seen as having a defect in its formality. Instead of the formula, this manuscript begins with the date and description of the timber harvest, which was not a common opening in writing a contract. Thus, a further test is needed concerning the third stage of substantiality. As noted previously, the content of the contract related to the confirmation of relations between shareholders—specifically, the allocation of the number of shares and the money accordingly. The content should at any rate be seen as recording some kind of jural relation, prescribing rights and obligations among those shareholders. In this case, as the rule provides, concrete substantiality can cure the small issue of formality (by the lack of a symbolic formula), and the marginal and borderline case can therefore still be classified as a contract.

6.2.3 Substantiality: Kitty Contracts and Tomb Contracts

Obviously, not everything or every type of relation can be managed and stipulated by a contract, but only those that are "jurally meaningful." Normally, a jural relation can easily be distinguished from other issues, as is shown by the aforementioned

---

[293]The emphasis on formality seems to be a common phenomenon in ancient law. Maine offered a clear statement regarding this issue: "Ancient law is still more suggestive of the distance which separates the crude form of Contract from its maturity. At first, nothing is seen like the interposition of law to compel the performance of a promise. That which the law arms with its sanctions is not a promise, but a promise accompanied with a solemn ceremonial. Not only are the formalities of equal importance with the promise itself, but they are, if anything, of greater importance; for that delicate analysis which mature jurisprudence applies to the conditions of mind under which a particular verbal assent is given appears, in ancient law, to be transferred to the words and gestures of the accompanying performance. No pledge is enforced if a single form be omitted or misplaced, but, on the other hand, if the forms can be shown to have been accurately proceeded with, it is of no avail to plead that the promise was made under duress or deception." Henry Sumner Maine, *Ancient Law*, 313.

[294]See Christian Daniels, Yang Yougeng, and Takeuchi Fusaji, *Kishū Myaozoku ringyō keiyaku monjo kaihen (1736–1950-nen)*, vol. 3, E-0050.

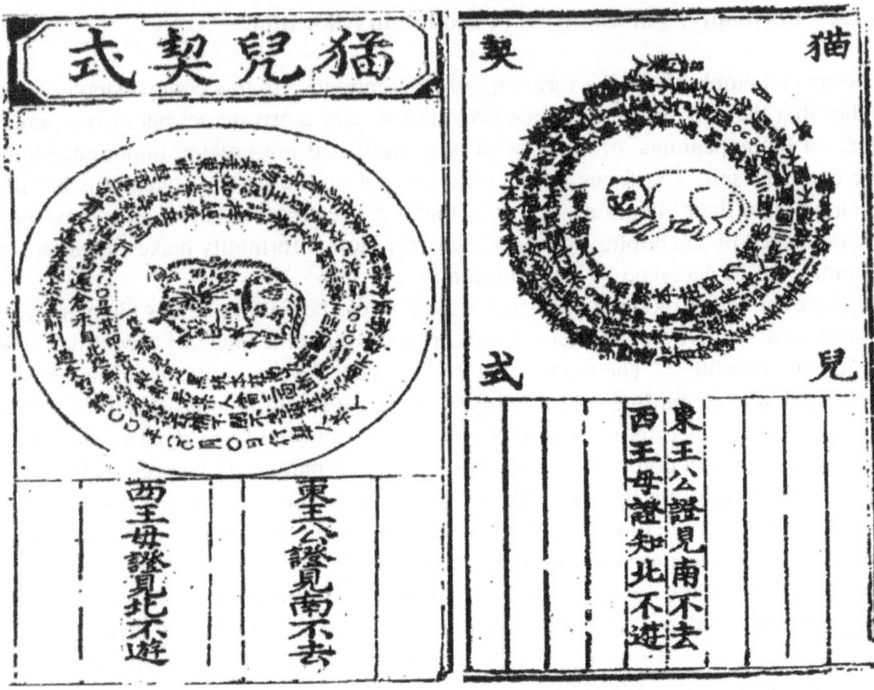

Fig. 4 Forms of kitty contracts

example of the agreement on the rising sun in the east. Admittedly, this is a loose standard, which explains the extreme diversity of social activities that a contract could include. However, this does not mean that it is practically useless. There were still some manuscripts that need a careful examination of their substantiality.

Kitty contracts (*mao'er qi*) could be one kind of these questionable manuscripts.[295] They fit the requirements of the first two stages perfectly, and the layout of these documents is more vivid (see Fig. 4)[296] than the commonly dull and boring contract form. According to the text contained within these contracts, the contract was concluded after the purchase of a kitty. Nevertheless, it is believed that the two parties were not the buyer and the seller, but the new owner (the buyer) and, interestingly, the cat.[297] The content is also interesting. The owner made a deal with the cat, stipulating that, for example, it should do its duty of catching rats and should not harm other livestock or steal food, or else it should willingly accept being punished. An even fancier feature of the manuscript is the indication of the witnesses of the contract: the Grandpa King of the East (*Dongwanggong*) and the Queen Mother of the West (*Xiwangmu*).

[295] For introduction and discussion of this kind of "contract," see Li [111], Qian and Wang [143].

[296] The left image, see Lin and Lin [116]. The right one, see Song et al. [160].

[297] See Li Ren-yuan, "Mao'er qi," 1.

Writing down the names of the Taoist god and goddess on the manuscript made it more unreal.

In the description of the contract's substantiality, a jural relation is stipulated to exist among parties, and not only the "jural relations" but also the "parties" shall be considered as real-life and as being able to bring actual changes. The "kitty contract" does not meet the standard of either one. The document, in this case, is not considered a contract by the proposed definition, and because of the non-reversing principle no other remedies can be given to the failure of its substantiality.

By analogy, the commonly seen tomb contracts (*maidiquan*) are not proper real-world contracts either.[298] This kind of document was supposed to be buried in tombs "for the purchase of grave plots" with gods,[299] and, by the late imperial period, they "were often written on paper and burned or buried with the body."[300] In the Qingshui River region, field research has shown that customs of funeral rites might generate similar manuscripts—underworld contracts (*yinqi*)—even though none have been found, since, in theory, these paper manuscripts were written to be burned in order to help the dead to obtain their properties even in the underworld.[301] As shown by a record in the Gazetteer of Anshun, Guizhou, the underworld contract could share the same purpose of purchasing grave plots as the tomb contract.[302] Although it is believed that tomb contracts "were heavily influenced by commercial contracts" of the real world, "they were always two distinct categories of property deeds;"[303] hence, the tomb contracts might not have a necessary connection with the secular contracts.[304]

The application of the criteria of substantiality has been exemplified by two types of contracts, i.e. kitty contracts and tomb contracts. As the final stage of the tripartite structure cannot be cured by efforts from earlier stages, the substantiality is therefore of decisive importance in defining contracts. In sum, when seeing the contract as a practical device, the tripartite structure of contracts can be used to explain thoroughly the three aspects of it. The proposed structure does not aim for perfect or standard contracts. Its task, as stated, is to identify those relatively few but difficult, and therefore significant, cases at the borderline.

---

[298] For studies of tomb contracts, see Valerie Hansen, *Negotiating Daily Life in Traditional China*, 149–221; Lu [126]; Zhang Chuanxi, *Qiyue shi maidiquan yanjiu*, 173 ff. Although it is mostly discussed within the context of earlier times, this type of document can still be found in late imperial China, see Lu Xiqi, *Zhongguo gudai maidiquan yanjiu*, 578 ff; Brown [18].

[299] Valerie Hansen, *Negotiating Daily Life in Traditional China*, 149.

[300] Tristan G. Brown, "The Deeds of the Dead in the Courts of the Living," 117.

[301] See Wang Zongxun, *Xunshi yiluo de jiyi*, 112. A seal specifically made for the production of underworld contracts was found preserved in the village of Yuhe.

[302] For a detailed description of the custom of writing and burning underworld contracts in Guizhou, albeit one from another area of Anshun, see Anshun shi difangzhi bianzuan weiyuanhui [9]. It is also claimed a stone tablet inscription that embodies a tomb contract was found. See Wang [193].

[303] Tristan G. Brown, "The Deeds of the Dead in the Courts of the Living," 121.

[304] See Lu Xiqi, *Zhongguo gudai maidiquan yanjiu*, 73–77.

7 Conclusion

After the investigation of materiality, formality, and substantiality of contracts in context, a tentative definition might finally be concluded and proposed. In the context of late imperial China, and particularly in the Qingshui River region during the Qing dynasty, a contract, in most cases, refers to a piece of paper, or other valid material carrier, with a text written on it in a certain form, concerning the establishment or/and confirmation of jural relations, i.e. those relating to rights and obligations, between parties.

This finding not only provides a practical definition of a contract in the given context but also, perhaps more importantly, offers a new understanding of traditional Chinese contracts in the specific context to a significant extent. These contracts were to some extent the rationalized expression of everyday life in the region, which served as the foundation of the (re)arrangement of social life. The seemingly theoretical discourses around them are firmly supported by vivid real stories that happened, and they can be used to account for more unexplored instances.

In this chapter the differences and similarities between contracts in the context of the Qingshui River region and their modern counterparts have been scrutinized through a comparative analysis and from both perspectives. However, it should always be kept in mind that, for most contracts in context, whether applying a modern definition or the one proposed in this chapter would not make a huge difference in terms of identification. The large degree of similarity between the two urges the use of the English term "contract" in this study, instead of creating a new term of, say, *hetong* or *ziyue* based upon its Chinese context. However, the anomalous details also matter. It is the seemingly slight differences at the margin that shape and reveal the nature of the contract in context and mark it off as a relatively unique notion which should be re-understood and for this purpose calls for a distinct definition.

References

1. Abbattista, Guido. 2017. Chinese law and justice: George Thomas Staunton (1781–1859) and the european discourses on China in the eighteenth and nineteenth centuries. In *Law, justice and codification in Qing China. European and Chinese perspectives essays in history and comparative law*, ed. Guido Abbattista, 1–138. Trieste: Edizioni Università di Trieste.
2. Aihara, Yoshiyuki. 2017. Jinping wenshu yu xingke tiben [Jinping documents and routine memorials to the Ministry of Justice]. In *Jinping wenshu yu fawenhua yanjiu* [Jinping manuscripts and the studies of legal culture], ed. Qicai Gao and Kui Wang, 291. Beijing: Zhongguo zhengfa daxue chubanshe.
3. Allee, Mark A. 1994. *Law and local society in late imperial China: Northern Taiwan in the nineteenth century*, 217. Stanford, California: Stanford University Press.
4. American Law Institute, ed. 1981. *Restatement (Second) of contracts*, Sect. 1, St. Paul, MN: American Law Institute Publishers.
5. Anonymous. [1837] 2012. *Zhi Zhe chenggui* [Established rules for governing Zhejiang], ed. Yifan Yang and Ducai Liu, facsimile ed., 15 vols., vol. 7, Reprinted in *Zhongguo gudai difang*

falü wenxian (bing bian) [Local legal documents in ancient China (the 3rd series)], 277–278. Beijing: Shehui kexue wenxian chubanshe.
6. Anonymous. c. 1907. *Huang Kechuo chao qishi ji* [A collection of contract forms transcribed by Huang Kechuo], Qu Jian's Collections.
7. Anonymous. 2005. Qiyue zhi xiang jingxian kuangshi zhenping qiyue [A valuable contract appears in Jinping (an extract from *Guizhou dang'an gongzuo xinxi*)]. *Hainan dang'an* (2): 43.
8. Anonymous. Jinping wenshu [Jinping manuscripts]. Archive treasures, vol. 3, National archives administration of China. Accessed July 27 2019. http://www.archives.gov.cn/zpda/zpdazgdawxycmldsj/201411/t20141116_344.html.
9. Anshun shi difangzhi bianzuan weiyuanhui, ed. 2010. *Anshun diqu zhi* [Gazetteer of the Anshun area], vol. 1, 347. Guiyang: Guizhou renmin chubanshe.
10. Barber, Steve. 1993. *Resource Manual for Legal Writing for Paralegals*, 147. Nashville: South-Western Publishing Company.
11. Beale, Hugh, Bénédicte Fauvarque-Cosson, Jacobien Rutgers, and Stefan Vogenauer. 2019. *Cases, materials and text on contract law*, 3rd ed, Sect. 5.1. Oxford and Portland, Oregon: Hart Publishing.
12. Blackstone, William. 2007. *Commentaries on the laws of England: In four books*, reprinted ed., 4 vols., vol. 2, ed. William Draper Lewis, 446. Clark, New Jersey: The Lawbook Exchange, Ltd.
13. Bodde, Derk. 1963. Basic concepts of Chinese law: The genesis and evolution of legal thought in traditional China. *Proceedings of the American Philosophical Society* 107 (5): 375.
14. Bohlander, Michael. 2009. *Principles of German criminal law*, 16–17. Oxford and Portland, Oregon: Hart Publishing.
15. Bourgon, Jérôme. 2009. Ditan shang de tu'an: Shilun Qing dai falü wenhua zhong de 'xiguan' yu 'qiyue' [Figures in the carpet: 'Customs' and 'contracts' in Qing legal culture]. (trans. Shijie Huang). In *Ming Qing falü yunzuo zhong de quanli yu wenhua* [Power and legal culture in legal activities under the Ming and Qing dynasties], ed. Pengsheng Qiu and Xiyuan Chen, 96–127. Taipei: Lianjing chuban gongsi.
16. Bourgon, Jérôme, Thomas Buoye, Claude Chevaleyre, Chiu Peng-sheng, Frédéric Constant, Maura Dykstra, Julie Erismann, et al. 2019. Legalizing Space in China Project, May 22, 2019. http://lsc.chineselegalculture.org/.
17. Brockman, Rosser H. 1980. Commercial contract law in late nineteenth-century Taiwan. In *Essays on China's Legal Tradition*, ed. Jerome Alan Cohen, R. Randle Edwards, and Fu-mei Chang Chen, 76–136. Princeton: Princeton University Press.
18. Brown, Tristan G. 2018. The deeds of the dead in the courts of the living: Graves in Qing law. *Late Imperial China* 39 (2): 109–155.
19. Buxbaum, David C. 1993. Contracts in China during the Qing dynasty: Key to the civil law. *Journal of Oriental Studies* XXXI (2): 195–236.
20. Caldwell, Ernest. 2018. *Writing Chinese law: The form and function of legal statutes found in the Qin shuihudi corpus*, 19–44. New York: Routledge.
21. Campbell, David, ed. 2001. *The relational theory of contract: Selected works of Ian Macneil*. London: Sweet & Maxwell.
22. Chen, Chong-Fang. 2016. Qianlong banian *Da Qing Lüli* de banxing [The promulgation of *The Great Qing Code* in 1743]. *Fazhishi yanjiu* 29 (6): 77–124.
23. Chen, Li. 2016. *Chinese law in imperial eyes: Sovereignty, justice, and transcultural politics*, 69–111. New York: Columbia University Press.
24. Chen, Linghai. *Da Qing Huidian* yu Qing dai 'dian-li' falü tixi [*Huidian* and 'dian-li' legal system of the Qing dynasty]. *Zhongwai faxue* 29 (2): 402–428.
25. Chen, Jinquan, and Liang Guo, eds. 2017. *Guizhou Wendouzhai Miaozu qiyue falü wenshu huibian—Yi Zunfa Jiang Qicheng deng jiacang susong wenshu* [The compilation of contractual and legal manuscripts of the Miao from Wendou Village, Guizhou—Litigation manuscripts from family collections of Yi Zunfa, Jiang Qicheng, etc.], 230. Beijing: Renmin chubanshe.

26. Chen, Jinquan, and Wanhua Du, eds. 2008. *Guizhou Wendouzhai Miaozu qiyue falü wenshu huibian—Jiang Yuanze jiacang qiyue wenshu* [The compilation of contractual and legal manuscripts of the Miao from Wendou Village, Guizhou—Manuscripts from Jiang Yuanze's family collection], 27. Beijing: Renmin chubanshe.
27. Chen, Shichuan, Shengqing Wang, and Mingli Wang. 1987. Jinping Chengguan wenhua jiaoyu shikuang [A history of the cultural education in Chengguan of Jinping]. In *Jinping wenshi ziliao xuanji (di yi ji)* [Selected collection of historical accounts of past events in Jinping County (Vol. 1)], ed. Guizhou sheng Jinping xian zhengxie wenshi yanjiu weiyuanhui, 118. Jinping: Zhongguo renmin zhengzhi xieshang huiyi Guizhou sheng Jinping xian weiyuanhui wenshi ziliao yanjiu weiyuanhui.
28. Cheng, Zeshi. 2011. *Qingshuijiang wenshu zhi fayi chutan* [A primary legal research on the Qingshui River manuscripts], 116. Beijing: Zhongguo zhengfa daxue chubanshe.
29. Cheng, Zeshi. 2012. 'Yao Baiwan' wugao moufan an yu jiaoyi gongping [The case about being falsely charged with treason by Yao Baiwan and fair trades]. *Yuanshengtai minzu wenhua xuekan* 4 (2): 46–53.
30. Cheng, Zeshi. 2017. *Hudong yu gongxiang: Qing dai Miao Jiang shehui zhuanxing zhi lisong tiaoshi* [Trial adjustment and social transition in Qing Miao areas], 259–273. Beijing: Zhongguo fazhi chubanshe.
31. Cheng, Lucie, and Arthur Rosett. 1991. Contract with a Chinese face: Socially embedded factors in the transformation from hierarchy to market, 1978–1989. *Journal of Chinese Law* 5 (2): 152.
32. Christopher, Russell L. 2007. Tripartite structures of criminal law in Germany and other civil law jurisdictions. *Cardozo Law Review* 28 (6): 2675–2695.
33. Cohen, Myron L. 1969. The role of contract in traditional Chinese social organizatio. In *Proceedings: VIIIth international congress of anthropological and ethnological sciences, Tokyo and Kyoto, 1968, Vol. 2, ethnology*, 130–132. Tokyo: Science Council of Japan.
34. Cohen, Myron L. 2004. Writs of passage in late imperial China: The documentation of practical understandings in Minong, Taiwan. In *Contract and property in early modern China*, ed. Madeleine Zelin, Jonathan K. Ocko, and Robert Gardella, 37–93. Stanford: Stanford University Press.
35. Cohen, Myron L. 2005. *Kinship, contract, community, and state: Anthropological perspectives on China*, 252–303. Stanford: Stanford University Press.
36. Committee for the Publication of the Rural Customs and Practices of China, ed. 1958. *Chūgoku nōson kankō chōsa* [Investigation of Rural Chinese Customs]. Tokyo: Iwanami shoten.
37. Corbin, Arthur L. 1921. Jural relations and their classification. *The Yale Law Journal* 30 (3): 226–238.
38. Cordier, Henri. 1910. Pierre Hoang (Huang Bolu) Houang Pe-lou (Fei Mei). *T'oung Pao* 11 (1): 139–141.
39. Dai, Shaoqiang, and Dongdong Wei. 2016. Qing dai Qingshuijiang liuyu de huozai jiqi shehui yingdui [Fires and its countermeasures in the Qingshui River Basin in the Qing dynasty]. *Guangxi keji shifan xueyuan xuebao* 31 (5): 92–94.
40. Daniels, Christian, Yougeng Yang, and Fusaji Takeuchi, eds. 2003. *Kishū Myaozoku ringyō keiyaku monjo kaihen (1736–1950-nen)* [Old forestry contracts of the Miao in Guizhou, 1736–1950], vol. 3, E-0050. Tokyo: Tōkyō gaikokugo daigaku Ajia Afurika gengo bunka kenkyūjo.
41. Deng, Hui. 2018. Lun hetong de biyao tiaokuan [On the necessary terms of contracts]. *Caijing faxue* (2): 111–125.
42. Deng, Jianpeng, and Kai Qiu. 2013. Cong heyi dao qiangzhi: Qing zhi Minguo Qingshuijiang jiufen wenshu yanjiu [From consensus to enforcement: A study on disputes manuscripts in the Qing and Republican periods]. *Gansu zhengfa xueyuan xuebao* 126 (1): 27.
43. Doleželová-Velingerová, Milena, and Rudolf G. Wagner, eds. 2014. *Chinese Encyclopaedias of New Global Knowledge (1870–1930): Changing Ways of Thought*. Heidelberg: Springer.
44. Duanhuang yanjiuyuan, ed. 2000. *Dunhuang yishu zongmu suoyin xinbian* [General index of Dunhuang texts, new edition], 57. Beijing: Zhonghua shuju.

45. Du Plessis, Paul J., and Andrew Borkowski. 2015. *Borkowski's textbook on roman law*, 5th ed., 296 ff. Oxford: Oxford University Press.
46. Elman, Benjamin. 2007. Collecting and classifying: Ming dynasty compendia and encyclopedias (Leishu). *Extrême-Orient, Extrême-Occident* hors-série (1): 152.
47. Faber, Wolfgang, and Brigitta Lurger, eds. 2011. *National reports on the transfer of movables in Europe: Germany, Greece, Lithuania, Hungary*, vol. 3, 20. Munich: Sellier. European Law Publishers.
48. Farnsworth, E. Allan. 2007. Comparative Contract Law. In *The oxford handbook of comparative law*, ed. Mathias Reimann and Reinhard Zimmermann, 990. Oxford: Oxford University Press.
49. Faure, David. 2001. Contractual arrangements and the emergence of a land market in the pearl river delta, 1500–1800. In *Qiyue wenshu yu shehui shenghuo (1600–1900)* [Contract documents and social life, 1600–1900], ed. Li-wan Hung and Chiu-kun Chen, 265–283. Taipei: Zhongyang yanjiuyuan Taiwan shi yanjiusuo choubeichu.
50. Faure, David, and Anthony Pang. 1996. The power and limit of the private contract in Ming-Qing China and today. In *Chinese business enterprise: Critical perspectives on business and management*, ed. Rajeswary Ampalavanar Brown, 282. London: Routledge.
51. Fauvarque-Cosson, Benedicte, and Denis Mazeaud, eds. 2008. *European contract law—materials for a common frame of reference: Terminology, guiding principles, model rules*, 3–21. Munich: Sellier. European Law Publishers, 2008.
52. Feng, Xuewei, ed. 2014. Qing keben 'Xieyue bu qiuren' [A Qing edition of the 'Instructions for writing contracts with no need for others' help']. *Falü wenhua luncong* 2: 122–129.
53. Feng, Xuewei. 2015. Zhongguo chuantong qishi chutan [A primary investigation on the traditional Chinese contract forms]. *Qinghua fazhi lunheng* 24 (2): 462–463.
54. Feng, Xuewei. 2015. *Ming Qing qiyue de jiegou gongneng ji yiyi* [The structure, function, and meaning of contracts in the Ming-Qing eras], 68–69. Beijing: Falü chubanshe.
55. Fletcher, George P. 2007. *The grammar of criminal law: American, comparative, and international*, vol. 1: Foundations, 43 ff. New York: Oxford University Press.
56. Foerste, Karla. 2000. Eine Methode der Streitvermeidung: Die» dritte Partei «bei Begründung und Durchsetzung von Verträgen im traditionellen China. *Rabels Zeitschrift für ausländisches und internationales Privatrecht* 64 (1): 126.
57. Fu, Rebecca Shuang. 2015. Women's literacy practices in late medieval China (600–1000). Doctoral dissertation, University of Pennsylvania, 118–127.
58. Gao, Hongjun. 2004. *Yisilan fa: Chuantong yu xiandaihua* [Islamic law: Tradition and modernization], revised ed., 430. Beijing: Qinghua daxue chubanshe.
59. Gardella, Robert. 2004. Contracting business partnerships in late Qing and Republican China: Paradigms and patterns. In *Contract and property in early modern China*, ed. Madeleine Zelin, Jonathan K. Ocko, and Robert Gardella, 330. Stanford: Stanford University Press.
60. Gardella, Robert. 2004. Enterprises, contracts and partnerships: A case for chinese customary legal traditions bridging the Nanyang. In *Maritime China in transition 1750–1850*, ed. Gungwu Wang and Chin-Keong Ng, 291. Wiesbaden: Harrassowitz Verlag.
61. Garner, Bryan A., ed. *Black's law dictionary*, 9th ed., 365–366. St. Paul, MN: West.
62. Ge, Yajun. 2002. *Hetong yingyu shouce* [Master English for contract], reprinted ed., 30–32. Tianjin: Tianjin keji fanyi chubanshe.
63. Giele, Enno. 2005. Signatures of 'Scribes' in early imperial China. *Asiatische Studien/Études Asiatiques* 59 (1): 381.
64. Graham, A.C. (trans.). 1990. *The book of Lieh-tzu: A classic of the Tao*, 179. New York: Columbia University Press.
65. Gu, Changsheng. 2013. *Chuanjiaoshi yu jindai Zhongguo* [Missionaries and modern China], 112. Shanghai: Shanghai renmin chubanshe.
66. Gu, Lu. [1830] 1986. *Qing jia lu* [Record (of customs) of the pure and the fine], 102. Shanghai: Shanghai guji chubanshe.
67. Guizhou sheng bianjizu, ed. 1988. *Dongzu shehui lishi diaocha* [Investigation into the society and history of the Dong people], 30–31. Guiyang: Guizhou minzu chubanshe.

68. Han, Shiyuan. 2018. *Hetongfa zonglun* [The law of contract], 4th ed., 3. Beijing: Falü chubanshe.
69. Hansen, Valerie. 1995. *Negotiating daily Llife in traditional China: How ordinary people used contracts, 600–1400*, 6–10. New Haven and London: Yale University Press.
70. Hart, H.L.A. 2012. *The concept of law*, 3rd ed, 4. Oxford: Oxford University Press.
71. Hase, Patrick H. 2013. *Custom, land and livelihood in rural South China: The traditional land law of Hong Kong's new territories, 1750–1950*, 1. Hong Kong: Hong Kong University Press.
72. Hayes, James. 1985. *Specialists and written materials in the village world*. In *Popular culture in late imperial China*, ed. David Johnson, Andrew J. Nathan, and Evelyn S. Rawski, 85–86. Berkeley, Los Angeles, London: University of California Press.
73. Hayton, David. 1996. The irreducible core content of trusteeship. In *Trends in contemporary trust law*, ed. A. J. Oakley, 47–62. Oxford: Clarendon Press.
74. He, Weifang. 1992. Qiyue' yu 'hetong' de bianxi [Discriminating 'qiyue' and 'hetong']. *Bijiaofa yanjiu* (2): 36–40.
75. He, Xiaopin. 2016. *Qing dai xiguanfa: Zudian guanxi yanjiu* [Customary law in the Qing: A study on the tenancy relationship], 53 ff. Beijing: Falü chubanshe.
76. Henderson, Dan Fenno, and Preston M. Torbert. 1992. Contract in the far East—China and Japan. In *International encyclopedia of comparative law: Volume VII: Contracts in general*, ed. Arthur von Mehren, 3–34. Tübingen: J. C. B. Mohr.
77. Hoanga Peter. 1889. A practical treatise on legal ownership. *Journal of the China Branch of the Royal Asiatic Society for the Year1888* 23: 118.
78. Hoang, Peter. 1922. A practical treatise on legal ownership. *China Law Review* 1 (2): 90.
79. Hoang, Peter. 1923. A practical treatise on legal ownership. *China Law Review* 1 (5): 232.
80. Hoang, Pierre, ed. 1882. *Qiquan huishi* [Forms of contracts for the use of prosecutors]. Shanghai: Cimutang.
81. Hoang, Pierre. 1920. *Notions techniques Sur La Propriété En Chine: Avec Un Choix d'Actes Et de Documents Officiels*, 2nd ed., 1. Zi-Ka-Wei—Chang-hai: Orphelinat de T'ou-sè-we.
82. Hoebel, E. Adamson. 1967. *The law of primitive man: A study in comparative legal dynamics*, 4th ed., 49–50. Cambridge, MA: Harvard University Press.
83. Hogg, Martin. 2011. *Promises and contract law: Comparative perspectives*, 1–2. Cambridge: Cambridge University Press.
84. Hohfeld, Wesley Newcomb. 1913. Some fundamental legal conceptions as applied in judicial reasoning. *The Yale Law Journal* 23 (1): 28–30.
85. Hohfeld, Wesley Newcomb. 1917. Fundamental legal conceptions as applied in judicial reasoning. *The Yale Law Journal* 26 (8): 710–770.
86. Hohfeld, Wesley Newcomb. 1923. *Fundamental legal conceptions as applied in judicial reasoning; and other legal essays*, ed. Walter Wheeler Cook. New Haven: Yale University Press.
87. Hohfeld, Wesley Newcomb. 2001. *Fundamental legal conceptions as applied in judicial reasoning*, ed. David Campbell and Philip Thomas. London and New York: Routledge.
88. Hsing, I-tien. 2011. Cong jiandu kan Han dai de xingzheng wenshu fanben: 'shi' [Observations of the sample manuscript of Han administrative documents from bamboo and wooden slips: '*shi*']. In *Zhiguo anbang: Fazhi, xingzheng, yu junshi* [Managing the country and keeping the state safe: The legal system, administration, and military affairs], authored by I-tien Hsing, 450–470. Beijing: Zhonghua shuju.
89. Huang, Philip C.C. 1990. *The peasant family and rural development in the Yangzi Delta, 1350–1988*, 155. Standford, California: Standford University Press.
90. Huang, Philip C.C. 1996. *Civil justice in China: Representation and practice in the Qing*, 54. Stanford, California: Stanford University Press.
91. Huang, Philip C.C. 2001. *Code, custom, and legal practice in China: The Qing and the republic compared*, 71–98. Stanford, California: Stanford University Press.
92. Huang, Philip C.C. 2001. *Qing dai de falü shehui yu wenhua: Minfa de biaoda yu shijian* [Civil justice in China: Representation and practice in the Qing], 54. Shanghai: Shanghai shudian chubanshe.

93. Huang, Philip C.C. 2010. *Chinese civil justice, past and present*, reprinted ed., 65–67. Lanham, Maryland: Rowman & Littlefield Publishers, Inc.
94. Huang, Philip C.C. 2013. *Qing dai yilai minshi falü de biaoda yu shijian: Lishi, lilun yu xianshi* [Representation and practice of civil law since the Qing: History, theory, and reality], 3 vols., vol. 1, 47. Beijing: Falü chubanshe.
95. Isett, Christopher. 2007. *State, peasant, and merchant in Qing manchuria, 1644–1862*, 69–70. Standford, California: Standford University Press.
96. Isett, Christopher. 2014. Customary and judicial practices as seen in criminal sales of land in Qing manchuria. In *Research from archival case records: Law, society and culture in China*, ed. Philip C.C. Huang and Kathryn Bernhardt, 197. Leiden: Brill.
97. Jiang, Ming. 2018. *Guizhou Cengong qiyue wenshu yanjiu* [A study on contract manuscripts in Cengong, Guizhou], 30–43. Guiyang: Guizhou renmin chubanshe.
98. Jiang, Yixu. 1906. *Shuqi bianmeng* [A handy primer on writing contracts], 3rd reprinted ed. Shanghai: Tushanwan cimutang.
99. Jinping xian difangzhi bianzuan weiyuanhui, ed. 2011. *Jinping xianzhi 1991–2009* [Jinping County gazetteer 1991–2009], vol. 2, 1263. Beijing: Fangzhi chubanshe.
100. Jinping xian linye zhi bianzuan weiyuanhui, ed. 2002. *Jinping xian linye zhi* [Jinping County forestry gazetteer], 468–469. Guiyang: Guizhou renmin chubanshe.
101. Jones, William C. (trans.). 1994. *The great Qing code*, 117. Oxford: Clarendon Press.
102. Kar, Robin Bradley, and Margaret Jane Radin. 2019. Pseudo-contract & shared meaning analysis. *Harvard Law Review* 132 (4): 1135–1219.
103. Kaötz, Hein. 2012. *Vertragsrecht*, 2nd ed, 39. Tübingen: Mohr Siebeck.
104. Kbötz, Hein. 2017. *European contract law*. (Trans. Gill Mertens and Tony Weir), 2nd ed., 17–18. Oxford: Oxford University Press.
105. Kcwan, Man Bun. 2004. Custom, the code, and legal practice: The contracts of changlu salt merchants in late imperial China. In *Contract and property in early modern China*, ed. Madeleine Zelin, Jonathan K. Ocko, and Robert Gardella, 294. Stanford: Stanford University Press.
106. Keliher, Macabe. 2016. Administrative law and the making of the first *Da Qing Huidian*. *Late Imperial China* 37 (1): 55–107.
107. Kishimoto, Mio. 1998. Ming Qing qiyu wenshu [Contract manuscripts in the Ming-Qing period]. (trans. Yaxin Wang). In *Ming Qing shiqi de minshi shenpan yu minjian qiyue* [Civil justice and civil contracts in the Ming-Qing period], ed. Yaxin Wang and Zhiping Liang, 280–314. Beijing: Falü chubanshe.
108. Kishimoto, Mio. 2015. Lijiao, qiyue, shengcun—Shixi Ming Qing minshi shenpan zhong de hengping yuanze [Moral ethics, agreements, and subsistence: An essay on equitable principles in civil justice during the Ming-Qing period]. *Fazhishi yanjiu* 27: 42.
109. Lepaulle, Pierre. 1932. *Traité Théorique et Pratique des Trusts en Droit Interne, en Droit Fiscal et en Droit International*, 113. Paris: Rousseau & Cie.
110. Li, Hongxiang. 2014. Xiang Qian Gui bilian didai lishi shiqi 'qi' yu wenshu de guanlianxing yanjiu [A relevant study of the historical 'deed' and documents in Xiang-Qian-Gui region], 84–85. *Guizhou daxue xuebao (shehui kexue ban)* 32 (3): 84–85.
111. Li, Ren-yuan. 2015. Mao'er qi [Kitty contracts]. *Zhongyang yanjiuyuan zhoubao* (1542): 1–2.
112. Li, Li, and Mingwu Liang. 2006. Qiandongnan diqu linye wenhua chutan [On forestry culture in southeastern Guizhou province]. *Beijing linye daxue xuebao (shehui kexue ban)* 5 (3): 8.
113. Liang, Qichao. [1904] 2012. Lun Zhongguo chengwenfa bianzhi zhi yange deshi [On the history and the success and failure of the compilation of China's codified laws]. In *Liang Qichao lun Zhongguo fazhishi* [Liang Qichao on Chinese legal history], 110–120. Beijing: Shangwu yinshuguan.
114. Liang, Zhiping. 1996. *Qing dai xiguanfa: Shehui yu guojia* [Customary law in the Qing: Society and state], 129. Beijing: Zhongguo zhengfa daxue chubanshe.
115. Lin, Fu. [c. 1796–1820] 1994. *Guzhou zaji* [Miscellanea of Guzhou], 646. Shanghai: Shanghai shudian.

116. Lin, Shaozhou, and Weisong Lin, eds. [c. 1368–1644] 1996. *Xinkan liqi xiangbian zuanyao santai bianlan tongshu zhengzong* [Newly published essential collections of detailed arguments on li and qi, and convenient reference for orthodox almanac of the three terraces], 20 vols., vol. 15, Reprinted in *Xuxiu siku quanshu* [The complete books in four treasuries, continued and revised], 791. Shanghai: Shanghai guji chubanshe.
117. Linshi Taiwan tudi diaochaju, ed. 1998. *Taiwan tudi guanxing yi ban* [A fragment of land customs in Taiwan], reprinted ed., vol. 3. Taipei: Nantian shuju.
118. Liping xian linye ju, ed. 1989. *Liping xian linye zhi* [Liping County forestry gazetteer], 170. Guiyang: Guizhou renmin chubanshe.
119. Liu, Daosheng. 2009. Ming Qing Huizhou hetong yu minjian heyue guanxi [Contracts and civilian agreements of Huizhou district in the Ming and Qing dynasties]. *Anhui daxue xuebao (zhexue shehui kexue ban)* 33 (1): 121–128.
120. Liu, Guangan. 2015. *Da Qing Huidian* sanwen [Three questions on the *Da Qing Huidian*]. *Huadong zhengfa daxue xuebao* (6): 140–147.
121. Liu, James J.Y. 1988. *Language-Paradox-Poetics: A Chinese perspective*, ed. Richard John Lynn, 16. Princeton, NJ: Princeton University Press.
122. Liu, Miao. 1996. *Ming Qing yanhai dangdi kaifa yanjiu* [A study on the development of *dangdi* in the Ming-Qing eras], 216–217. Shantou: Shantou daxue chubanshe.
123. Long, Jialiang. 1982. Jingui tang [Jingui pond]. In *Miaozu minjian gushi ji (di yi ji)* [Folk stories of the Miao (Vol. 1)], ed. Qiandongnan miaozu dongzu zizhi zhou minzu shiwu weiyuanhui and Qiandongnan miaozu dongzu zizhi zhou yishu yanjiushi, 77–80. Qiandongnan: Qiandongnan miaozu dongzu zizhi zhou minzu shiwu weiyuanhui & Qiandongnan miaozu dongzu zizhi zhou yishu yanjiushi.
124. Long, Linglie. 2016. Minjian xiguan yu guanfu guifan hutong huren de fanben—Qing Guangxu shisi nian 'Peiliang shanlin tiantu guanye zhizhao' [A sample for the mutual recognition between civil customs and official regulations: A license in the fourteenth year of Guangxu]. In *Jinping wenshu: Zouxiang shijie de shaxiang jiyi* [Jinping manuscripts: The memories of Jinping County], ed. Linglie Long, 107–108. Beijing: Zhongguo wenhua chubanshe.
125. Long, Denggao, Zhan Lin, and Bo Peng. 2013. Dian yu Qing dai diquan jiaoyi tixi [Dian (conditional sale) and the transaction system of land rights in the Qing dynasty]. *Zhongguo shehui kexue* (5): 125–141.
126. Lu, Xiqi. 2014. *Zhongguo gudai maidiquan yanjiu* [A study on tomb contracts in ancient China]. Xiamen: Xiamen daxue chubanshe.
127. Luan, Chengxian. 2005. Ming Qing qiyue wenshu de yanjiu jiazhi [The research value of contracts in the Ming and Qing dynasties]. *Shixue yuekan* (12): 7–9.
128. Luo, Yundan, Hongbo Chen, and Jinfeng Deng. 2015. Qingshuijiang wenshu fenleifa tantao [On the classification of Qingshui River manuscripts]. *Kaili xueyuan xuebao* 33 (2): 174, 177.
129. Macneil, Ian Roderick. 2000. Relational contract theory: Challenges and queries. *Northwestern University Law Review* 94 (3): 877–907.
130. Maine, Henry Sumner. 1861. *Ancient law: Its connection with the early history of society, and its relation to modern ideas*, 325. London: John Murray.
131. Mallat, Chibli. 2007. *Introduction to Middle Eastern Law*, 53. Oxford: Oxford University Press.
132. Mallat, Chibli. 2019. Comparative law and the Islamic (Middle Eastern) legal culture. In *The oxford handbook of comparative law*, ed. Mathias Reimann and Reinhard Zimmermann, 624 ff. Oxford: Oxford University Press.
133. Markesinis, Basil, Hannes Unberath, and Angus Johnston. 2006. *The German law of contract: A comparative treatise*, 2nd ed., 27–37. Oxford and Portaland, Oregon: Hart Publishing.
134. McSheffrey, Shannon. 2006. *Marriage, Sex, and civic culture in late medieval London*, 28–32. Philadelphia: University of Pennsylvania Press.
135. Mindai shi kenkyu shi hen, ed. 1975. *Chūgoku tochi keiyaku bunsho shiryō shū (Kin–Shin)* [A collection on Chinese land contracts (Jin–Qing)], 191–212. Tokyo: Tōyō bunko.

136. Mohammed, Noor. 1988. Principles of Islamic contract law. *Journal of Law and Religion* 6 (1): 127–128.
137. Niwa, Tomosaburō. 1968. Keiyaku shoshiki rei o tōshite mita Gendai sonraku seido ni kansuru ichi kōsatsu [A consideration concerning the village system in Yuan period, observed through the examples of the form of the contract]. *Hōseishi kenkyū* (18): 65–72.
138. Oberauer, Norbert. 2017. *Islamisches Wirtschafts- und Vertragsrecht*, 22–23. Würzburg: Ergon-Verlag.
139. Okada, Asatarō. [1912] 2013. *Xingfa fenze* [Specific provisions of criminal law], ed. Yuanhan Xiong and Fei Xia, 84. Shanghai: Shanghai renmin chubanshe.
140. Pan, Zhicheng, and Dahua Wu, eds. 2011. *Tudi guanxi ji qita shiwu wenshu* [Manuscripts on land relationship and other issues], vol. 1, 221–222. Guiyang: Guizhou minzu chubanshe.
141. Peel, Edwin. 2015. *Treitel the law of contract*, 14th ed., 1-001. London: Sweet & Maxwell Ltd.
142. Perrault, Stephen J., ed. 2008. *Merriam-Webster's advanced learner's english dictionary*, 355–356. Springfield, Massachusetts: Merriam-Webster.
143. Qian, Guangsheng, and Jingbo Wang. 2011. Mao'er qishi, maohua, fojing: E cang Dunhuang xiejuan дх. 00147v 'mao'er ti' lice [Kitty contracts, the pictures of cats, the Buddhist Scriptures: A primary study on the дх. 00147v 'mao'er ti' of Russian Dunhuang collections]. *Dunhuangxue jikan* (3): 31–40.
144. Qian Nanjing guomin zhengfu sifa xingzheng bu, ed. [1930] 2000. *Mingshi xiguan diaocha baogao lu* [Collection of reports of custom surveys on civil matters], 2 vols., vol. 1. Beijing: Zhongguo zhengfa daxue chubanshe.
145. Qu, Jian. 2012. Qing zhonghouqi Qiandongnan Wendou zhai Miaozu dianzhi yanjiu [A treatise on the dian of the Miaos in Wendou Village of southeastern Guizhou in the mid and late Qing dynasty]. *Minjian fa* 11: 205–206.
146. Qu, Jian. 2017. Toushi xueyi: Qiyue chuantong zhong de 'baishi' yu 'baizhi' [Apprenticeship and the tradition of contract in China]. *Quyi* (9): 36.
147. Qu, Jian. 2017. *Yikou daibi: Qing dai Wendou zhai falü shuxie de xianchang yu biaoda* [The scribe: The scenario and expression of legal writing practice in Wendou Village in the Qing dynasty]. In *Jinping wenshu yu fawenhua yanjiu* [Jinping manuscripts and the studies of legal culture], ed. Qicai Gao and Kui Wang, 185. Beijing: Zhongguo zhengfa daxue chubanshe.
148. Radin, Max. 1938. A restatement of Hohfeld. *Harvard Law Review* 51 (7): 1141–1164.
149. Redfield, Robert. 1947. The folk society. *American Journal of Sociology* 52 (4): 293–308.
150. Ren, Zhiqiang and Weijun Fang. 2009. 'Minjian zhiye, quanyi qiquan wei ping' zhiyi [Questioning the saying of 'the possession of the property in civil practice are entirely based on contracts']. *Zhongguo shehui jingjishi yanjiu* (2): 57–63.
151. Shan, Honggen. 2012. *Lüse jiyi: Qiandongnan linye wenhua shicui* [The green memories: Forestry culture in Qiandongnan], 85–86. Kunming: Yunnan renmin chubanshe.
152. Shan, Honggen. 2017. *Jinping wenshu yu Qingshuijiang linye shihua* [Jinping manuscripts and the history of the forestry industry in the Qingshui River region], 105–108. Beijing: Zhongguo zhengfa daxue chubanshe.
153. Shangwu yinshuguan bianyisuo, ed. 1990. *Da Qing Guangxu xin faling* [New laws of the Great Qing Dynasty of Guangxu era], 20 vols., vol. 20, 41. Shanghai: Shanghai shangwu yinshuguan.
154. Shen, Zhiqi, ed. [1715] 1998. *Da Qing lü jizhu* [The *Great Qing Code* with compiled annotations]. Beijing: Falü chubanshe.
155. Shi, Qigui. [1986] 2002. *Xiangxi Miaozu shidi diaocha baogao* [A report of field survey of the Miao in Xiangxi], revised and enlarged ed., 165. Changsha: Hunan renmin chubanshe.
156. Simmonds, Nigel E. 2001. Introduction. In *Fundamental legal conceptions as applied in judicial reasoning*, ed. David Campbell and Philip Thomas, xii–xvi. London and New York: Routledge.
157. Slingerland, Edward (trans.). 2003. *Confucius analects: With selections from traditional commentaries*, 139. Indianapolis/Cambridge: Hackett Publishing Company, Inc.

158. Smits, Jan M. 2017. *Contract law: A comparative introduction*, 2nd ed, 39–118. Cheltenham, UK: Edward Elgar Publishing Limited.
159. Song, Meiyun, ed. 2006. *Tianjin shangmin fangdi qiyue yu tiaopan anli xuanbian: 1686–1949* [A selected collection on commercial and civil contracts of house and land and mediation documents and judgments in Tianjin: 1686–1949], 1–121. Tianjin: Tianjin guji chubanshe.
160. Song, Luzhen, Shitai He, and Zongli Xiong, eds. [c. 1368–1644] 2002. *Leibian lifa tongshu daquan* [Great compendium of calendrical methods and almanacs, organized by categories], 30 vols., vol. 9, Reprinted in *Xuxiu siku quanshu* [The complete books in four treasuries, continued and revised], 215. Shanghai: Shanghai guji chubanshe.
161. Spear, Samuel Thayer. *The legal-tender acts, considered in relation to their constitutionality and their political economy*, 55. New York: Baker, Voorhis & Co., Publishers.
162. Staunton, Howard, ed. 1866. *The work of Shakespeare*, vol. 1, 399. London: George Routledge & Sons.
163. Staunton, George Thomas (trans.). 1810. *Ta Tsing Leu Lee; Being the Fundamental Laws, and a Selection from the Supplementary Statutes, of the Penal Code of China*. London: T. Cadell and W. Davies.
164. Stone, Richard, and James Devenney. 2015. *The modern law of contract*, 11th ed, 191. London and New York: Routledge.
165. Su, Yigong. 1999. *Ming Qing lüdian yu tiaoli* [The codes and substatutes in the Ming and Qing], 39–52. Beijing: Zhongguo zhengfa daxue chubanshe.
166. Sun, Jiahong. 2008. *Da Qing Lüli* bainian yanjiu zongshu [A literature review on studies of *Da Qing Lüli* in the past century]. *Falü wenxian xinxi yu yanjiu* (2): 2.
167. Sun, Peng. 2019. Jinqian 'zhanyou ji suoyou' yuanli pipan ji quanli liuzhuan guize zhi chongsu [A critique on the principle of 'money possession that is all' and reconstruction of the rule of 'money right transfer']. *Faxue yanjiu* 41 (5): 25–43.
168. Sweet, Jonathan J. 1993. *Avoiding or minimizing construction litigation*, 104. New York: Wiley Inc.
169. Tang, Honglin. 2008. Zhongguo chuantong minshi qiyue geshi yanjiu [A study on the format of traditional Chinese civil contracts]. Doctoral dissertation, East China University of Political Science and Law, 28.
170. Terada, Hiroaki. 1994. Zhongguo jinshi tudi suoyouzhi yanjiu [A study on the land ownership in early modern China], (trans. Xiao Feng). In *Zhongwai falü shi xintan* [New Exploration of Chinese and Foreign Legal History], ed. Yifan Yang, 428. Xi'an: Shaanxi renmin chubanshe.
171. Terada, Hiroaki. 2004. Gōi to keiyaku–Chūgoku kinsei ni okeru 'keiyaku' o tegakari ni [Agreements and contracts: An examination of 'contracts' in early modern China]." In Hikakushi no Ajia: Shoyū, keiyaku, shijō, kōsei [Asia in comprative perspective: Ownership, contracts, markets, fairness and justice], edited by Toru Miura, Mio Kishimoto and Teruo Sekimoto, 89–112. Tokyo: Tōkyō Daigaku Shuppankai.
172. Terada, Hiroaki. 2012. Ming Qing shiqi fazhixu zhong 'yue' de xingzhi [The nature of 'yue' in the legal order of Ming-Qing China]. (trans. Yaxin Wang). In *Quanli yu yuanyi: Sitian haoming Zhongguo fashi lunji* [Rights and injustice: Hiroaki Terada's essays on Chinese legal history], ed. Hiroaki Terada, 136–181. Beijing: Qinghua daxue chubanshe.
173. Terada, Hiroaki. 2019. 'Satoru rei songi' PDF risuto [A list of pdf of *Duli cunyi* (Doubts remaining after perusing substatutes)], May 22, 2019. http://www.terada.law.kyoto-u.ac.jp/dlcy/dlcy_pdf.htm.
174. Tian, Tao, and Qin Zheng, eds. 1999. *Da Qing lüli* [The great Qing code], 7. Beijing: Falü chubanshe.
175. Tiersma, Peter M. 2000. *Legal Language*, 1–6. Chicago and London: The University of Chicago Press.
176. Tomiya, Itaru. 2013. *Wenshu xingzheng de Han diguo* [The archival administration in the Han empire], (trans. Hengwu Liu and Libo Kong), 147 ff. Nanjing: Jiangsu renmin chubanshe.
177. Trombert, Éric. 1995. *Le crédit à Dunhuang: Vie matérielle et société en Chine médiévale*, Chap. 1. Paris: Collège de France, Institut des Hautes Études Chinoises.

178. Trombert, Éric. 2003. *Dunhuang de jiedai: Zhongguo zhonggu shidai de wuzhi shenghuo yu shehui* [Le crédit à Dunhuang: Vie matérielle et société en Chine médiévale], (trans. Xin Yu and Jianwei Chen), 4–5. Beijing: Zhonghua shuju.
179. UNIDROIT. 2016. *UNIDROIT principles of international commercial contracts*. Rome: International Institute for the Unification of Private Law.
180. United Nations. 2010. *United nations convention on contracts for the international sale of goods*. Vienna: English, Publishing and Library Section, United Nations Office at Vienna.
181. von Bar, Christian, Eric Clive, Hans Schulte-Nölke, Hugh Beale, Johnny Herre, Jérôme Huet, Matthias Storme, et al., eds. 2009. *Principles, definitions and model rules of European private law: Draft common frame of reference (DCFR)*, Online ed., 183. Munich: Sellier. European Law Publishers.
182. Vormbaum, Thomas. 2014. *A modern history of German criminal law*, (trans. Margaret Hiley), ed. Michael Bohlander, 131. Heidelberg: Springer.
183. Walton, F. P. 1925. Cause and consideration in contracts. *Law Quarterly Review* 41 (3): 306–328.
184. Wang, Kaiyu. 1936. *Dazhong qiyue chengshi* [Popular contract forms], 8–30. Shanghai: Dazhong shuju.
185. Wang, Hong. 2005. Hetong xingshi qianque yu lüxing zhiyu lun—Jianping *Hetongfa* di 36 tiao zhi guiding [Contractual defects in form and 'cure by performance'—An analysis of article 36 of the *Contract Act of the People's Republic of China*]. *Xiandai faxue* 27 (3): 81–88.
186. Wang, Hongliang. 2019. Lun hetong de biyao zhi dian [On the *essentialia negotii* of contracts]. *Qinghua faxue* 13 (6): 122–134.
187. Wang, Hui. 2007. *Yingwen hetong jiedu: Yuyong, tiaokuan ji wenben fanli* [Understanding English contracts], 37. Beijing: Falü chubanshe.
188. Wang, Kui, ed. c. 2017. *Jinping wenshu jiyi duben* [A memorial reader of Jinping manuscripts], 112–113. Jinping: Jinping County Archives.
189. Wang, Liming, and Yegang Wang. 2016. *Hetong fa* [Contract law]. Hong Kong: Xianggang chengshi daxue chubanshe.
190. Wang, Shuaiyi. 2012. *Ming Qing shidai guanfang duiyu qiyue de ganyu: Tongguo 'shuiqi' fangshi de jieru* [The official intervention to the contracts in the Ming-Qing eras: The intervention through 'tax deed']. *Zhongwai faxue* 24 (6): 1278–1291.
191. Wang, Xu. 2013. *Qizhi qiannian—Zhongguo chuantong qiyue de xingshi yu yanbian* [A thousand years of contract paper: The form and evolution of traditional Chinese contracts], 172 ff. Beijing: Beijing daxue chubanshe.
192. Wang, Xu, ed. 2016. *Zhongguo kuaiji bowuguan cangpin jicui: Qiyue juan* [China Accounting Museum's essential collections: The volume of deeds], foreword page. Shanghai: Lixin kuaiji chubanshe.
193. Wang, Zhengxian. 2000. *Qiyi de shitou shijie—Guizhou yanshi zaiti wenhua* [The fantastic world of stone: Material culture of stones in Guizhou], 256. Guiyang: Guizhou jiaoyu chubanshe.
194. Wang, Zhiqiang. 2003. Qing dai cheng'an de xiaoli heqi yunyong zhong de lunzheng fangshi—Yi *Xing'an Huilan* wei zhongxin [Leading cases in the Qing dynasty: Legal effect and method of justification in its application]. *Faxue yanjiu* (3): 146–160.
195. Wang, Zhiqiang. 2017. *Qing dai guojiafa: Duoyuan chayi yu jiquan tongyi* [State law in the Qing dynasty: Heterogeneous plurality and power centralization], 137 ff. Beijing: Shehui kexue wenxian chubanshe.
196. Wang, Zhenzhong. 2006. Qing dai qianqi Huizhou minjian de richang shenghuo—Yi Wuyuan minjian riyong leishu *Mulu shiliu tiao* wei li [Everyday life in Huizhou in the early Qing dynasty: A study based on the encyclopedia for daily use in Wuyuan, *Mulu shiliu tiao*]. In *Ming Qing yilai changjiang liuyu shehui fazhan shilun* [Historical study on the social development in the Yangtze River basin in the Ming-Qing eras], ed. Feng Chen, 719–726. Wuhan: Wuhan daxue chubanshe.
197. Wang, Zongxun. 2009. *Wendou: Kan de jian lishi de cunzhai* [Wendou: A village with visible history], 102. Guiyang: Guizhou renmin chubanshe.

198. Wang, Zongxun. 2013. Yao Baiwan de xingshuai [The rise and fall of Yao the Millionaire]. In *Qingshuijiang lishi wenhua tanwei* [Studies on the historical culture of the Qingshui River region], ed. Zongxun Wang, 224–232. Kunming: Yunnan meishu chubanshe.
199. Wang, Zongxun. 2013. *Qingshuijiang lishi wenhua tanwei* [Studies on the historical culture of the Qingshui River region], 158–159. Kunming: Yunnan meishu chubanshe.
200. Wang, Zongxun, ed. 2015. *Jiachi siheyuan wenshu kaoshi* [Collection and annotation of the Jiachi siheyuan manuscripts], 4 vols., vol. 4, 541–610. Guiyang: Guizhou minzu chubanshe.
201. Wang, Zongxun. 2015. *Xunshi yiluo de jiyi: Jinping wenshu zhengji shouji* [Finding the lost memories: A diary of collecting the Jinping manuscripts], 70–71. Guangzhou: Shijie tushu chuban Guangdong youxian gongsi.
202. Wang, Zongxun. 2017. *Qingshuijiang mushang guzhen—Maoping* [The old town of timber merchants along the Qingshui River—Maoping], 105–108. Guiyang: Guizhou minzu chubanshe.
203. Westen, Peter. 2018. Poor Wesley Hohfeld. *San Diego Law Review* 55 (2): 450.
204. Wolf, Manfred, and Jörg Neuner. 2016. *Allgemeiner Teil des Bürgerlichen Rechts*, 11th ed, 434–451. München: Verlag C. H. Beck oHG.
205. Wu, Caimao. 2016. Ming dai yilai Qingshuijiang wenshu shuxie geshi de bianhua yu minzhong xiguan de bianqian [The changes of the writing forms of Qingshui River manuscripts and the transition of popular customs since the Ming dynasty]. *Xinan daxue xuebao (shehui kexue ban)* 42 (4): 179–188.
206. Wu, Caimao. 2016. *Minjian wenshu yu Qingshuijiang diqu de shehui bianqian* [Folk documents and the social change in the Qingshui River region], 185. Beijing: Minzu chubanshe.
207. Wu, Dahua. 2013. *Qian fa tanyuan* [A study on the origin of laws in Guizhou], 211–215. Guiyang: Guizhou renmin chubanshe.
208. Wu, Huifang. 2005. *Wanbao quanshu: Ming Qing shiqi de minjian shenghuo shilu* [Wanbao quanshu: A truthful record of everyday life in the Ming and Qing periods], 2 vols., vol. 1, 247–257. Taipei: Hua Mulan wenhua gongzuo fang.
209. Wu, Liping. 2011. Ming Qing qiyue wenshu de souji he zhengli zongshu [A summary of the collection and sort-out of the contracts in the Ming and Qing dynasties]. *Qingdao daxue shifan xueyuan xuebao* 28 (3): 57–62.
210. Wu, Xiangxiang, ed. [1923] 1962. *Zhongguo minshi xiguan daquan* [A compendium of Chinese popular customs], 25–26. Taipei: Wenxing shudian.
211. Xu, Bin. 2016. Qingshuijiang wenshu zhong de 'zhizhao' yanjiu [A study on the 'license' in the Qingshui River manuscripts]. *Guizhou daxue xuebao (shehui kexue ban)* 34 (1): 128.
212. Xu, Xiaoguang. 2006. *Qingshuijiang liuyu linye jingji fazhi de lishi huisu* [A historical study on the forestry economic legal system in the Qingshui River Basin], 189–206. Guiyang: Guizhou renmin chubanshe.
213. Xu, Xiaoguang. 2014. *Qingshuijiang liuyu chuantong linye guize de shengtai renleixue jiedu* [An explanation of ecological anthropology on the traditional forestry rules in the Qingshui River basin], 185. Beijing: Zhishi chanquan chubanshe.
214. Xue, Yunsheng. 1906. *Duli cunyi* [Doubts remaining after perusing the substatutes]. Beijing: Hanmao zhai.
215. Xue, Yunsheng. 1970. *Duli cunyi chongkanben* [Doubts remaining after perusing the substatutes: A reprinted and annotated version], ed. Jingjia Huang. Taipei: Chengwen chubanshe.
216. Yan, Qiyan. 2018. Qingshuijiang liuyu gongshan guanli yu jingying de shengtai jiazhi—Yi beike ziliao wei zhongxin de kaocha [The ecological value of the management and operation of the collective forests in the Qingshui River Basin—Research mainly based on stone inscriptions]. *Zhongguo nongshi* (4): 105–114.
217. Yang, Bojun. 1979. *Liezi jishi* [Collected annotations for *Liezi*], 271. Beijing: Zhonghua shuju.
218. Yang, Guozhen. 1988. *Ming Qing tudi qiyue wenshu yanjiu* [On land-related contracts in the Ming-Qing period]. Beijing: Renmin chubanshe.

219. Yang, Guozhen. 2009. *Ming Qing tudi qiyue wenshu yanjiu (xiudingban)* [On land-related contracts in the Ming-Qing period], revised ed. Beijing: Zhongguo renmin daxue chubanshe.
220. Yang, Jing, ed. 2016. *International Business Contracts Bilingual Course*, 58–59. Dalian: Dongbei caijing daxue chubanshe.
221. Ye, Wenling, and Zhenguo Zhang. 2015. Wan Qing Xuhui gongxue xiaozhang Jiang Yixu shengping zhushu kao [A study on Jiang Yixu's life and works in the late Qing dynasty]. *Chengdu shifan xueyuan xuebao* 31 (4): 96–99.
222. You, Chenjun. 2013. *Falü zhishi de wenzi chuanbo: Ming Qing riyong leishu yu shehui richang shenghuo* [Written propagation of legal knowledge: The encyclopedia for daily use and social life in the Ming and Qing dynasties], 172. Shanghai: Shanghai renmin chubanshe.
223. Yu, Jiang. 2003. 'Qiyue' yu 'hetong' zhibian—Yi Qing dai qiyue wenshu wei chufadian [Qiyue and hetong: Forms of contracts in Qing China]. *Zhongguo shehui kexue* (6): 134–148.
224. Yu, Jiang. 2017. Tianxia hetong dou yiyang [All over the world the *hetong* is the same]. In *Huizhou hetong wenshu huibian* [A collection of *hetong* in Huizhou], ed. Jiang Yu. Guilin: Guangxi shifan daxue chubanshe.
225. Yu, Jiang, and Yunzhao Chen. 2014. Lun Qing dai hetong de leixing—Jiyu Huizhou hetong wenshu de shizheng fenxi [On the types of hetong in the Qing dynasty: Based on an empirical analysis of Huizhou hetong documents]. *Faxue* (6): 120–130.
226. Zelin, Madeleine. 1994. Merchant Dispute Mediation in Twentieth-Century Zigong, Sichuan. In *Civil Law in Qing and Republican China*, ed. Kathryn Bernhardt and Philip C.C. Huang, 263. Stanford, Calif.: Stanford University Press.
227. Zelin, Madeleine. 2004. A Critique of Rights of Property in Prewar China. In *Contract and Property in Early Modern China*, ed. Madeleine Zelin, Jonathan K. Ocko, and Robert Gardella, 23–26. Stanford: Stanford University Press.
228. Zelin, Madeleine, Jonathan Ocko, and Robert Gardella. 2004. Introduction. In *Contract and Property in Early Modern China*, ed. Madeleine Zelin, Jonathan K. Ocko, and Robert Gardella, 3. Stanford: Stanford University Press.
229. Zhang, Chuanxi. 1995. *Qin Han wenti yanjiu* [Studies on the Qin and Han dynasty], revised and enlarged ed., 189 ff. Beijing: Beijing daxue chubanshe.
230. Zhang, Chuanxi. 2008. *Qiyue shi maidiquan yanjiu* [Study on the history of contracts and tomb contracts], 26–32. Beijing: Zhonghua shuju.
231. Zhang, Junming. 2005. Dunhuang Xuanquanzhi tanfang T0309 chutu jiandu gaishu [An introduction to the bamboo and wooden slips from T0309 excavation unit in Xuanquanzhi, Dunhuang]. In *Changsha Sanguo Wujian ji bainian lai jianbo faxian yu yanjiu guoji xueshu yantaohui lunwenji* [Proceedings of the international conference on the discovery and study of Wu slips (Three Kingdoms) unearthed at Changsha and the slips and silks discovered in the last century], ed. Changsha wenwu kaogu yanjiusuo, 396–399. Beijing: Zhonghua shuju.
232. Zhang, Junming. 2009. Dunhuang Xuanquan Han jian suojian 'shi' yu 'shi' ling ['*Shi*' and the *ling* of '*shi*' in bamboo slips of Dunhuang Xuanquan in the Han dynasty]. *Lanzhou xuekan* (11): 16.
233. Zhang, Junming. 2014. Jiandu wenshu geshi chutan [A primary study on the forms of bamboo and wooden slips documents]. In *Jianduxue lungao: Jushapian* [Essays on bamboo and wooden slips], authored by Junming Zhang, 63–82. Lanzhou: Gansu jiaoyu chubanshe.
234. Zhang, Taisu. 2017. *The Laws and Economics of Confucianism: Kinship and Property in Preindustrial China and England*, 39. Cambridge: Cambridge University Press.
235. Zhang, Ting. Marketing Legal Information: Commercial Publications of the Great Qing Code, 1644–1911. In *Chinese Law: Knowledge, Practice and Transformation, 1530s to 1950s*, ed. Li Chen and Madeleine Zelin, 231. Leiden: Brill.
236. Zhang, Ting. *Circulating the Code: Print Media and Legal Knowledge in Qing China*, 11–83. Seattle: University of Washington Press.
237. Zhang, Xiaolin. 2000. *Qing dai Beijing chengqu fangqi yanjiu* [A study of real estate sale contracts in the city of Beijing in the Qing dynasty], 2. Beijing: Zhongguo shehui kexue chubanshe.

238. Zhang, Xinmin, ed. 2014. *Tianzhu wenshu* [Tianzhu manuscripts], vol. 1(2), 240. Nanjing: Jiangsu renmin chubanshe.
239. Zhang, Yingqiang. 2006. *Mucai zhi liudong: Qing dai Qingshuijiang xiayou diqu de shichang, quanli yu shehui* [The wood flow: Market, power, and society in the downstream sections of Qingshui River in the Qing dynasty], 159–173, 297–301. Beijing: Shenghuo, dushu, xinzhi sanlianshudian.
240. Zhang, Yingqiang, and Tengwen Hu. 2004. *Jinping* [Jinping], 141. Beijing: Shenghuo, dushu, xinzhi sanlian shudian.
241. Zhang, Yingqiang, and Zongxun Wang, eds. 2007. *Qingshuijiang wenshu* [Qingshui River manuscripts], vol. 1(12), 112. Guilin: Guangxi shifan daxue chubanshe.
242. Zhang, Yingqiang, and Zongxun Wang, eds. 2009. *Qingshuijiang wenshu* [Qingshui River manuscripts], vol. 2(2), 57–58. Guilin: Guangxi shifan daxue chubanshe.
243. Zhang, Yingqiang, and Zongxun Wang, eds. 2009. *Qingshuijiang wenshu* [Qingshui River manuscripts], vol. 2(1), 255, 256. Guilin: Guangxi shifan daxue chubanshe.
244. Zhang, Yingqiang, and Zongxun Wang, eds. 2009. *Qingshuijiang wenshu* [Qingshui River manuscripts], vol. 2(3), 179. Guilin: Guangxi shifan daxue chubanshe.
245. Zhao, Shouhui, and Richard B. Jr. Baldauf. 2008. *Planning Chinese Characters: Reaction, Evolution or Revolution?*, 34. Dordrecht: Springer.
246. Zheng, Qin, and Guangyuan Zhou. 1995. Pursuing Perfection: Formation of the Qing Code. *Modern China* 21 (3): 310.
247. Zhongguo shaoshu minzu shehui lishi diaocha ziliao congkan xiuding bianji weiyuanhui, ed. 2009. *Miaozu shehui lishi diaocha* [Investigation to the society and history of the Miao people], vol. 1, 57. Beijing: Minzu chubanshe.
248. Zhou, Liandi. 1919. *Shuqi chengshi* [The forms of writing contracts]. Shanghai: Ranlige shuju.
249. Zhou, Yaoming, ed. 1994. *Hanzu minjian jiaoji fengsu* [Social customs of the Han Chinese], 139–141. Nanning: Guanxi jiaoyu chubanshe.
250. Zimmermann, Reinhard. 1992. *The Law of Obligations: Roman Foundations of the Civilian Tradition*, reprinted ed., 546. Cape Town, Wetton, and Johannesburg: Juta & Co, Ltd.

Chapter 3
Middlemen

A contract can involve many people—for example, eleven names including four vendors, one vendee, one scribe, and, surprisingly, five middlemen, can be seen in one contract of sale.[1] However, as indicated, from a legal or contractual standpoint, only four classifications of participants are considered to partake in the contracting activity, i.e. the vendor, the vendee, the middleman, and the scribe. No matter how many vendors there actually were, they should all be understood as one party in a contractual sense.

While buyers and sellers have been examined thoroughly throughout the scholarly development of contract and contract law, the other two protagonists, namely the middleman and the scribe, seem not to be accounted for in existing legal doctrines of contracts. However, these were the two most fundamental and unique elements that a traditional Chinese contract embraced. If buyers and sellers were those who "used" the contract as a "device," middlemen and scribes were those who elaborately constructed the "device" and offered all the "services" that a contract could possibly provide, thereby forming a relationship between service consumers and providers. In this respect, as a crucial part of answering the questions of what the contract was and how it worked, careful analyses will be presented in this and the next chapter of these two critical components of the device of a contract.

1 Introduction: Understanding Middlemen Within a Contract

The workings of middlemen in traditional societies in late imperial China have attracted extensive attention from various perspectives in both Chinese and other

---

[1] See, e.g., Guizhou sheng dang'an guan, Qiandongnan zhou dang'an guan, and Jianhe xian dang'an guan [24].

J. Qu, *Social Order through Contracts*,
https://doi.org/10.1007/978-981-33-4947-6_3

languages in previous scholarship.[2] Among all these perspectives, the figure of a traditional Chinese middleman can normally be depicted against two different backgrounds: either against the background of society or that of a contract.[3] The middleman is firstly a concept directly derived from the practice of contract—the term *zhongren*[4] literally means the person in the middle between, generally speaking, two contracting parties.[5] Likewise, the concept of a middleman also bears a strong connection with its social environment, as is seen, for example, by the fact that those who are invited to act as middlemen in contracts usually have a relatively "high status" in local communities (i.e. people with "face," *mianzi*) or have certain relationships (e.g. friends or relatives) with contractors.[6] A reviewer of the existing research on middlemen would unsurprisingly find that the more favorable approach is the social approach (rather than the contractual approach), which focuses on describing the image of middlemen against their social background. A characteristic feature of this approach is the relation drawn between middlemen and dispute settlement, in which the middlemen's social status may have a role to play.[7]

However, this chapter attempts to avoid the temptation of seeking to discover middlemen's social or cultural stories beyond or behind the contract, and instead tries to understand them within the contract. In doing so, it will refrain from narrating as such: although the text of the contract records such a situation, in fact, beyond the contract, the relationship between the two parties is quite different. Both middlemen and contracts were deeply rooted in society, but they can also be analyzed separately from their social context. Rather than seeing the purpose of having a middleman in a contract as "personalizing an impersonal relationship,"[8] the contractual approach aims to depersonalize middlemen and to treat them as an intrinsic part of the contract instead of highlighting their social identities. Although it is impossible to see

---

[2]See Hsiao [37], Duara [18, 19], Huang [41], Liang [57], Li [53], Foerste [22], Wu [82], Li and Chen [54], Hu [38], Zeng [86], Zhou and Li [102], Chen [7], Chen and Wang [8], Liu and Qu [59], Terada [72], Mao [61], Hase [35], Zhou [103], Wang [75], Guo and Li [27], Guo [28]. For previous accounts of middlemen with a special focus on the Qingshui River region, see, e.g., Liang [55], Chen and Hou [9], Cheng [13], Qu [65], Zhou and Fu [104].

[3]For a discussion of the internal and external, in terms of within the contract or not, research approaches, see Wang Shuaiyi, "Ming Qing shidai de zhongren yu qiyue zhixu," 170–171.

[4]The term "middlemen" is used as a translation to the Chinese term of "*zhongren*," while *ren* should be understood as "person(s)" rather than simply "man/men." As she reminded in her book review to a collection on middlemen, women could also play a remarkable role in contractual transactions, "even if [they were] still relatively few in numbers." See Weiner [78]. For a comprehensive study of the activities of the Miao women in the Qingshui River region, see Wu [79].

[5]Some might imply that there were two kinds of middlemen, namely social middlemen as well as contractual middlemen. See Liang Zhiping, *Qing dai xiguanfa: Shehui yu guojia*, 120.

[6]See Prasenjit Duara, *Culture, Power, and the State*, 181 ff; Prasenjit Duara, "Elites and the Structures of Authority in the Villages of North China, 1900–1949," 268. Also, a summarization of former scholarship on this point can be seen in Guo [29].

[7]See, e.g., Huang [43]. For an earlier version of this chapter, see Huang [40].

[8]See Prasenjit Duara, *Culture, Power, and the State*, 181. Another study also asserts that, in the field of transactions where state law was less involved, the maintenance of contractual order depended on specific individuals. See Wang Shuaiyi, "Ming Qing shidai de zhongren yu qiyue zhixu," 171–172.

middlemen in complete isolation from their social aspects, this chapter aims to focus on the activities of middlemen that are limited to the contract and, so far as possible, to reveal the contractual or technical nature of the capabilities they demonstrate through these activities. Consequently, it is argued in this chapter that a middleman was not chosen as a middleman completely or mostly because of their status in local society, but because he or she owns the contractual or technical ability in demand. Hence, even if the root of his or her ability lies in social status, it still needs to be contractualized or transformed in the way that is needed by and could be embodied in the contract.

It is no secret that, although there are differences, the approach that solely focuses on the contract is obviously influenced by the pure theory of law and legal positivism,[9] which may carry the risk of being too idealized and unrealistic. However, compared to the often-emphasized importance of, among others, *mianzi*,[10] acquaintanceship,[11] or social status,[12] some attention might need to be paid to the boring side of the story—the tendency of a theoretical construction underpinned by the tedious contract text may be able to present a new take on understanding middlemen.

Despite the diverse customs and practice of middlemen in different regions,[13] this chapter mainly focuses on materials from the Qingshui River region, and Wendou Village in particular. In the following sections of this chapter, in order to try to construct a clear system of middlemen to whom various contractual activities are assigned, a dichotomy between the primary and the secondary will be explained at the outset in order to systematize the four roles that the middleman could play in a contract. Further, through a contract-based approach, the functions of the middleman are investigated individually, and middlemen's diverse abilities and characters are discussed accordingly. After this, the tension between the internal and external dimensions of the middleman system and the possibility of the system's extension and expansion are specifically considered. Finally, after incorporating many other third-party contractual figures, a partly open system is proposed as an explanatory description of the middlemen in context. In sum, this chapter aims to offer an account of the contractual figure of middlemen in the Qingshui River region and to provide a systematic and explanatory analysis concerning the long-standing and ongoing question of what a middleman was.

[9]For example, Hans Kelsen believed that jurisprudence must be distinguished from "cognition of social reality." See Kelsen [49], Bix [6].

[10]See Liang Zhiping, *Qing dai xiguanfa: Shehui yu guojia*, 152–166.

[11]See Wang Shuaiyi, "Ming Qing shidai de zhongren yu qiyue zhixu," 181.

[12]See Li [52].

[13]See Liang Zhiping, *Qing dai xiguanfa: Shehui yu guojia*, 121.

2 The Primary and the Secondary: Formation and Restoration

2.1 Four Roles

From the perspective of the contract, the significance of middlemen lies in their participation in the substance of the contract, or taking part in the establishment or confirmation of its jural relations. Their participation in contractual activities is often described as "middlemen's functions."[14] According to the renowned Chinese sociologist Fei Xiaotong, "[s]ocial actors are not necessarily aware of functions," but functions are actually "the result of analysis."[15] The discussion of middlemen's functions which follows in this chapter is also based on this understanding of "functions" in society.

In a traditional village society, middlemen could perform a variety of roles. Among them, it is commonly believed that there were four major roles that middlemen could play in a contract, namely introducers,[16] witnesses, guarantors, and mediators.[17] This understanding is based on the assumption that various kinds of middlemen-like figures who varied in terms of their designations could all be classified as middlemen.[18] Normally these designations included descriptions of the specific workings of the middleman. For example, *zhongjianren* means the middleman who witnessed. The aforementioned four roles also have their corresponding designations, namely *yazhong*[19] (introducers), *jianzhong* (witnesses), *baozhong* (guarantors), and *quanzhong* (mediators).[20] As designations or de facto descriptions of each distinctive role of the middleman,[21] one would be able to tell the different works that middlemen, as a whole, could do.

---

[14] See Li Tao and Chen Shengqiang, "Zhongren zai Qing dai siqi zhong gongneng zhi jiyin fenxi," 61; Mao Yongjun, "Gudai qiyue 'zhongren' xianxiang de fawenhua beijing," 107–108.

[15] Fei [21]. A translation can be found in Hamilton and Wang [31].

[16] The difference between "introducers" and the similar term "brokers" can be found in Patrick H. Hase, *Custom, Land and Livelihood in Rural South China*, 443. The later were mostly "professionals, making a living from this trade," and in this sense "introducers" could be a better translation.

[17] See Philip C. C. Huang, *Civil Justice in China*, 52–54; Li Zhuhuan, "Zhongguo chuantong minshi qiyue zhong de zhongren xianxiang," 141; Li Tao and Chen Shengqiang, "Zhongren zai Qing dai siqi zhong gongneng zhi jiyin fenxi," 61; Zhou Dao and Fu Mengna, "Qingshuijiang wenshu zhongren de juese yu gongneng tanxi," 12–14; Patrick H. Hase, *Custom, Land and Livelihood in Rural South China*, 143 ff.

[18] For studies on their designations, see Li Zhuhuan, "Zhongguo chuantong minshi qiyue zhong de zhongren xianxiang," 138–141; Guo [30].

[19] The name of "*yazhong*" is rarely seen but still exists in Qing contracts. One example can be found in Wang et al. [76].

[20] There were many other designations and only one term for each designation is given here as an example.

[21] Designations and their usages need to be taken seriously as the textual and phenomenological approaches are of special importance in the study of traditional Chinese civil law, see Liang [58], Kishimoto [50]. The phenomenological method is rooted in the belief that "[t]he way things appear

It should additionally be borne in mind that describing middlemen's works as their "functions" does not imply that every middleman was able to offer all kinds of services. As a matter of fact, different functions might be provided by different groups of middlemen. In these cases, it was not one single group of middlemen who had different "functions," but different roles in contracts were played by different middlemen. Surely there were inevitably overlaps—sometimes one middleman would take on two or more roles in one contract at the same time. However, in essence these four designations should be seen as representing different contractual roles as one contracting party can include many people in practice.

In sum, the middleman is treated as a superordinate concept over the other four, whether one understands these latter roles as four different kinds of subordinate concepts of the middleman or as four roles of the middleman, in cases in which they might come from groups that do not completely overlap with one another.

2.2 *Two Levels*

The contractual approach of middlemen requires one to analyze the degree to which and in what ways they became involved in contractual relations. Thus, the four roles shall be interpreted at two levels: the primary and the secondary.

This distinction is inspired by Hart's theory of law as the union of primary and secondary rules.[22] In simple terms, "[p]rimary rules are those that grant rights or impose obligations upon members of the community," while "[s]econdary rules are those that stipulate how, and by whom, such primary rules may be formed, recognized, modified or extinguished."[23] Similarly, although not exactly the same as in the Hartian interpretation of primary and secondary rules, a primary middleman is one who participates in the formation of contractual relations which "grant rights or impose obligations," while a secondary middleman is one who plays a crucial part in the restoration of relations or order through contracts.

Generally speaking, in a contractual relation there would be a previous primary middleman who helped to form it, and secondary middleman whose task it was to restore (to re-form, modify, or terminate) the relation if it has been breached. Only in some rare situations, such as when breaking a non-contractual order, might there be no corresponding primary middleman. Put succinctly, primary middlemen were involved in forming the contractual order or relation, while secondary middlemen were needed in its restoration when necessary. Therefore, in light of the distinction between formers and restorers, the three aforementioned roles of the introducer, witness, and guarantor should be placed at the primary level, whilst only middlemen who acted as mediators should be regarded as secondary.

---

is part of the being of things; things appear as they are, and they are as they appear." See Sokolowski [70].

[22] See Hart [34].

[23] Dworkin [20].

3 The Primary Level: Introducers, Witnesses, and Guarantors

The primary roles of middlemen in the contract include introducers (*yazhong*), witnesses (*jianzhong*), and guarantors (*baozhong*).[24] Middlemen at this level directly contributed to or participated in the formation of the contract. Each group of middlemen in this domain has a distinctive characteristic: introducers and guarantors are relatively more dependent on their advantages in contractual techniques and wealth, respectively, while witnesses are more non-technical and the key requirement might only be their presence.

3.1 Introduction

3.1.1 Matchmaking and Facilitation

As a definitionally in-between figure, a middleman firstly played the role of an introducer who helped the contracting parties with matching transactions.[25] This might have been people's first impression of a middleman as well as the most basic task that people would expect of one. This task of introduction was frequently reflected in formulaic expressions of contracts, such as "[the vendor] asked the middleman to sell [his property] to [the vendee]" (*qing zhong chumai yu*)[26] or "[the vendor] asked the middleman to find [a vendee who is willing to buy]" (*qing zhong wendao*).[27] It is conceivable that if, for example, someone wanted to sell his land but at the time did not know who might be the proper buyer, the best option for him was to ask an introducer to contact potential buyers for him and finally to match the suitable buyer with the seller.[28] Introducers who helped with making matches in transactions might

[24] Hereafter introducers, witnesses, and guarantors are used to translate the Chinese designations of *yazhong*, *jianzhong*, and *baozhong*, respectively.

[25] See Liang Cong, *Qing dai Qingshuijiang xiayou cunzhai shehui de qiyue guifan yu zhixu*, 120.

[26] See, e.g., Chen and Du [10].

[27] See, e.g., An and Pan[4].

[28] A detailed step-by-step description of the process, although using a manuscript from Huizhou, can be found in Guo Ruijun, "Huizhou qiyue suojian 'zhongren' chengwei," 48–49. The customs in Shaanxi show that people should first write and hand over a document of a middleman's invitation (*qingzhong zi*) to the middleman, whereupon the middleman would start to find buyers on behalf of the seller. See Wu [80]. A vivid presentation of the introduction process, though concerning a marriage rather than commercial transactions and told through the lens of the middleman himself, can be seen in a folk lyric of the Miao people. See Guizhou sheng minjian wenxue gongzuozu [25]. For a field investigation in southeastern Guizhou which described the works of a middleman as an introducer, see *Zhongguo shaoshu minzu shehui lishi diaocha ziliao congkan* xiuding bianji weiyuanhui [1].

be the most typical and central type of middlemen.[29] In some contracts, they were straightforwardly designated as "matchmaking middlemen" (*shuohe zhongren*),[30] which clearly manifests the content of their works.

Although relatively brief, sometimes the contract text also includes a record of the process of the middleman's introduction in certain cases:

> Manuscript 6: A contract of land sale (April 2, 1876)
>
> The establishers of the contract of sale of cemetery land, Chen Jianwen and Chen Jianfang, [established this contract] because of the lack of money [to pay for] living expenses and having no other way [to raise money]. The father and the son and brothers discussed [the situation] and are willing to sell the land...[we] asked the middleman to make the match and sell it to Jiang Peigang, who is from Jiachi Village, as the property under his name. The three parties discussed the price and agreed on 3,680 copper cashes, [and the sum was] paid out and handed over [to the vendee] exactly...
>
> Middleman: Jiang Fengyi
>
> Scribe: Sun Zhankui
>
> The vendors of the cemetery land: Chen Jianwen and Chen Jianfang
>
> Guangxu, second year, third month, eighth day (April 2, 1876), established.[31]

In this transaction, a family meeting of the selling party was first held, after which they went to find a middleman, whose name was indicated later in the contract as Jiang Fengyi. The middleman helped the vendors to find a buyer from another neighboring village,[32] who was willing to take over their property with an acceptable price.

It is noteworthy that, in addition to the matchmaking in the pre-contract phase, the middleman was involved in the substantive processes of bargaining as one of the "three parties" (*sanmian*),[33] and he probably oversaw the later payment. The presence of the middleman in negotiating the price was commonly and explicitly recorded in contracts from the region.[34]

At times other services, such as measuring the land[35] or orchestrating the rituals,[36] might also be expected from the middleman in order to facilitate the transaction. It is conceivable that there was a technical threshold for offering these services. For

[29]See Patrick H. Hase, *Custom, Land and Livelihood in Rural South China*, 143–144. However, Hase explains that "the main aim of the middleman" as an introducer is to avoid embarrassment between the vendor and potential purchasers.

[30]See, e.g., Zhang and Wang [90]. The term "*shuohe ren*" is also translated as "person talking into agreement" in Philip C. C. Huang, *Civil Justice in China*, 52.

[31]Zhang and Wang [91].

[32]Otherwise there might be no necessity to point out the specific name of the village where the buyer was from in the contract.

[33]It has been noted that in later contracts of the Republican period, the situation of only two parties participating in the price discussion appears to be more frequent. See Wu [81].

[34]Just to list a few other examples, see An Zunhua and Pan Zhicheng, *Tudi qiyue wenshu jiaoshi*, vol. 1, 9, 13, 15, 29.

[35]See Guo Ruijun, "Huizhou qiyue suojian 'zhongren' chengwei," 49.

[36]See Patrick H. Hase, *Custom, Land and Livelihood in Rural South China*, 144.

instance, supervision of the payment[37] required the special knowledge of how to recognize or measure the relative purity of silver and how to calculate the final sum based on the exchange rates between silver and copper coins, or, more importantly, silver in different purities,[38] not to mention the necessity of being skilled in specific techniques in measuring land. These skills all signify that an introducer was not only a matchmaker who functioned before the contracting parties met, but also that he or she acted as a facilitator or a "processor,"[39] in some cases, during the contracting ceremony itself.

In regard to these two aspects of being an introducer, matchmaking and facilitation (bargaining in particular), two characteristic kinds of middlemen in the area are worthy of being singled out: *duzhong* and *hanzhong*.

3.1.2 *Duzhong*

As a designation of the middleman which may only be seen in contract manuscripts in the Guizhou area,[40] *duzhong* has rarely been noticed in previous scholarship. The reason why *duzhong* should be considered as a special type of middleman is that, occasionally, this designation could be juxtaposed with another general middleman in a contract by its writer as *duzhong X* and *pingzhong Y*,[41] which clearly shows that the former was deliberately distinguished from general middlemen. As shown in Table 1,[42] which lists the appearance of *duzhong* in contracts from Wendou Village, half of the contracts (17/34) were concluded solely with the help of *duzhong*, while in the other contracts a general middleman was needed along with the *duzhong*.

Yet, seemingly, there is not a sufficiently sure explanation of what a *duzhong* was: some believe that *du* here means "to instigate" or "to persuade," since it has a similar

---

[37] It was suggested by Hase that it was the middleman's job to check the money to be "a full and fair payment." See ibid.

[38] A famous so-called "silver case" which took place in the Qingshui River region exactly involved people arguing over the purity of silver in transactions; for relevant primary sources on the case, see Pan et al. [62]. One of the many calculation methods in the area can be found in Jinping xian Sanjiang zhen renmin zhengfu [45]. Also, a more general description, see Chen and Cai [11].

[39] See Patrick H. Hase, *Custom, Land and Livelihood in Rural South China*, 145.

[40] See Kang [47].

[41] Examples can be found in Daniels et al. [15], Zhang and Wang [92], Chen Jinquan and Du Wanhua, *Jiang Yuanze jiacang qiyue wenshu*, 86, 167, 330, 344; Chen and Du [12], Pan et al. [63].

[42] For the indication of the identifier of the listed manuscripts, the capital letter, A or C, respectively refers to a publication of the Qingshui River manuscripts listed in the appendix part of this study; the numerals refer to the volume and page number of the manuscript in the corresponding publication. For the abbreviation of years, "QL 29" means "the twenty-ninth year of Qianlong era," while "JQ" means Jiaqing, "DG" means Daoguang, "XF" means Xianfeng, and "TZ" means Tongzhi; "JQ (?)" means that the exact year was not indicated in the contract but the estimated time could be in the Jiangqing reign.

Table 1 *Duzhong* in wendou village

Number	Contract titles	*Duzhong*	Other middlemen (if applicable)	Year
D2-005	Contract of Sale of Forest Land	Jiaogou	Jiang Wenke	QL 29
C1-12-013	Contract of Sale of Forest Land	Jiang Yangu	–	QL 33
C1-12-316	Contract of Sale of Fishpond	Jiang Dezhong/Gengu	–	QL 33
C1-12-020	Contract of Sale of Forest Land	Jiang Zongbao	Jiang Wenzuo	QL 35
C1-12-021	Contract of Sale of Forest Land	Jiang Qiaoxiang	–	QL 36
A-A0027	Contract of Sale of Forest Land	Jiang Qiwei	–	QL 49
C3-09-009	–	Jiang Yansheng	Jiang Yingming	QL 52
C3-08-233(2)	–	Jiang Guanke	–	QL 56
C1-12-243	Contract of Sale of Hillside Fields	Jiang Yansheng	–	QL 57
C3-09-335	Contract of Sale of Forest Land	Jiang Yansheng	–	QL 58
D1-048	Contract of Sale of Wet-rice Field	Jiang Yansheng	–	QL 58
D2-032	Contract of Sale of Fishpond	Jiang Jinbao	–	JQ 2
D1-086	Contract of Sale of Wet-rice Field	Jiang Bizhou	Jiang Laoyou/Chaoqing	JQ 12
C1-12-258	Contract of Sale of Forest Land	Jiang Gongxun	–	JQ 18

(continued)

Table 1 (continued)

Number	Contract titles	*Duzhong*	Other middlemen (if applicable)	Year
D1-143-2	Contract of Sale of Wet-rice Field	Wang Jicai	–	JQ 20
D1-153	Contract of Sale of Forest Land	Long Jinjiao	–	JQ 22
D1-167	Contract of Sale of Forest Land	Jiang Gongxun	Jiang Yuxing	JQ 23
D1-201	Contract of Sale of Wet-rice Field	Jiang Dezhao	Jiang Guangzhao/Yingke	JQ (?)
A-B0102	Contract of Sale of Forest Land	Jiang Yingzong	Jiang Xianglin	DG 1
A-B0074	Contract of Sale of Forest Land	Jiang Yingzong	Jiang Yingrong/Laotong	DG 3
A-B0092	Contract of Sale of Forest Land	Jiang Shaohe	Jiang Guanglian/Yunheng/Changli	DG 11
A-B0094	Contract of Sale of Forest Land	Luo Laolong	Jiang Rongwei	DG 11
D2-213	Contract of Sale of Forest Land	Zhu Laoxiao	Luo Laolong, Jiang Shaolue	DG 11
C3-09-361	Contract of Sale of Wet-rice Field	Jiang Yingfa	–	DG 13
C1-13-108	Contract of Sale of Vegetable Farm	Jiang Yingrong	–	DG 14
D2-235	Contract of Sale of Forest Land	Jiang Dashou	–	DG 14

(continued)

Table 1 (continued)

Number	Contract titles	*Duzhong*	Other middlemen (if applicable)	Year
D1-330-1	Contract of Sale of Mountain Woods	Jiang Dashou	Jiang Chaogan	DG 16
D1-344	Contract of Sale of Forest Land	Long Jiulian	Jiang Chaogan	DG 18
D1-401	Contract of Sale of Wet-rice Field	Jiang Dashou	Jiang Tongxuan/Chaoxuan[a]	DG 24
D1-415	Contract of Sale of Wet-rice Field	Fengming. Fengxiang	Hu Jiujiang	DG 29
E2-084-9	–	Long Changrong	–	XF 8
E2-088-1	–	Fan Benyu	Jiang Zhongqi	XF 10
D1-452	Contract of Sale of Timber's Shares	Jiang Yingyuan	–	TZ 3
E2-088-4	–	Huang Junhua	Jiang Zhongfang/Enzhao	TZ 4

[a]It may be noted that the ending part of this manuscript is not clear enough and there may be inaccuracies

meaning in the dialect of Guizhou province.[43] However, for this point it is necessary to take a look at the meaning of *du*, the key character in this word, in its context in the contract.

Other evidence shows that *du* was often used with *mai* in the main body of contracts[44] in order to form the word *dumai*. This phenomenon implies that *du* could actually mean *mai*, which means "to sell." In Chinese, *du* has the meaning of "transfer" or "pass," which is similar to the situation that the word "sell" describes—transferring goods from one party to another. In addition to the phrase *dumai*, the strongest evidence supporting this opinion is that there existed two manuscripts that are actually two versions of one contract.[45] These two manuscripts contain almost the same content with only slight differences in word choice—respectively they used *du* and *mai* in the corresponding same position of one sentence. The writers of the two manuscripts used them to express the same meaning of selling, which indicates

[43]Kang Caiyun, "Gudai qiyue wenshu de zhongbaoren chengwei yuci yanbian yanjiu," 42.

[44]See, e.g., Chen Jinquan and Du Wanhua, *Jiang Yuanze jiacang qiyue wenshu*, 201. A similar usage can be found in contracts from other areas, see Anonymous [5].

[45]See Chen Jinquan and Du Wanhua, *Jiang Yuanze jiacang qiyue wenshu*, 310, 311.

that these two words were interchangeable, and so conceivably synonyms of one another.[46] Thus, the *duzhong*, literally meaning "the middleman of selling," could be understood as the matchmaker for transactions, who was able to help the vendor to sell his property to an appropriate vendee on the market.

Two phenomena noted in Table 1 can be explained by this understanding of *duzhong*. Firstly, this makes clear why nearly all *duzhong* contracts listed in Table 1 are contracts of sale. Secondly, the phenomenon that one middleman was specifically designated as *duzhong*, while another general middleman was also appointed, can be understood as a cooperation of different intermediary service-providers: the *duzhong* assumes the role of a matchmaker and then mainly focuses on the transaction itself, while other middlemen play more general roles (witnessing, guarantee, etc.) in the entire process of contracting. In short, the existence of *duzhong* indicates a highly technical orientation in terms of matchmaking in the choice of the transactional middleman.

3.1.3 *Hanzhong*

While the designation of *duzhong* highlights the function of an introducer in matchmaking, another specialized type of middlemen, *hanzhong*, emphasizes the significance of introducers in providing facilitation for contract activities, principally the contract bargaining.

Han literally means "shouting" in Chinese, but it can be understood as "bidding" when its context is related to bargaining; in these contexts, it naturally refers to the scenario in which every participant in the marketplace shouts the price out under the organization of middlemen. Generally speaking, this was not an oft-used designation in the contract text, but occasionally the phrase *hanzhong* appears directly at the ending part of a contract[47] in order to indicate that the name after it was the middleman who was involved in bargaining. More frequently, the existence of the *hanzhong* is reflected in the narrative of the contract. For example, in another contract, the process of price negotiation is described as "the bid (*han*) was made and the price was decided according to [the will of] the middleman."[48]

As shown in the above expression, *hanzhong* certainly played a decisive role in price making.[49] Customarily, it was believed by the people of the region and at that time that the middleman, rather than the buyer and the seller, held the authority of finalizing the contract price; the old saying concerning this point is that "[although the contract price is as high as] a thousand pieces of gold, it can be decided by one

[46]For other examples which indicate that *du* can be understood as "sell," see ibid., 103; Christian Daniels, Yang Yougeng, and Takeuchi Fusaji, *Kishū Myaozoku ringyō keiyaku monjo kaihen (1736–1950-nen)*, vol. 2, B-0135.

[47]See Zhang and Wang [93]. Although this is a contract of the early Republican period, it may still help in demonstrating the phenomenon of employing the phrase *hanzhong* in contracts in a slightly earlier period of the Qing.

[48]Daniels et al. [16].

[49]See Liang Cong, *Qing dai Qingshuijiang xiayou cunzhai shehui de qiyue guifan yu zhixu*, 119.

word shouted (*han*) by [the middleman]."[50] Specifically, both the vendor and the vendee were expected to propose a price at their own will and try to find a meeting point during the bargaining process run by the middleman. However, if it turned out that one party insisted on his or her proposal and was unwilling to compromise even after a long-lasting negotiation, which can take several days, it was the middleman who held the "power in customs" to declare the price that he believed was appropriate for both sides, as well as the market, as the final price in order to facilitate and finalize the transaction.[51]

Naturally, this discretionary power in pricing would cause disputes and once in a while even tragedies—one who sustained losses in business after settling too low a price by the middleman later drowned himself in the river.[52] However, it was perceived that, even if the price settled by the middleman was considered "wrong," still it could not be changed once the price had been "shouted out."[53] Occasionally, this strong and absolute power was challenged by some self-confident commercial officials, who came to the frontier area and thought that, as representatives of legal and governmental authorities, they could and should be in charge of the bargaining process, although it turned out that they were too naïve and finally failed in the rivalry between them and the local middlemen.[54] When the power of *hanzhong* could not be challenged by even dynasty officials, then it was let alone by ordinary locals.[55]

What should be noted is that the influence of *hanzhong* was mainly seen in timber transactions in *Sanjiang*, which refers to several downstream villages where major timber markets of the region were located, as has already been noted in the story of Jiang Shichao.[56] In most situations, the formal occupation of these people was the so-called *zhujia*,[57] meaning a host of foreign merchants; the *zhujia* represented one type of *xiejia*,[58] who can be crudely understood as "brokers" in late imperial China. Thus, *hanzhong* were essentially brokers on the timber market, which shows that the seemingly "overbearing" customary power they held was actually technology- and market-oriented. This power can also be understood as a market-pricing mechanism which was embodied in the operation of the middleman, rather than a discretionary power which was exercised without any limits. Though middlemen in other fields were not as influential as they were in timber markets in *Sanjiang*, the role they played as introducers in facilitating contractual transactions was still significant.

---

[50]Guizhou sheng Jinping xianzhi bianzuan weiyuanhui [26].

[51]The process was delineated in Yu [85]. Similar records can be found in a manuscript of the Qing dynasty named *Caiyun huangmu andu*, see Qu [67].

[52]See Zhang and Wang [94].

[53]Ibid.

[54]For a detailed analysis of a case concerning this issue, see Qu [68].

[55]A tentative analysis of the source of this power will be given in Sect. 5 of this chapter.

[56]See Xu [84]; Pan Zhicheng, Wu Dahua, and Liang Cong, *Qingjiang si an yanjiu*, vol. 3, 9; Qu Jian, *Yanchu fasui*, 47.

[57]See Jinping xian Sanjiang zhen renmin zhengfu, *Sanjiang zhen zhi*, 254–255; Liang [56].

[58]See Hu [39].

In sum, the role of an introducer mainly contains of two parts, namely matchmaking and facilitation, which take place respectively before and during the formal contracting process. The analyses of the traditional designations of *duzhong* and *hanzhong* exactly reveal the functions of the introducer in each aspect.

3.2 Witnessing

As this designation suggests, a *jianzhong* was a middleman who was primarily present at the contractual event to see or witness the process. Therefore, "being present" (*zaichang*) was sometimes stressed specifically in the contract when mentioning the middleman.[59] Since the apparent core requirement of assuming a witness in a contract was simply to be present, it is conceivable that no strict pre-selection would be conducted; as long as one happened to be present or even just passed by when the contract ceremony was held, he or she might be invited to be a witness. An additional requirement for a witness could be only that he or she should have a good credit record at a minimum level or at least not be a well-known dishonest person in the community. In this case, compared to being an introducer, the requirement for becoming a witness was definitely much lower. Correspondingly, the witnesses were also less responsible. Whereas the introducer was a more technical middleman, the witness might be the most non-technical kind.

On the other hand, it is exactly because of this technicality-free characteristic that the composition of witnesses was far more complicated. Furthermore, the complexity of the composition of witnesses largely explains the complexity of the composition of middlemen, which has given rise to the long-lasting question of the middlemen's social status.

Although different ways of categorizing the middlemen's social identities have been offered in previous scholarship,[60] researchers have pointed out that it is still hard to answer the question of "who can be a middleman" precisely, since it seems that people of a diverse social status may all act as middlemen from time to time. For instance, not only people who had a relatively high status, such as the heads of local communities or clans, or those who maintained a closer relationship with the parties to the transaction, such as being relatives, but also those who were at that time considered to be from a lower social class, such as women,[61] servants, or tenant peasants, could serve as middlemen in contractual activities.[62] Middlemen with special

[59] See Zhang Yingqiang and Wang Zongxun, *Qingshuijiang wenshu*, vol. 1 (12), 236. The contract records that "the middleman who is present is Jiang Deyu."

[60] A literature review on this point can be found in Guo Ruijun, "Qing dai Huizhou qiyue wenshu suojian 'zhongren' shenfen tantao," 58–59.

[61] For the event of inviting women to be the middle(wo)men in Tianzhu County, see Wang and Zhao [74]. It is noted that its evidence is from the Republican period.

[62] See Wu Xin, "Ming Qing shiqi de zhongren jiqi falü zuoyong yu yiyi," 168–174.

status or occupations can also be found in Wendou Village, such as a bricklayer[63] or a hired laborer.[64] However, it is believed that these circumstances have never been the mainstream of middlemen. They were selected only because their moral, social, technical, or economical traits might occasionally meet the requirements of assuming a middleman, and on these occasions, they were more likely to act as "witnesses."[65] Therefore, the great differences of roles inherent in the concept of the middleman should be taken into account, so that the composition of middlemen in society does not become too complicated to explain.

In fact, the system of middlemen could generally find its open access-point to society through its role as a witness. In this case, almost everyone in society can be a middleman, or (more accurately) almost everyone, even without any special technical knowledge or social status, can at least be a witness of a contract, which is still one of the many important roles that a middleman could play. The complexity of middlemen's social status might largely be explained by the easiness of becoming a witness.

This point can also be explained by recourse to specific cases. Generally speaking, those who best meet the minimum requirements of "being present" are first and foremost relatives and neighbors to the contracting parties. The latter might naturally be the best option when choosing witnesses. A contract which involves four neighbors as witnesses can serve as an example[66]:

> Manuscript 7: A contract of reimbursement (July 15, 1821)
>
> The establishers of the contract of reimbursement,[67] Jiang Laoyun, [established this contract] because of the death of my wife and son, and therefore having no one to depend on. I willingly reimburse all my properties, including one share of five of Mountain Huangmucha, one share of five of Jiebi, one share of twenty of Duimenpo, and one share of ten of the place which is under Dongniuchangtian, four [shares] altogether, to my cousin Jiang Laoqiu as the property under his name. The price is four maces and five candereens exactly. On the day of the burial, all the people have been involved in the discussion, [thus both parties] should not back out or raise any dissenting voices. Fearing that no other thing can be proof in later times, this contract of reimbursement is hereby established for retention and reference.
>
> Postscript: ...
>
> According to many neighbors[68]: Jiang Tonghai, [Jiang] Zhenhai, [Jiang] Laoqiao, [Jiang] Xianzhong
>
> Scribe: Jiang Qiyi
>
> Daoguang, first year, sixth month, seventeenth day (July 15, 1821), established.

---

[63] See Christian Daniels, Yang Yougeng, and Takeuchi Fusaji, *Kishū Myaozoku ringyō keiyaku monjo kaihen (1736–1950-nen)*, vol. 1, A-0229.

[64] See Daniels et al. [17].

[65] See Wu Xin, "Ming Qing shiqi de zhongren jiqi falü zuoyong yu yiyi," 172–173.

[66] Christian Daniels, Yang Yougeng, and Takeuchi Fusaji, *Kishū Myaozoku ringyō keiyaku monjo kaihen (1736–1950-nen)*, vol. 1, A-0144.

[67] According to the content of the contract, this example is a contract of sale.

[68] The phrase used here clearly indicates that these people lived in the neighborhood of the establisher of the contract, rather than being the owners of the adjacent property of the establisher's land.

The most eye-catching part of this contract is that, in the position where the name of the middleman is normally written, the names of persons are found which are labeled as "neighbors." In other words, to judge from the writing style and the position where these neighbors' names appeared in this contract, they in fact assumed the role of middlemen though not under the name of it. But what job did they exactly do? The process of contracting is recorded as stating that, "[o]n the day of the burial, all the people have been involved in the discussion." It is conceivable that here "all the people" must include those neighbors and their job was to make sure that both parties would not "back out or raise any dissenting voices," since all the neighbors have witnessed what has been agreed. In this case, they might not be able to be the most typical middlemen, such as introducers or mediators, but they did play the role of witnesses due to the special "character" they possessed as neighbors of the contract establisher.

The situation of relatives was more complicated. Being a relative of the contracting party implies that he or she might have social, economic, and family or even emotional connections with the contractors, which could either enhance or weaken the effectiveness of his or her testimony when necessary. Choosing a witness was a delicate task which needed tactful judgment in interpersonal relationships. The chosen witness should be someone neither too close to the contractor (e.g., one's partner, father, and son) nor a complete stranger—people would probably question the reliability of their testimony when the witness's relationship with the contractor was either too close or too alienated. Thus, there existed a gradational relational system of witnesses, which can also be found in a genuine contract.[69] In this case, one contracting party returned six parcels of land, which was bought years ago from the other party, to their previous owner freely. The contract was then established before their "relatives, clan members, and friends." The contract categorized six witnesses into three types with different degrees of closeness in its ending part. It is worth noticing that even friends, along with neighbors, who might not have any substantial connection with the contractor, can be the witnesses of a contract. This re-confirms that no strict requirement had to be met for the status of being a contractual witness.

3.3 *Guarantee*

Some believe that, in essence, a guarantor was different from a middleman.[70] In a narrow sense, hardly any direct legal obligations would be imposed on a middleman, whereas a guarantor must bear the responsibility of guarantee. That is to say, the guarantor is the one who, among other things, is obliged to complete the payment of the loan or the performance of the tenant's obligations once the latter is unable to perform them. However, in rural society, these two roles were often viewed as

[69] See Zhang and Wang [95].

[70] See Li Jinzheng, "20 shiji shangbanqi Zhongguo xiangcun jingji jiaoyi de zhongbaoren," 105.

non-separate.[71] A significant indication of this point is that in contract practice guarantors were regularly called *zhongbaoren*, meaning that "the middleman was also a guarantor."[72] In this case, the guarantor should also be included in the concept of the middleman as one important role of the latter.

In the Qingshui River region, it appears that the guarantor was not a common figure in contracts. It is even asserted that "the role of the guarantor did not exist in contracts from Wendou Village."[73] However, a contract from Jiachi Village, which is a neighboring village of Wendou, clearly illustrates the existence of the guarantor in contracts of the region[74]:

> Manuscript 8: A loan contract (November 24, 1840)
>
> The establishers of the loan contract, Jiang Zhilian, [established this contract] because of the lack of money [to pay for] expenses in the *si*[75] and having no other way [to raise money], visited Mister Yang Guang... with willingness and borrowed [money] from him. The actual sum of the loan is twenty-four taels and four maces exactly, [and Jiang Zhilian] received the money with his own hands. After the money is borrowed, [both parties] agreed that there should be twenty percent interest added for every one tael, and the full amount shall be paid up by the twelfth month, tenth day of this year without fail. In case [the borrower] failed [to pay up], [Jiang Zhilian] should willingly mortgage one parcel of forest land which is located in a place named Yangbao, three parcels of fields in Yangbao, and eight piculs of grain [for the loan]. [Since] now [the creditor] wants to have a proof, this loan contract is hereby established for retention and reference.
>
> Two characters were added to, and one character was deleted from, the main text of [this contract].
>
> Middlemen and guarantors:
>
> Miaosui Village, Zeng Guangsheng;
>
> Yanwan Village, Fan Shaozhao;
>
> Jiachi Village, Jiang Guangxiu and [Jiang] Shilian
>
> Wendou Upper Village, Jiang Guang...
>
> *Zhujia*, Luo Tiancai and Yang Guanglin
>
> Daoguang, twentieth year, eleventh month, first day (November 24, 1840), written by Jiang Zhilian in his own handwriting.

Although this contract was preserved in Jiachi Village, it was actually a trans-village contract that was co-signed by guarantors from at least four nearby villages

---

[71] See Liang Zhiping, *Qing dai xiguanfa: Shehui yu guojia*, 123.

[72] Philip C. C. Huang, *Civil Justice in China*, 53. Other examples and discussions of *zhongbaoren* can be found in ibid., 27, 60; Cohen [14], Wakefield [73], Huang [42].

[73] Liang Cong, *Qing dai Qingshuijiang xiayou cunzhai shehui de qiyue guifan yu zhixu*, 122.

[74] See Zhang and Wang [96].

[75] According to Wang Zongxun's annotation from another contract from the same village that has the same phrase of "in the *si*" (*zaisi*), the *si* here refers to the Longli *zhangguan si* of Guizhou province. See Wang [77].

The term *zhangguang si* was a "common designation for a military-rank tusi official," and the "tusi" can be understood as a local administration by indigenous dignitaries. See Herman [36]. As for Longli, see ibid., 147. For another contract that uses the phrase *zaisi*, see Jinping xian difangzhi bianzuan weiyuanhui [46].

including Wendou. This shows the widespread existence of the guarantee system in the village society of the region.

This manuscript also reveals the basic situation of the use of a guarantee in a contract. The creditor's rights were well-protected under the terms and conditions set forth in the loan contract. Firstly, the interest was agreed at a relatively high level and the loan period was short—the time for repayment was strictly limited to before "the twelfth month, tenth day of this year," which means that the loan period was only 40 days. Secondly, not only a "personal guarantee" (seven guarantors from at least four villages) but also a "real guarantee" (one parcel of forest land, three parcels of field, and eight piculs of grain) were provided by the debtor for this short-term borrowing. It is generally believed that, "[w]hen loans were secured by land, there was usually no need for a guarantor."[76] In this case, although it was also not uncommon to guarantee the debt with movable or immovable property in Wendou,[77] requiring guarantors and property guarantees was rarely seen at the same time in a single contract. A possible reason for this might be that, although the loan period was rather short, the amount of the loan was large ("twenty-four taels and four maces"), and, most importantly, it seems that the debtor had to leave the village and go out for business, as indicated at the beginning of the contract text. Thus, a special insurance might be needed since the contractor would not be present in the village for a while. In this case, it is also conceivable that the guarantor was required by the contract to bear the corresponding guarantee responsibility if the debtor failed to come back and repay the loan on time and the collateral he provided could not be realized successfully.[78] Accordingly, the one who was able to be a guarantor must be someone with some standing or propertied at a rather high level.

It has to be stressed that there was another similar type of warranty obligation in the contract that might easily be confused with the guarantee responsibility. In this context, offering a warranty in a contract entailed the express promise that certain facts are as they are represented to be. In most cases, the vendor was the one who needs to warrant against any defects of the subject-matter of the contract.[79] For instance, in the case that the vendor might only hold the imperfect right of the property, e.g. if secretly in dispute with others, a complete contract was required to include the statement that, "[i]f there are any dissenting voices [raised by others], the vendor shall be in charge of them."[80] Nonetheless, it is believed that the warranty might also represent a part of the duty of the middleman under some circumstances.[81] In fact, every middleman who has his or her name recorded in the contract generally bears

---

[76] Philip C. C. Huang, *Civil Justice in China*, 53.

[77] See, e.g., Chen Jinquan and Du Wanhua, *Jiang Yuanze jiacang qiyue wenshu*, 389.

[78] Sometimes the guarantor "might try first to get an extension or to arrange for the borrower to work off the loan." See Philip C. C. Huang, *Civil Justice in China*, 53.

[79] See Qu [64].

[80] Chen Jinquan and Du Wanhua, *Jiang Yuanze jiacang qiyue wenshu*, 27. Other examples can be seen in Chen Jinquan and Du Wanhua, *Jiang Qigui jiacang qiyue wenshu*, 131, 132, 133.

[81] In regard to the warranty of the middleman, see Patrick H. Hase, *Custom, Land and Livelihood in Rural South China*, 157.

a certain degree of guarantee or (more precisely) warranty obligation. This type of obligation does not necessarily have to be a guarantee based on the middlemen's own properties, but it could also be a type of moral obligation in regard to the determinacy of the conclusion or the performance of the content of the contract.

However, it is undeniable that one cannot find guarantors in most of the contracts from Wendou; only in strictly secured loan contracts such as the one mentioned above can one see the figure of the guarantor. Thus, it can only be inferred that the guarantor constitutes a relatively marginal part of the middlemen's system in the region. As for everyday transactions, a personal guarantee might not necessarily be needed.

4 The Secondary Level: Arbitrators and Peacemakers

Contracts were formed with the assistance of the primary middleman. However, transactions based on these concluded manuscripts still "gave rise to a fair share of disputes,"[82] and the field in which the secondary middleman played a role was exactly that of the disputes which stemmed from contracts.[83]

In Wendou Village, the previous middlemen who were involved in the conclusion of the disputing contract generally would not be appointed as the mediators in subsequent events of arbitration. However, the so-called "original middlemen" (*yuanzhong*) did play a role in the dispute settlement and need to be discussed first.

Apart from the "original middlemen" as a reflection of the primary middlemen at the secondary level, the secondary roles of middlemen in the contract include arbitrators (*lizhong*) and peacemakers (*quanzhong*).[84] The division between the two is derived from the difference between using mainly contractual techniques and utilizing "face" in decision-making. In the practice of dispute settlement, the well-known tradition of contract-based reasoning in Wendou[85] undoubtedly made the arbitrator the main block of the mediator system. Although the line between the two might be indistinct, the task of this section is to try to separate the indigenous concept of peacemakers from arbitrators, or mediators as a whole, and thereby to clarify its connotations in its context.

---

[82] Philip C. C. Huang, *Civil Justice in China*, 52.

[83] For a general introduction to the dispute settlement with a focus on the Qingshui River region, see Jiang et al. [44].

[84] Hereafter arbitrators and peacemakers are used to translate the Chinese designations of *lizhong* and *quanzhong*, respectively. The word "peacemaker" is employed to describe a certain role of a middleman in Philip C. C. Huang, *Civil Justice in China*, 55.

[85] See Zhang and Hu [97].

4.1 The "Original Middleman"

In Wendou Village, the "original middlemen" should not be seen as a separate type of middleman; this designation was used in contracts to refer to the middleman who was present in the disputing (original) contract.[86] Therefore, he should essentially be categorized as the primary middleman, so that the "original middleman" was in truth a designation of the primary middleman in a secondary contract.

However, some researchers believe that, generally, the middleman of the disputing contract originally bears the responsibility of acting as a mediator once a conflict occurs.[87] In this case, the primary and the secondary middlemen were actually the same person who assumed two roles at different times. It is assumed that, once there is a contractual dispute, the one who first comes forward to mediate often is the middleman.[88] Thus, some consider that the middleman is invited to participate in the contracting process and to play a role in the possible dispute in the future if needed.[89]

As for the concept of "original middlemen" in Wendou Village, its appearance in the mechanism of dispute resolution was not common; this was only occasionally seen in the village's disputes records. One of the reasons for this could be that some contracts had been produced quite a long time before the dispute arose, and so the "original middleman" had sometimes already passed away or might no longer be able to carry out the work of mediation. In addition, a more important reason might belong to the technical level, namely that the technical ability of the "original middleman" to match transactions was not entirely suitable for the requirements of dispute settlement. The abilities required by the primary and secondary middlemen were dissimilar; making a match was strikingly different from making a judgment.

There were two main roles that an original middleman could play in the process of dispute resolution in Wendou. First, the original middleman was naturally the authenticator of the original contract. In this sense, the original middleman shared the same function as the contract manuscript itself: once the contract was disputed, the original text recorded on the paper manuscript came to constitute the evidence that can be checked, and the original middleman also took part in this process as a "living proof" (*huozhi*) who is accessible. For example, in a plaint (Jiang Guangyu v. Jiang Zhiyuan and Jiang Jizhao) dated to the sixteenth year of Daoguang (1836) from Wendou, it is stated that[90]:

---

[86]However, it is believed that, in the villages of Jiangsu and Zhejiang provinces, *yuanzhong* was a conception opposed to *jianzhong* (the witness). The former was essentially involved in the contracting process and needed to guarantee the performance of the contract, while the latter was only provisionally invited to participate in the event. In this case, the "original middleman" was limited to a combination of the above-mentioned introducers and guarantors while excluding witnesses. See Zhou [105].

[87]See Chen Shengqiang and Wang Jiahong, "Zhongren zai Qing dai tudi juemai qiyue zhong de gongneng," 448.

[88]See Terada Hiroaki, "Ming Qing shiqi fazhixu zhong 'yue' de xingzhi," 176.

[89]See ibid.

[90]Takeuchi [71]. The same manuscript can also be seen in Jinping xian difangzhi bianzuan weiyuanhui, *Jinping xianzhi, 1991–2009*, vol. 2, 1291–1292.

Manuscript 9: A plaint (Jiang Guangyu v. Jiang Zhiyuan & Jiang Jizhao, 1836)

In the seventh year of Daoguang (1827), we and...[others] bought a parcel of forest land, named Chongjiukuang, from his father Jiang Zhiyuan. The purchase price was 4,020 taels, [and was] agreed to be divided into two big shares...we hold one big share. [The earning of the sale of] the timber [on the land] is 7,440 taels. Apart from the monthly interest and the cost of lumberers, the total net income is over 1,900 taels. The middlemen, Jiang Yingguang and [Jiang] Zhi'an, were the living proof [of the previous statement].

As shown in the manuscript, when proof of the sale of wood and especially the details of the transaction were needed, the original middlemen were mentioned and considered as "living proof" of the deal. This illustrates that, whether technically a witness or not, the original middleman could be required to give evidence in later disputes.[91]

Second, just like the role that an arbitrator or peacemaker would play, the original middleman could also function in the formation of the judgment. In this case, there appears a mixture of "the original middleman" and "the secondary middleman" to a limited extent. The postscript of a contract dated to the seventh year of Xianfeng (1857) records and displays in detail a mediation in which both the original middlemen and the subsequent "secondary" middlemen were embroiled[92]:

Manuscript 10: A contract postscript (1857)

In the eighth year of Guangxu (1882), the sale of the timber of the land was stopped by Jiang Xing. When inviting middlemen for arbitration, his contract of buying was checked, recording that there were nine parcels of fields and wasteland; and his old contract was also checked...The original middlemen are Fachun, Hailong, and Zuomei. [They] made the decision by saying that, whereas your [request of] nine parcels of fields had been fulfilled, the remaining wastelands shall belong to Haiwen and Haizhi. [However, the middlemen] did not know that there are two more parcels of fields to the left of the big field, and there is another parcel of wasteland...Therefore, Bingzhi, Keqing, and Defang [were invited to] join the survey of the land.

This dispute came into being after someone stopped the intended sale of the standing timber, in which it seems that the exact land parcels that one party owned were under controversy. Therefore, the parties invited the three original middlemen and sought clarification of the property rights, though apparently they did not obtain a satisfying result. It appears as if they rather distrusted the technical skills in conducting the land survey that the original middlemen possessed and doubted that these middlemen truly had a clear understanding of the situation of the land. Consequently, they further invited three other middlemen, who were certainly not the "original," to join the investigation.

However, one party believed that two of the three middlemen were sided with the other party and then again refused to accept the second-round adjudication. In the end, the secondary middlemen announced that "the judgment had already been made," which indicated that it was conclusive and should not be changed again, but

[91] In some cases, it was believed that the original middleman "should be invited" to the process of dispute resolution, as in the plaint manuscript cited in Zhang [98].

[92] Christian Daniels, Yang Yougeng, and Takeuchi Fusaji, *Kishū Myaozoku ringyō keiyaku monjo kaihen (1736–1950-nen)*, vol. 3, D-0030.

"if anyone refused to abide by [the decision], both parties were allowed to appeal to the gods."[93] It has to be stressed that, even in the divine judgment, the middleman would still join and play a role in the process according to the records.[94]

The procedure of arbitration in general can be explained as follows. Once there arises an issue, although not necessary, the "original middleman" is the one who might be appealed to first if applicable; if the problem is not solved, the dissenter can then find other secondary middlemen, either arbitrators or peacemakers, for another formal round of mediation. In the case that the middleman was not able to settle the dispute, a divine judgment could then be an option.[95]

In sum, the "original middleman" was to some extent the intersection of the primary and secondary middlemen, but the primary middleman might not have any special status in the secondary field of finding the solution.

4.2 Arbitration

In general, "[a]lthough the Chinese did have occasion to go to court, their ideal remained for individuals to draft a private agreement without depending on the judicial system to enforce it."[96] The Qingshui River region shared this same convention. The relevant customary background and societal foundations were of great importance to the championing of private arbitration in the region.[97]

Lizhong, or the arbitrator, was actually not an indigenous designation in Wendou Village. The word *lijiang*,[98] however, was frequently mentioned in contracts and other related documents referring to the activities of arbitration.[99] On most occasions, both arbitrators and peacemakers were vaguely called middlemen, but this study tends to classify them into two types.[100] Accordingly, the arbitrator was distinguished in terms of the concept of *lijiang*.

---

[93] Ibid. As for the customs of appealing to the gods or divine judgment in the region, see Takeuchi Fusaji, "Narukami to nakan no aida," 83–120.

[94] The original middleman was involved in the appeal later, see Christian Daniels, Yang Yougeng, and Takeuchi Fusaji, *Kishū Myaozoku ringyō keiyaku monjo kaihen (1736–1950-nen)*, vol. 3, D-0030. Another contract also shows that the middleman would join the ritual of appealing, see Zhang and Wang [101].

[95] The two-step process of arbitration by the (secondary) middleman and then the divine judgment can also be seen in Zhang Yingqiang and Wang Zongxun, *Qingshuijiang wenshu*, vol. 2 (2), 176.

[96] Hansen [33].

[97] For an introduction to the custom and foundation, see Wu [83].

[98] The designation *lizhong* here means the middleman of *lijiang*.

[99] For manuscripts using the word *lijiang*, see, e.g., An Zunhua and Pan Zhicheng, *Tudi qiyue wenshu jiaoshi*, vol. 1, 100–101, 260–261; An and Pan [3]; Pan Zhicheng, Wu Dahua, and Liang Cong, *Linye jingying wenshu*, vol. 2, 157, 171, 172; Pan Zhicheng, Wu Dahua, and Liang Cong, *Qingjiang si an yanjiu*, vol. 3, 19. For the use of *lijiang* in manuscripts from other areas in the Qingshui River region, see, e.g., Gao and Tan [23].

[100] K. C. Hsiao's work somehow also implies the distinction between the settlement of disputes through arbitration and mediation, see Kung-ch'üan Hsiao, *Compromise in Imperial China*, 3, 39.

4.2.1 Fact-Finding

The core of arbitral activities is to clarify the facts; this is the basis even for making a compromise. For compromising means giving up on something that one originally insisted on having, while a clarification of facts could provide the knowledge of what one has given up. That is exactly the job of an arbitrator: to identify the issue, investigate the facts, and then make a decision on the basis of the clarified facts. For instance, a contract records the clarification of the shares of forest land with the help of the arbitrator[101]:

Manuscript 11: A contract of sale (November 12, 1810)

The establisher of the contract of innocent sale of forest land, Jiang Baofu, [established this contract] because [he intended to sell] the forest land, named Tuge, which was bought from the Laolan and Laozhu brothers of Ping'an Village in earlier years. At present, the number of shares [of the forest land] is unclear, [and the party] invited the middlemen for arbitration. [As a result,] the forest land is divided into 16 shares, and there is one share under Baofu's name. Thanks to the arbitration by the middlemen, [the shares were] clarified and complemented. [The share under Baofu's name can then be] sold to Ren De from Ping'ao Village to be as the property under his name. The price was discussed in the presence of the middleman and agreed to be four taels and five maces exactly. Baofu received the exact amount of money with his own hands. In the future, no dissenting voices can be raised [concerning] this forest land. The establishment of this contract of innocence is true.

Middlemen: Zhoucai, Yanhua, Shaolun

Scribe: Shaoya

Jiaqing, fifteenth year, tenth month, sixteenth day (November 12, 1810), established.

This is somewhat a strange contract regarding its designation—"the contract of innocent sale of forest land." It is essentially a contract of sale but needs to especially claim that the sale was innocent, which might refer to a statement that the rights which the vendor held have already been clarified and confirmed, according to the narrative of the contract, through the arbitration by the middlemen. It appears that no substantial dispute has ever occurred before, but merely at that time "the number of shares [of the forest land] is unclear," probably because the purchase of the property happened "in earlier years." It is possible that it was only the concern of the vendee regarding the unclear status of the subject-matter of the contract that led to the arbitration. This exemplifies that, as long as there was a need for defining contractual facts, the arbitrator could be asked for a formal clarification. Another contract, as a supplementary illustration, also shows that the ill-defined ownership of a mountain which was transferred in the early years was clarified after arbitration.[102]

As the foundation of arbitral decisions, the facts concerning the contract can be clarified by arbitrators by various means. In addition to hearing the words from both sides,[103] more concrete evidence was often needed, such as the contract and the result

[101]Christian Daniels, Yang Yougeng, and Takeuchi Fusaji, *Kishū Myaozoku ringyō keiyaku monjo kaihen (1736–1950-nen)*, vol. 3, F-0031.

[102]See ibid., F-0032.

[103]For the description of the process of the "hearing," see Chen Jinquan and Hou Xiaojuan, "Lun Qingdai Qiandongnan Miao zhai de jiufen jiejue," 22.

of the land survey. As for the contract, the comparative analysis between the current and previous contracts was often required,[104] for some disputes stemmed exactly from the incoherence of the description of the subject-matter in relevant contracts. Regarding the land survey, since many controversial issues were raised due to the blurred and muddled boundaries of lands, a careful and on-the-spot investigation sometimes had to be conducted by the arbitrator in person. A private letter elucidates the emphasis that was placed on contract examination and field investigation in regard to the settlement of land disputes[105]:

Manuscript 12: A private letter concerning litigation (no.1, 1902)

[The previous statement about the properties purchased during the Qianlong era (1736–1790)] had been clearly written in these contracts. In addition, concerning the timber that we harvested in the ninth year of Daoguang (1829), [we] have the contract of division and the contract of sale as references. The timber that was harvested in the tenth year of Tongzhi (1871) can be proven by the planter's contract from the Hus. Later the land was planted by [the planter], and he is still alive. The planter's contract is not fake. [We all have] seen this in person. Can there still be any objections? As for the timber that was harvested and sold in this year, Hu and the Jiang Dengcheng brothers suddenly deliberately misrepresented the contract regarding Wenhao's sale to Qihua, calling white black… By means of the examination of the contracts and the investigation of the forest land by the middleman, the two parties were allowed to respectively possess their own properties. The two parties both abided by the decision.

In another letter concerning the same issue, it adds[106]:

Manuscript 13: A private letter concerning litigation (no. 2, 1902)

On [Guangxu, twenty-eighth year,] fourth month, sixth day (May 13, 1902), the middleman came back from the field investigation and made the decision that the [two parties should] respectively possess their own properties. The two parties both abided by the decision.

The two letters were written in the twenty-eighth year of Guangxu (1902), while the history of the purchase of the property can be traced back to the Qianlong era, which was over a century earlier. Every alteration of the rights related to the forest land can be tracked through a series of contracts that were well preserved from earlier years. The process of the arbitration is briefly described in the letters. Although some might try to deny the true ownership or the established contractual relationship concerning the forest land, taking advantage of the long period of time that had passed and the vagueness it brought by "calling white black," once the contracts and the lands themselves were thoroughly checked by an arbitrator, the truth would easily emerge and the dispute would be resolved accordingly. It can be inferred that the middleman, here posturing as the arbitrator, largely relied on these contract manuscripts, as well as the personal field investigation, in the fact-finding and decision-making ("[b]y

[104] For instance, the aforementioned contract states that "[w]hen inviting middlemen for arbitration, his contract of sale was checked, …and his old contract was also checked." See Christian Daniels, Yang Yougeng, and Takeuchi Fusaji, *Kishū Myaozoku ringyō keiyaku monjo kaihen (1736–1950-nen)*, vol. 3, D-0030.

[105] Ibid., F-0037.

[106] Ibid., F-0038.

means of the examination of the contracts and the investigation of the forest land by the middleman").

4.2.2 Reasoning

It has been shown that facts were the ground of arbitration and finding them out, through the investigative approach of both contracts and lands, was therefore the aim of the arbitrator. However, sometimes the facts might not be the only issue.

From the viewpoint of modern law, a trial of disputes can be divided into roughly two aspects: the factual and the legal aspects. In the region in question, finding out the facts was enough for most disputes. As the above-mentioned cases have shown, the need for tangible evidence may likely arise in response to the solution of the factual issue, such as land-border disputes or issues concerning the existence of property rights caused by the authenticity of contracts. However, occasionally either legal or more theoretical and abstract issues could be heard by arbitrators.

In the postscript of a contract this type of "legal or contractual issue" is presented[107]:

> Manuscript 14: A contract postscript (ca. 1834)
>
> The Mountain of Gangwan was sold by the Jiang Chaoxiang brothers to Jiang Wei and later a second time to Fan Xianlin. Xianlin sold it again to Jiang Chongying. In Daoguang, fourteenth year, ninth month (October 1834), it was sold to Chen Laowu to harvest [the timber on it]. The two parties disputed [this]. Thanks to the intermediation of the middlemen, according to the contracts, this share of the mountain[108] was decided to be possessed by Jiang Jitai. This postscript was written according to the middlemen. [All the parties shall] possess properties based on the share [they have,] and no objections shall be raised anymore.

This was a classical problem of double sales, which involved selling one object twice or more. The property (one share of "the Mountain of Gangwan") was firstly sold by A ("Jiang Chaoxiang brothers") to B ("Jiang Wei"), and then to C ("Fan Xianlin") again. Later C sold it to D ("Jiang Chongying") and D sold it to E ("Chen Laowu") for the final harvest. The facts of the case were clear and undisputed (shown in Fig. 1). The issue was that the property was sold twice to B and C successively. In this case, who should be the real owner?

This was certainly not a factual question but a legal or theoretical one. In the end, the middlemen made the decision, "according to the contracts," that F ("Jiang Jitai") would hold the property in contention. No further details of the case were provided by the case brief in the postscript, so it is hard to speculate about the reason behind the judgment. One clue comes from the genealogy which shows that F and B (Jiang Jitai and Jiang Wei) were brothers,[109] implying that there was a possibility that F

---

[107]Christian Daniels, Yang Yougeng, and Takeuchi Fusaji, *Kishū Myaozoku ringyō keiyaku monjo kaihen (1736–1950-nen)*, vol. 1, A-0098.

[108]In fact, according to the main text of the contract, the subject matter was only one small share of the mountain, or approximately 5.56% of the whole property. See ibid.

[109]See the genealogical diagram of Jiang's family in Wendou in Aihara [2].

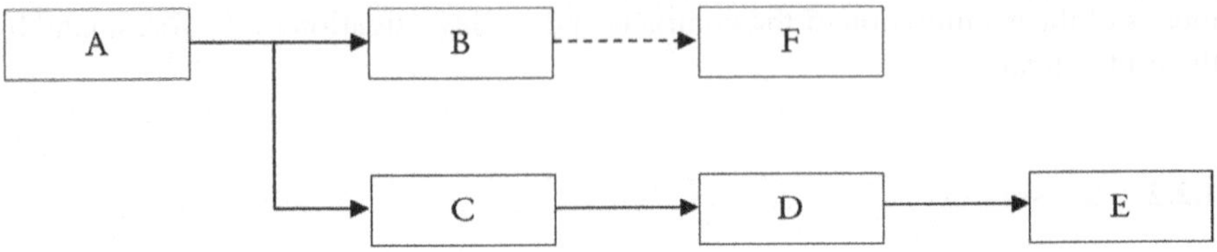

Fig. 1 A diagrammatic sketch of the case of double sales

was B's successor or they were joint owners of the property. Thus, it appears that the arbitrator's opinion was that all the following transactions, including A to C, C to D, and D to E, should be invalidated and the property should return to the first purchaser B.

Unlike the notion of face-based compromise in dispute settlement, all of the above reveals that the basic characteristic of the arbitrators who were heavily active in the region was their contract-based reasoning in dealing with both factual and legal issues; they made decisions by means of analyzing the evidence. The process of this type of reasoning is repeatedly presented in contracts.[110] It is this basic feature that emphasizes the requirement of techniques in, for example, examining contracts or investigating lands for being arbitrators, rather than the power, influence, financial resources, etc. that one would generally imagine.

Undoubtedly, a special knowledge was necessary for determining the authenticity of a contract, conducting land surveys, and reasoning on the basis of the factual findings. Although this is not to say that the arbitrators were complete technicians, it is undeniable that they must have had an advantage over other common people in the techniques used for determining facts, and this technological advantage could reduce people's demands for their high social status.[111]

4.3 Mediation

Quanzhong, the peacemaker, was in fact a unique designation in the middlemen system of Wendou Village. Although there have been copious discussions about the mediation of the middleman in the region, the role of the peacemaker has been ignored for a long time as one distinctive function of the middleman from many. For scholars tend to equate the peacemaker to the middleman regarding mediation.

As in general private dispute settlements, the mediation that the peacemaker helped to apply included "a wide range of subtle and not-so-subtle pressures, the use

[110]See, e.g., Christian Daniels, Yang Yougeng, and Takeuchi Fusaji, *Kishū Myaozoku ringyō keiyaku monjo kaihen (1736–1950-nen)*, vol. 1, A-0205.

[111]Its historical root might be found in the convention of *lishi*, "the master of arbitrating," who was able to settle disputes not because of his political or economic privileges in the village but because he was familiar with traditional customary norms and taboos and was considered to be eloquent and fair. See Liu [60].

of moralistic language, and in some cases even material inducements."[112] Unlike the arbitrator, who tended firstly to observe the facts and secondly to adjudicate on the grounds of the result of investigation and reason, if it was not (customary) law, peacemakers aimed "to establish peace and harmony based on customary ethical values" by means of achieving "some form of compromise," which was sometimes believed to be "more important than adjudicating right and wrong."[113] This job-description exactly reflects the dichotomy between the arbitrator and the peacemaker as secondary types of middleman.

The peacemaker was not a made-up concept, but was itself distinguished from other middlemen by the villagers of the time. For example, in a contract of the twenty-seventh year of Daoguang (1847), it is written that "we actually invited the middlemen Jiang Zongyou, [Jiang] Wenguang and the peacemaker (*quanzhong*) Jiang Huaiyi, and we made an appointment to tomorrow, the sixth day, in the morning."[114] The writer of this contract explicitly distinguished the peacemaker from other general middlemen.

The specific process of peacemaking by *quanzhong* is occasionally presented in contracts themselves[115]:

> Manuscript 15: A contract of innocence (March 7, 1833)
>
> The establishers of the contract of innocence are the Jiang...brothers and Jiang Kaiming and his son. The two parties bought one parcel of forest land, named Ran... Mountain, from the Xinlong and Xingui brothers...[Afterwards,] the two parties came into conflict [over the forest land]. Thanks to the mediation and persuasion[116] by the middlemen, the three landlord's shares[117] of the standing timber [on the land] were divided into two [equal] parts: the...brothers take one and a half share, [while] Kaiming and his son take one and a half share. The two parties willingly established two duplicates of the contract of innocence, and each of them holds one piece in order to prevent further troubles. This is true and for reference.
>
> Postscript: The two planter's shares of the old standing timber of this time are held by Shihong.
>
> The establishment of the contract of innocence is true.[118]
>
> Peacemakers (*quanzhong*): Long Xiancai, Jiang Shi'an
>
> Scribe: Jiang Shihe
>
> Daoguang, thirteenth year, first month, sixteenth day (March 7, 1833), established.

---

[112]Katz [48].

[113]Ibid.

[114]Christian Daniels, Yang Yougeng, and Takeuchi Fusaji, *Kishū Myaozoku ringyō keiyaku monjo kaihen (1736–1950-nen)*, vol. 3, F-0033.

[115]Zhang and Wang [99].

[116]Literally, *quanzhong* means the middleman of persuasion.

[117]The landlord's share and the latter planter's share were two types, or classes, of share in the forestry industry which were commonly seen in the region. Normally the landlord would share the profit of the production of the forest land, i.e. the standing timber, with the planter. In this contract, the landlord held 3/5 of the whole and the planter held the other two shares. For the multiple share classes in the Qingshui River region, see Qu [66].

[118]This sentence was written at the junction of the edges of two sheets of paper, so only the right part was written on this manuscript.

The background of the conflict in this contract is that the two parties bought one parcel of forest land together, but for some reason failed to allocate their respective portions. The respective claims of the two parties are not known, but once there was a conflict between them over one property, it is conceivable that either one or both parties claimed more than a half of the property. However, the dispute was later settled by the middleman as a peacemaker who tried to smooth things over by letting the two parties split the forest land fifty-fifty. Even though it was originally divided into three shares, the middleman assigned it as one and a half shares for each. No further facts were given in this contract, such as the amount or ratio of the contributions of the two parties in buying the property. At any rate, it appears that, according to this manuscript, the problem was solved by mediation and persuasion, not by facts and reasoning.

Rather than adjudicating right from wrong, reconciling the parties was the primary concern of mediation.[119] Another contract is a satisfactory illustration of this point[120]:

Manuscript 16: A division contract (January 17, 1829)

The establisher of the division contract, Fan Xingxiu and [Fan Xing]jue and four others from Zhanghua Village, and Jiang Zhihao and Jiang Kairang, who are uncle and nephew, from Jiachi Village, [established this contract] because, in earlier years, the Fans bought the mountain, named Jiashitang, from Jiang Guanlüe of…Wendou. The boundary of the mountain is close to Zhihao['s mountain], and there is a parcel of the mountain on the branch of the mountain range. The two parties came into conflict [over the parcel of the mountain] and could not distinguish [the boundary between the two mountains]. Thus, [the two parties] went to Wendou Village together and invited the middlemen for arbitration. Thanks to the persuasion and mediation by the many relatives and friends, [they] let [the Fans] give up this forest land and let the Jiangs conserve [the forest]. [The Jiangs and the Fans] each possess their own property according to the boundary… [This is] discussed publicly in the presence of the many [middlemen]. The two parties should not back out in the future. If this situation happens, the many [middlemen] will enforce the decision fairly and will not be partial to and side with [any party]. Two duplicates of the division contract are specially established, and each of them holds one piece for reference in the future.

One character was added to and one character deleted [from the main text of this contract].

This contract is proof.[121]

Middleman: The vendor Jiang Laotuan

Peacemakers (*quanzhong*): Jiang Xianzu, [Jiang]…, [Jiang] Chaogan, [Jiang] Kaixiang from Wendou Village; Jiang Shilian, [Jiang] Guangxiu from Jiachi Village.

Scribe: Yang Zhiyi

Daoguang, eighth year, twelfth month, thirteenth day (January 17, 1829), established.

Similarly to the previous case, the two parties in this contract also argue about one parcel of the mountain, but in this case because of the unclear boundary. Logically speaking, the mediator's task should be to conduct the land survey and define the clear boundary between the two mountains according to the survey results. For an

[119]See Philip C. C. Huang, *Civil Justice in China*, 64.

[120]Zhang and Wang [100].

[121]This line was written at the junction of the edges of two sheets of paper, so only the left part was written on this manuscript.

arbitrator, the issue could be solved in this way. However, the peacemaker in this case might tend not to make a clear decision by drawing a fine line between the two. The final solution was somewhat surprising, since one party agreed to disclaim their rights and the other party accordingly took all of the land which was at stake. Further, the middlemen declared that they "will not be partial to and side with [any party]."

The resolution of this dispute, as in the previous case, was not derived from a careful examination of relevant contracts or an on-the-spot investigation of the boundaries of the mountain. The fact that one party "voluntarily" transferred the disputed mountain to the other party also reflects that the peacemakers, as well as the two parties, might not be pursuing absolute objective facts. Instead, a certain balance has been reached thanks to the persuasion and mediation from friends and relatives. It is also noteworthy that, as previously, this is a trans-village contract, and peacemakers were from two neighboring villages. This indicates that the land dispute might not be the whole issue, but that this story may have been just one part of a larger, yet unknown picture across villages. Ultimately, regardless of what actually happened, the dispute was solved by peacemakers in a contractual way.

In sum, if the tag of an arbitrator was "reasoning," then that of a peacemaker might be the so-called "face." A manuscript from the early Republican period is more explicit on this point, stating "[we did this] because of you two middlemen's face."[122] By means of the "face," maintaining the peace of the community became the major concern, and compromising became the main method of the mediation, "though generally with a frame set by law and by the community's sense of right and wrong."[123] The distinction between these two profoundly different secondary middlemen highlights both the somehow long-ignored technicality of middlemen and the two quite different approaches in the restoration of contractual relationships in the community.

5 The Middleman as the Third Party and the Third Party as the Middleman

5.1 The Involvement of the Middleman in a Contract

How was a middleman involved in a contract? Previous sections in this chapter have already presented the four—or five, if the arbitrator and peacemaker count as two—different roles that middlemen could play in contractual activities in the Qingshui River region. Moreover, according to the previous analyses, it is not difficult to uncover that the middleman could greatly facilitate the establishment of the contract in various respects. But what was the exact position of a middleman in a contract?

---

[122]Christian Daniels, Yang Yougeng, and Takeuchi Fusaji, *Kishū Myaozoku ringyō keiyaku monjo kaihen (1736–1950-nen)*, vol. 3, F-0040.

[123]Philip C. C. Huang, *Civil Justice in China*, 61.

Was the middleman merely an outsider, helper, or service provider, or was he or she actually an insider who was essentially involved in the contract?[124]

The essential involvement in a contract indicates the direct expression of one's will in the core content of a contract. Traditionally, the substantial part of a contract is the consent which is the result of the meeting of wills from both parties. In the context in question, as has been discussed, the content of a contract was the jural relations that were established or confirmed by the contract. Thus, in regard to the establishment or confirmation of the jural relations, whose wills or intentions were reflected in the contract? Were the vendor and the vendee, for example, the only determiners of a contract of sale?

Despite many other factors, the answer is "yes" in most cases in the eyes of modern contract law, since only the contracting parties can determine the contract. As mentioned, this is called the principle of "freedom of contract." However, it has been known that the case might be completely different in the context where a middleman constantly existed—here, the middleman's will should be considered seriously and sometimes the intention of the non-trading party could even surpass the wills of the vendor and the vendee. In this sense, the middleman should be deemed the third party of a contract: not the type of "third" that ranks after the two parties in its degree of importance and stands outside of the central decisive circle, but the type of "third" which stands in the middle and might sometimes even be superior to the first and the second.

The most obvious examples have been examined in the above analyses at the two levels of the middleman. For primary middlemen, *hanzhong* seems to denote the type of middleman with the greatest influence on the contract. For the content of a contract of sale, the price is perhaps one of the most important and essential clauses.[125] However, even this core part of the consent of the contract was not entirely decided by the buyer and seller.[126] Differently from the general understanding of "freedom of contract," the middleman was the one who held the "power in customs" to make the final decision. It might be hard to investigate the exact normative source of this "power,"[127] but the privilege must rest somewhere in the society or industry that is external to the specific contract activity. It is conceivable that, for the conclusion of the final price in a timber market, not only the wills of the parties but also the interests of the middlemen and even the sustainable development of the whole industry should be taken into account. Specifically, a lower price would harm the benefit of upstream suppliers (i.e. forest workers), while a higher price might scare off downstream customers (i.e. timber merchants). A balance is thus needed in the middleman's intervention. Generally, owing to both social influence and technical capabilities, he

---

124 A similar distinction is also considered regarding "political middlemen," for it is believed that "[s]ome middlemen are mere messengers, go-betweens without initiative or responsibility," while "[o]ther middlemen...play roles that influence the pace and direction of change in the societies in which they exist." See Rodman and Counts [69].

125 See Kötz [51], Han [32].

126 For the case of unilateral price-fixing, see Hein Kötz, *European Contract Law*, 45.

127 For a tentative theory on this point, see Qu Jian, *Yanchu fasui*, 84.

or she should then act as an adjuster in contracts, representing the conflicting but also mutually necessary interests in and beyond the specific transaction. In this sense he or she may justifiably obtain the arbitrary power to finalize the negotiation.

The case might be more explicit at the secondary level. In their original intentions, arbitrators and peacemakers might not seek to create new contracts but rather to fix the old ones. However, in fact, while trying to restore the order of the original contract, secondary middlemen actually exercised the arbitrary power to reconstruct the contractual relations—the arbitration agreements are de facto new contracts—but through different approaches. On the one hand, the effort of fact-finding marks the intention of an arbitrator to restore in one sense, or to create in another, the order based on the accessible objective facts and his reasoning instead of the wills of the parties concerned. On the other hand, the contractually creative work of a peacemaker could be more evident: a peacemaker could even directly ignore the evidence provided and produce a somewhat groundless new contract in an "arbitrary" way. One might wonder why they were considered to have such decisive powers. The answer could be the corresponding technical advantage or social status they held, which turned them into representatives of community values. As the puzzle of the power of *hanzhong* shows, they were chosen or invited because of some particular characteristics they held. But what is important is that, with these characteristics, they were able to assume the role of the middleman who could substantively intervene in the formation of contracts.

Witnesses and guarantors seem to be less influential compared to the previous types of middlemen. However, their wills are also reflected in the contract. The appearance of the witness not only means that he or she endorses the authenticity of the contract, but also indicates that he or she has at least a non-objective attitude towards the content of the contract. In many cases, this is even an expression of approval. The guarantor can actually be regarded as an enhanced witness. A guarantor not only endorses the contract content with his or her own credit or social status, but in some cases even his or her own property. If the middleman can be regarded as a representative of the community,[128] then obviously a transaction that was not viewed with at least a non-objective attitude from the community seems difficult to make successful.

In a nutshell, the middleman was generally the ever-present third party who was essentially involved in a contract as the representative of external interests and, to some extent, the one who acted as the channel or junction point by which social forces could be introduced into contracts.

[128]See Patrick H. Hase, *Custom, Land and Livelihood in Rural South China*, 143–157.

5.2 Incorporating Various Third Parties as Middlemen

Middlemen can be regarded as the third party to a contract; however, it should be noted that not all the contractual third parties were designated as "middlemen." In contracts from Wendou Village, the indication of the third party in a contract text was usually the word "*ping*," and therefore the middleman was normally mentioned as "*pingzhong*."[129] The complete meaning of what this expression intends to express could be that the contract is established according to, by virtue of, or in the presence of the middleman. In this case, the term *ping* could be deemed a textual indicator of the appearance of the middleman in the contract.[130]

Following this path, various designations other than the middleman can be found mentioned right after the character *ping* in different types of contracts, such as the family head or clan head in the case of the family division,[131] the matchmaker in the case of marriage,[132] the geomancer in the case of a funeral,[133] or the "prime minister" in a case of profit allocation.[134] Consequently, it is hard to define their contractual status on the theory that only the middleman is accepted to be involved in a contract.

A broader theory is needed to incorporate these unfamiliar contractual figures. These figures were the third parties to the contract but should also be considered as middleman-like, not only because they were mentioned right after the indicating word *ping* as the middleman, but also because they played a similarly essential role to the middleman. For instance, the geomancer should be seen as the key figure in formulating a contract of funeral-related issues. For most third parties, which is actually a slightly broader concept than the middleman, these individuals assume one or several roles of the middleman. In this sense, if the strictly defined middleman is not a suitable term for describing the diverse variations of contract facilitators, these figures should at least be placed under the re-defined concept of the middleman. More third-party contractual figures could be seen as one type of—or at least one part of the system of—the re-defined middleman. Thus, the two types—the middleman as the third party and the third party as the middleman—are merged into the broader concept of middlemen in the following discussions.

[129] See, e.g., Chen Jinquan and Du Wanhua, *Jiang Qigui jiacang qiyue wenshu*, 63.

[130] This point will be further discussed in detail in Sect. 4.1 of Chap. 5.

[131] See, e.g., Zhang and Wang [87].

[132] See, e.g., Zhang and Wang [88].

[133] See, e.g., Christian Daniels, Yang Yougeng, and Takeuchi Fusaji, *Kishū Myaozoku ringyō keiyaku monjo kaihen (1736–1950-nen)*, vol. 3, D-0055. A contract of the invitation of a geomancer can be found in Zhang [89].

[134] See Christian Daniels, Yang Yougeng, and Takeuchi Fusaji, *Kishū Myaozoku ringyō keiyaku monjo kaihen (1736–1950-nen)*, vol. 3, E-0048. The "prime minister" refers to the head of local troops in Wendou during the late Qing dynasty.

5.3 A Partly Open System of Middlemen

In this sense, a system of middlemen with appropriate explanatory power can be descriptively constructed and the enduring question of what a middleman was might be answered to a large extent through this system.

The most significant feature of this system of middlemen is that it is a partly open system. It was firstly an open system, implying that almost everyone in the community was able to become a middleman under certain circumstances. As noted above, the role of witnesses could act as an open access point of the middlemen system to the whole society, since it was extremely easy to be a witness to a contract. In addition, the emphasis of the contractual techniques on the middleman made it possible for people to become middlemen by acquiring these techniques without being restricted by social status. Compared with social identity, the approach of skill learning seems to be more feasible for ordinary people. In other words, there was a possibility, in principle, for all society members to access this system of middlemen.

Nonetheless, the system was after all a *partly* open system, which means that the requirement for becoming a middleman might be low, but still existent. Each role of the middleman placed a particular emphasis on different issues, such as technical advantages (introducers, arbitrators), property advantages (guarantors), and advantages of social identity (peacemaker). As for witnesses, they were certainly expected to have a minimum degree of, among other things, honesty that can be accepted by the contracting parties. These requirements define the professionalism of a standard middleman to some extent, and the specific characteristics they possess would justifiably empower them to participate in the formation and restoration of the contractual order more effectively.

Thus, within the partly open system shown in Table 2, the population of middlemen could range from persons with special characteristics in terms of techniques or social or economic status to ordinary people who only meet the minimum requirements of, say, conditional honesty. Given the constructed fact that the extremely wide range of middlemen, from core cases to peripheral cases, can be included in the system, the possibility existed to equate the group of middlemen with all society members. However, the enactment of this possibility remains to be discussed in Chap. 5 with regard to the justification of the rightfulness of contracts.

Table 2 The partly open system of middlemen/third parties

Levels	"Professionals"	"High-ups"	"Nonprofessionals or every-men"
Primary middlemen	Introducers	Guarantors	Witnesses
Secondary middlemen	Arbitrators	Peacemakers	
Other third parties	E.g., geomancers, matchmakers	E.g., heads of the family, clan, local troops	E.g., relatives, neighbors, friends

Put succinctly, the partly open system of middlemen suggests that, as a whole, the middleman should not simply be understood as an agent within the bureaucratic hierarchy, who acted as a go-between in bringing messages from one party to another on behalf of the other side. Rather, owing to the characteristics of both convergence and divergence, the middleman is both sufficient to provide professional services and was not limited to a highly concentrated closed group.

6 Conclusion

Contemporary scholarship on traditional Chinese middlemen tends to view them in terms of their background and the way in which they were embedded in the social sphere. However, rather than capturing their lively social lives, this chapter presented and explained the figure of middlemen within the dull and mechanical framework of contracts.

According to this approach, middlemen of the Qingshui River region were discussed at the two levels, the primary and secondary, and the four roles to which they are assigned at these two levels were examined at length. A focus was especially given to on their neglected technical aspect: the genuinely technical introducer is pointed out and the arbitrator is also specially separated from peacemakers. These findings all suggest that a middleman could be a vital constructional element of the contract mechanism even without the "face" or other social relations, but through various other ways, such as when their technicality served as the "open sesame" for entering into contracts.

The essential participation of the middleman in contracts marks their role as the third party. Other atypical middleman-like contractual figures who acted as third parties are incorporated into a re-defined concept of middlemen, thereby making the middleman a representative of all third-party contracting participants. Ultimately, the partly open system is established and used to elucidate the social source of middlemen.

Although this chapter is devoted to understanding middlemen within the context of contracts, after a thorough clarification of the contractual middleman, it has been revealed that the middleman acted as a medium of communication between the inside and outside worlds of the contract. This aspect will be of crucial importance in the following discussion, which concerns the relationship between contracts and the social order.

References

1. *Zhongguo shaoshu minzu shehui lishi diaocha ziliao congkan* xiuding bianji weiyuanhui, ed. 2009. *Miaozu shehui lishi diaocha* [Investigation to the society and history of the Miao people], vol. 1, 57. Beijing: Minzu chubanshe.

2. Aihara, Yoshiyuki. 2003. Shindai Chūgoku Kishū Shō Shimizu Kō ryūiki niokeru ringyō keiei no ichi sokumen—'Kishū Myaozoku ringyō keiyaku monjo kaihen' Ping'ao Zhai bunsho o jirei toshite [Forest management in the Qingshui River Basin in Guizhou province in Qing China: A case study of the documents from Ping'ao Village]. In *Kishū Myaozoku ringyō keiyaku monjo kaihen (1736–1950-nen)* [Old forestry contracts of the Miao in Guizhou, 1736–1950], ed. Christian Daniels, Yougeng Yang, and Fusaji Takeuchi, 127. Tokyo: Tōkyō gaikokugo daigaku Ajia Afurika gengo bunka kenkyūjo.
3. An, Zunhua, and Zhicheng Pan, eds. 2016. *Tudi qiyue wenshu jiaoshi* [Collation and annotation of land-related contract manuscripts], vol. 2, 126–127, 184–185, 218–219. Guiyang: Guizhou minzu chubanshe.
4. An, Zunhua, and Zhicheng Pan, eds. 2016. *Tudi qiyue wenshu jiaoshi* [Collation and annotation of land-related contract manuscripts], vol. 1, 14–15. Guiyang: Guizhou minzu chubanshe.
5. Anonymous. 1918. Dazheng qinian maiduren Chenshiman chifen tudi maimai yuyue shu (No. LBA259291) [A contract of sale in 1918]. Academia Sinica (digitalarchives.tw), Feng Chia University. Accessed 8 Oct 2020. http://catalog.digitalarchives.tw/item/00/5e/37/b7.html.
6. Bix, Brian H. 2018. Kelsen, hart, and legal normativity. *Revus* 34: 1–17.
7. Chen, Feng, and Guobin Cai. 2013. *Zhongguo caizheng tongshi—Qing dai caizheng shi* [A general history of finance in China—Financial history in the Qing dynasty], vol. 7, 664. Changsha: Hunan renmin chubanshe.
8. Chen, Jinquan, and Wanhua Du, eds. 2008. *Guizhou Wendouzhai Miaozu qiyue falü wenshu huibian—Jiang Yuanze jiacang qiyue wenshu* [The compilation of contractual and legal manuscripts of the Miao from Wendou Village, Guizhou—Manuscripts from Jiang Yuanze's family collection], 344. Beijing: Renmin chubanshe.
9. Chen, Jinquan, and Xiaojuan Hou. 2010. Lun Qing dai Qiandongnan Miao zhai de jiufen jiejue—Yi Wendou Miao zhai cizhuang wei duixiang de yanjiu [Brief analyses of disputes settlement in Miao villages in Qiandongnan in the Qing dynasty—On the basis of legislation documents of Wendou Village]. *Xiangtan daxue xuebao (zhexue shehui kexue ban)* 34 (1): 18–23.
10. Chen, Jinquan, and Wanhua Du, eds. 2015. *Guizhou Wendouzhai Miaozu qiyue falü wenshu huibian—Jiang Qigui jiacang qiyue wenshu* [The compilation of contractual and legal manuscripts of the Miao from Wendou Village, Guizhou—Manuscripts from Jiang Qigui's family collection], 5, 213. Beijing: Renmin chubanshe.
11. Chen, Shengqiang. 2010. Zhongren dui Qing dai tudi juemai qiyue de yingxiang jiqi jiejian yiyi [The impact of middlemen to land contracts of absolute sale in the Qing dynasty and its referential value]. *Faxue pinglun* (3): 155–160.
12. Chen, Shengqiang and Jiahong Wang. 2010. Zhongren zai Qing dai tudi juemai qiyue zhong de gongneng—Jian yu xiandai xiangguan gainian de bijiao yanjiu [Functions of middlemen in the contract of absolute sale of land in the Qing dynasty—And a comparative study with its modern counterpart]. *Falü wenhua yanjiu* 6: 438–451.
13. Cheng, Zeshi. 2011. *Qingshuijiang wenshu zhi fayi chutan* [A primary legal research on the Qingshui River manuscripts], 120–121. Beijing: Zhongguo zhengfa daxue chubanshe.
14. Cohen, Myron L. 1992. Family management and family division in contemporary rural China. *The China Quarterly* 130: 377.
15. Daniels, Christian, Yougeng Yang, and Fusaji Takeuchi, eds. 2001. *Kishū Myaozoku ringyō keiyaku monjo kaihen (1736–1950-nen)* [Old forestry contracts of the Miao in Guizhou, 1736–1950], vol. 1, A-0133. Tokyo: Tōkyō gaikokugo daigaku Ajia Afurika gengo bunka kenkyūjo.
16. Daniels, Christian, Yougeng Yang, and Fusaji Takeuchi, eds. 2002. *Kishū Myaozoku ringyō keiyaku monjo kaihen (1736–1950-nen)* [Old forestry contracts of the Miao in Guizhou, 1736–1950], vol. 2, B-0092, B-0094, B-0102. Tokyo: Tōkyō gaikokugo daigaku Ajia Afurika gengo bunka kenkyūjo.
17. Daniels, Christian, Yougeng Yang, and Fusaji Takeuchi, eds. 2003. *Kishū Myaozoku ringyō keiyaku monjo kaihen (1736–1950-nen)* [Old forestry contracts of the Miao in Guizhou, 1736–1950], vol. 3, D-0031. Tokyo: Tōkyō gaikokugo daigaku Ajia Afurika gengo bunka kenkyūjo.

18. Duara, Prasenjit. 1988. *Culture, Power, and the State: Rural North China, 1900–1942*, 181–191. Stanford, California: Stanford University Press.
19. Duara, Prasenjit. 1990. Elites and the structures of authority in the villages of North China, 1900–1949. In *Chinese local elites and patterns of dominance*, ed. Joseph W. Esherick and Mary Backus Rankin, 261–281. Berkeley, Los Angeles, Oxford: University of California Press.
20. Dworkin, Ronald M. 1967. The model of rules. *The University of Chicago Law Review* 35 (1): 19.
21. Fei, Xiaotong. 1985. *Xiangtu Zhongguo* [Rural China], reprinted ed., 88. Beijing: Shenghuo, dushu, xinzhi sanlian shudian.
22. Foerste, Karla. 2000. Eine Methode der Streitvermeidung: Die »dritte Partei« bei Begründung und Durchsetzung von Verträgen im traditionellen China. *Rabels Zeitschrift für ausländisches und internationales Privatrecht* 64 (1): 123–142.
23. Gao, Cong, and Hongpei Tan, eds. 2013. *Guizhou Qingshuijiang liuyu Ming Qing tusi qiyue wenshu, Jiunan pian* [Tusi contract manuscripts in the Qingshui River Basin of Guizhou during the Ming-Qing eras, Jiunan volume], 141, 445, 451. Beijing: Minzu chubanshe.
24. Guizhou sheng dang'an guan, Qiandongnan zhou dang'an guan, and Jianhe xian dang'an guan, eds. 2017. *Guizhou Qingshuijiang wenshu, Jianhe juan* [Qingshui River manuscripts, Jianhe County volume], 5 vols., vol. 1, 51. Guiyang: Guizhou renmin chubanshe.
25. Guizhou sheng minjian wenxue gongzuozu, ed. 1985. *Minjian wenxue ziliao, Dian Qian Xiangxi Miaozu geyao ji* [Materials of folk literature, a collection of Miao folk songs in Yunnan, Guizhou, and west Hunan], vol. 29, 299–300. Guiyang: Zhongguo minjian wenyi yanjiuhui Guizhou fenhui.
26. Guizhou sheng Jinping xianzhi bianzuan weiyuanhui, ed. 1986. *Jinping xianzhi* [Jinping County gazetteer], 521. Guiyang: Guizhou renmin chubanshe.
27. Guo, Ruijun. 2014. Huizhou qiyue wenshu 'zhongren' yanjiu huimou yu sikao [A literature review of studies on middlemen in Huizhou contract documents]. *Huaihua xueyuan xuebao* 33 (12): 18.
28. Guo, Ruijun. 2017. Qing dai Huizhou qiyue wenshu suojian 'zhongren' shenfen tantao [A study on the status of middlemen in Huizhou contract documents in the Qing dynasty]. *Dang'anxue tongxun* (4): 32–41.
29. Guo, Ruijun. 2017. Huizhou qiyue suojian 'zhongren' chengwei [Designations of middlemen in Huizhou contract documents]. *Huaibei shifan daxue xuebao (zhexue shehui kexue ban)* 38 (1): 47–50.
30. Guo, Ruijun, and Lingqi Li. 2016. Qing dai Huizhou qiyue wenshu suojian 'zhongren' baochou [The research on zhongren's reward in Huizhou documents of the Qing dynasty]. *Zhongguo jingjishi yanjiu* (6): 32–41.
31. Hamilton, Gary G. and Zheng Wang. 1992. *From the soil, the foundations of Chinese society: A translation of Fei Xiaotong's Xiangtu Zhongguo, with an introduction and epilogue*, 139. Berkeley, Los Angeles, London: University of California Press.
32. Han, Shiyuan. 2018. *Hetongfa zonglun* [The law of contract], 4th ed., 115. Beijing: Falü chubanshe.
33. Hansen, Valerie. 1995. *Negotiating daily life in traditional China: How ordinary people used contracts, 600–1400*, 5–6. New Haven and London: Yale University Press.
34. Hart, H. L. A. 2012. *The concept of law*, 3rd ed., 79–99. Oxford: Oxford University Press.
35. Hase, Patrick H. 2013. *Custom, land and livelihood in rural South China: The traditional land law of Hong Kong's new territories, 1750–1950*, 143–156. Hong Kong: Hong Kong University Press.
36. Herman, John E. 2006. The cant of conquest: Tusi offices and China's political incorporation of the Southwest frontier. In *Empire at the margins culture, ethnicity, and frontier in early modern China*, ed. Pamela Kyle Crossley, Helen F. Siu, and Donald S. Sutton, 139. Berkeley, Los Angeles, London: University of California Press.
37. Hsiao, Kung-ch'üan. 1979. *Compromise in Imperial China*. Seattle: School of International Studies, University of Washington.

38. Hu, Qian. 2008. Zhongren tiaochu yu Qing dai minshi jiufen jiejue [The mediation of middlemen and the civil dispute settlement in the Qing dynasty]. *Yantai daxue xuebao (zhexue shehui kexue ban)* 21 (3): 51–54.
39. Hu, Tieqiu. 2015. *Ming Qing xiejia yanjiu* [A study on *xiejia* in the Ming and Qing dynasties], 68. Shanghai: Shanghai guji chubanshe.
40. Huang, Philip C.C. 1993. Between informal mediation and formal adjudication: The third realm of Qing civil justice. *Modern China* 19 (3): 251–298.
41. Huang, Philip C.C. 1996. *Civil justice in China: Representation and practice in the Qing*, 52 ff. Stanford, California: Stanford University Press.
42. Huang, Philip C.C. 2010. *Chinese civil justice, past and present*, reprinted ed., 26. Lanham, Maryland: Rowman & Littlefield Publishers, Inc.
43. Huang, Philip C C. 2014. Between informal mediation and formal adjudication: The third realm of Qing civil justice. In *The history and theory of legal practice in China: Toward a historical-social jurisprudence*, ed. Philip C.C. Huang and Kathryn Bernhardt, 184. Leiden/Boston: Brill.
44. Jiang, Ming, Caimao Wu, and Chunjun Yang, eds. 2015. *Quyu shehui shi gailun* [General introduction to regional social history], 137–138. Chengdu: Xinan jiaotong daxue chubanshe.
45. Jinping xian Sanjiang zhen renmin zhengfu, ed. 2011. *Sanjiang zhen zhi* [Sanjiang town gazetteer], 840. Jinping: Jinping xian Sanjiang zhen renmin zhengfu.
46. Jinping xian difangzhi bianzuan weiyuanhui, ed. 2011. *Jinping xianzhi 1991–2009* [Jinping County gazetteer 1991–2009], vol. 2, 1269. Beijing: Fangzhi chubanshe.
47. Kang, Caiyun. 2013. Gudai qiyue wenshu de zhongbaoren chengwei yuci yanbian yanjiu [The diachronic evolution of mediator appellation words in ancient contract documents]. Master dissertation, Shaanxi Normal University, 48.
48. Katz, Paul R. 2009. *Divine Justice: Religion and the Development of Chinese Legal Culture*, 47. Abingdon: Routledge.
49. Kelsen, Hans. 1941. The pure theory of law and analytical jurisprudence. *Harvard Law Review* 55 (1): 44–70.
50. Kishimoto, Mio. 1998. Ming Qing qiyu wenshu [Contract manuscripts in the Ming-Qing period], (trans. Yaxin Wang). In *Ming Qing shiqi de minshi shenpan yu minjian qiyue* [Civil justice and civil contracts in the Ming-Qing period], ed. Yaxin Wang and Zhiping Liang, 301–302. Beijing: Falü chubanshe.
51. Kötz, Hein. 2017. *European contract law*, (trans. Gill Mertens and Tony Weir), 2nd ed., 19. Oxford: Oxford University Press.
52. Li, Jinzheng. 2003. 20 shiji shangbanqi Zhongguo xiangcun jingji jiaoyi de zhongbaoren [Middlemen in economic transactions in Chinese villages in the first half of the 20th century]. *Jindaishi yanjiu* (6): 116–120.
53. Li, Zhuhuan. 1997. Zhongguo chuantong minshi qiyue zhong de zhongren xianxiang [The phenomenon of middlemen in traditional Chinese civil contracts]. *Faxue yanjiu* (6): 138–143.
54. Li, Tao, and Shengqiang Chen. 2008. Zhongren zai Qing dai siqi zhong gongneng zhi jiyin fenxi [A genetic analysis on functions of middlemen in private contracts in the Qing dynasty]. *Henan shehui kexue* 15 (5): 61–63.
55. Liang, Cong. 2008. *Qing dai Qingshuijiang xiayou cunzhai shehui de qiyue guifan yu zhixu* [Contractual norm and order in the village society of the lower reaches of Qingshui River in Qing China], 118–122. Beijing: Renmin chubanshe.
56. Liang, Mingwu. 2012. *Ming Qing shiqi mucai shangpin jingji yanjiu* [A study on timber commodity economy of Ming and Qing eras], 154–155. Beijing: Zhongguo linye chubanshe.
57. Liang, Zhiping. 1996. *Qing dai xiguanfa: Shehui yu guojia* [Customary law in the Qing: Society and state], 120–126. Beijing: Zhongguo zhengfa daxue chubanshe.
58. Liang, Zhiping. 1998. Pinglun [Commentaries]. In *Ming Qing shiqi de minshi shenpan yu minjian qiyue* [Civil justice and civil contracts in the Ming-Qing period], ed. Yaxin Wang and Zhiping Liang, 442–456. Beijing: Falü chubanshe.
59. Liu, Gaoyong and Qi Qu. 2011. Lun Qing dai tianzhai qiyue dingli zhong de disanfang qunti: Gongneng jiqi yiyi [The third party in land and house contracting in the Qing dynasty: Functions and meanings]. *Xibu faxue pinglun* (3): 16–20.

60. Liu, Zhenyu. 2011. Qing dai Qiandongnan Miaozu shehui bianqian yu minjian jiufen jiejue—Yi Wendou zhai jiefen wenshu wei yanjiu duixiang [Social change and civil dispute settlement of the Miao in Qiandongnan during the Qing dynasty—Evidence from the dispute settlement manuscripts in Wendou Village]. *Jiangsu jingguan xueyuan xuebao* 26 (3): 104.
61. Mao, Yongjun. 2012. Gudai qiyue 'zhongren' xianxiang de fawenhua beijing—Yi Qing dai tudi maimai qiyue wei li [The legal cultural background of the phenomenon of 'middlemen' in traditional contracts—Based on the land contracts of sale in the Qing dynasty]. *Shehui kexuejia* (9): 107–110.
62. Pan, Zhicheng, Dahua Wu, and Cong Liang, eds. 2012. *Linye jingying wenshu* [Manuscripts on forestry management], vol. 2, 88. Guiyang: Guizhou minzu chubanshe.
63. Pan, Zhicheng, Dahua Wu, and Cong Liang, eds. 2014. *Qingjiang si an yanjiu* [Studies on the four cases in the Qingshui River region], vol. 3, 51–61. Guiyang: Guizhou minzu chubanshe.
64. Qu, Jian. 2012. Qing zhonghouqi Qiandongnan Wendou zhai Miaozu dianzhi yanjiu [A treatise on the dian of the Miaos in Wendou Village of southeastern Guizhou in the mid and late Qing dynasty]. *Minjian fa* 11: 203–204.
65. Qu, Jian. 2013. Qing dai Wendou zhai zhongren zhidu [The zhongren system of Wendou Village in the Qing dynasty]. *Minjian fa* 12: 260–282.
66. Qu, Jian. 2018. Qingshuijiang linye qiyue zhong de caifaquan: Guifan jiqi shijian [Harvesting rights in forestry contracts of Qingshui River region: Norms and practices]. *Guizhou daxue xuebao (shehui kexue ban)* 36 (3): 51 ff.
67. Qu, Jian. 2019. *Yanchu fasui: Caiyun huangmu andu jiaojian yu yanjiu (xia)* [Taking promulgated words as law: Collation, annotation, and study of 'Records of the procurement of imperial timber'], 2 vols., vol. 2, 230. New Taipei City: Hua Mulan wenhua shiye youxian gongsi.
68. Qu, Jian. 2019. *Yanchu fasui: Caiyun huangmu andu jiaojian yu yanjiu (shang)* [Taking promulgated words as law: Collation, annotation, and study of 'Records of the procurement of imperial timber'], 2 vols., vol. 1, 83–87. New Taipei City: Hua Mulan wenhua shiye youxian gongsi.
69. Rodman, William L., and Dorothy Ayers Counts, eds. 1983. *Middlemen and Brokers in Oceania*, vii. Lanham: University Press of America.
70. Sokolowski, Robert. 2000. *Introduction to Phenomenology*, 14. Cambridge: Cambridge University Press.
71. Takeuchi, Fusaji. 2003. Narukami to nakan no aida—Shindai Kishū Myaozoku ringyō keiyaku bunsho ni miru nae zoku no shūzoku to funsō shori [Between divine judgment and lawsuit in court: Dispute resolution among the Miao people as seen in the forestry contracts in Qing Guizhou]. In *Kishū Myaozoku ringyō keiyaku monjo kaihen (1736–1950-nen)* [Old forestry contracts of the Miao in Guizhou, 1736–1950], ed. Christian Daniels, Yougeng Yang, and Fusaji Takeuchi, 107–108. Tokyo: Tōkyō gaikokugo daigaku Ajia Afurika gengo bunka kenkyūjo.
72. Terada, Hiroaki. 2012. Ming Qing shiqi fazhixu zhong 'yue' de xingzhi [The nature of 'yue' in the legal order of Ming-Qing China], (trans. Yaxin Wang). In *Quanli yu yuanyi: Sitian haoming Zhongguo fashi lunji* [Rights and injustice: Hiroaki Terada's essays on Chinese legal history], ed. Hiroaki Terada, 174 ff. Beijing: Qinghua daxue chubanshe.
73. Wakefield, David. 1998. *Fenjia: Household division and inheritance in Qing and republican China*, 55. Honolulu: University of Hawai'i Press.
74. Wang, Fengmei, and Yonglun Zhao. 2013. Qingshuijiang wenshu shuxie chengshi de zongzu xing tantao—Yi Tianzhu xian Gaoniang zhen Diliang cun qiyue wenshu weili [A probe into the patriarchal clans from the writing style in the Qingshui River manuscripts: Based on Diliang Village, Gaoniang Town in Tianzhu County]. *Guizhou daxue xuebao (shehui kexue ban)* 31 (4): 68.
75. Wang, Shuaiyi. 2016. Ming Qing shidai de zhongren yu qiyue zhixu [Zhongren and the contract order of the Ming and Qing dynasties]. *Zhengfa luntan* 34 (2): 170–182.
76. Wang, Zhiyuan, Yourong Shang, Qiang Wang, and Fuliang Liu, eds. 2007. *Guzhi shiyi* [A collection of old paper manuscripts], vol. 2, 53. Xi'an: Sanqin chubanshe.

77. Wang, Zongxun, ed. 2015. *Jiachi siheyuan wenshu kaoshi* [Collection and annotation of the Jiachi siheyuan manuscripts], 4 vols., vol. 1, 294. Guiyang: Guizhou minzu chubanshe.
78. Weiner, Annette B. 1983. Cultural: Middlemen and Brokers in Oceania. William L. Rodman and Dorothy Ayers Counts, eds. *American Anthropologist* 85 (2): 444.
79. Wu, Caimao. 2014. Lijiang, mingshen yu mingguan: Minjian wenxian suo jian Ming Qing Qiandongnan jiufen jiejue jizhi de duoyuanhua yanjiu [Arbitration, proceeding to the gods, and complaint to the official: Dispute resolution from the local historical documents in Qiandongnan area in the Ming and Qing dynasties]. *Zhongguo shehui lishi pinglun* 15: 271–277.
80. Wu, Caimao. 2016. Ming dai yilai Qingshuijiang wenshu shuxie geshi de bianhua yu minzhong xiguan de bianqian [The changes of the writing forms of Qingshui River manuscripts and the transition of popular customs since the Ming dynasty]. *Xinan daxue xuebao (shehui kexue ban)* 42 (4): 185.
81. Wu, Caimao. 2017. *Qing dai Miaozu funü de hunyin yu quanli: Yi Qingshuijiang wenshu wei zhongxin* [Marriage and rights of the Miao women in the Qing dyanasty: Evidence from the Qingshui River manuscripts]. Guiyang: Guizhou minzu chubanshe.
82. Wu, Xiangxiang, ed. [1923] 1962. *Zhongguo minshi xiguan daquan* [A compendium of Chinese popular customs], 40, 65. Taipei: Wenxing shudian.
83. Wu, Xin. 2004. Ming Qing shiqi de zhongren jiqi falü zuoyong yu yiyi—Yi Ming Qing Huizhou difang qiyue weili [Zhongren in the Ming-Qing eras and its legal functions and meaning—Based on local contracts of Huizhou in the Ming-Qing eras]. *Nanjing daxue falü pinglun* (Spring): 116–180.
84. Xu, Xiaoguang. 2006. *Qingshuijiang liuyu linye jingji fazhi de lishi huisu* [A historical study on the forestry economic legal system in the Qingshui River Basin], 33. Guiyang: Guizhou renmin chubanshe.
85. Yu, Weiyuan. 1986. Wo dui guangmu de renshi [My understanding about *guangmu*]. In *Changzhou shi mucai zhi (1800–1985)* [Changzhou timber gazetteer (1800–1985)], ed. Changzhou shi mucai gongsi, 131–132. Changzhou: Changzhou shi mucai gongsi.
86. Zeng, Xianyi. 2009. Mediation in China—Past and present. *Asia Pacific Law Review* 17 (Special on Mediation): 1–30.
87. Zhang, Guanghong. 2017. Mingshen yu mingguan: Qing dai Qingshuijiang liuyu minjian jiufen duoyuan jiejue jizhi shitan [Appealing to the gods or to the court: The multiple mechanisms of civil dispute settlement in the Qingshui River Basin in the Qing dynasty]. *Guizhou daxue xuebao (shehui kexue ban)* 35 (2): 30.
88. Zhang, Xinmin, ed. 2014. *Tianzhu wenshu* [Tianzhu manuscripts], vol. 1(10), 80. Nanjing: Jiangsu renmin chubanshe.
89. Zhang, Yingqiang, and Tengwen Hu. 2004. *Jinping* [Jinping], 123. Beijing: Shenghuo, dushu, xinzhi sanlian shudian.
90. Zhang, Yingqiang, and Zongxun Wang, eds. 2007. *Qingshuijiang wenshu* [Qingshui River manuscripts], vol. 1(8), 317. Guilin: Guangxi shifan daxue chubanshe.
91. Zhang, Yingqiang, and Zongxun Wang, eds. 2007. *Qingshuijiang wenshu* [Qingshui River manuscripts], vol. 1(13), 91. Guilin: Guangxi shifan daxue chubanshe.
92. Zhang, Yingqiang, and Zongxun Wang, eds. 2007. *Qingshuijiang wenshu* [Qingshui River manuscripts], vol. 1(11), 222. Guilin: Guangxi shifan daxue chubanshe.
93. Zhang, Yingqiang, and Zongxun Wang, eds. 2007. *Qingshuijiang wenshu* [Qingshui River manuscripts], vol. 1(12), 20. Guilin: Guangxi shifan daxue chubanshe.
94. Zhang, Yingqiang, and Zongxun Wang, eds. 2007. *Qingshuijiang wenshu* [Qingshui River manuscripts], vol. 1(10), 164. Guilin: Guangxi shifan daxue chubanshe.
95. Zhang, Yingqiang, and Zongxun Wang, eds. 2007. *Qingshuijiang wenshu* [Qingshui River manuscripts], vol. 1(1), 40. Guilin: Guangxi shifan daxue chubanshe.
96. Zhang, Yingqiang, and Zongxun Wang, eds. 2007. *Qingshuijiang wenshu* [Qingshui River manuscripts], vol. 1(4), 45. Guilin: Guangxi shifan daxue chubanshe.
97. Zhang, Yingqiang, and Zongxun Wang, eds. 2009. *Qingshuijiang wenshu* [Qingshui River manuscripts], vol. 2(2), 176. Guilin: Guangxi shifan daxue chubanshe.

98. Zhang, Yingqiang, and Zongxun Wang, eds. 2011. *Qingshuijiang wenshu* [Qingshui River manuscripts], vol. 3(10), 105. Guilin: Guangxi shifan daxue chubanshe.
99. Zhang, Yingqiang, and Zongxun Wang, eds. 2011. *Qingshuijiang wenshu* [Qingshui River manuscripts], vol. 3(7), 177. Guilin: Guangxi shifan daxue chubanshe.
100. Zhang, Yingqiang, and Zongxun Wang, eds. 2011. *Qingshuijiang wenshu* [Qingshui River manuscripts], vol. 3(9), 286–287. Guilin: Guangxi shifan daxue chubanshe.
101. Zhang, Yingqiang, and Zongxun Wang, eds. 2011. *Qingshuijiang wenshu* [Qingshui River manuscripts], vol. 3(8), 150. Guilin: Guangxi shifan daxue chubanshe.
102. Zhou, Dao and Mengna Fu. 2014. Qingshuijiang wenshu zhongren de juese yu gongneng tanxi [A study on the role and function of middlemen in the Qingshui River manuscripts]. *Wenshi bolan (lilun)* (8): 12–14.
103. Zhou, Jin. 2013. Qing dai tudi juemai qiyue zhongren de shuangxiangxing jujian gongneng [The bidirectional function of middlemen in land contracts of absolute sale in the Qing dynasty]. *Changjiang daxue xueao (shehui kexue ban)* 36 (5): 28–31.
104. Zhou, Jin and Tao Li. 2009. Tongxing zhongren zai Qing dai tudi juemai qiyue zhong de falü juese yanjiu—Cong yu maifang de guanxi tantao [A study of the legal role of middlemen from the same clan in land contracts of absolute sale in the Qing dynasty—From the perspective of their relationship with the vendor]. *Guizhou shehui kexue* 239 (11): 132–136.
105. Zhou, Yaoming, ed. 1994. *Hanzu minjian jiaoji fengsu* [Social customs of the Han Chinese], 126, 139. Nanning: Guanxi jiaoyu chubanshe.

Chapter 4
Scribes

1 Introduction: Taking Scribes Seriously

1.1 Scribes and the Writing of Contracts

As one of the two core pillars of the contract system, the scribe has not received as much academic attention as the middleman. The research materials for scholars on the Ming and Qing dynasties have been greatly enriched by the new emergence of contract manuscripts, but to some extent the process of producing these manuscripts seems to be often overlooked. Another frequently ignored fact is that the contractual relationships and societal circumstances that scholars have intended to explore through these manuscripts were written on the paper character by character by someone who was most likely a scribe. This process of "writing" indicates that, compared with the printed book, its nature of being a "manuscript" determines that the contract's text is mostly original and personal, and thus more accurately reflects the everyday life of ordinary people.[1] In other words, it must be borne in mind that contracts were produced and should therefore be understood within their unique writing contexts. There were certainly many factors that played a role in these contexts, even including the broader historical and spatial backgrounds, but, among many other factors, the key protagonist in the production process was undoubtedly the group of writers that was for the most part formed by scribes. For they organized the various information from the contracting parties and beyond, and transformed and expressed it in a satisfactory written form, thereby conclusively making it a contract.

As is widely acknowledged, apart from a limited number of holographic contracts,[2] many more contracts were written by scribes (*daibi* or *daibiren*), who thus became, along with the middleman, in-between figures in contract activities.

---

[1] See Zhang [121].

[2] The different ways of writing contracts will be analyzed in detail later in this chapter.

J. Qu, *Social Order through Contracts*,
https://doi.org/10.1007/978-981-33-4947-6_4

As a matter of fact, scribes are also commonly seen in contract activities in other societies throughout different eras. Apart from the Chinese world, provisions and records related to contractual scribes can be found in both Roman and Islamic worlds, respectively in *The Institutes of Justinian* and *The Qur'an*:

> [W]here there is a written contract, we have enacted that a sale is not to be considered completed unless an instrument of sale has been drawn up, being either written by the contracting parties, or at least signed by them. [I]f written by others; or if drawn up by a *tabellio*,[3] it must be formally complete and finished throughout.[4]

> O you who believe! When you contract a debt for a fixed period, write it down. Let a scribe write it down in justice between you. Let not the scribe refuse to write as Allâh has taught him, so let him write. Let him (the debtor) who incurs the liability dictate, and he must fear Allâh, his Lord, and diminish not anything of what he owes. But if the debtor is of poor understanding, or weak, or is unable to dictate for himself, then let his guardian dictate in justice...Let neither scribe nor witness suffer any harm, but if you do (such harm), it would be wickedness in you.[5]

These provisions and descriptions of scribal activities concerning contracts originate from completely different times and have completely different backgrounds, yet on the whole there was unsurprisingly no substantial difference between the aforementioned two instances and the situation in a Qing village. In all eras and regions with a relatively low level of literacy and contractual knowledge, the expert scribe was a key link for contractual transactions based on written documents, which presents a real significance from the perspective of functionalism.

However, as noted, the contractual scribe in late imperial China has not enjoyed an academic attention that is commensurate with its importance.[6] Unlike the middleman, the scribe was a figure of much less popularity in previous accounts regarding the activities of traditional Chinese contracts.[7]

This situation may have been caused by several factors. First and foremost, although the number of contracts in existence from the Ming and Qing dynasties is huge, the material on scribes is extremely scarce. The most obvious evidence for studying scribes is merely the signatures given by them at the end of each contract, which makes the research task rather difficult. Second, under certain circumstances, some might confuse the conceptual boundaries between the middleman and the scribe and subordinate the latter within the former,[8] which obviously weakens the importance of the scribe as an independent research subject. Third, unlike manuscripts in

---

[3] A scrivener/legal clerk/notary under the Roman Empire who draws up legal documents, e.g. contracts and testaments.

[4] Sandars [72].

[5] Al-Hilâlî and Khân [2].

[6] As a comparison, for studies on scribes in early China, see, e.g., Giele [26], Smith [76], Richter [69], Ma [53]. It needs to be stressed that, in the context of the ancient world, scribes were understood as "writing specialists" who "not only composed and made copies of texts, but also carried out most of the daily administrative tasks which ensured the proper functioning of a state." See ibid., 1.

[7] For discussions which touch on contractual scribes in Ming-Qing China and their writing practice, see Zhao [122], Feng [23], Wu [91]. The first chapter of Wu's work mainly focuses on the "official scribes" in Qing Taiwan, and only discusses contractual scribes in its fourth section of the chapter.

[8] See, e.g., Guo [28].

earlier times (mostly bamboo slips and silk), the scholarly importance of the materiality of paper manuscripts in late imperial China has not seemingly attracted enough attention, as noted in Chap. 2, and therefore the scribe has not yet been taken seriously in previous studies.

In fact, although direct materials seem to be lacking, from another angle, as most contracts were written by the scribe, every single piece of the manuscript can be seen as direct evidence for discussing the writing practice of the scribe. As it is believed that "writing was central to early modern Chinese legal culture,"[9] the process of production might to some degree determine the essential aspect of the contract. Thus, a better understanding of contracts requires more attention to be paid to not only the content of the contract but also the practice of writing it.

1.2 *Contractual Scribes, Official Scribes, and Litigation Lawyers*

As this chapter focuses on contract writing, it is necessary to distinguish it from several other similar styles of writing. Those writers who write contracts on behalf of contracting parties, in circumstances in which the latter might not be capable to do it by themselves, were commonly designated as scribes (*daibi*), or contractual scribes[10] in particular. The contractual scribe was different from the other two easily confused types of writers: the official scribe[11] (*guandaishu*) or so-called "scrivener" (*daishu*)[12] and the litigation lawyer[13] (*songshi*). The former term refers to those professionals who were "selected by the yamen on the basis of an examination" and "issued a seal signifying quasi-official status"[14] to write accusations or petitions for complaints by the letter of the law,[15] while the latter could also provide a similar service of writing plaints and made money out of it even though they did not possess an official status.[16]

The differences of these two figures from the contractual scribe are firstly connected to the distinction between urban and rural areas. As has been noted, "there was probably not enough demand among the villagers in a smallish area to support a

---

[9]Hegel and Carlitz [32]. It has to be noted that this opinion, in its original context, is based on the facts that "law codes are written documents" and "legal procedure engendered so much writing.".

[10]Their writing activities were also described as "writing civil contracts on behalf of others" (*daixie minjian qizi*), see Chun-Ying Wu, "Taiwan daishu de lishi kaocha," 157.

[11]On "the yamen scribes," see Huang [34]. Also, for scribes in the bureaucratic system and "canton scribes" at the county level in late imperial China, see Li [40].

[12]See Scogin [73], Allee [3].

[13]Sometimes the term is translated as "litigation masters," see Zhou [125]. Alternatively, they have been called "litigation instigators," see Philip C. C. Huang, *Civil Justice in China*, 152.

[14]Mark A. Allee, *Law and Local Society in Late Imperial China*, 176.

[15]See Wu [93]; Philip C. C. Huang, *Civil Justice in China*, 164.

[16]See You [103].

full-time plaint-writer or legal advisor," while "[i]n large towns and cities like county seats, on the other hand, professional plaint-writers may have been quite common."[17] Evidence of a similar discrepancy between the village and the city can be seen in the customs survey. For instance, in the rural areas of Yun County of Hubei province, 3% of the contract amount was normally taken as the scribe's fee, while the survey report underscored that such customs did not exist in the urban areas of the same place.[18]

Apart from the distinction between the village and the city, the most essential difference between the two alternative kinds (official scribes and litigation lawyers) and contractual scribes was that the former were more "official," as indicated by the appearance of their names, while the latter were relatively speaking more "private" or "civil." Official scribes and litigation lawyers were both litigation-oriented, insofar as they were involved private disputes that were ready to go to the official court for adjudicating; the documents they wrote (mostly plaints and related documents) acted as the link between the civilian and the official. In contrast, what a contractual scribe needed to face was more private, since in most cases both parties of the contract were private subjects. If one may draw a comparison with modern lawyers, the difference between the two is similar to the difference between litigation and non-litigation legal services.[19] Further, the official scribe and litigation lawyer primarily needed to consider the policies and regulations issued by the authorities, while contractual scribes seem to have been more concerned about local customs.[20] This aspect also relates to the fundamental difference between the two writing practices. In view of this, this study mainly focuses on the contractual scribes and their writing practices in village societies, and, unless otherwise specified, the term "scribe" refers to a contractual scribe in this chapter.

1.3 *The Institution of Scribes and Its Operation*

The contract cannot be separated from its production process, which is a process of writing, and the scribe certainly played a pivotal role in it. But what was the exact role that a contractual scribe played?

Some think that the contractual scribe only acts as a "printer" which makes paper copies of the information that is the object of input, thereby describing the role

[17]Philip C. C. Huang, *Civil Justice in China*, 164.

[18]See Wu [95].

[19]In modern China, a lawyer may "[accept] authorization to provide non-litigation legal services," and "[w]hen acting as an agent in litigation or non-litigation legal matters, a lawyer shall, within the limits of authorization, protect the lawful rights and interests of the client." See Law of the People's Republic of China on Lawyers, Art. 28 (7), Art. 30 (2007). As for the scope of service of non-litigation lawyers, see Ren [68].

[20]It is believed that "while writing contracts for others, [contractual scribes] were based on civil, unwritten, and local customs, and the government's written regulations on land sales do not seem to be considered." See Chun-Ying Wu, "Taiwan daishu de lishi kaocha," 59.

of the scribe as a simple and mechanical one.[21] This opinion seems to be widely accepted in previous scholarship and, in particular, in the study of customs surveys. For example, in a report of the customs in Taiwan, it is stated that "the scribe can only prove the existence of the contract but has nothing to do with the disputes raised [by the contract] later and is not responsible for the correctness of the content."[22] Also, it is believed that "the content of the contract had nothing to do with the scribe himself but was merely written in accordance with the agreement for the contracting parties."[23] As for scribes in the Qingshui River region, it is considered that "a scribe generally shall only be responsible to the writing."[24] In this case, were they employed or invited by contracting parties only to make written copies of what they were told?

It is clear that the scribe was an important figure in contract activities, but what has not yet been clarified is how, and to what extent or in what sense, scribes participated in contract activities. Thus, this chapter aims firstly to explore the institution[25] of contractual scribes, understood as a significant practice or custom in a society, that was formed as a result of the long-term contract practice in villages of the Qingshui River region. In doing so, it will also try to discuss how the institution operated. Further, the all-round functions of scribes in the formulation of a contract can be examined based on ample evidence of the scribal institution and the extent to which contractual scribes were involved in a contract can be demonstrated.

This chapter is organized chronologically in accordance with the typical activity of a contractual scribe in the region, with a special focus on the village of Wendou. The scribal demand will be discussed firstly in the following section, as this is the phrase used before a scribe is invited to formally join a contract activity. After appointing the scribe, the writing process of a contract will be explored and the two modes of drafting contracts are demonstrated in detail in the third section. The scribe will not leave the stage immediately after the completion of the contract for the scribe's fee might need to be paid—this issue will be analyzed in the fourth section, before the conclusion of the chapter.

2 The Demand for Scribes

The existence of the institution of contractual scribes undoubtedly stemmed from the demand for scribes in contractual activities. Every piece of contract has its producer materially, but not all of them were made by scribes—some contractors preferred and were capable to write the contract with their own hands. In this case, the question

[21] See Liu and Qu [51], Li [43].

[22] Okamatsu [59]. See also Rinji Taiwan Kyūkan Chōsakai [71]. A similar statement can also be seen in Linshi Taiwan tudi diaochaju [46].

[23] Cheng [10]. Quoted from Chun-Ying Wu, "Taiwan daishu de lishi kaocha," 51.

[24] Gao and Tan [25].

[25] The term "institution" is used in this chapter as a significant custom or system of a given society that has existed for a long time.

of the extent to which contractual scribes were needed in contract activities becomes important in the pre-contract phase.

2.1 The Typology of Contract Writers

It is commonly believed that the signature of the producer constitutes an essential element for the establishment of a contract in late imperial times,[26] although the descriptions or titles before the signature differed. In general, there were two types of contracts in terms of their production process: holographic (*qinbi*) contracts and allographic (or scribe-written) contracts.[27] The former means that the contract was written down completely by the contractor him- or herself, while the latter refers to those made by another person who was invited to do so on behalf of the contracting party. The report of a customs survey on "scribes of the contract of sale" indicates the existence of both situations:

> The contract of sale of land and houses can be written either by the vendor personally or by the third party who does the actual writing on behalf of [the vendor]; both situations are common practice.[28]

As for the effectiveness of both situations, it was recorded in the customs survey that "whether a contract of sale was written by some other one who was invited, or was written holographically [by the vendor], they are equally effective."[29]

The division between the two situations, holographic and allographic, seems to be clear enough and there might not be any other situation regarding contract production. However, in practice this issue was far more intricate, and therefore the essence of scribal works needs to be clarified.

The key difference between holographic contracts and those written by scribes is whether the one who does the actual writing is contractually obliged to do so or not. The concept of the obliged writer differs from the concept of contracting parties; it is obvious that not everyone involved in the contract relation was obliged to draw

---

[26] See Chen [7]. In addition, a study of the Huizhou manuscripts found that there exist some "contracts without scribes," and that these account for 5.51% (13/238) of the whole sample. The explanation of this phenomenon is that the production of the contract might have included the petty official because of the changes of the tax system in the early Qing times, so scribes were no longer needed. See Zhao Siyuan, "19 shiji Huizhou xiangcun de tudi shichang, xinyong jizhi yu guanxi wangluo," 95. However, the "contracts without scribes" might actually refer to "contracts without producers' name indicated," for the contract surely has its maker who would be seen as a scribe as long as he or she was not one of the contracting parties.

[27] The terms "holographic" and "allographic" can normally be seen in the law of succession, in order to mark that "[a] will might be either public or private, general or special, written, or verbal, holographic or allographic;" "[a] holographic will was, of course, one entirely written by the testator in his own hand; where it was taken down at his dictation, either by slaves, freemen, friends, lawyers or other persons, it was styled allographic." See Scott [74].

[28] See "The provincial customs of Hunan," Wu Xiangxiang, *Zhongguo minshi xiguan daquan*, 28.

[29] "The provincial customs of Heilongjiang," Qian Nanjing guomin zhengfu sifa xingzheng bu [62].

up the contract. Generally speaking, the obliged writer was the establisher (*liqiren*) or initiator of the contract. For example, for the most familiar type of contract, the contract of sale, "the establisher [of the contract] is the vendor,"[30] and therefore the scribe wrote on behalf of and for the vendor.[31] As mentioned in Chap. 2, the formulaic beginning of *li* can usually be used to indicate the establisher of a contract. Occasionally the name of the establisher would be repeated again in the ending part of the contract. For instance, a contract in the seventeenth year of Jiaqing (1812) starts with a statement that "the establisher of the contract of sale of forest land, Jiang Baowu," and ends with the reconfirmation that "[the contract was] established by the vendor, Jiang Baowu."[32] The actual producer of this contract was named Jiang Shaoya, who was not obliged to do so as he was not the establisher of the contract, and therefore he self-identified as a "scribe."

In general, the contract writer would not be one of the unobligated contracting parties. In the case of a contract of sale, the actual writer would normally not be the vendee (one of the contracting parties but not the establisher) as the vendor is the obliged establisher. Nevertheless, there existed a few exceptions. In a tenancy contract of forest land,[33] the tenant planter (the establisher) was Jiang Faxiang, while the land was co-owned by five landlords. Following convention, the contract should have been written by the tenant planter Jiang Faxiang, but in fact it was written by someone named Jiang Guangzong, who was one of the five landlords and who described himself as a scribe. In this case, the effect of distinguishing concepts is shown: if a holographic contract is defined as the contract made by one of the contracting parties, then it is a holographic one; but if the definition which applies to only a contract made by the obliged contracting party (the establisher) is counted as holographic, then this contract should be seen as allographic.

There is another similar contract which was also written by one of the landlords,[34] but here the difference is that, in the contract, immediately after the signature of the scribe (the landlord) there was another signature of the tenant (the obliged establisher). This situation partially matches the record of the customs survey which states that "[in the case of] a contract of sale, the personal signature [of the vendor] is essential, but the contract does not need to be written holographically [by the vendor]".[35] Although the contract was not entirely written by the establisher, it bore his signature.

At this point, it is already clear that a contract can be written by the obliged contracting party (a holographic contract) or the unobligated contracting party (an

---

[30] A [1].

[31] According to the survey report in Taiwan by the "Temporary Office for the Investigation of Taiwan Land Tenure," generally, a scribe would be invited only when the "vendor" was illiterate. See Rinji Taiwan Tochi Chōsakyoku [70].

[32] Zhang and Wang [114].

[33] See Daniels et al. [17].

[34] See Chen and Du [11].

[35] "The provincial customs of Heilongjiang," Qian Nanjing guomin zhengfu sifa xingzheng bu, *Mingshi xiguan diaocha baogao lu*, vol. 1, 118.

atypical allographic contract) or a scribe who previously had nothing to do with the contract relation at all (a typical allographic contract).

Apart from these three situations, however, there was another more special type, namely that the contract could be written by a single person out of many from the obliged contracting party. In this case, it seems that the contract was situated right between the categories of holographic and allographic which have been discussed.

For example, in a contract regarding the sale of timber,[36] the establishers/vendors were Jiang Shilian and Jiang Shiyuan, while the other party, who was Jiang Zhongying, intended to buy the timber. The signature of the producer at the end of the contract indicated that the contract was solely written by Jiang Shiyuan, one of the two establishers. It is noteworthy that the title of the writer was not *daibi* (scribe) or *qinbi* (holograph), but the combination of both types—*qindaibi* roughly meaning the "holographic scribe." This unusual title stems from the fact that the contract establisher was more than one person and therefore it became a crossing field of both types of contract writing. On the one hand, for Jiang Shilian (the other establisher/vendor), the contract was an allographic one since he did not write it; but, on the other hand, for Jiang Shiyuan, it was definitely a holographic contract. The descriptive title of "holographic scribe" also explicitly signifies its nature in-between holographic and allographic.

In fact, this was not an uncommon situation in the contract writing practice of Wendou Village.[37] The descriptive title before the signature of the writer did not need to be "holographic scribe," but sometimes it could also be written as "holograph"[38] or "scribe,"[39] indicating that the writer might not be fully aware of the situation. An even less common expression was that "[the contract was written by] the scribe Xiangrong[40] holographically,"[41] which mixed up two mutually contradictory phrases.

In sum, Table 1 shows the typology of contract writers in practice and highlights the overlaps of the holographic and allographic. In addition, it should be noted that, oftentimes, the scribe of a contract could be the middleman of the contract at the same time, and a combinatorial term "middlemen-scribes (m-s)" (*zhongbi*) would be used in this situation.[42] Nonetheless, a holographic contract would not find its writer serving as the middleman since he or she should be one of the contracting parties and a middleman cannot be a buyer or seller at the same time—the third party should be independent.

---

[36]Chen and Du [4].

[37]For other cases, see, e.g., Christian Daniels, Yang Yougeng, and Takeuchi Fusaji, *Kishū Myaozoku ringyō keiyaku monjo kaihen (1736–1950-nen)*, vol. 2, B-0020; Zhang and Wang [117].

[38]For example, the establishers of a contract were A and B but indicated that the contract was written holographically by B. See Daniels et al. [16].

[39]For example, the establishers of a contract were A and B but indicated that the contract was written by A as a scribe. See Chen Jinquan and Du Wanhua, *Jiang Yuanze jiacang qiyue wenshu*, 565.

[40]Xiangrong was one of the three vendors in this contract.

[41]Chen Jinquan and Du Wanhua, *Jiang Qigui jiacang qiyue wenshu*, 244.

[42]See, e.g., Chen Jinquan and Du Wanhua, *Jiang Yuanze jiacang qiyue wenshu*, 459; Chen Jinquan and Du Wanhua, *Jiang Qigui jiacang qiyue wenshu*, 360, 444.

Table 1 The typology of contract writers

Being involved in the contract relation			Not being involved in the contract relation	
The obliged contracting party/establisher		The unobligated contracting party		
Only one person of the party	Written by one of many people of the party		Being the scribe and middleman	Solely being the scribe
Typical holographic	Holographically allographic	Atypical allographic	Typical allographic	
Holographic				
	Allographic			

2.2 *The Number of Scribes*

In principle, and indeed in most cases there was only one scribe for one contract.[43] However, this impression cannot be taken for granted. Exceptions can be seen in the following report of a customs survey:

> In Changsha and other counties, apart from the aforementioned two situations,[44] occasionally the vendor of the property would co-write the contract with the third man; this is also a custom. The way to do it is that the first few characters or the first one or two lines of [the contract of] sale shall be written by the vendor holographically, the rest [of the contract] can be written by others as the scribe, giving clear indication [of the situation] at the end of the contract.[45]

In this case, the establisher and the scribe might write the contract together, so the actual writers of the contract could be plural. For example, a contract with three scribes could be found in a Japanese collection of Chinese contracts and it is believed that the reason for having three scribes in this was is that this marked a way to show the cautiousness and effectiveness of the contract.[46]

Among the contracts found in Wendou Village, however, the scribe did not seem to appear in the plural in any contract; there exist only a few easily confused examples which need to be discussed. One contract of dispute settlement indicates two middlemen as well as two scribes, "Zhu Dacai and [Zhu Da]quan."[47] These two names can be found in other contracts in Wendou: Zhu Dacai has been frequently invited as a scribe,[48] while there is only one record extant for Zhu Daquan in a

---

[43] See Feng Xuewei, *Ming Qing qiyue de jiegou gongneng ji yiyi*, 28.

[44] The "aforementioned two situations" refer to "holographic" and "allographic" in the context of the citation.

[45] Wu Xiangxiang, *Zhongguo minshi xiguan daquan*, 28.

[46] Fan [22].

[47] Pan and Wu [60].

[48] See, e.g., Zhang Yingqiang and Wang Zongxun, *Qingshuijiang wenshu*, vol. 1 (12), 291, 299; Chen Jinquan and Du Wanhua, *Jiang Qigui jiacang qiyue wenshu*, 341.

holographic contract.[49] Hence, it is clear that both were literate and knew how to write a contract. However, the handwriting of the contract seems to be coherent and, therefore, although the reason for signing two names is unknown, the contract seems to be written by one person alone.

Thus, the contract maker typically has a one-to-one correspondence with each contract and, generally, only one scribe was needed in the writing process of a single contract in Wendou Village.

2.3 The Proportion of Holographic Contracts and the Extent of Scribal Demand

The most direct way to discuss the demand for scribes is to examine the ratio of "holographic contracts" to "allographic contracts." What this ratio represents is how many people within a village in the Qing dynasty who ever needed to write a contract were capable of doing so by themselves, and, from another angle, what percentage of the contracts were written with the help of a scribe.

In the database of Group A of complete contracts in Wendou Village, 2,045 contracts provide valid and sufficient information regarding the situation of contract writers.[50] It should be noted that the description of "holographic" or "allographic" written at the end of the contract does not necessarily mean that the actual situation is as it is claimed, and further scrutiny is needed.[51] Therefore, the statistics are not straightforwardly based on the calculation of the labeling of "holographic" or "allographic" in the contract but rather on the de facto typology of contract writers, as mentioned above.

Accordingly, in light of the classification above, among all examined contracts, 1,338 pieces are allographic (including "middlemen-scribes") and account for 65.43%; 364 pieces are de facto holographic and account for 17.75%; and, in addition to these two cases, there are a total of 344 pieces situated in-between as "holographically allographic," and account for 16.82% (see Fig. 1). If the proportion of allographic contracts is calculated in a broad sense, comprising allographic and "holographically allographic" contracts, 82.25% of the contracts included the factor of scribes; by contrast, holographic contracts only account for less than 20%.[52]

As for the holographic contract, another situation is worth further consideration. In the village, when a "professional scribe" intended to purchase or rent a parcel of

---

[49] See Zhang and Wang [113].

[50] 64 pieces of contracts were eliminated, for the information of their writers was missing. The main reason was that these papers were damaged or ink-stained, which makes them unrecognizable.

[51] Sometimes the contract claimed that it was written by a scribe but in fact it was a holographic contract, and vice versa. For the first situation, see, e.g., Chen Jinquan and Du Wanhua, *Jiang Qigui jiacang qiyue wenshu*, 29. For the second situation, see, e.g., Chen Jinquan and Du Wanhua, *Jiang Yuanze jiacang qiyue wenshu*, 41.

[52] It needs to be clarified that there is no significant difference concerning the temporal distribution within the Qing dynasty.

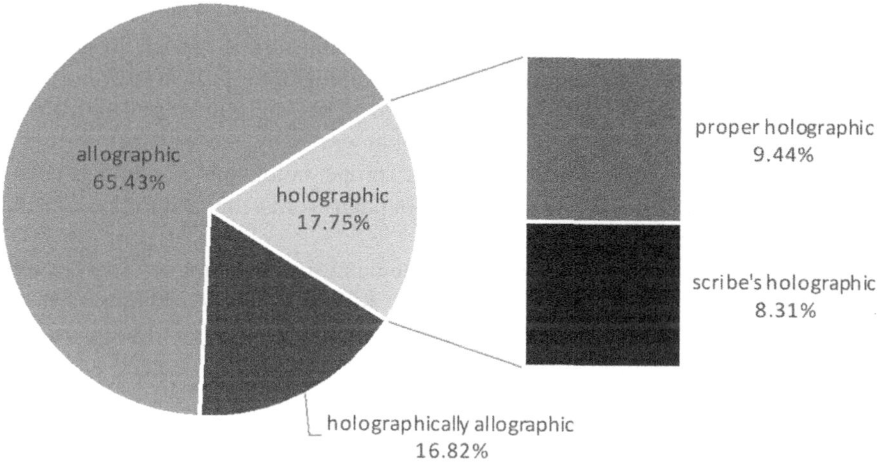

Fig. 1 The proportion of holographic and allographic contracts

land and therefore needed to draft a contract, he would surely not sign as a scribe on the contract of which he himself was the establisher. In this case, the writing would be labeled "holographic," and only rarely was the arrangement written in full as the contract was "holographically written by a scribe."[53] Therefore, these contracts would fall under the type of holographic contract in the previous quantitative analysis, even though these people may appear as scribes in other contracts, and some were even frequently invited by other villagers. Thus, to some extent, the holographic contracts written by the somewhat "professional scribe" should not be deemed "proper" holographs.

On the other hand, some of the names are recorded as holographic writers and have not yet been found as scribes in other contracts in the current database.[54] This shows that in the village there was a group of people who had the ability to make contracts but who were not inclined to serve as the scribe for others; they only wrote their own contracts. In this sense, this situation should be considered as "proper holographic"

[53] A loan contract indicating that it was "holographically written by a scribe," dated the nineteenth year of Guangxu reign (1893), can be found at the Koxinga Museum in Tainan City.

[54] For example, Jiang Benshen often appeared as a holographic writer but has not been found as a scribe so far. For the contracts that Jiang Benshen has participated in, see Chen Jinquan and Du Wanhua, *Jiang Yuanze jiacang qiyue wenshu*, 189, 208, 238; Chen Jinquan and Du Wanhua, *Jiang Qigui jiacang qiyue wenshu*, 139; Christian Daniels, Yang Yougeng, and Takeuchi Fusaji, *Kishū Myaozoku ringyō keiyaku monjo kaihen (1736–1950-nen)*, vol. 1, A-0183. In stark contrast, his contemporaries or probably even brothers according to the naming rules, Jiang Benqing and Jiang Benwang, were both invited to be the scribe in other contracts. For the contracts that Jiang Benqing and Jiang Benwang have participated in, see, e.g., Zhang Yingqiang and Wang Zongxun, *Qingshuijiang wenshu*, vol. 1 (12), 280; Christian Daniels, Yang Yougeng, and Takeuchi Fusaji, *Kishū Myaozoku ringyō keiyaku monjo kaihen (1736–1950-nen)*, vol. 1, A-0183. Admittedly, here the possibility that relevant contracts have not yet been seen has been ruled out.

as those writers had no relation with the institution of village scribes—they neither needed assistance from other scribes nor did they offer scribal service for others.

In view of the above, by comparing the labeled holographic writers with those who appeared on at least one contract in the name of the scribe and eliminating the overlapping part (viz. "contracts labeled holographic but written by 'professional' scribes"), the total number of contracts belonging to the "proper holographic" contracts is 193, which accounts for only 9.44% (see Fig. 1). In other words, the scribe appears in the over 90% of the remaining contracts.

In summary, each contract represents a demand for a writing service, but only less than ten percent of the demand could be fulfilled entirely without assistance from a scribe. This reveals both the level of literacy in the village to some extent[55] and signifies that, under most circumstances, there was a large demand for scribes in Wendou Village.

2.4 The Demand for Scribes in Different Kinds of Contracts

In general, as shown, there was a high demand for scribes when drafting contracts in the Qing village,[56] but the level of demand varied for different kinds of contracts. Four categories of contracts, namely contracts of sale (which mainly refer to the absolute sale, in contrast to conditional sale, *dian*), tenancy contracts, loan contracts (including contracts of conditional sale),[57] and contracts of apology (including other contracts of disputes settlement),[58] are singled out and their writers are examined separately, as shown in Table 2.[59]

[55]The issue of literacy will be discussed again in Chap. 5 based on the data presented here.

[56]In an interview of a centenarian scribe in Taiwan, it is said that a scribe was normally needed concerning land transactions since few people were literate and knew how to manage the issue. See Lin et al. [45].

[57]In fact, the loan contract, the contract of conditional sale, the contract of pawn, and other kinds of contract included in this category are all different from each other. However, they are classified as "loan contracts" because they are all related to financing though by diverse means. For the differences between these contracts, see "footnote 4," Qu [65].

[58]The criteria for the classification are mainly based on the self-claimed title of the contract. These four categories are selected since they cover nearly 90% of the total contracts; the remaining few types of contracts are, for example, those related to household division and profit allocation. The sample size of each remaining type of contract is relatively small and is therefore not suitable for statistical analysis.

[59]"A" refers to "allographic" contracts other than the situation of "A (m-s)," which means "allographic contracts while the scribe acted also as middleman;" "H" means "holographic" contracts, "H-A" and "H (p)" represent "holographically allographic" and "proper holographic" respectively.

Table 2 The demand for scribes in different kinds of contracts

Sorts	In total		Sale		Tenancy		Loan		Apology	
A	1,026	50.17	674	47.97	171	54.98	38	46.34	18	42.86
A (m-s)	312	15.26	201	14.31	60	19.29	10	12.20	6	14.29
H-A	344	16.82	236	16.80	55	17.68	10	12.20	6	14.29
H	363	17.75	294	20.93	25	8.04	24	29.27	12	28.47
H (p)	193	9.44	151	10.75	14	4.50	13	15.85	6	14.29
	–	–	–	–	–	–	–	–	–	–
In total	2,045	100%	1,405	100%	311	100%	82	100%	42	100%

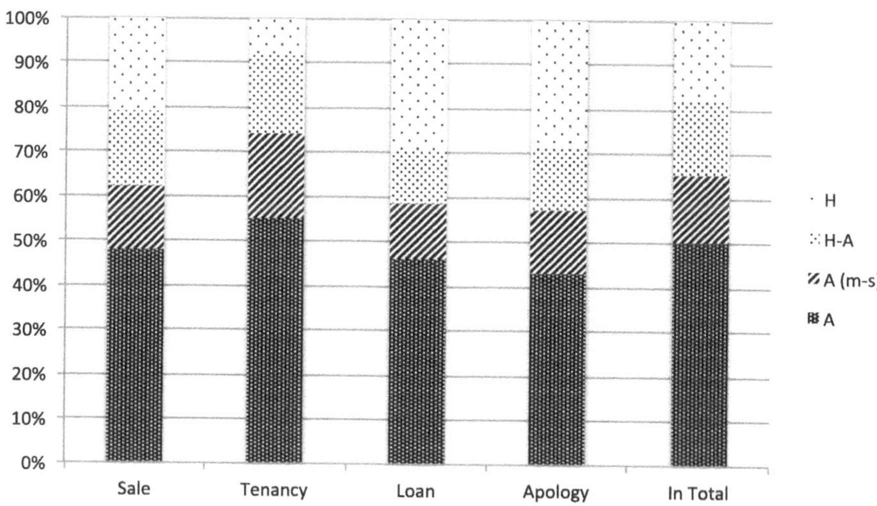

Among all these four kinds of contracts, the contract of sale accounts for the largest proportion at 69.14%, followed by the tenancy contract at 15.31%. The "allographic-holographic, A-H" distribution of the specific type of the contract of sale shows little difference from the overall situation. However, for the tenancy contract, the proportion of "holographic" is extremely small, with only 8.04%, which is nearly half of the figure of the overall situation (17.47%). Moreover, its ratio of "proper holographic" at 4.5% is also lower than the overall figure (9.44%).

Two reasons can be cited for why people preferred allographic over holographic writing in respect of tenancy contracts. Firstly, the establishers of tenancy contracts were mainly tenant farmers or planters who wanted to rent a wet-rice field or especially forest land and, therefore, in contrast to the establishers (vendors) of sales contracts, they usually belonged to a somewhat lower economic level. Being a seller of land or forests in the transactions indicates that one was propertied at least once, but most tenants chose to rent land from landlords largely due to the predicament that what they owned cannot sufficiently support their living expenses.[60] It is conceivable that they might be relatively poorly educated due to financial stress and not able to write the contract by themselves, which accounts for the low percentage of holographic writing.

Secondly, among these tenant farmers or planters in Wendou, a substantial number were newcomers who moved to the village to clear forested lands for agricultural purposes and to earn their living from it. Ever since the forest and mountains near Wendou were reclaimed, the contradiction between the increase in cultivated land area and the shortage of manpower has provided opportunities for many people elsewhere.[61] Consequently, "people from many other places, especially from the region of the lower reaches of the Qingshui River, came to the Wendou area to rent mountains for planting cunninghamia trees since the middle of the Qing dynasty."[62] Researchers have shown that quite a large number of those newcomers were "poor peasants coming from Hunan, Jiangxi, Fujian, Anhui, Zhejiang, Jiangsu, and other provinces, and also some other places, such as Tianzhu, in the [Guizhou] province."[63] In fact, the surrounding villages of Wendou, such as Zhongyang or Jiuyou, were naturally formed after those newcomers, as well as other tenants, gradually settled down; residents of these villages were described by Wendou villagers as "outcomers" (*lairen*), which referred to the poor and destitute both economically and socially who came from other places outside Wendou.[64] For those non-local tenants, regardless of the allocation of the final harvest or other terms in the contract, the treatment given by the landlord was extremely demanding.[65] In this context, it is conceivable that, when drafting the tenancy contract, even if the newcomer had the ability to write the contract, the landlord in Wendou might still be more willing to ask a local scribe for help.[66] In general, due to various aspects linked to these two reasons, the degree of demand for scribes in connection with tenancy contracts in Wendou Village was obviously greater than the normal level.

Conversely, the holographic proportions regarding loan contracts and contracts of apology are excessively high, at 29.27% and 28.47% respectively, in contrast to the overall number of 17.75%.[67] The commonality between these two types of

[60]It has to be noted that in Wendou Village there were also some tenant planters who were at the same time the landlords of another parcel of forest land. For an introduction and explanation of this phenomenon, see Wang [89], Zhang and Hu [110].

[61]See Wang Zongxun, *Wendou*, 34.

[62]Zhang Yingqiang and Hu Tengwen, *Jinping*, 121.

[63]Wang Zongxun, *Wendou*, 41.

[64]See ibid., 34–35.

[65]See Guizhou sheng bianjizu [27].

[66]In an interview record of a field research conducted on October 4, 2013, Yi Zunfa, the former director of Wendou Village, mentioned that, when outcomers came to buy mountains in Wendou and needed to find the middleman and the scribe for drafting contract, it was the opinion of the local seller that mattered, and usually the seller was inclined to choose a local scribe. See "Appendix 2: Field Research Report," He [31].

[67]Another statistic in Huizhou has also shown similarly that the holographic proportion in the categories of "receipt for a loan" and "conditional sale" (44 pieces of documents in total) is 22.73%,

contracts is that the establisher, the debtor or the one who apologized might be the relatively weaker party in the contractual relationship and might be asked to provide some type of guarantee, whether this involved repaying the loan or doing no wrong again. Therefore, on these occasions, the contracts were preferred to be written by the establishers themselves in order to enhance their effectiveness. Also, compared with the tenants, they might have reasonably better credits in the local society, or else they would not be able to ask for a loan.

A case of loan dispute in Shaanxi province during the Daoguang era might offer evidence supporting the opinion that one should generally write the loan contract holographically. The magistrate of Fengyang Prefecture said in his judgment:

> [I have] investigated the customs of Shaanxi province and found that there are only middlemen and witnesses in a loan contract, and the contract will not be required to be written holographically. I have arrived at the job in Shaanxi since the second year of Daoguang (1822) and [I was] shocked by the fact that the contract was not written holographically when hearing loan disputes.[68]

The magistrate was "shocked" by the special customs in Shaanxi[69] which might rather illustrate that the loan contract should be written holographically in other places in general.

On top of this, another loan dispute in Jiangsu province during the Tongzhi era can provide further relevant evidence. The defendant of a case questioned the authenticity of the allographic loan contract that concerns the debt, which he had denied by arguing that, "since I am literate, there is no need to invite a scribe."[70] A similar argument brought forward by the defendant can also be seen in the above case in Shaanxi, in which the defendant said "since I am literate, why didn't I write it by myself?"[71] The response of the judge to these statements was similar too: "The reason why you refused to write [the loan contract] by yourself is that you harbored malicious intentions."[72] Conversely, a creditor of goodwill who planned to repay his debt would either be required to or of his own will try to write the contract by himself, unless it was beyond his ability. All these reports and the logic behind them show that, as a rule, a holographic loan contract seemed to be the preferred option.

The abnormal figures concerning different types of contracts, whether they are too high or too low compared with the total level, are all explicable in light of the dissimilar characteristics of each category. But it still needs to be stressed that, even for loan

---

which is higher than the average ratio at 15.68%. See Zhao Siyuan, "19 shiji Huizhou xiangcun de tudi shichang, xinyong jizhi yu guanxi wangluo," 95.

[68]Qiu [64].

[69]In addition, there was even a custom that no signature was needed in loan contracts in Qian County of Shaanxi, regardless of the signature of the middleman, the debtor, or the writer. See Qian Nanjing guomin zhengfu sifa xingzheng bu [63].

[70]Chen [12].

[71]Qiu Huang, *Fupan Lucun*, 12–13.

[72]Chen Yuanqi, *Yongxianzhai biji*, 57. In the above case in Shaanxi, the magistrate explained that the reason given was that the defendant did not want to keep a holographic contract as a handle against him. See Qiu Huang, *Fupan Lucun*, 13.

contracts and apology contracts as the types that are preferred to be written holographically, the rates of proper holographic contracts are only 15.85% and 14.29% respectively, which points to the overwhelmingly high demand for scribes even if a holographic document was strongly encouraged. On all accounts, the demand for scribes was rather high in a general way but the extent varied regarding different types of contracts.

3 Drafting of a Contract by a Scribe

3.1 Appointing the Scribe

The appointment of the scribe formally marks the inception of the production process of a contract. However, it is not mentioned in the main text of most contracts and only a few words before the signature of the scribe indicate that the scribe was invited.[73] Fortunately, some cost list manuscripts record the activity of inviting scribes. For example, one mentioned that "[I/We] invited Mister Scribe (*daishu xiansheng*)[74] three times [...]."[75] Sometimes, as in an example from Tianzhu County, one is said to have been "begging Shu Shaoji to be the scribe,"[76] using a phrasing which highlights the importance of the role that the scribe played in the contracting activity. The question that arises from the description of this invitation is who, among all contracting parties, the inviter was or by whom the scribe was appointed.

Generally speaking, since the establisher was obliged to write the contract, he or she should also be responsible to appoint a scribe if no one was able to write it holographically. This point can be confirmed by some contracts of sale which explicitly state that the scribe was invited by the vendor.[77] For example, one contract about selling shares of forest land says that "Wang invited the scribe Fan Xishou," in

[73]It was written as "inviting A as the scribe." See, e.g., Chen Jinquan and Du Wanhua, *Jiang Qigui jiacang qiyue wenshu*, 345; Christian Daniels, Yang Yougeng, and Takeuchi Fusaji, *Kishū Myaozoku ringyō keiyaku monjo kaihen (1736–1950-nen)*, vol. 2, B-0179.

[74]Here the scribe was called Mister (*xiansheng*), showing that the profession of the scribe was well respected. In addition, it could also be a general title for people who were learned or were at least literate. It also has to be noted that *daishu* could be slightly different from *daibi* depending on the context.

[75]See No. JYZ-7-P1010076, collected from Jiang Yuanze's family in Wendou Village, Guizhou; courtesy of Prof. Chen Jinquan and Prof. Pan Zhicheng. This manuscript is unfortunately not dated. But since the currency the writer mentioned in it includes copper cash, it could very likely be dated as a Qing manuscript.

[76]See Zhang [108].

[77]See, e.g., Zhang Yingqiang and Wang Zongxun, *Qingshuijiang wenshu*, vol. 1 (12), 12, 114; Chen Jinquan and Du Wanhua, *Jiang Yuanze jiacang qiyue wenshu*, 565.

which the surname "Wang" refers to the vendor "Wang Shikui."[78] Another contract contains a few more words about the process of invitation: "I went to Jiang Qiwei's home to invite him in person to write [the contract]."[79]

In addition to the manner of appointing the scribe by one of the contract parties, there was also another special case called "dual invitation." For example, in a contract of sale, it is clearly indicated that "the scribe Jiang Tianxiang was invited by both parties."[80] More frequently, "dual invitation" can be seen in indentures (*hetong*) or contracts of dispute settlement, for these kinds of contracts were initiated by both parties. One "contract of compromise and innocence," for example, says that "the scribe Jiang Tongxue was invited by both parties of their own accord."[81] In another example, an agreement stipulating the profit allocation of the future harvest of the timber between the landlord and the tenant planter, it is emphasized that "the scribe Jiang Tingzhou was invited by the two [parties]."[82] These examples of "dual invitation" indicate that the scribe might not only be the representative of, or the only one hired by, one of the contract parties but could have a connection with all parties, whoever initiated or was substantially involved in the contractual relation.

3.2 Sources for Writing Contract Content: Words and Drafts

It is certainly true that the process of writing was of crucial importance to the operation of the institution of contractual scribes. When a scribe was invited by one or both contract participants to be present on the occasion of contracting, he would soon notice that what he faced was a combination of uniformity and uniqueness that should be simultaneously incorporated into his writing of the contract. This marks the particularity of contract writing: on the one hand, the uniformity entails that all contracts were generally the same in forms and writing styles,[83] while on the other hand the uniqueness refers to the perception that each contract was about a unique event and reflected specific jural relations. In this case, what a scribe needed to do was exactly to express the unique facts in an identical way. The content of the vivid story should be edited and encased in a dull and contract-shaped box; this is how a contract was made.

This perception brings with it the following question: what was the basis of the writing in the production process of a contract? Further, in light of the form-content

78 Zhang Yingqiang and Wang Zongxun, *Qingshuijiang wenshu*, vol. 1 (12), 120. It is also noteworthy that this and the above-mentioned three contracts were all written by the scribe Fan Xishou. It might be his own habit to record the situation of invitation since it was infrequent.

79 Zhang and Wang [118].

80 Christian Daniels, Yang Yougeng, and Takeuchi Fusaji, *Kishū Myaozoku ringyō keiyaku monjo kaihen (1736–1950-nen)*, vol. 1, A-0002.

81 Daniels et al. [18].

82 Christian Daniels, Yang Yougeng, and Takeuchi Fusaji, *Kishū Myaozoku ringyō keiyaku monjo kaihen (1736–1950-nen)*, vol. 2, C-0014.

83 See Zhu [126], Yu [104].

dichotomy, what was a scribe's source when writing the contract content and what did he or she need to conform to in terms of contract form?

3.2.1 *Yikou* or "According to the Spoken Words"

How was a contract written? This question is hard to answer since almost no direct materials can be found in the contract text. It is generally assumed that, due to the formalization of the contract, more vivid factors such as the scene of contracting, the process of negotiation, verbal agreements made by the parties, or even the atmosphere of the event were not reflected in the contract text.[84] Four characters, as a formulaic expression, should be highlighted in this case, for they might be the only few words that straightforwardly describe the action of the scribe. In principle, a scribe could gather all the information needed by means of hearing the words of the contracting parties. This was recorded by the term "*yikou daibi*," which means "to write [as a scribe] according to the mouth (which here means the verbal expression or spoken words)." These four characters can frequently be seen before the scribe's signature at the end of the contract,[85] seemingly to give the impression that the writing of the contract was a process of dictation and faithfully transcription of the speaking participants of the contracting event.

This term or description for the writing of private contracts might stem from its counterpart in the field of writing official documents. A similar description can be seen in plaints written by official scribes.[86] In an exhortative book or handbook for officials, it is said that "if [the plaint] was written according to the spoken words, then a clear indication should be given."[87] Moreover, as an official institution, the *Great Qing Code* also wrote that "anyone who instigates an action is obliged to make the plaint by himself; in case he is not capable of writing by himself, it is permitted for him to dictate and let the official scribe transcribe his words faithfully; if there are any details added or omitted deliberately, the official scribe shall be punished according to the law."[88] According to the narrative in law, a plaint could be dependably written by a certified official scribe based on the words of the plaintiff.[89] Hence, in the case of writing litigation documents, the process of dictation-transcription might be a proper description.

However, the situation was slightly different with regard to the writing of contractual scribes. Here, what an official scribe faced was only one party of the litigation

[84] See Du [21].

[85] There are more than 50 contracts across different time periods containing the phrase and its variations. See, e.g., Chen Jinquan and Du Wanhua, *Jiang Yuanze jiacang qiyue wenshu*, 3, 9, 45, 126, 178, 204, 207, 275, 345, 463.

[86] For example, in the plaints in Huizhou of the Qianlong era, the term was used when the source of the plaint needed to be specified. See Zheng [123].

[87] Yu [105].

[88] See Xue [98]. See also Mark A. Allee, *Law and Local Society in Late Imperial China*, 176.

[89] See Xue Yunsheng, *Duli cunyi*, Art. 340.10.

(viz. the plaintiff), but a contractual scribe also needed to respond to both parties of the contract (see Fig. 2[90]). If the term *yikou daibi* implies that the process of writing was a dictation, then to whom should the scribe listen?

In order to understand the term *yikou daibi*, the first thing to be noted is that the contract was merely the output of one small, albeit vital, step in the lengthy procedure for forming and maintaining the contractual relationship.[91] Many factual details, especially those of pre-contract dealings, have not been reflected directly or have been omitted on purpose in the contract text. What can be seen in most contracts is the reflection of the scene of the final negotiation. In other words, the context of this four-character idiom, or even the whole contract text, was the final step of a series of long negotiations.

The process of the negotiation in land transactions, for example, can be summed up as follows.[92] At first, the vendor claims his reason for selling the land, and asks an introducer to be his representative to find a potential vendee; subsequently, after a suitable one was found, the introducer then talks over the transaction with the vendee, and they negotiate the issues of the conveyance of the land and, if all goes well, comes to a preliminary arrangement; then, a scribe is invited at this point of time when the final agreement is about to be reached, and a written contract of sale is therefore drawn up by the scribe with all witnesses and introducers (middlemen) present. This process was also commonly recorded, albeit only briefly, in several contracts from Wendou.[93] Thus, it seems that the scribe came on the stage only at the final step. But did he show up during the substantive negotiation, such as the bargaining, or did he merely participate in the event as a part of the overelaborate formalities, after all vital issues had been settled?

Occasionally, a few more lines concerning the presence of a scribe in the contracting activity can be found in litigation documents. In a litigation recorded in the Dan-Xin archives,[94] a testimony from a middleman, Yang Kuai, mentioned his colleague in the same contracting event, a contractual scribe:

> I am Yang Cheng's kin. At the time when [he] was about to sell the wet-rice field, the two parties went to the shop to negotiate the price; and asked [me] to be the middleman and guarantor, [asked] Yang Qinchi to write the contract as the scribe.[95]

This description suggests that, spatially or chronologically speaking, the bargaining process and the writing of the contract were coherent and closely

---

[90] An illustration in a "complete book of myriad treasures," *Xinke yejia xincai wangbaoquanshu*, vol. 9, ca. 1614. This figure is a very rare image in a daily encyclopedia that concerns the contractual scribe in late imperial China, although it was printed in the Ming dynasty. It clearly illustrates that a scribe faced both parties of the contract, in this image the two brothers involved in the household division.

[91] See Du Zhengzhen, "Cong susong dang'an huidao qiyue huodong de xianchang," 119.

[92] See Chen [8].

[93] See, e.g., Chen Jinquan and Du Wanhua, *Jiang Qigui jiacang qiyue wenshu*, 18.

[94] The Dan-Xin archives are "a collection of administrative and judicial records of the Danshui sub-prefecture and the Xinzhu County" in northern Taiwan dated from 1789 to 1895. A detailed introduction can be found in Chen et al. [6].

[95] Wu [94].

Fig. 2 A contractual scribe writing a household division contract in front of his two clients

connected. It is noted that the formulaic expressions in the contract text also indicated that there was a process of negotiation, especially concerning the price, right before the formal contract was drawn up.[96] Accordingly, the scribe was involved in the bargaining process, at least sitting in on the discussion,[97] and at any rate present at the event. This is also consistent with the normal requirement of holding the contract event with "all four persons present."[98] The successive activities of all participants in a contract event can be sketched out by a record in the customs survey: "The middleman negotiated a price between two parties, then the scribe wrote the contract

[96]See Fan Jinmin, "'Caoyi' yu 'yidan': Qing dai Jiangnan tianzhai maimai wenshu de dingli" 86.

[97]An example concerning house division can be seen in Yu-ju Lin et al., *Daishu bi, shangren feng*, 61.

[98]Zhou [124].

according to the negotiation, and all witnesses checked [the contract] and signed or made their marks on it."[99]

Compared to *yikou daibi*, the nuance of this sentence should be noted, since it says that a scribe would write the contract according to the "negotiation," rather than according to the "mouth/words." It offers the alternative explanation that, compared to the situation in official scribal writings in which one should follow the words of one party, *yikou* in contract writings might actually mean "according to the spoken words of all participants," including both contracting parties and the middlemen (introducers, witnesses, and whoever else was involved), and even the opinion of the scribe himself might be considered.

Evidence can also be seen in various manuscripts of Wendou Village which explicitly recorded the process of negotiation and claimed that the scribe wrote according to the negotiation of all participants.[100] An adjective was added in front of *kou* in another contract to give *yizhongkou*, meaning "according to all [people's/participants'] mouths/words."[101] This expression implies that more voices should be considered, as it is believed that, although based on contracts in Hainan, *yikou* means writing according to the spoken words of both contracting parties.[102] Only rarely would a contract state that it was written by a scribe "according to the spoken words of the vendor."[103] In most cases, *yikou* indicates diverse sources of information. In the above-mentioned interview, the interviewee happened to mention the meaning of *yikou*: "There are two levels of meaning when using *yikou* in these manuscripts. Firstly, it means the contract was written based on the words of both parties of the transaction. Secondly, all participants of the contracting feast shall be the witness in case of any future dispute."[104]

In light of this understanding, as well as other related evidence, it is conceivable that the sources for the contract content were plural, and a scribe, apart from his duty of writing, should at first deal with the information he received at the event. Consequently, while processing these messages, the unique role of a scribe gradually emerged—he was the one who either requested or rejected the information which he needed as the representative of legal and customary norms.

Put succinctly, the so-called *yikou* in contracts refers to the situation in which a scribe writes the contract according to what has been agreed on in the final negotiation, such as the final price; conversely, it seems that only when the consensus was written down by the scribe could it be deemed confirmed.[105] It was in this sense that a scribe was involved in the finalization of the deal—from "mouth" to "paper," or

---

[99]Wu Xiangxiang, *Zhongguo minshi xiguan daquan*, 40.

[100]See Zhang Yingqiang and Wang Zongxun, *Qingshuijiang wenshu*, vol. 1 (12), 307.

[101]Ibid., 330.

[102]Li [38].

[103]Zhang Yingqiang and Wang Zongxun, *Qingshuijiang wenshu*, vol. 1 (12), 113.

[104]"Appendix 2: Field Research Report," He Yumei, "Qing dai Minguo shiqi Qiandongnan Wendou zhai de linye jingji xisu yanjiu," 57.

[105]It is said that all the "argy-bargies" would finally be settled in the contract text. See Yu-ju Lin et al., *Daishu bi, shangren feng*, 61.

from verbal words to written text. A scribe thus "intervened" by editing the information that the negotiation provided, which was the sole power that the process of transcription bestowed on him.

3.2.2 *Yigao* or "According to the Draft"

For an official scribe in the Qing dynasty, apart from *yikou* or according to the "oral description,"[106] another way to write formal documents could be based on the draft provided by the litigant[107]; this type of draft was called *zilaigao* or a self-provided draft.[108] Correspondingly, although rare, a similar situation can also be found concerning the contractual scribe.[109] In Wendou Village, for example, one contract stated that it was written by the scribe according to a draft (viz. *yigao*)[110]; additionally, the same indication can also be seen in a contract from the neighboring village of Ping'ao.[111]

In fact, *yikou* and *yigao* could be deemed two scribal methods of writing contracts. According to a renowned field research conducted in Huangyan, Zhejiang province, *yiyan daibi*, which is a rephrasing of *yikou daibi*, and *yigao daibi* were found in parallel in a sample contract preserved by an experienced scribe.[112] The juxtaposition of these two phrases in a model contract, which had all potential situations listed, might suggest the two possibilities for a scribe to write the contract content, based on the on-site negotiation or the *gao*, respectively.

However, what did this *gao* or draft exactly refer to? There were several terms related to the *gao* concerning contract writing. Firstly, there was one type of so-called *guanfa qigao,* or the "officially issued contract draft," which existed in some areas during the Qing dynasty. But this type of document should be filled out when using it,[113] which was apparently not the situation in the discussion. Secondly, *gao* could mean one type of precontract documents,[114] which were different from the real contract in their forms, subjects, times, etc.[115] In this case it was possible, when both

---

106 Mark A. Allee, *Law and Local Society in Late Imperial China*, 176.

107 See Zheng Xiaochun, "Qing dai daishu zhidu yu jiceng sifa," 38.

108 It is believed that the origin of a self-provided draft was detected by asking the scribe who used it. See Liu [47].

109 For the evidence of *yigao daibi* in the Huizhou manuscripts, see Liu [49].

110 See Christian Daniels, Yang Yougeng, and Takeuchi Fusaji, *Kishū Myaozoku ringyō keiyaku monjo kaihen (1736–1950-nen)*, vol. 1, A-0191. It should be noted that originally the character *gao* was written wrongly but has been corrected in the transcription by the editor.

111 See Christian Daniels, Yang Yougeng, and Takeuchi Fusaji, *Kishū Myaozoku ringyō keiyaku monjo kaihen (1736–1950-nen)*, vol. 2, B-0194.

112 Tian [81].

113 See Zhang [106].

114 Some considered this document as a type of agreement concerning the breach of contract but categorized it as a "pre-contract document." See Feng Xuewei, *Ming Qing qiyue de jiegou gongneng ji yiyi*, 49–54.

115 See Fan Jinmin, "'Caoyi' yu 'yidan': Qing dai Jiangnan tianzhai maimai wenshu de dingli" 86.

parties agreed to sign the formal contract on another day, that the vendor first handed over a precontract document in exchange for the earnest money agreed from the vendee.[116] Nevertheless, a precontract and a real contract should be regarded as two independent contracts that deal with one type of contractual relationship separately. Thirdly, *gao* could indicate the unsigned rough draft of a formal contract, which was about to be edited further and transcribed, by a scribe, into a clear, proper, and so effective contract.

The characteristics of a rough draft have been thoroughly discussed in studies concerning bamboo and wooden manuscripts in early times. It was defined as the original and fundamental document for further discussion and revision,[117] and the three major characteristics of it are: (1) that the handwriting could be rather sloppy with quite a lot of smearing and interpolations; (2) the personal name should be replaced by a fixed mark or a character that can help to keep the document anonymous; and (3) the date of the document might remain vacant.[118] Some interpreters argue further that the main features of a rough draft are marks of adding and removing, marks of replacing, and sloppy handwriting, although the latter two might not be necessary.[119] Even though the focus of these researches is not Qing contracts, these authors do point out the general character of the draft, so that it can also be used for analyzing the contract drafts from Wendou Village.

Thus, the third possibility—*gao* as the rough contract draft—may be in line with the present situation; accordingly, a few sets of manuscripts, including the contract drafts and their corresponding formal versions, can be singled out as evidence for the existence of this type of *gao* in the production process leading towards a final contract.

Yet, it was not easy to find these examples since the connection between the manuscripts was difficult to clarify; only an obvious high degree of similarity of the texts written in different manuscripts can link them together. For example, Fig. 3[120] shows a set of two pieces of manuscripts concerning the sale of forest land. Textually, the two are largely identical in respect to all clauses and major information with only nuances, which indicates that both manuscripts actually bore the same text, or, rather, variations of the same text.

However, if one looks more closely at the details, especially those regarding the handwriting and the formality of expression, the differences are significant. Firstly, the name of the vendor is indicated as "△△" in three places in the left manuscript, but in the formal contract his full name "Jiang Tingwei" was written. Secondly, unlike in the formal contract, the draft does not include any information concerning the middleman and scribe or the contracting date. Thirdly, a postscript was added at the end of the formal version, mentioning the text correction at length. Fourthly,

---

[116]See Yang [100].

[117]See Li and Liu [39].

[118]See ibid., 165–166.

[119]See Hsing [33].

[120]For the rough draft, see Chen Jinquan and Du Wanhua, *Jiang Yuanze jiacang qiyue wenshu*, 203. For its corresponding formal contract, see ibid., 131.

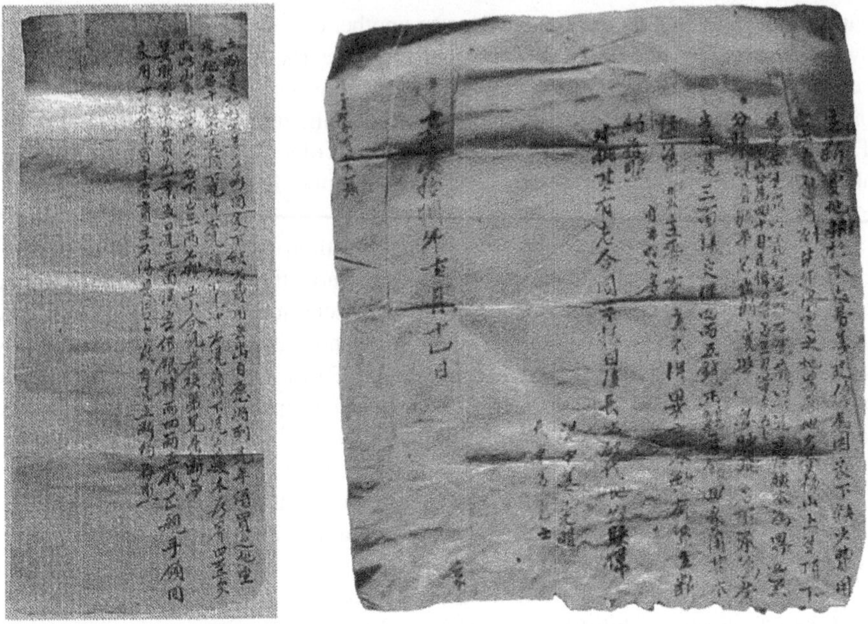

Fig. 3 A rough draft (left) and the corresponding formal contract (1)

compared with the draft version, the expression in the final contract appears to be more sophisticated and formal, and specifically concerning the layouts of the two manuscripts that can be seen from the provided pictures, the left seems to be a note rather than a formal contract. In sum, the left manuscript stands in accordance with the major characteristics of a draft as given above, and thus should be a draft of the formal contract on the right. It shows that, in some cases in Wendou Village, a draft might be prepared when drawing up a contract.

Another set of manuscripts which concerns the tenancy issue offered further details on the production process of a contract (see Fig. 4).[121] Above all, these two manuscripts accord with the four differences between a draft and a formal contract mentioned above. In addition, the handwriting of the rough draft was definitely much sloppier. The most noticeable point is that the draft contains many signs of erasure or correction, which provide ample information regarding the formation of the final text.

Out of many corrections present, two are relatively important. The first is the alteration of the contract title. Initially the title was drafted as "establishing a division contract (indenture) of cultivating land and planting cunninghamia trees (*li zhongdi fenhetong zai shamu zi*)." The wording of this contract title was later altered using correction marks to "establishing a tenancy contract (indenture) of cultivating

[121] The rough draft, see ibid., 476. For its corresponding formal contract, see Zhang Yingqiang and Wang Zongxun, *Qingshuijiang wenshu*, vol. 1 (12), 133.

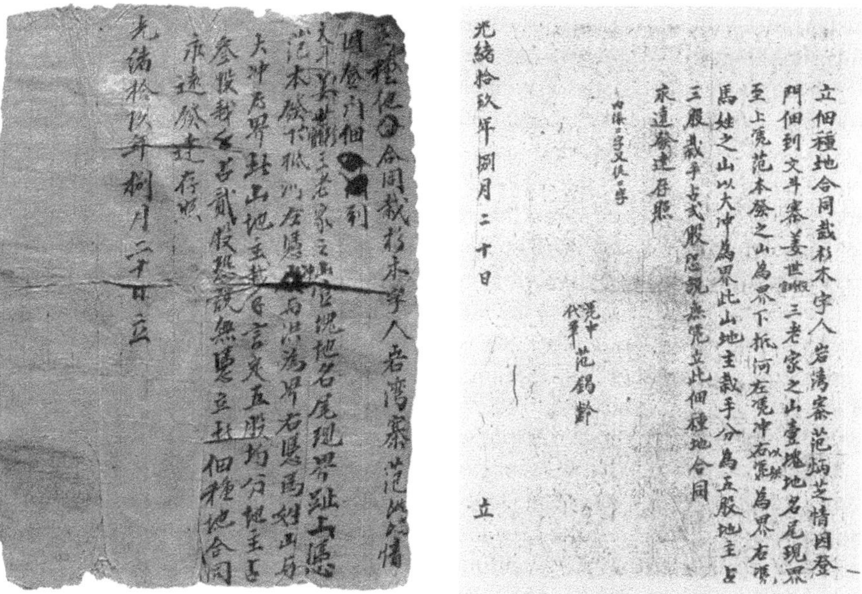

Fig. 4 A rough draft (left) and the corresponding formal contract (2)

land and planting cunninghamia trees (*li dian zhongdi hetong zai shamu zi*)." The latter replaced the expression "division" with "tenancy," which is obviously a better summary of the nature of the contract. In addition, no other contracts whose titles solely contain "planting (*zhongdi*)" were found in Wendou, while all other related contracts added one more word, "tenancy," in front of it as "*dian zhongdi* (tenant planting)."[122] Thus, it seems that the revision was more professional in the context of Wendou.

The second correction is related to the modification of the boundary of the forest land in the contract. The forest land was determined by the *sizhi* or "the four boundaries or ends," in this case the upper, the lower, the left, and the right. Among these four boundaries, the left boundary has been modified from "the mountain ridge (*ling*)" to "the valley (*chong*)." Indirectly, this correction probably reflects the process of confirming or reconfirming the boundary by both parties in the production of the contract. A similar situation concerning two parcels of forest land can be found in another manuscript, which specified the four boundaries of the first forest land and the upper and the lower boundaries of the second forest land, but left the right and the left boundaries of the second parcel undefined (written as "△△").[123] This may also reflect that, at the time when this manuscript was drafted, the specific boundaries of

[122] See, e.g., Christian Daniels, Yang Yougeng, and Takeuchi Fusaji, *Kishū Myaozoku ringyō keiyaku monjo kaihen (1736–1950-nen)*, vol. 2, C-0050.

[123] See Chen Jinquan and Du Wanhua, *Jiang Yuanze jiacang qiyue wenshu*, 542.

the two sites had not yet been fully clarified, so the unclear part was written as "△△." This should be replaced with a clearer description after further investigation.

On the above grounds, the writing process of *yigao* can be reconstructed as starting from a rough draft to a formal and deliberate contract. The first step also required a process of negotiation considering the plentiful signs of erasure or correction which remained in the draft. All the issues that had been discussed and confirmed by both sides at the time could be taken down in advance, but for those items that had not yet been determined (such as the transaction price),[124] they could be left blank and were to be filled up when the formal contract was concluded.[125]

The second step was to have the prepared draft transcribed,[126] by a formal scribe at the event, into a more legible and well-presented contract. This also represented a procedure of finalizing the negotiation. As it was believed that one could back out of the draft agreement and modify it,[127] the clauses in the draft were not determined until the writing of the final contract was finished.

In sum, a scribe has two ways to gather the basic information for writing contract content, namely either *yikou* or *yigao*. Although the latter was not as common as the former, both ways reflected the process from the preliminary negotiation to the contracts' finalization. In the meantime, the scribe was introduced to the final stage and played a vital role even in the contract negotiations.

3.3 Communicating Knowledge of Contract Forms

After collecting all the necessary information on the contract content, the scribe's job was then to use his knowledge of contract forms to express the content in a proper and contractual way. It is considered that in the Ming and Qing dynasties scribes had sufficient awareness concerning the typology of transactions and the question of which contract form should be employed in each case.[128] As the form was such an important matter to the contract writing, some scribes would even specifically prepare "form scripts/fill-in forms" in advance that covered all general terms, while later the specific information could be filled in according to the actual situation.[129] This shows that merely being literate was not enough to serve as a contractual scribe, and that "what is more important is that they know the 'rules,' and they possess 'form scripts'

---

[124] For example, the aforementioned contract draft says that "the contract price was agreed at △ taels," which does not indicate the specific number. See ibid.

[125] A similar situation in which one could write an anonymous draft contract prior to the formal one when transferring land was also recorded in the customs survey report of Zhongmou County, Henan province. See Wu Xiangxiang, *Zhongguo minshi xiguan daquan*, 64.

[126] A rarely seen contract suggests that, in some circumstances, there was one person who was specially assigned to prepare the draft, while another person, the scribe, had the task of transcribing the contract text. See Li [36].

[127] See Fan Jinmin, "'Caoyi' yu 'yidan': Qing dai Jiangnan tianzhai maimai wenshu de dingli" 92.

[128] See Wang [86].

[129] See Tian Tao, *Huangyan susong dang'an ji diaocha baogao*, 35–36.

that can be used [for contract writing]."[130] Therefore, not only the material of "form scripts" but also the invisible "rules" embodied the scribal knowledge of contract forms. The contractual knowledge was the symbolic element of a qualified scribe. But how was this knowledge communicated, especially to frontier areas such as Wendou Village? The question can be discussed at two levels: firstly, the knowledge transmitted from the hinterland to the frontier area, and, secondly, the utilization of the knowledge of contract forms within the village society.

3.3.1 Knowledge Communication from the Hinterland to the Frontier Area

The influence from the official side was limited in the communication of contractual knowledge since it is generally believed that there were no statutory contract forms.[131] Judging from the contracting practice in the Qing dynasty, contracts of (for example) real estate were concluded according to the rules of the folk society rather than the official law.[132] However, this does not mean that no official efforts were made in this regard. In 1727, Tian Wenjing (1622–1732), who was acknowledged to be the best provincial governor by the Yongzheng emperor,[133] initiated the so-called "*qizhi qigen zhi fa*,"[134] which was to issue "official contract forms with their stubs" and to "[provide] that all real estate transactions were to be written down on these official contract forms in order to be considered valid."[135] However, the reform of introducing official contract forms was short-lived, since it was revoked in 1736, soon after Emperor Qianlong ascended to the throne.[136] Local initiatives taken to promote official contract forms do not seem to have ended immediately after the demise of Tian's reform at the central government level. For example, in Fujian province, in order to "stop counterfeiting contracts and then quell litigation,"[137] contracts of real estate transactions were required to apply the officially issued contract forms.[138]

However, the most important component in promoting the application of contract forms and unifying these forms might not have been the official regulations but the folk customs in the society.[139] Even in places where official contract forms had been

[130] Wang Xu, *Qizhi qiannian*, 234.

[131] See Li [41].

[132] See Liu [50].

[133] See Mote [56].

[134] For more details, see Kungang et al. [35].

[135] Gabbiani [24].

[136] See Kungang et al., *Qinding da Qing huidian shili*, vol. 763.

[137] Taiwan yinhang jingji yanjiushi [79].

[138] See ibid. Another example of local provisions on contract forms can be found in a document from She County, Anhui province of 1906, see Tian et al. [82]. Applying the official contract forms in China was not implemented again in practice at a central level until the end of the Qing dynasty. See Sun [78].

[139] See You [102].

stressed repeatedly, such as the above-mentioned Fujian province, the government in its official communication still had to admit the local customs of contract writing and accept people's contracts written according to their own rules.[140] At the village level, such as Wendou, the change of the national policy concerning contract forms barely had any visible effect on the local contract writing practice. It rather seems that, based on evidence from Taiwan, scribes did not necessarily consider the official regulations when writing contracts but continued to adhere to the unwritten and indigenous folk customs.[141]

Nevertheless, one crucial part of the folk customs concerning contract forms was not indigenous in the Qingshui River region. Although contracts from the region present an evident feature of using contract forms, it is widely believed that the communication of knowledge from the hinterland to the frontier area concerning contracts was critical to the cultivation of this practice.[142] Due to the lack of concrete evidence, the process of disseminating and promoting contracts has not yet been examined thoroughly, but a likely explanation is that the contract practice came down to "the influx of garrison troops and other Han incomers" during the Ming-Qing periods.[143] Historical evidence found in the *Gazetteer of Dushan Sub-prefecture*[144] partially elucidates the connection between the communication of knowledge, including concerning contracts, in the Miao area and the contact, whether formal or informal, between the Han and the Miao people:

> The trespass of the Han people into the Miao villages has long been forbidden according to the regulation. [Now they] go so far as to incite litigations... Recently, there are more and more Miao people who became literate, some of them even took part in the imperial examination and went to schools; it is not prohibited by the regulation that [the Miao people] invite teachers to teach their sons... [I] investigated and found out that there were unworthy *shengyuan* (licentiates) who eked out their livelihood in Miao villages; from the outset, they taught the children how to write litigation documents and sale contracts of field.[145]

This material directly explains how the Miao people acquired the knowledge of writing legal instruments, including contracts, from their Han teachers, and the close relationship between learning the writing of the language[146] and its application in contracts and other formal documents.

A source in English also illustrates the same issue of knowledge communication through language learning in the Miao frontier from another angle. A Protestant missionary, Samuel R. Clarke (1853–1946), who had lived in the Miao region for

---

[140]See Taiwan yinhang jingji yanjiushi, *Taiwan sifa wuquan bian*, vol. 3, 592–593.

[141]See Chun-Ying Wu, "Taiwan daishu de lishi kaocha," 59.

[142]The process of communication is later called "contract documents coming from the east" by scholars since the region is located to the southwest of the hinterland. See Xu [96], Cheng [13], Deng and Qiu [20], Xu and Cheng [97].

[143]Wu [90].

[144]Dushan Sub-prefecture, or Dushan County nowadays, is also located in the central region of the Miao territory; its straight-line distance to Jinping County is around 190 km.

[145]Liu et al. [48].

[146]For the diffusion of Chinese characters in the Miao territory, see Wang and Zhang [85].

decades from the late nineteenth century to the early twentieth century, offered a detailed account of the relationship between the Chinese language and the contract in the Miao society, in his book published in the last year of the Qing dynasty (1911):

> At the present time there are schools in the Miao villages where Chinese literature is taught... When we opened a school at Panghai[147] some years ago, and offered to teach the scholars to write their own language in the Roman script, the parents would not consent, but wished their children to learn to read and write Chinese. Their way of looking at the matter is not hard to understand. What writing they have to do must be done for them in Chinese. Any Miao who can read and write passably may easily make his living among his neighbours by doing their reading and writing for them. All proclamations and official notifications, all pleas and counter-pleas in law cases have to be written in Chinese. When a Miao headman receives a dispatch from the magistrate, he has to find some one to read it for him and write his reply. All their contracts, mortgages, and deeds of sale or rental are written in Chinese, and not one in a hundred of them when he buys a piece of land is able to read the deed of sale when it is written.[148]

In this description, the main reason why the parents of Miao villages wanted their children to learn Chinese was to enable them to read and write various formal documents including the contract, thereby enabling them to make a living from it in the village. In general, it seems that the process of disseminating the Chinese language in Miao villages was also the process of disseminating contracts and related documentary knowledge.

Apart from the direct teacher-student learning reflected in both the Chinese and English materials, contract forms in daily-use encyclopedias and, later, the separated contractual manuals also played an important role in the process of communicating knowledge in the Miao territory, as they did in other regions during the Ming-Qing times.[149] Although no printed contractual manual has yet been found in Wendou, it cannot be ruled out that the contracts in the village were not affected by those handbooks. An un-dated hand-written booklet containing form manuscripts for the use of weddings and funerals was found in the village (See Fig. 5),[150] illustrating that, though not including any scripts concerning contracts, manuals of contract forms as a related genre of documentary forms might have existed in the village at the time.

Another body of evidence (see Fig. 6) includes two manuscripts extracted from two completely different sources: the first is an ignored slip of paper that was put in a booklet from Wendou Village,[151] and the second is a model manuscript excerpted by the author from a popular daily-use encyclopedia printed in the early Qing dynasty.[152]

---

[147] The place is located in the southeast of Guizhou.

[148] Clarke [15].

[149] See Wang [88].

[150] Courtesy of Prof. Chen Jinquan and Prof. Pan Zhicheng, No. JTQ-1-P1010001 & P1010002, Collected from Jiang Tingqing in Wendou Village, Guizhou.

[151] The broken oblong scrip, or note, seems to have been photocopied accidentally by the editor since it was sandwiched between two other pages of a booklet and there are even other unrelated characters written on it. See Zhang and Wang [120].

[152] See Li et al. [42].

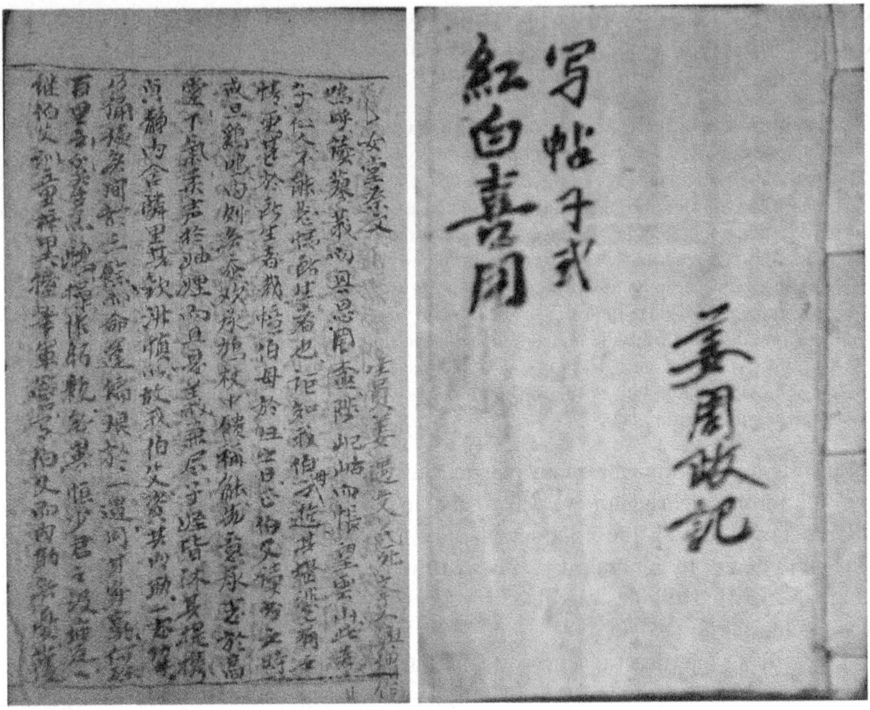

Fig. 5 A booklet of form manuscripts for the use of weddings and funerals

As shown, the left slip is in fact a typical invitation once sent by Jiang Xihao[153] and his niece, with characters written in regular script in a neat and legible way, using a sophisticated and literary language that obviously came from prevailing handbooks of forms. Likewise, the right text, which is an excerpt from a well-known manual of forms, can be used to verify the link between the form book and its application in actual writings.

It is easy to tell the influence of the daily-use encyclopedia on the invitation letter simply from their similar layouts—a few lines written on the left and right sides of the upper part of the paper with a line written below. Almost all words and phrases

---

[153]In Wendou, Jiang Xihao was also frequently invited as a middleman and scribe from the tenth year to the thirty-third year of Guangxu (1884–1907), and one manuscript signed as "Xihao" was dated to the fourteenth year of Daoguang (1834). See Christian Daniels, Yang Yougeng, and Takeuchi Fusaji, *Kishū Myaozoku ringyō keiyaku monjo kaihen (1736–1950-nen)*, vol. 3, F-0006; Zhang Yingqiang and Wang Zongxun, *Qingshuijiang wenshu*, vol. 1 (12), 137, 140; ibid., vol. 1(13): 41, 248, 351; Zhang Yingqiang and Wang Zongxun, *Qingshuijiang wenshu*, vol. 3 (10), 3; Chen Jinquan and Du Wanhua, *Jiang Yuanze jiacang qiyue wenshu*, 474, 477, 480; Chen Jinquan and Du Wanhua, *Jiang Qigui jiacang qiyue wenshu*, 442, 447; Chen and Guo [5].

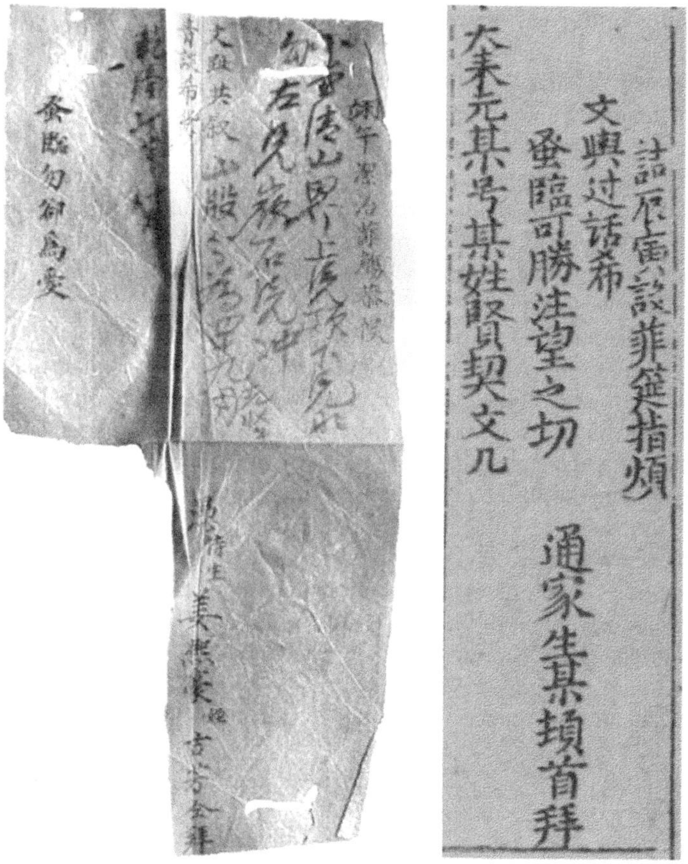

Fig. 6 An invitation from Wendou Village (left) and a model invitation in a daily-use encyclopedia

that the invitation used can be found in these popularly used encyclopedias in Ming-Qing China. For example, a *Wanbao quanshu* printed in the Qianlong reign includes almost all the invitation-related vocabulary of the Wendou letter.[154]

The possible interaction between the two manuscripts and the widespread circulation of encyclopedias shows the profound influence of documentary forms from the hinterland on the writing practice of remote Miao villages, and, concomitantly as a necessary part of those form books, illustrates the process of the knowledge of contract forms which entered the social life of the villages. Both the teacher-student language learning and the spreading of form manuals represented key links of knowledge communication from the hinterland to the frontier area.

[154]See Mao [54].

3.3.2 Using Contract Forms in Villages: Application and Imitation

The typical way of exercising the contract manuals was to find the suitable contract form from manuals and to apply this form to the real situation in the writing, replacing over-general language with precise diction, eliminating inapposite words and sentences, and adding proper descriptions that suited the given situation. This approach also explains why they were often named *huotao*,[155] which can be translated literally as "running knot" but actually means "flexible formulas,"[156] indicating that those forms shall be further edited according to the real situation by a scribe who applies it in his writings.

An often-overlooked fact in this connection is that, in addition to the application of contract forms, imitating other actual contracts rather than those fictional and general forms might have played an important role in the scribal writing. This explains somewhat why a prodigious number of contracts were found in Wendou with an incommensurately small number of materials related to contract forms—contract forms might not be necessary if another actual contract can be consulted. Moreover, scribes in the village not only accepted the contract forms but also generated, perhaps not deliberately, new contract forms which were improved by being region-specific.[157] More generally, this explains how the scribe became a crucial figure in the development of the whole institution of Chinese contracts.[158]

Although, as mentioned, no collected and printed handbooks of contract forms have been found in Wendou Village so far, there are a few pieces of manuscripts that can be taken as evidence for the production of contract forms through actual contracts.

A manuscript (see Fig. 7)[159] concerns the sale of a child bride which was once considered as "a probable contract form"[160] by the editor, while some further believe that it was "apparently a contract form taken from daily-use encyclopedias."[161] The most obvious feature of the contract forms made based on an actual contract is that they often retain some specific details which can be traced to their original text, while replacing most personal information by certain fixed characters;[162] this feature can be seen in this manuscript. In addition, at the end of the manuscript, it is suggested to the reader or user of the manuscript that he or she can "either write the contract

[155]See, e.g., Wu [92].

[156]See Unschuld and Zheng [83].

[157]It is believed that more regional and ethnological features were gradually added into the forms of contracts in the Qingshui River region. See Wu Caimao, "Ming dai yilai Qingshuijiang wenshu shuxie geshi de bianhua yu minzhong xiguan de bianqian," 187.

[158]See Wang Xu, *Qizhi qiannian*, 232.

[159]Chen Jinquan and Du Wanhua, *Jiang Yuanze jiacang qiyue wenshu*, 543. The same manuscript is also included in another publication, see Pan Zhicheng and Wu Dahua, *Tudi guanxi ji qita shiwu wenshu*, vol. 1, 93. The transcriptions in the two books are slightly different.

[160]The editor, however, finally concluded that it was a "draft." See Pan Zhicheng and Wu Dahua, *Tudi guanxi ji qita shiwu wenshu*, vol. 1, 93.

[161]Liang [44].

[162]A similar situation can be seen in bamboo slips of early times, see Zhang [107].

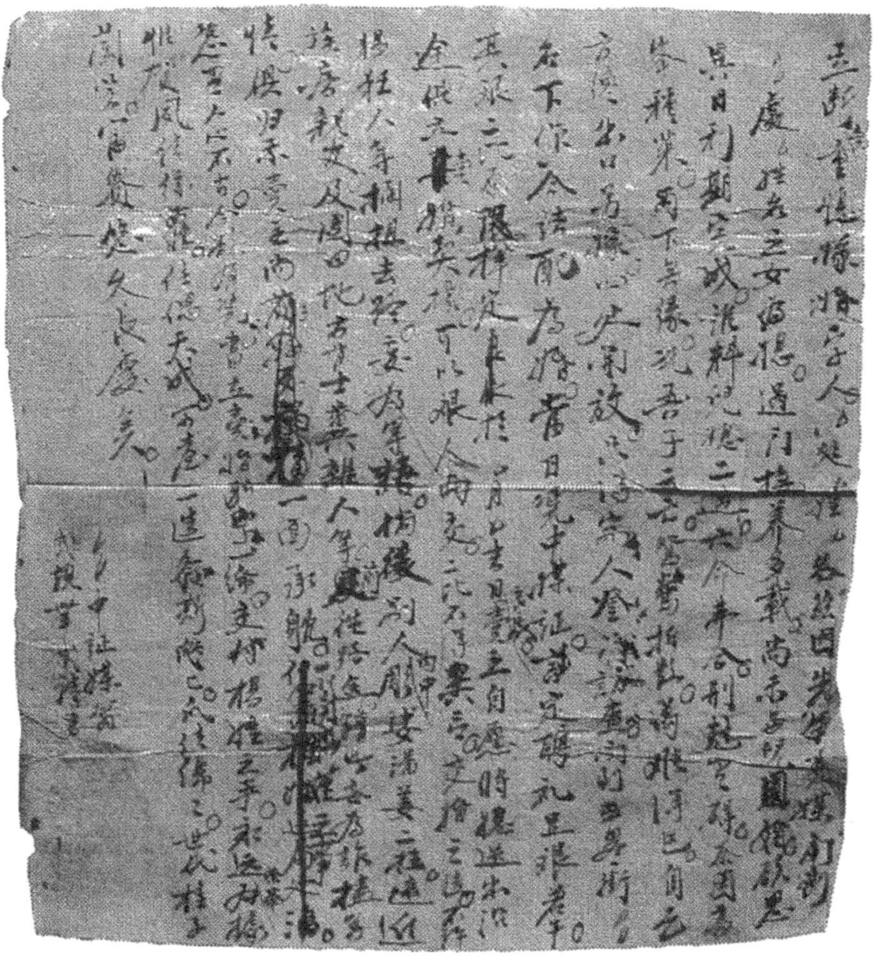

Fig. 7 A contract form for the sale of a child bride in Wendou

holographically or invite a scribe." This evidently signifies that it was a contract form that included all possible situations and so proposed the suggestion of how to apply it.

As a comparison, another version of this manuscript with only slight textual differences has been found in Wendou (see Fig. 8).[163] The existence of the two versions of one original text in a village proves that a reality-based and newly generated contract form has been disseminated and was probably being used in the village society by the scribe.

---

[163]Courtesy of Prof. Chen Jinquan and Prof. Pan Zhicheng, No. JYZ-9- P1010091. Collected from Jiang Yuanze in Wendou Village, Guizhou

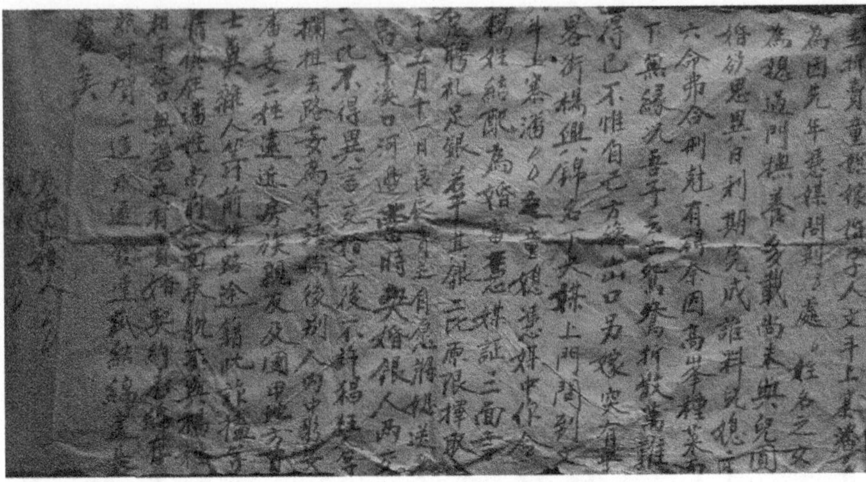

Fig. 8 Another contract form for the sale of a child bride in Wendou

In sum, the process can be described as follows. Firstly, the knowledge of contract forms in the village society of the Miao people possibly came from the hinterland by means of the entry of Han people (teacher-student learning) and the spread of contract manuals along with other daily-use encyclopedias. Secondly, the learned scribe in the frontier areas could either apply the contract form from the handbooks or imitate an existing actual contract to write a new one.[164] Thirdly, by accumulating experience in this exercise, village scribes gradually added more practical and local-oriented elements into the contract form when they tried to create new forms that were born out of actual contracts. This process of localization with respect to contracts signifies that, in a developmental sense, imitation might represent the most important tool for writing contracts.

3.4 *Postscripts and Signatures*

Apart from the main body, the subordinate parts are also indispensable to the effectiveness of the contract; the postscripts and signatures are especially vital.

The purpose of a postscript is normally to explain the correction of the main text of the contract, including deleting and adding characters.[165] A typical postscript will

[164] It was not easy for normal people to get access to the actual contract owned by other people. That is also a reason why scribes liked to write down a manuscript in the form of "contract form," eliminating personal and private information, for reference. This issue of accessibility will be discussed again in Sect. 5.2 of Chap. 5.

[165] Other information would be added in a postscript from time to time, such as the scribe's fee. Also, one may notice another type of "postscript" at the end of a contract which stated the later situation or transaction in regard to the property recorded in the contract, such as that the forest on

indicate at length how many characters were deleted from and how many were added to the main text. It is conceivable that the postscript was added by the scribe after he or she had completed the writing and checking of the main text of the contract. When the scribe found out that some minor issues were miswritten, he or she was allowed to modify the text of the original contract directly, instead of writing a new contract. In this case, the postscript could be seen as an editor's note to the final version.

The writing of the postscript might be related to the reading stage of the contracting ritual. In the customs of the hinterland, there was a procedure of reading after completion of the writing of the contract, which demands that "the whole contract text should be read out publicly by the scribe," and, if no objection was raised by any participant after hearing of the contract, it could then be signed.[166] Although no explicit record of the reading procedure is seen in the contracts of Wendou, clues appear in one document of dispute settlement: "The Jiang knew that the contract of innocence had been read aloud face to face with me, Wang Chengbang, in the presence of the invited middleman."[167] This action was taken in order to check the terms originally recorded in the contract. In the dispute settlement, both sides chose the method of reading aloud, "face to face," to examine the text of the contract, and it is conceivable that this could also be a commonly used way of checking contracts which were already written. A postscript might then entail an exercise in proofreading the contract text.

Furthermore, in general, the signature is a crucial prerequisite in proving the authenticity of a text.[168] In a litigation document, "Yao Tingbiao vs. Shaoxiang," which was widely circulated in villages of the Qingshui River area, it is mentioned that, whenever a shareholder claimed his or her dividend of a sold property, the recipient should "sign or make his or her own mark right after receiving the money."[169] This shows that, under certain circumstances, signatures were considered probative and necessary. Another example is the commonly seen *hetong*, or "indenture," which is often written in duplicate, or infrequently triplicate,[170] on several pieces of paper with a specific phrase. Often these phrases were not names but lucky words written

---

the forest land had later been harvested for three times and now a tenant would rent the land again. See, e.g., Christian Daniels, Yang Yougeng, and Takeuchi Fusaji, *Kishū Myaozoku ringyō keiyaku monjo kaihen (1736–1950-nen)*, vol. 2, B-0004. However, this is not a "postscript" to the original contract but an explanation of the further situation concerning the contract property added by the preserver for reference.

[166] Zhou Yaoming, *Hanzu minjian jiaoji fengsu*, 139–140.

[167] Pan et al. [61].

[168] Today, the signature is generally used as evidence that "1. the signatory has personally seen what he or she signed; 2. he or she acknowledges or even accords with its contents; 3. thereby taking responsibility for its accuracy as well as; 4. lending authority to it (as much as his or her position in relation to the issue allows)." However, the signature of early imperial China might not conform to those features. See Enno Giele, "Signatures of 'Scribes' in Early Imperial China," 361.

[169] Zhang [109].

[170] A contract in triplicate, with the propitious phrase "[concluding] the contract [will bring] forever prosperity" written on the junctions of the edges, can be found in Zhang Yingqiang and Wang Zongxun, *Qingshuijiang wenshu*, vol. 1(13), 46; Zhang and Wang [119]; Chen Jinquan and Du Wanhua, *Jiang Yuanze jiacang qiyue wenshu*, 472.

across the junctions of the edges of two or three sheets of paper, which were akin to a parchment document "chirograph" designed to prove the contract's authenticity.[171] Thus, it is believed that "signatures or marks made by contracting parties were the indication of the consensus and also a vital step for the contract to go into effect."[172]

Most contracts in Wendou Village indeed bear the name of their contracting parties and, generally, the name of the establisher of the contract, namely the vendor or tenant, which appears at the end of the whole document.[173] But can these names be regarded as signatures? If the handwriting of the names, which is exactly the individuality that a signature should provide, is taken into account, one will soon notice that on most occasions the handwriting of the whole contract is consistent. This shows that the whole text was written by one single person, including the names of all the parties involved in the ending part of the contract.[174] In the case of an allographic contract, the "signature" is normally written by the scribe, so it cannot be deemed a real "signature." Similar customs also existed in the hinterland where the names of the contracting parties did not necessarily have to be signed by them personally but could be written by the scribe instead.[175]

In Wendou, even if one of the contract participants was able to sign by himself, his name, along with the names of other participants, would possibly be written by the scribe all together. For example, Jiang Shaoya, who was a familiar scribe in contracts from Wendou,[176] once joined a contract as a middleman,[177] but the handwriting of his name in the contract appears to be different from his signatures in other contracts written by himself as the scribe; the writing of the whole contract was consistent. As one of the most important scribes in the village, Jiang Shaoya was obviously literate and knew every rule of concluding contracts, but even though he himself was an expert in contract writing, his name was also written by someone else who was appointed as the scribe of this contract. This indicates that in the area the names on the contracts were not, and at least not required to be, "signatures."

In general, instead of signatures, specific marks were drawn and appended to the contract immediately below the names of the parties.[178] It was also a custom in the

---

[171] A contract suggests that the writing of this part of the contract, called a "half character," might be specially assigned to a person whose name is indicated at the end of the contract. See Li Bin, *Guizhou Qingshuijiang wenshu, Liping wenshu*, vol. 12, 93.

[172] Liang Cong, *Qing dai Qingshuijiang xiayou cunzhai shehui de qiyue guifan yu zhixu*, 69. Also, the signature of the vendor in the case of the sale of real estate was required by the custom according to the survey in the hinterland. See Qian Nanjing guomin zhengfu sifa xingzheng bu, *Mingshi xiguan diaocha baogao lu*, vol. 1, 106.

[173] In another region, many participants, including the witnesses, would signed their names at the end of a contract. See Li Ren-yuan, "Making Texts in Villages," 314.

[174] This seems to imply that, in extreme cases, a scribe could freely "create" any contract at will. But this is hardly possible, given the social context in which the contract takes place. This will be discussed in detail in Chap. 5.

[175] See Wu Xiangxiang, *Zhongguo minshi xiguan daquan*, 26, 34–35.

[176] The career of the scribe in the village will be discussed in detail in Sect. 5.4.2 of Chap. 5.

[177] For the example, see Chen Jinquan and Du Wanhua, *Jiang Qigui jiacang qiyue wenshu*, 206.

[178] In Dunhuang manuscripts, a peculiar form of finger-seal was commonly used. See Chen [9].

hinterland that, "when establishing a contract, the names [of the parties] should be written and the marks should be drawn."[179] In this case, it seems that the affixed names were not necessarily holographic, but the marks should be drawn autographically.

Although far from common, drawing marks as a way of signing also existed in contracts of Wendou Village. In the hinterland, apart from the signature written by the literate, these marks drawn by the illiterate could be "circles, dots, or crosses."[180] In contracts of Wendou, five types of signing or drawing are concluded as follows (see Table 3).

(1) Writing the character(s) *ya* or *yafada*.[181] These two phrases literally mean "signed" and "signed for prosperity."
(2) Drawing non-literal marks, such as circles, crosses, and dots.[182]
(3) Using the paraph, or "stylized signature"[183] (*huaya*).[184] This was deemed an important anti-counterfeiting method,[185] but it might be too difficult to be used even for some literate people.
(4) Using the handprint[186] or fingerprint.[187] Normally, it is believed that handprints or fingerprints would not appear in land transfers. They were used in transactions related to personal relations, such as selling a wife, repudiation, or buying and selling adopted children.[188] However, sample 3 is a contract of a transaction on timber shares but bears a fingerprint, indicating that it was the print of the middle finger of the left hand of the vendor.
(5) Using the private seal.[189] In general, private seals were rarely used in contracts.[190] People from the region did not even seem to value the official

[179] Wu Xiangxiang, *Zhongguo minshi xiguan daquan*, 32. See also Qian Nanjing guomin zhengfu sifa xingzheng bu, *Mingshi xiguan diaocha baogao lu*, vol. 1, 442.

[180] Wu Xiangxiang, *Zhongguo minshi xiguan daquan*, 70.

[181] Samples 1–3 of type (1) are from Zhang Yingqiang and Wang Zongxun, *Qingshuijiang wenshu*, vol. 1 (12), 260.

[182] Samples 1–3 of type (2) are from Chen Jinquan and Du Wanhua, *Jiang Qigui jiacang qiyue wenshu*, 7; Chen Jinquan and Du Wanhua, *Jiang Yuanze jiacang qiyue wenshu*, 13.

[183] For the translation, see Mark A. Allee, *Law and Local Society in Late Imperial China*, 177.

[184] Samples 1–3 of type (3) are from Zhang Yingqiang and Wang Zongxun, *Qingshuijiang wenshu*, vol. 3 (7), 226; Zhang Yingqiang and Wang Zongxun, *Qingshuijiang wenshu*, vol. 1(13), 92, 94.

[185] See Feng Xuewei, *Ming Qing qiyue de jiegou gongneng ji yiyi*, 105–107; Liu Daosheng, *Ming Qing Huizhou zongzu wenshu yanjiu*, 77.

[186] For a discussion of contracts with handprints, see Sommer [77].

[187] Samples 1–3 of type (4) are from Wang Zongxun, *Wendou*, 104; Chen Jinquan and Guo Liang, *Yi Zunfa Jiang Qicheng deng jiacang susong wenshu*, 256; Christian Daniels, Yang Yougeng, and Takeuchi Fusaji, *Kishū Myaozoku ringyō keiyaku monjo kaihen (1736–1950-nen)*, vol. 2, B-0183.

[188] See A Feng, *Ming Qing shidai funü de diwei yu quanli*, 111.

[189] Samples 1–2 of type (5) are from one contract from the collection of Jiang Tingqing in Wendou, Guizhou, No. Z-001; the picture was taken by the author in September 2015.

[190] There was an examination of one collection of more than two thousand contracts in the Ming-Qing periods preserved in one branch of the National Library of China; it turns out that, though a few of them used signatures, not even one single piece of contract used the private seal. See Yang [99].

Table 3 Samples of types of signing contracts in Wendou

Types	Sample 1	Sample 2	Sample 3
(1)			
(2)	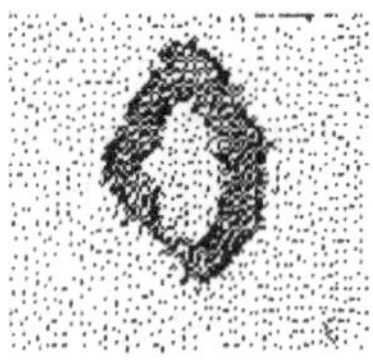		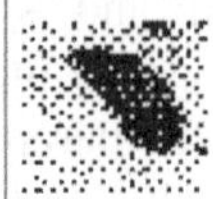
(3)			
(4)			
(5)			–

seal and the legitimacy and authority it represented.[191] However, in a contract dated 1898 collected by the author in Wendou Village, the establisher affixed his seal twice, firstly on the top of the paragraph about the price and then at the end of the main text.

[191] See Li and Hu [37].

In addition, it should be noted that, in certain cases, drawing marks would cost money, which was called *huazi qian* or "money for drawing marks" in the hinterland.[192] Although this phenomenon is yet to be seen in Wendou, it appears in a contract in Jiunan, another place within the Qingshui River area, whereby a special person was appointed, according to the commentaries to the contract by the editor, to be in charge of drawing marks. Furthermore, when required, this specially appointed person was obliged to teach the contracting parties how to draw the marks and verify, at the same time, that the marks were truly drawn by the contracting parties personally.[193] In this case, he or she was deemed one type of middleman and was paid for his or her job.

In sum, what needs to be emphasized is that, after examining the rare cases of using personalized marks, signing or drawing marks was far from common practice in Wendou. By means of signatures or marks, the effectiveness of the contract surely could be reinforced, but it was not a compulsory procedure in concluding contracts.

4 The Scribe's Fee

The physical product of the scribal service is the piece of paper with the final version of the contract written on it. But was there a fee to pay after the product had been handed over? If the scribal service could be deemed professional or at least "semi-professional,"[194] the corresponding remuneration should be an essential element for supporting this professionalism.[195] In the case of urban "professional plaint-writers," their remuneration has been explored in a tentative way through individual case

[192]See Qian Nanjing guomin zhengfu sifa xingzheng bu, *Mingshi xiguan diaocha baogao lu*, vol. 1, 543. For a special discussion in this regard, see Liu Gaoyong, "Qing dai maimai qiyue yanjiu," 134–144.

[193]See Gao Cong and Tan Hongpei, *Guizhou Qingshuijiang liuyu Ming Qing tusi qiyue wenshu, Jiunan pian*, 103.

[194]See Zhao Siyuan, "19 shiji Huizhou xiangcun de tudi shichang, xinyong jizhi yu guanxi wangluo," 96. Also, in his introduction to the second part "The City in Space," G. William Skinner marked rural scribes as "occupational specialists" (together with traders, artisans, religious specialists, pettifoggers, geomancers, and so forth) when discussing the concepts of the Great Tradition and the Little Tradition relating to the urban-rural division in Chinese society. See Skinner [75].

[195]The long-standing uncertainty of the professionalism of rural scribes and middlemen caused many arguments. For instance, it is assumed that the role of the scribe cannot be seen as professional, at least in dispute settlement procedures, for the scribe and the contracting parties may come from the same village or kinship family in most cases. See Deng [19]. Also, some believed that "[i]t should be remembered that there were no professional writers or lawyers available to villagers in this period." See Hase [29].

descriptions;[196] as for rural scribes, however, the current understanding is not yet sufficient.[197]

Thanks to the survival of some scribal notes, even though their number is extremely limited, an examination of the proper amount of the scribe's fee is possible. In particular, when combined with other relevant sources, a series of questions related to the scribe's fee and its payment, including the necessity, the method, the timing of the payment as well as the payer of the fee, can be posed.

4.1 *To Pay or not to Pay?*

In the relatively scarce scribal notes found in Wendou contracts, which served as the main materials for this section, the remuneration of scribes was designated *biyin*, literally translated as "the silver for penning."[198] In most cases, the scribe would directly add a note under his or her name; for example, "[the scribe] accepted [a certain amount of] silver" (*shouyin*),[199] "[the scribe] ate (took) [a certain amount of] silver" (*chiyin*),[200] "[a certain amount of] kun silver [had been paid or taken]" (*kunyin*),[201] or simply wrote that "[a certain amount of] silver [had been paid or taken]" (*yin*).[202]

These notes clearly point to the payment and receipt of the scribe's fee after the contract has been completed by the hired scribe. Apparently, it does not imply that only with these notes can one say that the scribal costs were incurred in transactions. In practice, in terms of the hinterland's convention of contract writing, the scribe's fee would presumably not be recorded in the contract[203]; this could only occasionally be

[196]See Philip C. C. Huang, *Civil Justice in China*, 164–165. It is believed that professional plaint-writers in large towns and cities such as county seats, although they differed notably from the contractual scribe, might have charged for their services. The discussion is based on materials from Gangyi's *Muling xuzhi* or "*What a magistrate should know.*".

[197]It is noticed that, in a study based on materials from Hong Kong, the writers of contracts "were paid for their trouble," though no further elaboration is offered. See Hayes [30].

[198]For example, at the end of Jiang Xingyu's contract of sale of farmland, the writer uses the term *biyin* and indicates that "Scribe Jiang Tingzuo's 'silver for penning (*biyin*) [is] two candareens exactly," see Chen Jinquan and Du Wanhua, *Jiang Yuanze jiacang qiyue wenshu*, 11.

[199]See e.g., Christian Daniels, Yang Yougeng, and Takeuchi Fusaji, *Kishū Myaozoku ringyō keiyaku monjo kaihen (1736–1950-nen)*, vol. 1, A-0006.

[200]See e.g., ibid., A-0005.

[201]See e.g., Zhang Yingqiang and Wang Zongxun, *Qingshuijiang wenshu*, vol. 1(13), 101. The exact meaning of "kun silver" (*kunyin*) still remains to be explained. Literally, however, *kun* means "threshold" as a noun and "to tie up" as a verb, which appear to be totally irrelevant. But *kunyin* together seemed to refer to the "intermediate costs" of transactions in Wendou's contracts, meaning more specifically "the scribe's fee" when it was written under the signature of a scribe.

[202]See e.g., Chen Jinquan and Du Wanhua, *Jiang Yuanze jiacang qiyue wenshu*, 10.

[203]For the question whether the scribe's fee will be noted in the contract or not, the author scanned through some other contemporary contract manuscripts, also during the Qing dynasty, in Huizhou, Taiwan, and other regions. Although the numerous manuscripts have not been reviewed one by

referred to in the postscript part.[204] The contracts of Wendou Village seem to share the same tradition since it was uncommon to record the scribe's fee within the main body of a contract. After analyzing several contracts of Wendou Village, it has previously been argued that a scribe's "remuneration generally would not be written explicitly in the contract, though there might be some exceptions."[205] However, certain do's and don'ts with respect to the circumstances under which the scribe's fee would be noted in a contract might not exist in practice.[206]

---

one, generally speaking it is very clear that indicating the scribe's fee directly in the main text of a contract was a less common situation. For the examined manuscripts, see Mindai shi kenkyu shi hen [55], Wang et al. [87], Choi [14], Taiwan shiliao jicheng bianji weiyuanhui [80].

[204] In a contract of the eighth year of Daoguang (1828), the writer indicated that "the scribe's fee (*bizi*, similar to *biyin*, literally translated as the "fee for penning") [is] eight candareens of silver exactly" in its postscript part. See Mindai shi kenkyu shi hen, *Chūgoku tochi keiyaku bunsho shiryō shū (Kin–Shin)*, 12. In addition, a Jiaqing-era booklet named *Hetong wenyue tengqibu* (*Transcription of Indentures and Contracts*) published in the 11th volume of the foregoing *Huizhou qiannian qiyue wenshu* contains quite a few contracts in which their intermediate costs are recorded. However, since the booklet is a transcribed version, it is not clear whether these notes of the intermediate costs, including the scribe's fee, were written in the original contract or not. See Wang Yuxin and Zhou Shaoquan, *Huizhou qiannian qiyue wenshu: Qing, Minguo bian*, 189–379.

[205] See Guizhou sheng bianjizu, *Dongzu shehui lishi diaocha*, 14.

[206] One of the satisfactory illustrations might be a set of two mutually related contracts found in Wendou Village, which were written on the same day, i.e. "the tenth day of the eighth month in the fifty-eighth year of Qianlong (September 14, 1793)" (incidentally, it is exactly the same day that George Macartney's delegation met with the Qianlong Emperor in Beijing), and by the same scribe "Jiang Bizhou." For the first manuscript, it indicated that the scribe's fee was "one mace," while the second one only recorded the scribe's name without any further information about his remuneration. Moreover, these two contracts share the same vendees, the "Jiang Chaojin brothers." Thus, it is conceivable that these two contracts can be considered as being written on the same occasion. As for the contract price, the first one's price is "three taels and eight maces," while the price of the second one (without the note of the scribe's fee) is only "four maces." Provided that the writing of these two manuscripts could be seen as a continuous process on one single occasion, it became rather difficult to explain why the scribe's fee did not appear in one of these "same" manuscripts. One explanation could be that, in the second case, that the amount of the contract price was too small to charge an additional scribe's fee from it. In that circumstance, it was quite reasonable that the scribe wrote nothing about his remuneration. But there is another contract written by the same scribe which was finished some two months earlier, i.e. "the thirtieth day of the sixth month in the fifty-eighth year of Qianlong (July 20, 1793)," and its contract price was only "five maces and eight candareens exactly," which was at the same level as in the second one. However, it indicated that the scribe's fee was "three candareens," which implies that there might not be any strong relationship between the low contract price and the payment of the scribe's fee. In

Since the note on the scribe's fee might represent the sole direct material available for analyzing the payment for scribes, contracts containing the note in Wendou Village were tracked down as far as possible and listed in Table 4. These contracts mainly concentrate on the early period from the reign of Qianlong to the reign of Jiaqing, except for one contract from a later period of Daoguang. However, it needs to be stressed that this does not necessarily mean that there was no need to pay the fee in later periods.[207] As the customs survey of the hinterland in later times suggests, scribes were still paid in contractual activities,[208] even though it was commonly not stated in the contract text.

In addition to the remuneration-related notes in contracts, descriptions concerning the scribe's payment could also be found in some manuscripts of "cost lists." As shown in Fig. 9,[209] the content partly reads: "Mr. Scribe wrote the *dispute settlement report* on behalf of [me/us], and it costs one thousand [copper] cashes (*wen*)." The scribe's fee was deemed an item in the cost list similarly to travel expenses, the costs of buying shoes, melons, and beans. Hence, it might have been common knowledge that, just as one pays for other goods, one should also pay to enjoy the service provided by the scribe.

On the basis of such limited materials, it is hard to define clearly the circumstances under which the contracting parties should pay the scribe. Nevertheless, the custom in the hinterland was that, "in case of writing a contract of sale, a certain amount of remuneration needs to be paid for inviting the middleman and the scribe," but, "for other kinds of contract relationships, remuneration for the middleman and the scribe are not necessary;" however, "if the peasant [that you] meet is kind enough, then [he/she] would give them (the middleman and the scribe) a 'red envelope' [as a reward]."[210] Similarly to the description of the hinterland's customs, except for the "contract of *dian*," which can also be seen as a "conditional sale of land," all other manuscripts recording the scribe's fee in Table 4 refer to the sales of forest land, shares, farmland, etc.

Thus, it seems that scribes were generally paid, albeit in different ways, for providing their services, especially in sales transactions. However, the scribe's fee was not always reflected in the texts of the contract.

---

addition, no further notes of the scribe's fee can be found in all other contracts written by the scribe Jiang Bizhou in the database of Wendou. Accordingly, to some extent, whether a scribe will record his remuneration in the contract or not could be relatively random. For the first, second, and third manuscripts, see Christian Daniels, Yang Yougeng, and Takeuchi Fusaji, *Kishū Myaozoku ringyō keiyaku monjo kaihen (1736–1950-nen)*, vol. 1, A-0046, A-0047; Chen Jinquan and Du Wanhua, *Jiang Qigui jiacang qiyue wenshu*, 311.

[207] A similar situation happens to the middleman's fee too. In later times, as with the notes of the scribe's fee, it is also very hard to find notes concerning the middleman's fee within the contract manuscript. However, there remains sufficient evidence which shows that the middleman's fee is a longstanding institution even in the later period of the Qing dynasty. See Qu [66].

[208] See Wu Xiangxiang, *Zhongguo minshi xiguan daquan*, 38–40.

[209] Courtesy of Prof. Chen Jinquan and Prof. Pan Zhicheng, No. JYZ-7- P1010076. Collected from Jiang Yuanze in Wendou Village, Guizhou.

[210] Zhou Yaoming, *Hanzu minjian jiaoji fengsu*, 139–140.

Table 4 The scribe's fee in Wendou Village during the Qing dynasty

Number	Contract title	Price	Scribe[a]	Scribe's fee		Middleman's fee		Year
D1-003	Contract of Sale of Forest Land	9	Jiang Qixiang	0.01	0.11%	0.05	0.56%	QL 13
D1-004	[Contract of] Sale of Forest Land	1.3	Jiang Dezhong	0.05	3.85%	–	–	QL 16
D2-004	[Contract of] Sale of Forest Land	2.2	Jiang Dezhong	0.05	2.27%	–	–	QL 16
A-A0005	Contract of Sale of Forest Land	5.25	Jiang Shaoyu	0.1	1.90%	0.1	1.90%	QL 31
A-A0006	Contract of Sale of Timber's Shares	2.3	Jiang Tingwei	0.05	2.17%	0.05	2.17%	QL 31
A-A0008	Contract of Sale of Forest Land	17	Jiang Hongwen	0.15	0.88%	0.2	1.18%	QL 32
D1-010[b]	Contract of Sale of Wet-rice Field	32	Jiang Zhoulong	0.2	0.63%	0.4	1.25%	QL 32
D1-011	Contract of Sale of Wet-rice Field	38	Jiang Tingzuo	0.2	0.53%	–	–	QL 32
D1-016	Contract of Sale of Wet-rice Field	6	Jiang Tingzuo	0.1	1.67%	0.1	1.67%	QL 35
D1-025	Contract of Sale	7.3	Chen Shimin	0.1	1.37%	0.1	1.37%	QL 43
A-A0038	Contract of Sale of Timber's Shares	6.8	Jiang Qiwei	0.03	0.44%	–	–	QL 53
D2-019	Contract of Sale of Camellia Farm	0.58	Jiang Bizhou	0.03	5.17%	0.02	3.45%	QL 58

(continued)

Table 4 (continued)

Number	Contract title	Price	Scribe[a]	Scribe's fee		Middleman's fee		Year
A-A0047	Contract of Sale of Timber's Shares	3.8	Jiang Tingzuo	0.1	2.63%	0.1	2.63%	QL 58
A-B0014	Contract of Sale of Timber's Shares	6.2	Wang Weicheng	0.06	0.97%	0.06	0.97%	JQ 6
C1-13-101	Contract of Sale of Timber's Shares	17	Zhang Youyuan	0.1[c]	0.59%	0.2	1.18%	JQ 14
C1-12-360	Contract of Sale of Timber's Shares	1.5	Teng Jiaxing	0.05	3.33%	–	–	JQ 22
C1-12-361	Contract of Sale of Timber's Shares	29	Teng Jiaxing	0.3	1.03%	0.4	1.38%	JQ 22
D1-400[d]	Contract of *Dian* of Wet-rice Field	5.5	Jiang Kaiyuan	–	–	0.1	1.82%	DG 24

Unit Tael

[a]The scribal note in manuscript A-A0008 indicates that it is an autograph writing. The note in C1-12-360 also indicates the same situation while it was actually written by the scribe. Moreover, the notes, respectively, say that the scribe is the little brother (in C1-12-360) and the son (C1-12-361) of one of the vendors

[b]In manuscript A-B0014 and C1-13-101, there are four middlemen in the transaction, while there are three in D1-016 and D1-003, and two in D1-010

[c]At the end of this manuscript, there is a character "seven" written closely next to the note "the scribe Zhang Youyuan['s] *kunyin* [is] one mace" between the "one" and the "mace." This probably means that the amount of the scribe's fee is "one mace and seven [candareens];" alternatively it could be seen as some scribal mistakes of redundant words. According to the analysis of the overall context, in this table, the figure keeps "0.1" with a footnote attached to it

[d]The scribal note of manuscript D1-400 indicates that the scribe acted as a middleman at the same time. Thus, the fee is not simply paid to the person for being a scribe, but might also include the part of the hosting (*dongdao*) fee according to the note

4.2 *How Much?*

It is generally acknowledged that the amount of the scribe's fee was in principle determined by certain percentages of the contract price. However, these percentages differed from place to place. According to a customs survey, the percentages of the

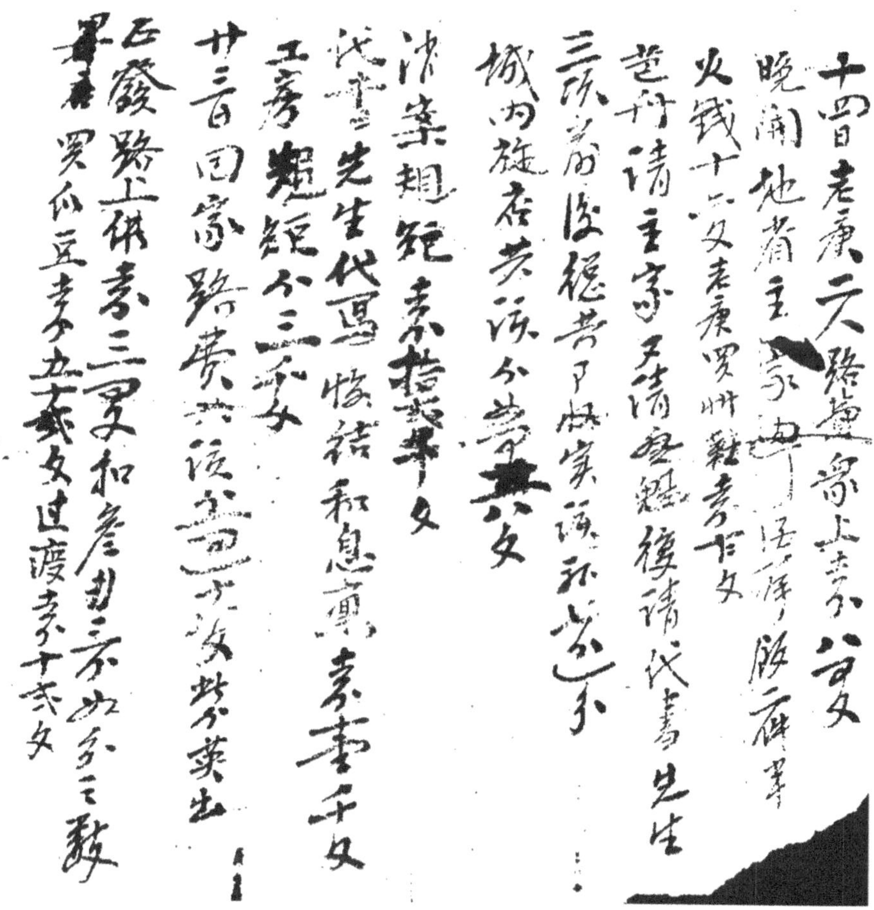

Fig. 9 A cost list manuscript containing information of inviting scribes

scribe's fee in Taiwan ranged from "fifty *qian* per hundred *yuan*" to "eight *yuan* per hundred *yuan*" among different parts of the island at the same time.[211] Nevertheless, the most frequent figure is "2%" in the customs survey of the hinterland.[212] In Table 4, the minimum scribe's fee is one candareen and the maximum are three maces. The proportion of the contract price varies from 0.11% to 5.17%, and the mean value of these numbers is 1.74%, which is a little bit lower than the earlier 2%.

Was there a fixed percentage? As far as Table 4 shows, it seems that the amount of the scribe's fee in Wendou Village was not set at a certain percentage of the contract price. The data presented in the table shows that typically vendors or vendees did

[211] The detailed customary percentages of the scribe's fee in Taiwan could be found in Rinji Taiwan Tochi Chōsakyoku, *Taiwan tochi kankō ippan*, vol. 3, 158–162.

[212] For example, in Zhuxi County of Hubei province, "the fee for writing contracts is two percent [of the contract price]." See Wu Xiangxiang, *Zhongguo minshi xiguan daquan*, 38–39.

Table 5 The charging model of the scribe's fee in Wendou Village

Intervals of contract prices	Scribe's fee charged	Percent (roughly) (%)
<1	≈0.03	<3
1–5	≈0.05	≈1–5
5–20	≈0.1/0.15	≈0.5–3
20–40	≈0.2/0.3	≈0.67–1.%

Unit Tael

not have a customary percentage of the scribe's fee in mind from which they tried to calculate a suitable and fixed amount. In two contracts which were both written by a scribe named "Jiang Dezhong,"[213] the contract prices are differently noted as "one tael and three maces" and "two taels and two maces," while the scribe's fee is "five candareens" in both cases. In this example, the scribe's fee was not adjusted to the change of the contract price. Moreover, these two manuscripts were written on the same day, "the twentieth day of the fourth month in the sixteenth year of Qianlong (May 15, 1751)." Consequently, it seems that the charging model of the scribe's fee is that, when the difference of contract prices is marginal, then the scribe's fee is relatively fixed. Taking all cases in Table 4 into account, the charging model can be reconstructed and summarized, as is shown below in Table 5.

Roughly speaking, the scribe's fee would stay under five candareens if the contract price was low, meaning that less than one tael was in common; when the contract price was one to five taels, the scribe's fee would be around five candareens; when the contract price ranged from three taels to twenty taels, the scribe's fee could normally reach one mace; when the contract price was as high as twenty or thirty taels, the scribe's fee would be raised accordingly to two or three maces. Surely, there were some exceptions,[214] but there is still a tendency of an orderly progression of the scribe's fee in the light of the contract price. The main difference between calculations with a set or floating percentage and the following progressive amounts of the scribe's fee is that the scribe's fee would be comparatively stable within the corresponding interval of the contract price.

The charging model in Table 5 can be re-examined by comparison with contracts from other nearby villages in the Qingshui River region that have previously not been taken into consideration as materials in the forming of this model. As noted above, these villages had strong civil and commercial connections with each other and therefore shared similar customs and traditions. For example, in Ping'ao Village, when the contract price was twenty-four taels, the scribe's fee was three maces[215];

[213] See Chen Jinquan and Du Wanhua, *Jiang Yuanze jiacang qiyue wenshu*, 4; Chen Jinquan and Du Wanhua, *Jiang Qigui jiacang qiyue wenshu*, 4.

[214] In Table 3, there are four contracts, i.e. D1-003, A-A0038, A-A0047, and A-B0014, which are exceptions and so do not fall into the model of Table 4.

[215] See Christian Daniels, Yang Yougeng, and Takeuchi Fusaji, *Kishū Myaozoku ringyō keiyaku monjo kaihen (1736–1950-nen)*, vol. 1, A-0001.

when the contract price was lower than three taels and eight candareens, the scribe's fee correspondingly fell to five candareens[216]; when the contract price continued to drop to two taels, the scribe's fee remained as five candareens[217]; when the contract price was only five maces and five candareens, the scribe's fee was three candareens as listed in the table,[218] etc. For other examples in Jiachi Village, when the contract price was eight taels, the scribe's fee was one mace[219]; when the contract price rose to ten taels, the scribe's fee was still one mace[220]; when the contract price reached the level of twenty-two taels, the scribe's fee also rose to two maces,[221] etc. Consequently, the charging model which is determined on the basis of materials from Wendou seems to be suitable in other neighboring villages too.

Surely not all contracts fitted the standard that Table 5 shows, but at least this table gives a charging model in the rough. More importantly, it illustrates that at least in Wendou and nearby villages the calculation of the scribe's fee was different from what the hinterland population did according to descriptions in the customs survey. The simple reason for this difference could be that a relatively fixed amount of the scribe's fee in each interval of the contract price would be more practical for Qing villagers than multiplying the contract price by a certain percentage to calculate the exact or rounded number of the scribe's fee.[222]

4.3 *Which Is Higher? Comparison of the Scribe's and the Middleman's Fees*

In a contractual transaction during the Qing dynasty, the scribe's fee was included as a primary part of the intermediate costs along with the middleman's fee.[223] There was a certain proportion between the two kinds of fees.

The customs survey shows that the scribe's fee usually would not be listed separately but was generally mentioned together with the middleman's fee. Standardly the proportion between the two was "3% as the middleman's fee and 2% as the

[216] See ibid., A-0002.

[217] See Zhang and Wang [116].

[218] See ibid., 2.

[219] See Zhang and Wang [115].

[220] See Zhang and Wang [111].

[221] See Zhang and Wang [112].

[222] Issues of calculation in the Qingshui River manuscripts have been discussed in relation to the profit allocation of timber harvest, see Nam [57].

[223] The concept of "intermediate costs," or "*zhongzi*" (costs in the middle), can be understood as "transaction costs" in contracts of sale. It refers not only to the middleman's fee, but also to other costs and remuneration for people who are involved in the contractual activities other than contracting parties (i.e. vendors and vendees). These figures included scribes, middlemen (as witnesses, brokers, guarantors, or mediators) or other possible participants.

scribe's fee,"[224] but there were slight differences among regions. For instance, in Hubei province, the customary rules were as follows:

> Yun County: In the countryside of Yun County, [the intermediate costs] are calculated as 5% of the selling price, and [it] shall be apportioned as 3% for the middleman and 2% for the scribe.
>
> Guanji County: In the case of the house [selling], [the intermediate costs] are calculated as 8% of the contract price, [and it shall be apportioned as] 5% for the middleman and 3% for the scribe; in the case of landed property [selling], [the intermediate costs] are calculated as 5% of the contract price, [and it shall be apportioned as] 3% for the middleman and 2% for the scribe.
>
> Zhushan County: [The intermediate costs] are calculated as 5% of the contract price, [and it shall be apportioned as] 3% for the middleman and 2% for the scribe.
>
> Badong County: [the intermediate costs shall be apportioned as] 5% for the middleman and 1% for the scribe.[225]

In addition, in Shaanxi province:

> Nanzheng County: [The custom of] purchasing lands and houses among civilian people [is]: When [people] have come to an agreement on the [contract] value, 5% [of it] shall be taken out [as the intermediate costs] according to the value of the [contract], 3% shall be paid to the middleman as a reward, and 2% shall be given to the scribe who wrote the contract of sale.[226]

Although the proportions differed from each other, the middleman's fee was generally higher than the scribe's fee.[227] This is also broadly in line with the understanding of the importance of the middleman in transactions which was presented in the previous chapter.

Of all the contracts which record notes of the middleman's fee in Wendou Village,[228] the percentage of the middleman's fee of the contract price ranges between 0.42%[229] and 3.45%; the mean value of these numbers is 1.69%, which is slightly lower than the mean percentage of the scribe's fee (1.74%). In addition, in the overwhelming majority of contracts, there was only one scribe but possibly

---

[224] The "3%" and "2%" here refer to 3% or 2% of the contract price.

[225] See Wu Xiangxiang, *Zhongguo minshi xiguan daquan*, 38–39.

[226] See ibid., 40.

[227] In a statistical table based on *Zhongguo minshangshi xiguan diaocha baogaolu* (Abstracts of reports on investigations of civil and commercial customs in China) and *Zhongguo minshi xiguan daquan*, customary standards are listed in 41 different places from Heilongjiang in the north to Fujian in the south, with no case indicating that the scribe's fee is higher than the middleman's fee. See Table "Changjian de disanfang canyuren de baochou e'du [The amount of the remuneration of the common third parties]," in Liu Gaoyong, "Qing dai maimai qiyue yanjiu," 96–98.

[228] Other than the 13 contracts with the middleman's fee listed in Table 3, there are 6 more contracts recording only the middleman's fee. For this reason, they are not included in the previous table. For these 6 manuscripts, see Chen Jinquan and Du Wanhua, *Jiang Yuanze jiacang qiyue wenshu*, 5, 50, 92; Christian Daniels, Yang Yougeng, and Takeuchi Fusaji, *Kishū Myaozoku ringyō keiyaku monjo kaihen (1736–1950-nen)*, vol. 1, A-0012, A-0064; Zhang Yingqiang and Wang Zongxun, *Qingshuijiang wenshu*, vol. 1 (12), 232.

[229] See Chen Jinquan and Du Wanhua, *Jiang Yuanze jiacang qiyue wenshu*, 50.

several middlemen. The middleman's fee could be either equally[230] or unequally[231] distributed among all middlemen. But, when counting the percentage of the per capita middleman's fee, the mean value fell to 1.24%. It is generally believed that the middleman as the one directly involved in the transaction seems to be more important than the scribe. If the proportion of the remuneration is taken to reflect, partially or fully, one's status or importance in the transaction, then the lower proportion of the middleman's fee is not only inconsistent with relevant descriptions in the hinterland's customs survey, but also with the general impression of the middleman's fundamental importance in transactions.[232]

Admittedly, the number of samples being analyzed here is quite small. Nevertheless, by looking at the details of 12 manuscripts that contain records of both the middleman's fee and the scribe's fee, it can be shown that, for one manuscript the scribe was paid higher than the middleman, for six of them the scribe gained a remuneration equal to the middleman's, and for the remaining five of them the middleman's fee was higher than the scribe's fee, though three of them have more than one middleman. More precisely, in terms of per capita income, the scribe was paid higher in four manuscripts, in five manuscripts the scribe received an equal payment, and only in three cases did the middlemen have a higher remuneration.[233] In one contract manuscript of Wendou's neighboring village Ping'ao,[234] two middlemen shared "two maces of silver" as remuneration, while the scribe "accepted three maces of silver" alone, which is triple the amount of the per capita middleman's fee.[235]

---

[230]Another example of equal remuneration could be found in Jiang Yingbao's contract of sale of farmland, in which the amount was "two candareens of silver." See ibid.

[231]The most obvious "unequal" example is in a contract of timber shares established by Liu Chaoyuan. There were four middlemen in total, of which "Jiang Laosi's [middleman's fee is] one mace of silver," while the other "three people shared one mace." See Zhang Yingqiang and Wang Zongxun, *Qingshuijiang wenshu*, vol. 1(13), 101.

[232]For the "general impression," see e.g. Li Zhuhuan, "Zhongguo chuantong minshi qiyue zhong de zhongren xianxiang," 138–143; Wang [84].

[233]In these three contracts, two of the scribes had a close relationship with their contracting parties; one scribe was also one of the many vendors in the transaction and the other was the son of one of the vendors. As for the third manuscript, the amounts of the scribe's fee (one candareen) and the middleman's fee (five candareens for three middlemen) were extraordinarily small. But according to the photocopy of the manuscript, the amount of the scribe's fee could possibly be "one mace," instead of "one candareen" in light of the annotation. However, it is still difficult to confirm which is the right amount since the photocopy is too blurred to identify the figure with certainty. Thus, the number remains as "one candareen" here according to the annotation. For these three manuscripts, see Christian Daniels, Yang Yougeng, and Takeuchi Fusaji, *Kishū Myaozoku ringyō keiyaku monjo kaihen (1736–1950-nen)*, vol. 1, A-0008; Zhang Yingqiang and Wang Zongxun, *Qingshuijiang wenshu*, vol. 1 (12), 361; Chen Jinquan and Du Wanhua, *Jiang Yuanze jiacang qiyue wenshu*, 3.

[234]Although this manuscript was found in Ping'ao Village, it can still be seen as a Wendou manuscript since the vendor in this contract is from Wendou. See Christian Daniels, Yang Yougeng, and Takeuchi Fusaji, *Kishū Myaozoku ringyō keiyaku monjo kaihen (1736–1950-nen)*, vol. 1, A-0046, A-0001.

[235]It is noteworthy that this number is not abnormally high but a reasonable amount according to the charging model in Table 4. Its contract price is twenty taels, so the scribe's fee should be about two to three maces.

According to the analysis above, unlike the situation in the hinterland, the scribe's fee in areas centered on Wendou Village was either roughly equal or slightly higher than the middleman's fee in amount, which reflects the equal or greater importance of the scribe than the middleman in transactions.

4.4 *Who Pays?*[236]

In a typical contract of sale at least two parties are involved: the vendee and the vendor. Who is obliged to pay the transaction costs (including the scribe's fee in this case) or how are the costs distributed between different parties?

In the hinterland, the payment proportion between the vendee and the vendor in a contract of sale is "3 to 2."[237] This proportion was somehow officially confirmed. A section of the "Regulations for Deed Writing and Tax Declaration" (*Xieqi toushui zhangcheng*) attached to an official deed (*guanqi*) in Guangxu reign reads: "As for the fees for the commission agent, middleman and scribe, it is permitted to pay 5% of the contract price [for these fees, of which] 3% should be paid by the vendee and 2% should be paid by the vendor."[238] However, differences still existed among regions. In Anhui and Fujian province the proportion was set as follows:

> Guangde County, Shucheng County, etc.: [The custom of] purchasing and selling lands and houses among civilian people [is]: the intermediate costs are 5% of the value of the land or house, which should be paid by the vendee alone, including 3% for the middleman and 2% for the town criers (*dongshi* and *dibao*)[239]; as for the scribe, there is also some remuneration, more or less.[240]

> Shucheng County: The remuneration for the middleman and the scribe should be calculated according to the contract price. 5% for the middleman and it should be paid by the vendee; 2% for the scribe and it should be paid by the vendor.[241]

> Shunchang County: [When] purchasing or selling houses, mountains, and lands [...] the intermediate costs are 5%, and the vendee should pay for it; this is called a "cash gift" (*jianliyin*) for the middleman and the scribe.[242]

---

[236] The same question was also discussed in laws of the *Halakhah*: in a writ of divorce, the husband pays the fee; in a writ of indebtedness, the borrower pays the scribe's fee; in a writ of sale, the purchaser pays the scribe's fee; in the documents of betrothal and marriage, the husband pays the scribe's fee; in the documents of tenancy and sharecropping, the tenant pays the scribe's fee; in the documents of arbitration or any document drawn up before a court, both litigants pay the scribe's fee. See Neusner [58].

[237] See Wu Xiangxiang, *Zhongguo minshi xiguan daquan*, 38–39.

[238] Zhang Chuanxi, *Zhongguo lidai qiyue huibian kaoshi*, 1467.

[239] For positions of local governance in the Qing dynasty, including *dongshi* and *dibao*, an introduction could be found in Yang [101].

[240] Wu Xiangxiang, *Zhongguo minshi xiguan daquan*, 40.

[241] Ibid.

[242] Ibid.

As for Wendou Village, unfortunately nothing in the surviving manuscripts serves as a smoking gun of who should pay the remuneration. Generally speaking, however, the scribe's fee was likely to be paid by the one who invited the scribe, and, if the scribe was invited by both parties, they might have to pay the scribe's fee together.[243]

To be more specific, the foregoing discussion only considers the distribution of the intermediate costs as a whole between parties; it does not clarify how the scribe's fee alone was distributed. Under some circumstances, the scribe's fee appears to be seen as a fee beyond "the intermediate costs." As in the quotation noted above, "as for the scribe, there is also some remuneration, more or less," it seems that the scribe's fee was not included in the intermediate costs. One of the reasons for this might be that there was not always a scribe's fee involved. For example, in addition to scribal writings, the scribe's fee would not incur in transactions if contracts were drafted holographically. Nonetheless, one can investigate the question of "who should pay the fee" exactly from the starting-point of "who does not need to pay the fee."

As mentioned above, in transactions of lands and houses in the hinterland the distribution of the intermediate costs is "3% by the vendee and 2% by the vendor;" at the same time, the composing of the intermediate costs is generally "3% for the middleman and 2% for the scribe." Additionally, the writing of the contract could be a duty of the one who initiates the contractual activity, namely the vendor as the establisher of the contract. Accordingly, the two figures above can be understood to show that the middleman's fee (3%) was paid by the vendee and the scribe's fee (2%) was paid by the vendor. Obviously, provided that this assumption was followed in practice, then 2% of the scribe's fee would no longer incur when the contract was written holographically, so the vendor can save a part of his or her transaction costs by writing the contract him- or herself. As evidence, descriptions like "if the contract of sale was written by the vendor him- or herself, then this 2% [as the scribe's fee] remain with the vendor" can also be found in the customs survey.[244]

It should be noted that, again, the scribe could be one of many vendors; or, to put this point differently, one of the vendors could write the contract as a scribe for other vendors. Therefore, two more examples in this regard will be presented.

The first example is a contract of sale of forest land.[245] The vendors in this transaction are Jiang Yuncai, Jiang Hongwen, and some other individuals. The note of the scribe's fee states that "Jiang Hongwen [took] one mace and five candareens of silver," while the middleman's fee is "two maces." According to Table 4, in the case in which only one middleman was involved, the remuneration of the middleman and the scribe is the same or similar in amount. It is conceivable that the scribe might have charged the same amount of money as the middleman, i.e. "two maces." However, since the scribe himself was one of the vendors, the scribe's fee was reduced to "one mace and five candareens," so in this case Jiang Hongwen did not need to pay himself.

---

[243]The invitation of the scribe has been discussed in the preceding section.

[244]See Wu Xiangxiang, *Zhongguo minshi xiguan daquan*, 40.

[245]See Christian Daniels, Yang Yougeng, and Takeuchi Fusaji, *Kishū Myaozoku ringyō keiyaku monjo kaihen (1736–1950-nen)*, vol. 1, A-0008.

The second example occurs in Teng Wanming's contract of sale of timber's shares.[246] In this transaction, there were four vendors: Teng Wanming, Teng Haiming, Zhang Guofu, and Zhang Guoyao. The middleman's fee was "four maces" and the scribe's fee was "three maces." The scribe is identified as "the son Teng Jiaxing," which indicates that he is the son of one of the vendors, whether of Teng Wanming or Teng Haiming. This might be the reason why the scribe's fee is one mace lower than the middleman's fee: the father did not need to pay, or could pay less, to his son.

These examples once again illustrate that the scribe's fee was at least relatively close to the middleman's fee in Wendou Village. Secondly, since the scribe's fee could be reduced if the scribe had some relation with the vendor, it seems that the vendor or establisher was the one who was originally obliged to pay the scribe's fee.

4.5 *How and When to Pay?*

In addition to the cash payment, feasting the middleman and the scribe could also be one part or one type of payment. The feast after the transaction might have a certain implication of publicity.[247] In a certain sense, holding the feast is necessary for both ritual and practice since anyone who is invited to the feast can act as the witness to the signing of the contract.[248] This type of feast was called "*chizhong*" (literally translated as "[invite] the middleman to eat") in Wendou Village and according to field research finds it remains in place until today.[249]

In the hinterland, there also existed the same tradition of "*chigeshi*" (literally translated as "to eat the cut food"):

> Nanzheng County, Xunyi County, Liquan County, etc. (Shaanxi): In all activities of purchasing or selling lands and houses, on the day of signing the contract and paying the price, the vendee should prepare for a feast, and invite the vendor, the middleman, the scribe, relatives, and neighbors to enjoy the feast together.[250]

A bill manuscript found in Wendou Village lists all items needed (e.g. pork, beef, rice, wine, tobacco, oil, tofu, salt) for preparing several feasts at length, and, apparently, many of these were costly.[251] Another contract manuscript directly says:

---

[246] See Zhang Yingqiang and Wang Zongxun, *Qingshuijiang wenshu*, vol. 1 (12), 361.

[247] An introduction to the tradition of holding a feast in contractual activities could be found in Ren [67]. A further discussion on this point will be offered in Chap. 5.

[248] See Liu Gaoyong, "Qing dai maimai qiyue yanjiu," 95.

[249] See Liang Cong, *Qing dai Qingshuijiang xiayou cunzhai shehui de qiyue guifan yu zhixu*, 115. The scribe here could also be seen as one type of generally defined middlemen.

[250] See Wu Xiangxiang, *Zhongguo minshi xiguan daquan*, 34.

[251] See Chen Jinquan and Du Wanhua, *Jiang Yuanze jiacang qiyue wenshu*, 570.

"The price had been paid, including [the costs of] the feast."[252] This signifies that the costs of the feast could also become an important part of the intermediate costs.[253]

Lastly, it is worth noting a rather unique phenomenon in contractual conventions of the hinterland regarding the middleman's fee and the scribe's fee in transactions. In some cases one person might falsely sign two different names, respectively as the middleman and as the scribe, in one contract in order to earn payments for both positions. This case can be found as a custom in the counties of southern Jiangxi province:

> The scribe, who writes the instrument, could normally also be the middleman who makes the match. Thus, one person might sign two names, like Zhao Jia as the name of the scribe, and Zhao Yi as the name of the middleman. The reason for signing two names is to earn both the middleman's fee in the name of the middleman and the scribe's fee in the name of the scribe at the same time.[254]

This phenomenon has not been found within contracts in Wendou Village. In a contract of *dian* established by Jiang Xianzong, however, its postscript part contains the following information[255]:

> The hosting fee and the middleman's fee are one mace together; the fees remain to be paid at the time when the farmland is redeemed in the future.

In this contract, the middleman Jiang Kaiyuan was also the scribe at the same time. However, he received only the middleman's fee according to the postscript. Thus, it seems that he did not receive more remuneration by his holding two positions.

This scribal note also gives a clue to the timing of the payment: normally the intermediate costs should be paid right after the transaction is completed. Otherwise a special note has to be attached to the contract manuscript in order to remind the obligor of the remuneration needing to be paid. In the case of a contract of *dian*, since "*dian*" is to be identified as one type of conditional sales, it is then easy to understand why the intermediate costs can be paid after the subject of the contract was redeemed, i.e. after the transaction was truly completed.

It should be stressed that there is an enormous difference between paying after the contract manuscript is completed (evidential or material aspect) and paying after

---

[252] Luo [52]. This manuscript was found in Jinping County according to the collector, but it is not yet clear whether it was found in Wendou Village or not.

[253] According to a field research interview (Oct. 4, 2013), when the interviewee was answering the question "Are the middleman and the scribe normally paid?" he said, "Generally their services are unpaid [in cash], [you] only need to invite them for a meal. But if the vendee is from other places, and came to Wendou to buy forest land, then he has to pay the scribe and the middleman; because after he left, these local people need to deal with all the possible troubles." This interview illustrates that, as least in the local elder's memories, not all the scribe's fee needs to be paid in cash, but some could be paid with feasting. See "Appendix 2: Field Research Report," He Yumei, "Qing dai Minguo shiqi Qiandongnan Wendou zhai de linye jingji xisu yanjiu," 57.

[254] See Wu Xiangxiang, *Zhongguo minshi xiguan daquan*, 26.

[255] This note says nothing about the scribe's fee, although the middleman performed a scribe's work. The middleman's fee could then be seen as including the scribe's fee as a part of it. See Chen Jinquan and Du Wanhua, *Jiang Yuanze jiacang qiyue wenshu*, 400.

the transaction is completed (legal or essential aspect). This distinction implies that the scribe's service is not limited to the production of the document, but also enters into the essential content of the contracting process.

In sum, the various aspects of the scribe's fee have now been presented and discussed in detail. The issue of the scribe's fee may seem trivial at first glance, but it is only through the elucidation of facts that the conceptual construction based on it is possible. In addition, through the comparison between the customs involving the scribe's fee in the Qingshui River region and in the hinterland, it seems that, in frontier areas, the scribe was more important than the previous scholarly impression has allowed. This and the previous chapter further emphasize the image of the middleman and the scribe as two equally fundamental figures in the construction of the contractual relationship. Whether for the professional description of the contract intermediaries or the emphasis on the importance of the scribe, the clarification of the scribe's fee can play a significant role in it.

5 Conclusion

The discussion in this chapter provides a thorough account of the scribe as a critical contractual element that has not been valued by previous scholarship. In contrast to the impression of being a "printer," the multiple roles of the scribe in the contract activities, including but not limited to contract writing, have been examined in three phases: before, during, and after the process of writing. The discussions of each role give a clear impression of the scribe at each stage. Specifically, although some might be able to write the contract by themselves, most of the villagers still needed the service provided by the scribe from the outset; after a scribe was invited, he or she would find that there were two methods, either according to the spoken words or the draft, to confirm the content of the contract, and it was the scribe who definitively organized the information in a certain way to meet the requirement of the contract form, which has been introduced into the frontier area from the hinterland and started to evolve in the new context. Finally, when the contract was finished, the scribal service needed to be paid in various ways by the appropriate parties.

Moreover, through these discussions the often-overlooked aspects of how a scribe was involved in the contract emerge, such as through participation in the substantial negotiation, editing and transcribing the oral descriptions, accepting and applying conventional contract forms, and generating locally oriented new forms. Thus, the operation of the institution of contractual scribes has been presented at length.

Due to the successful operation of his or her activity, the scribe substantively contributed to the formation of each contract beyond the practice of writing. The importance of the scribe can be reflected in four aspects: (1) the high demand for scribes in village societies, (2) the substantial participation of scribes in contract activities, (3) the comparable contractual status of the scribe to the middleman, as reflected by the intermediate costs, and finally (4) the key role that the scribe played in the evolution of contract forms and contractual tradition. A scribe might not be as "powerful" as the middleman in terms of the immediate "discretionary power" one could hold in the negotiation, but he or she possesses another type of "soft power" of writing in the long run. In this sense, the scribe deserves his status as one of the two underpinnings of a contract.

References

1. A, Feng. 2009. *Ming Qing shidai funü de diwei yu quanli: Yi Ming Qing qiyue wenshu susong dang'an wei zhongxin* [Women's status and rights during the Ming and Qing periods: With a focus on contracts and legal documents from the Ming and Qing periods], 89. Beijing: Shehui kexue wenxian chubanshe.
2. Al-Hilâlî, Muhammand Taqî-ud-Dîn, and Muhammad Muhsin Khân. 1994. *The Holy Qur'an: English Translation of Meanings and Commentary*, 65–66. Madinah, K.S.A.: King Fahid Complex for the Printing of the Holy Qur'an.
3. Allee, Mark A. 1994. *Law and local society in late imperial China: Northern Taiwan in the nineteenth century*, 176–177. Stanford, California: Stanford University Press.
4. Chen, Jinquan, and Wanhua Du, eds. 2015. *Guizhou Wendouzhai Miaozu qiyue falü wenshu huibian—Jiang Qigui jiacang qiyue wenshu* [The compilation of contractual and legal manuscripts of the Miao from Wendou Village, Guizhou—Manuscripts from Jiang Qigui's family collection], 312. Beijing: Renmin chubanshe.
5. Chen, Jinquan, and Liang Guo, eds. 2017. *Guizhou Wendouzhai Miaozu qiyue falü wenshu huibian—Yi Zunfa Jiang Qicheng deng jiacang susong wenshu* [The compilation of contractual and legal manuscripts of the Miao from Wendou Village, Guizhou—Litigation manuscripts from family collections of Yi Zunfa, Jiang Qicheng, etc.], 253. Beijing: Renmin chubanshe.
6. Chen, Szu-Pei, Jie Hsiang, Hsienh-Chang Tu, and Micha Wu. 2008. On building a full-text digital library of historical documents. In *Asian digital libraries. looking back 10 years and forging new frontiers: 10th international conference on asian digital libraries, ICADL 2007, Hanoi, Vietnam, December 10–13, 2007 Proceedings*, ed. Dion Hoe-Lian Goh, Tru Hoang Cao, Ingeborg Torvik Sølvberg, and Edie Rasmussen, 53. Berlin & Heidelberg: Springer.
7. Chen, Xuewen. 2005. Tudi qiyue wenshu yu Ming Qing shehui jingji wenhua de yanjiu [Land contracts and the studies on the society, economy, and culture during the Ming and Qing dynasties]. *Shixue yuekan* (12): 9–10.
8. Chen, Xuewen. 2006. Qing dai tudi suoyouquan zhuanyi de fazhihua—Qing Daoguang sanshi nian Shanxi Xugou xian Wang Yao tianqi (siqi, guanqi, qiwei) de kaoshi ji qita [The legalization of the transfer of land ownership in the Qing dynasty: An annotation to a contract of 1850]. *Zhongguo shehui jingjishi yanjiu* (4): 25.
9. Chen, Yongsheng. 2000. Dunhuang maimai qiyue falü zhidu tanxi [Law system seen in sale contracts from Dunhuang]. *Dunhuang yanjiu* (4): 97.
10. Cheng, Hung-Chi. 1998. Cong qizi kan Taiwan falüshi shang youguan tudi maimai de falü guifan [Land transferring regulations in Taiwan's legal history: Analysis of land deeds]. Master dissertation, National Taiwan University, 81.
11. Cheng, Jinquan, and Wanhua Du, eds. 2008. *Guizhou Wendouzhai Miaozu qiyue falü wenshu huibian—Jiang Yuanze jiacang qiyue wenshu* [The compilation of contractual and legal manuscripts of the Miao from Wendou Village, Guizhou—Manuscripts from Jiang Yuanze's family collection], 151. Beijing: Renmin chubanshe.
12. Cheng, Yuanqi. [1873] 1989. *Yongxianzhai biji* [Notes from the studio of idleness], 57. Beijing: Zhonghua shuju.
13. Cheng, Zeshi. 2011. *Qingshuijiang wenshu zhi fayi chutan* [A primary legal research on the Qingshui River manuscripts], 18. Beijing: Zhongguo zhengfa daxue chubanshe.

14. Choi, Chi-cheung, ed. 1995. *Kyo Jo hakase shozo shoyo oyobi tochi keiyaku bunsho: Kantairyū bunsho (1): Chaoshan diqu tudi qiyue wenshu* [Business documents and land deeds collected by Dr. James Hayes: Kin Tye Lung document Vol. 1: Land deeds of the Chaoshan region], vol. 65. Tokyo: Tōkyō Daigaku Tōyō Bunka Kenkyūjo Fuzoku Tōyōgaku Bunken Sentā.
15. Clarke, Samuel R. 1911. *Among the Ttibes in South-west China*, 38–39. London: Morgan & Scott.
16. Daniels, Christian, Yougeng Yang, and Fusaji Takeuchi, eds. 2001. *Kishū Myaozoku ringyō keiyaku monjo kaihen (1736–1950-nen)* [Old forestry contracts of the Miao in Guizhou, 1736–1950], vol. 1, A-0002. Tokyo: Tōkyō gaikokugo daigaku Ajia Afurika gengo bunka kenkyūjo.
17. Daniels, Christian, Yougeng Yang, and Fusaji Takeuchi, eds. 2002. *Kishū Myaozoku ringyō keiyaku monjo kaihen (1736–1950-nen)* [Old forestry contracts of the Miao in Guizhou, 1736–1950], vol. 2, C-0058. Tokyo: Tōkyō gaikokugo daigaku Ajia Afurika gengo bunka kenkyūjo.
18. Daniels, Christian, Yougeng Yang, and Fusaji Takeuchi, eds. 2003. *Kishū Myaozoku ringyō keiyaku monjo kaihen (1736–1950-nen)* [Old forestry contracts of the Miao in Guizhou, 1736–1950], vol. 3, F-0043. Tokyo: Tōkyō gaikokugo daigaku Ajia Afurika gengo bunka kenkyūjo.
19. Deng, Jianpeng. 2013. Qing zhi Minguo Miaozu linye jiufen de jiejue fangshi—Yi Qingshuijiang 'rencuozi' wenshu weili [The forestry dispute settlement of the Miao from Qing to Republican—A case study of 'rencuozi' manuscripts in Qingshui River]. *Hubei daxue xuebao (zhexue shehuikexue ban)* 40 (4): 89.
20. Deng, Jianpeng, and Kai Qiu. 2013. Cong heyi dao qiangzhi: Qing zhi Minguo Qingshuijiang jiufen wenshu yanjiu [From consensus to enforcement: A study on disputes manuscripts in the Qing and Republican periods]. *Gansu zhengfa xueyuan xuebao* 126 (1): 34.
21. Du, Zhengzhen. 2014. Cong susong dang'an huidao qiyue huodong de xianchang—Yi wan Qing Min chu de Longquan sifa dang'an wei li [Reproduce the contracts activities through reading judicial archives: Taking the Longquan judicial archives in late Qing and early Republic of China as an example]. *Zhejiang shehui kexue* (1): 119.
22. Fan, Jinmin. 2015. 'Caoyi' yu 'yidan': Qing dai Jiangnan tianzhai maimai wenshu de dingli [Draft agreements and documents: Concluding property contracts in the Jiangnan region under the Qing]. *Lishi yanjiu* (3): 84.
23. Feng, Xuewei. 2015. *Ming Qing qiyue de jiegou gongneng ji yiyi* [The structure, function, and meaning of contracts in the Ming-Qing eras], 28–29. Beijing: Falü chubanshe.
24. Gabbiani, Luca. 2013. Taxing for Profit? The title-deed tax in eighteenth century China from a fiscal and legal perspective. Paper presented at the fourth international conference on sinology: Exploring the archives and rethinking Qing studies, Academia Sinica, Taipei, 706–707.
25. Gao, Cong, and Hongpei Tan, eds. 2013. *Guizhou Qingshuijiang liuyu Ming Qing tusi qiyue wenshu, Jiunan pian* [Tusi contract manuscripts in the Qingshui River Basin of Guizhou during the Ming-Qing eras, Jiunan volume], 103. Beijing: Minzu chubanshe.
26. Giele, Enno. 2005. Signatures of 'Scribes' in early imperial China. *Asiatische Studien/Études Asiatiques* 59 (1): 353–387.
27. Guizhou sheng bianjizu, ed. 1988. *Dongzu shehui lishi diaocha* [Investigation into the society and history of the Dong people], 17–19. Guiyang: Guizhou minzu chubanshe.
28. Guo, Ruijun. 2014. Cong Qimen Lingshi 'Hetong wenyue teng qi bu' kan Qing dai Huizhou 'zhongren' de zhongzi [Middlemen's fee in Qing Huizhou, evidence from 'Hetong wenyue teng qi bu' of Qimen Lingshi]. *Mudanjiang daxue xuebao* 23 (6): 22.
29. Hase, Patrick H. 2013. *Custom, land and livelihood in rural South China: The traditional land law of Hong Kong's new territories, 1750–1950*, 148. Hong Kong: Hong Kong University Press.
30. Hayes, James. 1985. Specialists and written materials in the village world. In *Popular culture in late imperial China*, ed. David Johnson, Andrew J. Nathan, and Evelyn S. Rawski, 87. Berkeley, Los Angeles, London: University of California Press.

31. He, Yumei. 2014. Qing dai Minguo shiqi Qiandongnan Wendou zhai de linye jingji xisu yanjiu [The research on the customs of forestry economy of Wendou Village in Qiandongnan during the Qing dynasty and the Republican era]. Master dissertation, Guangxi Normal University, 57.
32. Hegel, Robert E., and Katherine Carlitz, eds. 2007. *Writing and law in late imperial China: Crime, conflict, and judgment*, ix. Washington: University of Washington Press.
33. Hsing, I-tien. 2011. Han dai jiandu gongwen shu de zhengben, fuben, caogao he qianshu wenti [Han dynasty wooden slips containing official documents and the problems of original versions, copies, drafts, and signatures]. *Zhongyang yanjiuyuan lishi yuyan yanjiusuo jikan* 82 (4): 666.
34. Huang, Philip C.C. 1996. *Civil justice in China: Representation and practice in the Qing*, 163. Stanford, California: Stanford University Press.
35. Kungang, et al., eds. 1899. *Qinding da Qing huidian shili* [Collected statutes and precedents of the Qing during the reign of Guangxu], 1220 vols., vol. 763.
36. Li, Bin, ed. 2017. *Guizhou Qingshuijiang wenshu, Liping wenshu* [Guizhou Qingshui River Manuscripts, Manuscripts in Liping County], vol. 12, 93. Guiyang: Guizhou minzu chubanshe.
37. Li, Bin, and Tingduo Hu. 2017. Qianyan [Preface]. In *Liping wenshu* [Liping manuscripts], ed. Bin Li, 5. Guiyang: Guizhou minzu chubanshe.
38. Li, Jingxin. 2013. Hainan Sanya Yacheng Li zu minjian diqi chutan [A preliminary study on the folk title deeds of Li nationality in Yacheng of Sanya]. *Hainan daxue xuebao (renwen shehui kexue ban)* 31 (4): 87.
39. Li, Junming, and Jun Liu. 1999. *Jiandu wenshu xue* [Study of bamboo and wooden documents], 164. Nanning: Guangxi jiaoyu chubanshe.
40. Li, Ren-yuan. 2014. Making texts in villages: Textual production in rural China during the Ming-Qing period. Doctoral dissertation, Harvard University, 114–121.
41. Li, Wenzhi, ed. 1957. *Zhongguo jindai nongye shi ziliao* [Source materials on modern Chinese agricultural history], vol. 1, 50. Shanghai: Shenghuo, dushu, xinzhi sanlian shudian.
42. Li, Zhi, Meigong Chen, and Baigu Wang, eds. 1669. *Zengbu Suweng zhizhang zazhu quanji* [An enlarged edition of Suweng encyclopedia for daily-use contracts and documents], 3. Shulin qianfu tang.
43. Li, Zhuhuan. 1997. Zhongguo chuantong minshi qiyue zhong de zhongren xianxiang [The phenomenon of middlemen in traditional Chinese civil contracts]. *Faxue yanjiu* (6): 141.
44. Liang, Cong. 2008. *Qing dai Qingshuijiang xiayou cunzhai shehui de qiyue guifan yu zhixu* [Contractual norm and order in the village society of the lower reaches of Qingshui River in Qing China], 112. Beijing: Renmin chubanshe.
45. Lin, Yu-ju, Tay-Sheng Wang, Pintsang Tseng, Mei-hui Wu, and Yu-ju Lin. 2008. *Daishu bi, shangren feng—Baisui renrui Sun Jianghuai xiansheng fangwen jilu* [The writing brush of a scribe, the demeanour of a merchant: An interview record of a centenarian, Sun Jianghuai], 61. Taipei: Yuanliu chuban gongsi.
46. Linshi Taiwan tudi diaochaju, ed. 1998. *Taiwan tudi guanxing yi ban* [A fragment of land customs in Taiwan], reprinted ed., vol. 3, 156. Taipei: Nantian shuju.
47. Liu, Heng. [1838] 1997. Lisong shitiao [Ten principles of trial]. In *Muling shu* [The book of magistrates], ed. Dong Xu, Reprinted in *Guanzhen shu jicheng* [The collection of handbooks for officials], vol. 7, 387. Hefei: Huangshan shushe.
48. Liu, Dai, Mao Ai, and Tingxun Xie, eds. [1769] 2006. *Dushan zhouzhi* [Gazetteer of Dushan Sub-prefecture], vol. 9, Reprinted in *Zhongguo difangzhi jicheng, Guizhou fuxian zhi ji* [A collection of gazetteers in China: Gazetteers of prefectures and counties in Guizhou province], 211–212. Chengdu: Bashu shushe.
49. Liu, Daosheng. 2008. *Ming Qing Huizhou zongzu wenshu yanjiu* [On lineage documents and files of Huizhou in the Ming-Qing dynasties], 132. Hefei: Anhui renmin chubanshe.
50. Liu, Gaoyong. 2008. Qing dai maimai qiyue yanjiu [A study on the sale-memorandums in the Qing dynasty]. Doctoral dissertation, China University of Political Science and Law, 25–26.
51. Liu, Gaoyong and Qi Qu. 2011. Lun Qing dai tianzhai qiyue dingli zhong de disanfang qunti: Gongneng jiqi yiyi [The third party in land and house contracting in the Qing dynasty: Functions and meanings]. *Xibu faxue pinglun* (3): 18.

52. Luo, Hongyang. 2004. Guizhou Jinping linqi jingxuan [A selection of forestry contracts in Jinping, Guizhou]. *Minjian fa* 3: 510.
53. Ma, Tsang Wing. 2017. Scribes in Early Imperial China. Doctoral dissertation, University of California Santa Barbara.
54. Mao, Huanwen, ed. 1746. *Zengbu wanbao quanshu* [An enlarged edition of the complete book of myriad treasures], vol. 5. Jinchang shuye tang.
55. Mindai shi kenkyu shi hen, ed. 1975. *Chūgoku tochi keiyaku bunsho shiryō shū (Kin–Shin)* [A collection on Chinese land contracts (Jin–Qing)]. Tokyo: Tōyō bunko.
56. Mote, Frederick W. 2003. *Imperial China, 900–1800*, 892. Cambridge, Massachusetts: Harvard University Press.
57. Nam, Mingu. 2017. Qingshuijiang wenshu suojian famu fenyin wenti de tantao [Research on the profit allocation of timber harvest in the Qingshui River manuscripts]. In *Jinping wenshu yu fawenhua yanjiu* [Jinping manuscripts and the studies of legal culture], ed. Qicai Gao and Kui Wang, 221–230. Beijing: Zhongguo zhengfa daxue chubanshe.
58. Neusner, Jacob. 2000. *The Halakhah: An encyclopaedia of the law of judaism*, vol. 3, 151–152. Leiden: Brill.
59. Okamatsu, Santaro. [1900] 1971. *Provisional report on investigations of laws and customs in the Island of Formosa*, reprinted ed., 36. Taipei: Ch'eng Wen Publishing Company.
60. Pan, Zhicheng, and Dahua Wu, eds. 2011. *Tudi guanxi ji qita shiwu wenshu* [Manuscripts on land relationship and other issues], vol. 1, 118. Guiyang: Guizhou minzu chubanshe.
61. Pan, Zhicheng, Dahua Wu, and Cong Liang, eds. 2014. *Qingjiang si an yanjiu* [Studies on the four cases in the Qingshui River region], vol. 3, 113. Guiyang: Guizhou minzu chubanshe.
62. Qian Nanjing guomin zhengfu sifa xingzheng bu, ed. [1930] 2000. *Mingshi xiguan diaocha baogao lu* [Collection of reports of custom surveys on civil matters], 2 vols., vol. 1, 118. Beijing: Zhongguo zhengfa daxue chubanshe.
63. Qian Nanjing guomin zhengfu sifa xingzheng bu, ed. [1930] 2000. *Mingshi xiguan diaocha baogao lu* [Collection of reports of custom surveys on civil matters], 2 vols., vol. 2, 718. Beijing: Zhongguo zhengfa daxue chubanshe.
64. Qiu, Huang. [1839] 2008. *Fupan Lucun* [Recordings of magistrate decisions], ed. Benshe yingyinshi, vol. 1(19), Reprinted in *Ming Qing fazhi shiliao jikan* [Collection of legal material from the Ming and Qing], 11–16. Beijing: Guojia tushuguan chubanshe.
65. Qu, Jian. 2012. Qing zhonghouqi Qiandongnan Wendou zhai Miaozu dianzhi yanjiu [A treatise on the dian of the Miaos in Wendou Village of southeastern Guizhou in the mid and late Qing dynasty]. *Minjian fa* 11: 215.
66. Qu, Jian. 2013. Qing dai Wendou zhai zhongren zhidu [The zhongren system of Wendou Village in the Qing dynasty]. *Minjian fa* 12: 269.
67. Ren, Zhiqiang. 2010. Chuantong shehui qiyue de qianding yishi tanwei [The contract signing ceremony in traditional society]. *Huangshan xueyuan xuebao* 12 (2): 33–36.
68. Ren, Jihong, ed. 2014. *Lüshi shiwu yu zhiye lunli* [Lawyer affairs and professional ethic], 173–177. Beijing: Zhongguo zhengfa daxue chubanshe.
69. Richter, Matthias L. (2013). *The Embodied Text: Establishing Textual Identity in Early Chinese Manuscripts*. Leiden & Boston: Brill.
70. Rinji Taiwan Tochi Chōsakyoku, ed. 1905. *Taiwan tochi kankō ippan* [Overview of Taiwan land usage customs], 3 vols., vol. 3, 156. Taihoku (Taipei): Rinji Taiwan Tochi Chōsakyoku.
71. Rinji Taiwan Kyūkan Chōsakai, ed. 1995. *Taiwan shiho* [Civil law in Taiwan], vol. 1.1, 181. Taipei: Nantian shuju.
72. Sandars, Thomas Collett. 1876. *The institutes of Justinian; with english introduction, translation, and notes*, 441. Chicago: Callaghan & Company.
73. Scogin, Hugh T. 1990. Between heaven and man: Contract and the state in Han Dynasty China. *Southern California Law Review* 63 (5): 1369.
74. Scott, S.P., ed. 2001. *The civil law, including the twelve tables, The Institutes of Gaius, The Rules of Ulpian, The Opinions of Paulus, The Enactments of Justinian, and The Constitutions of Leo: Translated from the Original Latin, Edited, and Compared With All Accessible Systems of Jurisprudence Ancient and Modern*, 188–189. New Jersey: The Lawbook Exchange, Ltd.

75. Skinner, G William. 1995. Introduction: Urban and Rural in Chinese society. In *The city in late imperial China*, ed. G. William Skinner, 265. Taipei: SMC Publishing Inc.
76. Smith, Adam. 2012. The evidence for scribal training at Anyang. In *Writing and literacy in early China*, ed. Feng Li and David Prager Branner, 173–205. Seattle & London: University of Washington Press.
77. Sommer, Matthew H. 2015. *Polyandry and wife-selling in Qing dynasty China: Survival strategies and judicial interventions*, 15, 138, 141. Oakland, California: University of California Press.
78. Sun, Qingling. 2003. Lüelun Qing dai de shuiqi wenti [On the issue of the title deed of the Qing dynasty]. *Fujian shifan daxue xuebao (zhexue shehui kexue ban)* (6): 110–113.
79. Taiwan yinhang jingji yanjiushi, ed. 1963. *Taiwan sifa wuquan bian* [Civil law in Taiwan, part of real right], vol. 3. Taipei: Taiwan yinhang.
80. Taiwan shiliao jicheng bianji weiyuanhui, ed. 2005, 2006, 2007. *Taiwan zongdufu dang'an chaolu qiyue wenshu* [The archival contract documents of the Office of the Taiwan Governor-General], vol. 1 & 2. Taipei: Xingzhengyuan wenhua jianshe weiyuanhui.
81. Tian, Tao. 2004. *Huangyan susong dang'an ji diaocha baogao* [The judicial archives of Huangyan and a field report], 2 vols., vol. 2, 35–36. Beijing: Falü chubanshe.
82. Tian, Tao, Hugh T. Scogin, and Qin Zheng. 2001. *Tian cang qiyue wenshu cuibian* [The Tian collection of traditional Chinese contracts and related documents], vol. 1, 6. Beijing: Zhonghua shuju.
83. Unschuld, Paul U., and Jinsheng Zheng. 2012. *Chinese traditional healing: The Berlin collections of manuscript volumes from the 16th through the early 20th century*, 3 vols., vol. 3, 1802. Leiden and Boston: Brill.
84. Wang, Shuaiyi. 2016. Ming Qing shidai de zhongren yu qiyue zhixu [Zhongren and the contract order of the Ming and Qing dynasties]. *Zhengfa luntan* 34 (2): 170–182.
85. Wang, Qinmei, and Yingqiang Zhang. 2016. Wenzi shuxie yu xingdong celüe—Yi Guizhou Miao ren tusi jiapu Longshi diguang lu wei zhongxin de tantao [Text writing and action strategies: A discussion centered on the genealogy of the Miao people's Longshi diguang lu]. *Beifang minzu daxue xuebao (zhexue shehui kexue ban)* (2): 13–14.
86. Wang, Xu. 2013. *Qizhi qiannian—Zhongguo chuantong qiyue de xingshi yu yanbian* [A thousand years of contract paper: The form and evolution of traditional Chinese contracts], 229. Beijing: Beijing daxue chubanshe.
87. Wang, Yuxin, and Shaoquan Zhou, eds. 1994. *Huizhou qiannian qiyue wenshu: Qing, Minguo bian* [Huizhou millennium contract documents: Qing and Republican]. Shijiazhuang: Huashan wenyi chubanshe.
88. Wang, Zhenzhong. 2005. Shouji, zhengli he yanjiu Huizhou wenshu de jidian sikao [Reflections on collecting, collating, and studying Huizhou manuscripts]. *Shixue yuekan* (12): 16.
89. Wang, Zongxun. 2009. *Wendou: Kan de jian lishi de cunzhai* [Wendou: A village with visible history], 42. Guiyang: Guizhou renmin chubanshe.
90. Wu, Caimao. 2016. Ming dai yilai Qingshuijiang wenshu shuxie geshi de bianhua yu minzhong xiguan de bianqian [The changes of the writing forms of Qingshui River manuscripts and the transition of popular customs since the Ming dynasty]. *Xinan daxue xuebao (shehui kexue ban)* 42 (4): 187.
91. Wu, Chun-Ying. 2010. Taiwan daishu de lishi kaocha [A historical study on scribes in Taiwan]. Master dissertation, National Chengchi University, 57–62.
92. Wu, Huifang. 2005. *Wanbao quanshu: Ming Qing shiqi de minjian shenghuo shilu* [Wanbao quanshu: A truthful record of everyday life in the Ming and Qing periods], 2 vols., vol. 1, 254. Taipei: Hua Mulan wenhua gongzuo fang.
93. Wu, Jiyuan. 1994. Qing dai de daishu yu songshi [Official scribes and lawyers in the Qing dynasty]. *Wenshi zazhi* 3: 48.
94. Wu, Micha, ed. 2006. *Dan Xin dang'an* [Administrative archives of the Danshui Sub-prefecture and the Xinzhu County], vol. 18, 43. Taipei: National Taiwan University Library.

95. Wu, Xiangxiang, ed. [1923] 1962. *Zhongguo minshi xiguan daquan* [A compendium of Chinese popular customs], 38. Taipei: Wenxing shudian.
96. Xu, Xiaoguang. 2006. *Qingshuijiang liuyu linye jingji fazhi de lishi huisu* [A historical study on the forestry economic legal system in the Qingshui River Basin], 157–163. Guiyang: Guizhou renmin chubanshe.
97. Xu, Xiaoguang, and Zeshi Cheng. 2015. Qingshuijiang wenshu yanjiu zhengyi wenti pingshu [A review of controversial issues in the studies of the Qingshui River manuscripts]. *Yuanshengtai minzu wenhua xuekan* 7 (1): 46.
98. Xue, Yunsheng. 1906. *Duli cunyi* [Doubts remaining after perusing the substatutes], Art. 340.12. Beijing: Hanmao zhai.
99. Yang, Deqiao. 2012. Ziranren shumian qiyue quxin fangshi yanjiu [Research on the natural person's credit system in written contracts]. *Beifang faxue* 6 (2): 16.
100. Yang, Guozhen. 2009. *Ming Qing tudi qiyue wenshu yanjiu (xiudingban)* [On land-related contracts in the Ming-Qing period], revised ed., 189. Beijing: Zhongguo renmin daxue chubanshe.
101. Yang, Jinping. 2011. Kang Yong Qian shiqi Taiwan de xiangzhi [Local governance in Taiwan in eras of Kangxi, Yongzheng, and Qianlong]. In *Shengshi shehui yu Yangzhou yanjiu* [Prosperous society and Yangzhou studies], ed. Mingzhu Feng, 462–463. Taipei: Yuan-Liou Publishing Co., Ltd.
102. You, Chenjun. 2013. *Falü zhishi de wenzi chuanbo: Ming Qing riyong leishu yu shehui richang shenghuo* [Written propagation of legal knowledge: The encyclopedia for daily use and social life in the Ming and Qing dynasties], 59. Shanghai: Shanghai renmin chubanshe.
103. You, Chenjun. 2015. Qing dai songshi tanli xingxiang de duochong jiangou [Construction of image of greedy lawyers in the Qing dynasty]. *Faxue yanjiu* (5): 182–189.
104. Yu, Jiang. 2017. Tianxia hetong dou yiyang [All over the world the hetong is the same]. In *Huizhou hetong wenshu huibian* [A collection of hetong in Huizhou], ed. Jiang Yu, 1. Guilin: Guangxi shifan daxue chubanshe.
105. Yu, Qian. [1838] 1997. Zailun gedai shupai [Once again on the *shupai* in different dynasties]. In *Muling shu* [The book of magistrates], ed. Dong Xu, Reprinted in *Guanzhen shu jicheng* [The collection of handbooks for officials], vol. 7, 398. Hefei: Huangshan shushe.
106. Zhang, Chuanxi, ed. 1995. *Zhongguo lidai qiyue huibian kaoshi* [The collection and annotations of Chinese contracts from imperial times], 1429. Beijing: Beijing daxue chubanshe.
107. Zhang, Junming. 2005. Dunhuang Xuanquanzhi tanfang T0309 chutu jiandu gaishu [An introduction to the bamboo and wooden slips from T0309 excavation unit in Xuanquanzhi, Dunhuang]. In *Changsha Sanguo Wujian ji bainian lai jianbo faxian yu yanjiu guoji xueshu yantaohui lunwenji* [Proceedings of the international conference on the discovery and study of Wu slips (Three Kingdoms) unearthed at Changsha and the slips and silks discovered in the last century], ed. Changsha wenwu kaogu yanjiusuo, 396–399. Beijing: Zhonghua shuju.
108. Zhang, Xinmin, ed. 2014. *Tianzhu wenshu* [Tianzhu manuscripts], vol. 1(1), 206. Nanjing: Jiangsu renmin chubanshe.
109. Zhang, Yingqiang. 2006. *Mucai zhi liudong: Qing dai Qingshuijiang xiayou diqu de shichang, quanli yu shehui* [The wood flow: Market, power, and society in the downstream sections of Qingshui River in the Qing dynasty], 300. Beijing: Shenghuo, dushu, xinzhi sanlianshudian.
110. Zhang, Yingqiang, and Tengwen Hu. 2004. *Jinping* [Jinping], 122. Beijing: Shenghuo, dushu, xinzhi sanlian shudian.
111. Zhang, Yingqiang, and Zongxun Wang, eds. 2007. *Qingshuijiang wenshu* [Qingshui River manuscripts], vol. 1(7), 6. Guilin: Guangxi shifan daxue chubanshe.
112. Zhang, Yingqiang, and Zongxun Wang, eds. 2007. *Qingshuijiang wenshu* [Qingshui River manuscripts], vol. 1(8), 2. Guilin: Guangxi shifan daxue chubanshe.
113. Zhang, Yingqiang, and Zongxun Wang, eds. 2007. *Qingshuijiang wenshu* [Qingshui River manuscripts], vol. 1(13), 276. Guilin: Guangxi shifan daxue chubanshe.
114. Zhang, Yingqiang, and Zongxun Wang, eds. 2007. *Qingshuijiang wenshu* [Qingshui River manuscripts], vol. 1(12), 58. Guilin: Guangxi shifan daxue chubanshe.

115. Zhang, Yingqiang, and Zongxun Wang, eds. 2007. Qingshuijiang wenshu [Qingshui River manuscripts], vol. 1(3), 5. Guilin: Guangxi shifan daxue chubanshe.
116. Zhang, Yingqiang, and Zongxun Wang, eds. 2009. *Qingshuijiang wenshu* [Qingshui River manuscripts], vol. 2(1), 1. Guilin: Guangxi shifan daxue chubanshe.
117. Zhang, Yingqiang, and Zongxun Wang, eds. 2011. *Qingshuijiang wenshu* [Qingshui River manuscripts], vol. 3(7), 98. Guilin: Guangxi shifan daxue chubanshe.
118. Zhang, Yingqiang, and Zongxun Wang, eds. 2011. *Qingshuijiang wenshu* [Qingshui River manuscripts], vol. 3(8), 174. Guilin: Guangxi shifan daxue chubanshe.
119. Zhang, Yingqiang, and Zongxun Wang, eds. 2011. *Qingshuijiang wenshu* [Qingshui River manuscripts], vol. 3(10), 8. Guilin: Guangxi shifan daxue chubanshe.
120. Zhang, Yingqiang, and Zongxun Wang, eds. 2011. *Qingshuijiang wenshu* [Qingshui River manuscripts], vol. 3(9), 67. Guilin: Guangxi shifan daxue chubanshe.
121. Zhang, Yongquan. 2013. *Dunhuang xieben wenxianxue* [Documentation studies on Dunhuang manuscripts], 13. Lanzhou: Gansu jiaoyu chubanshe.
122. Zhao, Siyuan. 2015. 19 shiji Huizhou xiangcun de tudi shichang, xinyong jizhi yu guanxi wangluo [Land market, credit mechanism, and relational network in Huizhou villages during the nineteenth century]. *Jindaishi yanjiu* (4): 95–96.
123. Zheng, Xiaochun. 2010. Qing dai daishu zhidu yu jiceng sifa [The proctor system of the Qing dynasty and judicial practice]. *Shixue yuekan* (6): 38.
124. Zhou, Yaoming, ed. 1994. *Hanzu minjian jiaoji fengsu* [Social customs of the Han Chinese], 139–141. Nanning: Guanxi jiaoyu chubanshe.
125. Zhou, Guangyuan. 1995. Beneath the law: Chinese local legal culture during the Qing Dynasty. Doctoral dissertation, University of California, Los Angeles, 72.
126. Zhu, Yingui. 2013. Cong Guizhou Qingshuijiang wenshu kan jindai Zhongguo de diquan zhuanyi [The transfer of land ownership in contemporary China reflected in Qingshuijiang documents in Guizhou]. *Guizhou daxue xuebao (shehui kexue ban)* 31 (6): 70.

Chapter 5
The Functioning Mechanism of Contracts in the Society

1 Introduction: Contracts in Their Context

1.1 Revisiting the Contract within the Society

The relationship between social order and contracts can only be constructed as a result of the successful and effective operation of the latter in the society. Previous chapters have attempted to foreground the understanding of contract and its fundamental figures from a desocialized or decontextualized perspective. Conversely, the focus of this chapter will lie on the interaction between contract and its specific social environment—how the device of the contract was treated by the people in the society and why they perceived the contract in this way.

The successful operation of a contract in a society inevitably requires the acceptance of social members concerning not only the content of the contract but also the contract itself. As collective acceptance is widely acknowledged to be important to the construction and maintenance of social order,[1] a study of the functioning mechanism of contracts invites a social-psychological approach to examine the notion of contract that was held by the common people in the regional society.

It is difficult to explore directly the public psychology regarding contracts in a regional society in the past, but what people perceived at that time is to some extent reflected in the text of the contract and its related activities. Therefore, a detailed analysis of the contract text and relevant social practice in villages becomes necessary. After having examined the contract as a practical device in the previous chapters, the revisit of the contract in this chapter will attempt to put it back into its social context. Specifically, through an interpretive structure of a series of familiar contract factors, an explanatory theoretical framework of the contract's functioning mechanism in the society will be developed. In this way, the link between contract and the contractual order in its context can be more properly understood.

---

[1] See Tuomela [149].

J. Qu, *Social Order through Contracts*,
https://doi.org/10.1007/978-981-33-4947-6_5

1.2 The Functioning Mechanism of Contracts

The logical justification of "social order through contracts" depends on a successful and effective contract system in the society. The social order can be considered firmly established when most people abide by the contract which was employed to organize various relations among members of society. However, just like the social order itself, the question whether the operation of the contract is successful or not is not a theoretical assumption but an "empirical fact,"[2] which as such is a result of observation whether from a historical or social perspective. The task for a researcher is, then, to try to explain the functioning mechanism and the inner logic of this system of contract based on "empirical facts."[3]

This chapter aims to offer a tentative answer to the long-standing question of why people in the region honored contracts and to explain the workings of contracts in the society. To put it simply, if a "box" can be taken as a metaphor for a "contract," then this chapter attempts to answer the question "why people honor the 'box'." This question can itself be divided into a series of sub-questions as follows: (1) What is actually in the box and what is its rightfulness[4] per se? (2) Why do the potentially rightful contents of the box need to be packed into the box and how are they packed? (3) Why do people believe that the box will protect the contents in it from being tampered with, once they are put inside?

On the basis of the above metaphorical sub-questions, the remainder of the present chapter unfolds as follows. The following section begins with an examination of the issue of contract compliance in the Qingshui River region. It then provides a critical, albeit brief, survey of oft-mentioned approaches, both in the general sense and within the specific context, in explaining the question of honoring contracts, and thereafter proposes a different fashion of justification that does not follow the logic of enforcement. Following this path, Sect. 3 tries to discuss the rightful grounds of the contract by means of analyzing the self-justifiable contract text, taking the contractual formation of property rights as an example, and introducing an explanatory framework based on the understanding of the contextual limitation of recognition. After clarifying the contents of the "box," Sect. 4 then addresses the question why the recognition should be represented by a contract and how the process of representation could be achieved through the help of the middleman and the scribe. Subsequently, Sect. 5 underscores the importance of the authenticity of a contract, proposing a noncentral trust network of contracts inspired by the innovational solution of blockchain. In

[2]See Mielke et al. [110].

[3]This issue has attracted a lot of scholarly attention. One explanation of the functioning mechanism of contracts in Wendou Village is offered in three parts, focusing on the middleman, the institution of guarantee, and the influence of human relationships, customs, and moral pressure from public opinion in the village society, respectively. See Liang [86].

[4]Instead of "legitimacy," the term "rightfulness" is chosen in this study, for those contracts in question had little relation with "legal/law" but a norm concerning whether the issue involved was rightful or not.

addition to the construction of the explanatory framework, Sect. 6 tackles the challenges of breaches and forgeries and sets out the role that contracts played in the restoration of order. Further, the application of contracts in the public sphere will be examined in Sect. 7, revealing the intrinsic interactions between contracts and order in the region. Lastly, a possible limitation of the theorization of these findings will be considered within its larger context, followed by a short conclusion.

2 The Question of Honoring Contracts: Departing from the myth of Enforcement

Why do people honor contracts? This seems to be a perennial question ever since the first appearance of the contract in society, provoking academics to offer a bewildering array of answers from moral, theological, legal, economic, and sociological perspectives (and others still). Among them, a preferable approach in the context of the Qingshui River region will be raised after an examination of existing theories; but, in order to lay the groundwork for the task ahead, the state of contract compliance for people in the region during the Qing period should be assessed at the outset.

2.1 Contractual Order as an Empirical Fact

Is it a historical and empirical fact that people at that time and place generally observed the contracts which they forged and thus maintained the order formed by these seemingly legally unenforceable manuscripts? The answer, even though it has to some extent not yet been properly proved, is widely believed to be yes. In current studies and reports on the Qingshui River manuscripts, the term "spirit of contract," is frequently mentioned.[5] Despite other explanations of it as an English term,[6] this expression primarily lays emphasis on the principle of the sanctity of contracts (*Pacta sunt servanda*[7]) in its Chinese context, implying that the people in the past evidently adhered to the "spirit of contract"[8] and thus tended to observe the contract terms. Admittedly, people did believe that they ought to abide by contracts as a moral obligation, but since the gap between "is" and "ought" is no longer imperceptible,[9] this contributes little to the proof of the historical fact—it does not necessarily mean that people at that time and in that region generally observed contracts in practice.

---

[5] See, e.g., Zhu and Su [216], Zhong [213]. For a study of the spirit of contract in the general context of ancient China, see Huo [67].

[6] See, e.g., Speidel [143].

[7] See Wehberg [164], Sharp [139].

[8] See Zhong Yiwei, "Zhongguo chuantong qiyue zhong de 'qiyue ziyou' yu 'zhuti pingdeng'," 43.

[9] See Hume [66].

However, a slightly altered approach in analyzing the same materials will be helpful. It is difficult to undertake a quantitative investigation in the general situation of contract compliance in the Qingshui River region where contracts were extensively produced. But what is often overlooked is that the qualitative analysis of this situation can find good and solid evidence based upon exactly the same source. The fact a large number of contracts in the region exists best proves that contracts have been universally observed in the society, for otherwise it would be impossible to imagine that such a mass of contract manuscripts was produced and well preserved until the present, even though many were damaged accidentally.[10] It should be noted that both the production and the preservation of contracts were not without expense.

It is evident that these contracts were widely used and properly preserved ever since they were originally made. Their careful preservation indicates an emphasis on the value of contracts as evidence of the order of, for example, property. Even until today, villagers of the region still tend to keep these aged manuscripts in case of any disputes.[11] The existence and extensive application of contracts, especially in dispute resolution, in the society suggests people's overall recognition of the order constructed upon contracts.

Admittedly, there are plenty of examples of contract breaches in the existing materials, which has unsurprisingly attracted a fair amount of scholarly attention.[12] However, it seems that the emergence of these disputes is not sufficient to affect the overall effectiveness of the contract system in the region, just as a certain incidence of crimes in society does not necessarily affect the effectiveness of the whole criminal law system of the country. From another perspective, if defaults happened so often that people no longer trust that others would abide by the contract, then it would be meaningless for villagers to care about the preservation of these manuscripts. Obviously, this situation did not occur. This signifies that the risk of default during Qing times in the region was still limited to a low or tolerable level.

Every system of effectiveness may have its own designs of tolerating faults, and the fact that the system of the contract ran continuously indicates that the danger caused by the faults did not exceed the limits of fault tolerance. The contractual order which prevailed in the region can thus be considerably proved by the extensive existence and application of contract materials. The task in the remainder of this chapter is rather to explain this empirical fact, based on the fundamental understanding of the effectiveness of the contractual order. It should be borne in mind in

[10]For the preservation of a family's contract manuscripts in Wendou Village, as well as its damage throughout history, see Wang [159].

[11]During an archival research conducted on April 11, 2018, at the Jinping County Archives, Guizhou, the author personally participated in the negotiation concerning a dispute of forestry property rights as one of the mediators. The two elders, as representatives of the two disputing parties, came to the archives to inquire about their contracts of the forest land in question, which were previously collected by the government as historical documentation and thus preserved at the archives. In the eyes of contemporary people of the region, though not necessarily accepted by the law in force, contracts that were stipulated in older times are still deemed incontrovertible proof of their current property rights.

[12]See, e.g. Wu [172], Zhang [191], Zhong [212], Wu [168], Deng and Qiu [32].

all subsequent discussion that, no matter how many examples of breach of contract occur, relative to the substantial number of unrecorded cases of contract compliance, these counter-examples are just the few that they fail to endanger the overall system. The effectiveness of the contractual order in the Qingshui River region is largely beyond doubt.

2.2 *Generic and* Sui Generis*: The Logic of Enforcement*

In a general sense, previous studies on contract theory have been extremely rich.[13] However, it should be noted that great limitations emerge in their direct application in the context of the Qingshui River region. A large number of contract theories should therefore be considered as the result of thought-experiments and theoretical derivations within a limited and simplified environment. In particular, it is unavoidable that problems occur when applying these general theories to explain specific contracts and the societies in which they are situated, for not enough attention has been paid to countless unique details that need to be emphasized. In this context, the gap between general theories and the *sui generis* reality of the Qingshui River region can be analyzed through the following two main aspects.

First, there are differences regarding the setting of contract law. Many contract theories originated in the age of contract law,[14] in which setting observing the contract was a legal requirement without doubt. In this case, what needs to be explained is not why the contract should be observed, but rather why in the general sense people should abide by the law. This surely includes the provision of observing contracts that are legally binding.[15] More profoundly, there is no need to explain why people should comply with the contract, but rather a need to discuss directly the legal remedies that the law should provide, once the contract is not observed.[16] Moreover, in the theory of

---

[13]Chronologically, the development of contract theory (which is mostly but not necessarily law-related) in modern times can be summarized into three phases: the era of classical contract law, the era of neo-classical contract law, and the rising of relational contract theory, which is considered as "one of the latest steps in the scholarly project of responding to the inadequacies of classical contract law." See Feinman [40]. For three eye-catching monographs in the developmental trajectory of contract theory, see Gilmore [45], Macneil [105], Uchida [150]. As a summary, the so-called "meta-theories" of contract, compared to the classical contract theory as a general theory, are concluded as falling into three groups, namely promissory theories, reliance theories, and transfer theories. The neo-classical contract theory lays more emphasis on "reliance" than "promise" as the motivation of contract enforcement. See Austen-Baker and Zhou [6].

[14]For a critical overview of theories of contract under the background of contract law, see Hogg [61].

[15]When facing the state coercion, the question of "why the state should enforce a contract against the wishes of a party to it" arises. This is considered as "[a] perennial question in contract law." See Schwartz and Scott [137].

[16]See, e.g., Farnsworth [37].

efficient breach of contract which separates law and morality,[17] the contract does not necessarily need to be observed as long as there are sufficient liquidated damages to be charged.[18] However, in the context of the Qingshui River region, the contract faced a situation that obviously no clear and positive contract law existed, i.e. "contract without contract law" as described in the second chapter. Therefore, the question of honoring the contract cannot simply be explained by the requirement of law.

Second, the setting of the understanding of contracts is also different. An example that highlights the fundamental difference on this point is the relational contract theory. Here, the future aspect is especially stressed since the contract is broadly defined as "the relations among parties to the process of projecting exchange into the future."[19] Conversely, contracts seem to have a more backward-looking nature in the *sui generis* context of the Qingshui River region.

However, this is not to say that previous theories are completely unsuitable for the situation under discussion; on the contrary, they are actually quite inspirational when situated within a specific context. In this case, beyond the general theory, when focusing specifically on the context of the Qingshui River region, the question can be re-framed to account for a regional and historical experience[20]: why did people honor contracts in that context?

In previous contextual studies, this question is often asked together with a further, often implicit one: what would happen to those people who did not abide by the contract? The implication of this inquiry is that it is believed that the de facto reason why people opted to abide by the contract is nothing but the fear or aversion of the consequences of the breach. In other words, people are deemed to be forced to oblige contractually since they, in fact, did not have a choice. This approach extensively exists in general theories. For instance, it is believed that the reason which people adhere to the contract, or law,[21] is that it is enforceable, and, from both social and economic perspectives, the forces of coercion, apart from the police force, generally include pressure, deterrence, and utility calculations.[22]

This logic also enjoys great popularity in the scholarship concerning the Qingshui River manuscripts. For example, regarding the dispute settlement in the region, some scholars assert that it relied on the pressure of enforcement from the village head or

---

[17]For a summary of the theory, see Linzer [93].

[18]An impressive remark on this point from Justice Holmes is that "[t]he duty to keep a contract at common law means a prediction that you must pay damages if you do not keep it—and nothing else." See Holmes [62].

[19]Ian Roderick Macneil, *The New Social Contract*, 4. The "awareness of future," along with "society," "specialization of labor and exchange," and "choice," are listed by Macneil as the "four primal roots of contract" in exploring the nature of contract. See ibid., 1–4.

[20]It is believed that the situation or ratio of people honoring contracts can be seen as a matter of specific social conditioning. See Kato [78].

[21]From the perspective of social psychology, the starting points as to why people abide by the law and why they keep the contract may be similar, for contracts have long been regarded as having the same effect as law, although they are only binding on the parties to the contract. They are also regarded as the cornerstone of the birth of national law in social contract theory.

[22]See Xiao [174].

government,[23] and that the source of effectiveness of the dispute solution agreement, which is one kind of contract in the context, includes authorities and coercion that respectively stem from customary law and national law.[24] Some stress the decisive role that the coercive force of the state has played in contract disputes,[25] while still others emphasize that there was in effect no coercive force from external forces, namely the government, in the Qingshui River region,[26] but instead mention internal authorities and coercive measures as key factors.[27] Although some acknowledge the role that trust and integrity have played in contract practice, they emphasize that this integrity is a kind of "calculable" integrity, which is principally based on the rational calculation of the low-cost operation of the contract system.[28] On this view, beyond the contract, what played a decisive role was the game of power and interests, as well as people's considerations and trade-offs on real-life issues.[29]

Overall, these generic and *sui generis* interpretations, whether based on the fear of legal coercion, social pressure, or the avoidance of adverse results after rational game-theory-like calculations,[30] can be regarded as supported by the logic of enforcement.

2.3 A Weaker "Gunman" and a Better "Bad Man"? Shifting to "The Internal Point of View"

If someone is threatened "with unpleasant consequences if he refuses,"[31] then he is in what is called a "gunman situation" in the Hartian sense[32]: "The gunman orders his victim to hand over his purse and threatens to shoot if he refuses."[33] This is an

---

[23]See Deng Jianpeng and Qiu Kai, "Cong heyi dao qiangzhi," 32–35.

[24]See Cheng [23].

[25]See Cheng [24].

[26]See Yan [182].

[27]See ibid., 20–22.

[28]See Xu [177].

[29]See Jiang [70].

[30]For a study of social order in a game-theoretical approach, see Calvert [13]. As for a typical analysis on the question of observing contracts using game theory, see Sang [135]. Approaches of rational calculation have also been applied in the discussion of social order in specific contexts. As an example of the application of the rational calculation in another area, it is believed that the establishment of the order of fishery in Boyang Lake in late imperial times originated from people's realization of the high cost of violent conflicts after either direct or indirect experience, and then turned to find a peaceful way to reach agreements concerning everybody's interests in general. It seems that people observed those agreements in order to avoid endless armed combats after rational calculation. See Liu [94].

[31]Hart [52].

[32]The "gunman situation" was proposed by Hart to set it against John Austin's "command theory," with which he was dissatisfied. See ibid., 18 ff.

[33]Ibid., 6.

extreme illustration suggesting that the orderly situation is created and backed by the gunman's ability and the possibility of using force.

At the same time, however, the order of the bank in which the gunman's heist occurs cannot be maintained without the "cooperation" of the bank clerk. Rather than choosing to be a "hero," the clerk casually makes a quick rational calculation that results in him giving up resistance after hearing the gunman's threat to "[h]and over the money or I will shoot."[34] In this case, the victim shall to some extent also be a "bad man" in the sense of Justice Holmes' theory. According to Holmes' description, a bad man is someone who "cares nothing for an ethical rule which is believed and practised by his neighbors," but cares only for the predictable "material consequences."[35] For instance, since he "has as much reason as a good one for wishing to avoid an encounter with the public force," he is likely "to care a good deal to avoid being made to pay money, and will want to keep out of jail if he can."[36] A good man, on the contrary, is someone who "finds his reasons for conduct, whether inside the law or outside of it, in the vaguer sanctions of conscience."[37] Supposing that the gunman is facing a good man, who should be extremely "good" in this case (as it is an extreme emergency) and good to such an extent that he would rather risk his life than resignedly "hand over his purse" (which is something that a good man would believe to be wrong), it is conceivable that the heroic, or irrational, bank clerk would at least try to resist wholesale obedience of the intimidator. However, as an amoral man, a bad man would follow the command from the gunman since he can foresee the "material consequences" of not doing so, even if it is evidently ethically wrong from a good man's point of view.

In this way, two analytical approaches have emerged. First, people are forced to abide by the contract because they cannot bear the consequences of breaching it; and, second, people honor the contract because they themselves internally accept it as a rule and believe that it is the right thing to do. In other words, the difference between these two approaches is whether the choice to comply with the contract is principally rooted in the profit or the rightfulness of doing so.[38]

As to the first situation, as mentioned above, both protagonists are indispensable in forming the order: the "gunman" who is powerful enough and the "bad man" who is good at judging situations. However, it seems that, in the context of the Qingshui River region, neither of these points renders a satisfying explanation.

First, as has been repeatedly mentioned above, the system of coercive forces in the Qingshui River region during the Qing period seems to have been neither powerful nor systematic. On the basis of the available evidence, it seems that the coercive force that could be exerted by the governmental/legal authority, the local moral authority,

---

[34]Ibid., 19.

[35]Oliver Wendell Holmes, "The Path of the Law," 459.

[36]Ibid.

[37]Ibid.

[38]The game-theoretic analysis asserts that following the rules, including observing the contract, is in truth a smart choice for maximizing benefits. See Sang Benqian, "Qiyue weihe bixu zunshou," 28.

the religious authority, or the clan authority was insufficient to systematically support the thorough implementation of the rule, if any, of observing contracts. Therefore, in terms of his capability to using force, with such a relatively weak "gunman," there was little possibility of successfully securing order in the whole society based on the logic of enforcement. Practical deficiencies existed in the application of coercive force in guaranteeing social order. However, this is not to say that the coercive force did not exist or was not important at all for the region. For example, as some scholars have realized, although there were lawsuits, they were far from being the main means to resolve disputes.[39] The Miao frontier seems to be too remote a place for the arm of the imperial court to reach. Hence, the explanatory power of the logic of enforcement in this region should become questionable.

Second, to judge from both documentary evidence and the results of field research,[40] when it comes to the topic of honoring contracts, the social-psychological attitude concerning contracts in the region seems to be far from a mere measurement of the pros and cons under coercion. On the contrary, the doctrine of good faith has repeatedly been emphasized by the people of the region since long ago.[41] The power of morality and conscience cannot be ignored in a village society where, as noted, divine judgment still occasionally existed.[42] In this case, whether analysts portrayed those villagers as honest and simple or shrewd and crafty, they were far from being "bad men" in the full sense. That is not to say that no rational calculation ever appeared in their minds, but they seem to be a little "better" at least.

Since the logic of enforcement could be problematic in the context of the Qingshui River region, where a crowd of slightly better "bad men" with a relatively weaker "gunman" watching them lived, this chapter opts for a different analytical approach, by attempting to explain the question of honoring contracts based on the investigation of people's internal acceptance of the contract. This approach reflects the Hartian "internal point of view," which refers to the situation in which one is concerned with the rules as "a member of the group which accepts and uses them as guides to conduct," rather than "merely as an observer who does not himself accept them."[43] The weakness of the myth of enforcement lies precisely in the distrust of the premise that honoring contracts has been generally "accepted and used" by the locals as a "rule" in contracting behavior in the region.

In people's eyes at the time, the contract had gained a status which was much higher than just a civil agreement; as mentioned in the discussion of the contracts' materiality, villagers honored and even sanctified the contract to some degree. A

[39] See Deng Jianpeng and Qiu Kai, "Cong heyi dao qiangzhi," 33.

[40] Admittedly, the results of today's field research cannot fully mirror the situation in previous times. However, it may still be of some help for understanding the sociopsychological environment which to some extent still exists in the same region. An internal critical examination on this point can be seen in Szonyi and Peng [144].

[41] This phenomenon can be found as a result of field research conducted in the 1930s, see Shi [141]. For a much later example of field research which illustrates the doctrine of good faith in contracting, see Xu [178].

[42] See Takeuchi [145].

[43] H. L. A. Hart, *The Concept of Law*, 89.

scenario which repeatedly appears in the folk tales circulating in the local area of the Miao is as follows: two contracting parties, regardless of their social status and capability, choose to fight over the text of the contract, since the one who considers himself to be unfairly treated would normally try to balance his interests through the sometimes improper modification or interpretation of the contract text, instead of seeking to overthrow the contract directly or by wrestling in other fields beyond the contract.[44]

In several of these stories, the more socially influential and powerful party chooses, albeit reluctantly, to abide by the contract that works against him, even though the contract was, according to his narrative, wrongly signed by him. The general plot of one of these stories is as follows. A long-term hired hand has been exploited by a rich man for years, being driven away without paying wages since he did not have any labor contract at that time. Later, following the instruction from an expert, the long-term worker made a written contract with the rich man, stipulating that, no matter what the employer does, the worker must follow suit, and, in the case that the employer wants to dismiss the worker, the rich must offer double his wages. In the following days, the long-term worker performed the contract strictly according to the literal meaning, not only working with the employer as required, but also imitating him to enjoy the banquet prepared for the guests, and even quarrelling with the employer's wife as the employer did. In the end, the rich man, being made impatient, chose to dismiss the worker, and of course, paid double the wages according to the contract.[45] The socially powerful rich man who, in the eyes of ordinary people, could have completely overturned the agreement, just as he had done previously when there was no contract, eventually made the "unexpected" decision to abide by the contract terms. This plot-line illustrates that the calculation of benefits is not the whole story, and that the notion of honoring contract itself is a vital element.[46] It seems to indicate that the local people, regardless of their social status, tended to believe that a contract ought to be kept as long as it is a contract, even if one might personally see it as an inequitable one and have the capability to overturn it. Unlike the well-known maxim "*lex iniusta non est lex*," it seems that, in this case, an "unfair" contract is still believed to be a contract that needs to be observed, even there might have a "trap" in its terms.[47]

---

[44] See, e.g., Tianzhu xian minzu shiwu weiyuanhui and Tianzhu xian wenhuaguan [148], Wang [158].

[45] Multiple versions of this story can be seen in collections of folk literature, see, e.g., Yan [181], Miaozu wenxueshi bianxiezu [109], Miaozu wenxueshi bianxiezu [108].

[46] To a certain extent, it can also be said that the wealthy man still performed a certain degree of measuring his own benefits, albeit of a different kind. It is believed that the decision pattern of a good man should be differentiated from that of a "bad man," since the good man "is willing to pay something to perform his legal obligation." In order to "find out how much a citizen is willing to pay," one "must look inward and consult his intrinsic values," which is "the internal point of view." See Cooter [27]. In this story, the wealthy man was willing to pay double wages in exchange for fully performing his obligation in the contract.

[47] Hart believes that one important character of "social rules," which can be likened to "contract" here, is that "where there are such rules, not only is such criticism in fact made but deviation from the standard is generally accepted as a *good reason* for making it." See H. L. A. Hart, *The Concept of Law*, 55.

Put succinctly, "*force ne fait pas droit* (might is not right)."[48] Those people abided by the contract not (or not only) because it was in their interest to observe the contract, but because honoring the contract, as a social rule, itself was primarily considered right instead of profitable. The missing or overlooked but more important part of the story can be revealed through the examination of "the internal point of view" of the locals: why was it right to comply with the contract? An investigation into the phenomenon of honoring the contract from "the internal point of view" then firstly requires the exploration of the rightfulness of the contract in its context.

3 Recognition and the Rightfulness of the Contract

It is believed that, although the contract is "a complex legal institution," it "can be traced to and is determined by a small number of basic moral principles."[49] This assertion supports the understanding that it is feasible to explain the rightfulness of the contract based on its more fundamental doctrines.[50] Thus, the task ahead is to clarify these basic principles in the specific social context that the contract is rooted in.

3.1 Contract Text as Justification

It is known that the reasons why people in the Qingshui River region abided by the contract were not based solely on calculations of interest, but more so on the rightful grounds of the contract. However, it is difficult for a modern scholar to investigate, or rather speculate about, the genuine perception of a contractor at that time concerning the rightfulness of the contract. Still, since the personal intention of a contractor to observe a certain contract is not the focus of the discussion, more attention should be placed on the general or public discourse of a contract's rightful grounds, which, to a large extent, could and should be reflected somehow by the contract text.

On the basis of the previous analysis of the content or substantiality of the contract, its characteristically more backward-looking nature within the Qingshui River region has been shown. Hence, what a contract records in its text mainly concerns the relationship that has been previously established or established right by this contract. In the meantime, given the publicity that a contract could generate,[51] the contract

---

[48] Rousseau [133]. For the English translation, see Rousseau [134].

[49] Fried [43].

[50] It is believed that the question of why a contract must be kept is also a question of where the validity of the contract comes from, see Sang Benqian, "Qiyue weihe bixu zunshou," 22. Many theories answer this question by referring to some more fundamental principles. A critical summary of related theories can be found in Li [84].

[51] See Liang Cong, *Qing dai Qingshuijiang xiayou cunzhai shehui de qiyue guifan yu zhixu*, 121.

text itself should be considered as a part of public discourse in the village society. A contract could therefore to some extent be seen as a declaration that was situated in the public sphere[52] of a rural village or beyond, so that it ought to be persuasive to its potential readers. For this reason, the text of a contract must not only include a description of the fact but in most cases could also provide a justification for honoring the established or confirmed factual relations. In this scenario, the text of a contract is in truth a refined narrative. For readers of the contract, by selecting the description of facts and the use of declarative discourse, the contract text can offer not only a brief record of the contractual facts but also the values behind it; it can explain why it needs to be observed, or, to some extent, convince its readers to follow what has been written down. Thus, the contract appears to be a self-justifying document when facing the public, and the reasons it announces must necessarily be widely accepted by the general public, or else those reasons would not be written into this realistically effective instrument. To put it more specifically, among various contract terms, only those that are more general, non-specific, and commonly found can better reflect the general perception of the village society regarding observing and retaining the contract.

In light of the above understanding, rightful grounds should exist, explicitly or implicitly, in the general text of the contracts, especially the formulaic expressions as they are the most used terms.

3.2 *Behind the Text: Willingness and Estoppel*

A careful textual analysis is necessary to reveal the rightful grounds that are hidden in the contract context. For the convenience of further examination and given the extreme diversity of contract types in the region, the contract of property, especially of sale,[53] will be selected as an illustration, since such contracts account for the vast majority of all contracts in quantity and the property order constructed by them undoubtedly acts as the foundation of civil and commercial order in the society.

In general, the main content of property sales contract texts is a formatted description of a series of events[54]: for some reason (normally the shortage of living expenses),[55] the vendor intended to sell his, say, wet-rice field (a detailed clarification

[52]On the debate about the existence of the "public sphere" in China before the nineteenth century, see Chow [25].

[53]In the Qingshui River region, the methods of property transfer include not only sale, though it was the most popular one, but also conditional sale (*dian*), mortgage, household division, etc. See Zhu [215].

[54]It is believed that "the existence of a contract exemplifies *event-based institutional facts*." See Hage [48].

[55]Though some may argue that these reasons might not be the reality but merely a formulaic excuse, evidence shows that, at least under certain circumstances, the shortage of living expenses was the real cause for transferring properties. See Qu [125]. Sometimes the reason written in the contract would be specific, such as the lack of legal costs at yamen, see Chen and Du [20]. Therefore, even if

of the specific conditions of the property should be added, such as its boundaries); then, through the participation of the middleman, a suitable vendee emerged; the price was settled after negotiation, the money was paid and collected; and, finally, the contract was written down for reference.[56] These factual descriptions rarely involved expressions of the individual will (intention) of the contractor.[57] However, a careful textual analysis reveals that in property sales contracts there are two key expressions related to personal intention hidden in the formatted text: the "willingness" which is normally stated at the beginning of the contract and the "estoppel" at the end.

3.2.1 Willingness

At the beginning of most property sales contracts, after introducing the basic personal information of the contractor and the reason for the sale, the contractor would normally emphasize his or her willingness with respect to the entire process of sale before the formal narrative of the whole event begins.[58] As an random set of instances, the first 50 contracts of sale in Jiang Qigui's family collection are taken for examination,[59] and the result shows that 48 of them contain an expression of willingness, with only two exceptional cases.[60] Most of them use the phrase *ziyuan*,[61] while other expressions—*ziji*,[62] *zi*,[63] *qinshen*,[64] *qingyuan*,[65] and *ziji qingyuan*[66]—also appear from time to time. All of these terms, whether simple or complex, are used to underscore that the following acts were performed willingly by the contractor.

---

the contract text should not be treated as entirely true records, it should be considered as a narrative of fact; in a certain sense, the way the fact is narrated may be more important than the fact itself.

[56]The formatted description is commonly seen in contracts of sale in the Qingshui River region. For an example using the above-mentioned style of description, see Chen and Du [21].

[57]In the theory of legal transaction (*Rechtsgeschäft*), which derived from "the more specific notion of a contract," the individual will or intention is of crucial importance. Arguably, it is observable that "a contract is normally formed on the basis of will (intention) and declaration of it." See Jaap Hage, "What is a Legal Transaction?," 103. Therefore, it is essential to distinguish between pure descriptions of events and expressions of intention in the contract text, since the latter implies the justification of the contract at the normative level.

[58]A study on contracts from Zigong, Sichuan province also notes the importance of expressing the willingness of contracting parties in contract text, see Zhang [193].

[59]These contracts can be found in Chen Jinquan and Du Wanhua, *Jiang Qigui jiacang qiyue wenshu*, 3–57. In this corpus, page 9 includes two contracts, and of which six are not contracts of sale, see ibid., 16, 31, 44, 49, 52–53. Therefore, 50 contracts of sale remained after eliminating the six.

[60]See ibid., 35, 38.

[61]See ibid., 3, 8, 13, 14, 17, 19, 20–21, 24–25, 27–30, 32–34, 36, 39, 40, 42–43, 45–47, 50–51, 54, 56–57.

[62]See ibid., 4, 6, 12, 15, 18, 23, 41, 48, 55.

[63]See ibid., 7, 11, 26.

[64]See ibid., 5.

[65]See ibid., 9, 10, 22, 37.

[66]See ibid., 9.

Admittedly, there are different interpretations on this point. Previous scholarship tends to presume that these expressions of willingness were de facto cover-ups—they are very poor lies that just reveal the truth. Since the more one tries to hide, the more is exposed, it is therefore alleged, albeit without concrete evidence, that these statements of willingness demonstrate in reality that the contractor was often reluctant.[67] A mediation manuscript which clearly states that the parties were voluntarily participating in the mediation and not forced to do so by the middleman is often cited to illustrate this issue.[68] However, this kind of statement emphasizing the absence of coercion is in fact rarely seen in contracts, especially in sales contracts. The reason for this might precisely be that these expressions were rarely written into contracts, so that they become more eye-catching; modern readers start to imagine the real intention of the contractor in order to explain the sudden appearance of the wording. However, even if one agrees that there were some other stories hidden behind the text, a question that still needs to be considered is why, under the circumstances of possible coercion, the writer of the contract should still emphasize the aspect of willingness.

Contracts made under duress, whether in pre-modern or modern times, are invalid in both common and legal sense.[69] The emphasis of willingness by contract writers in the Qingshui River region exactly shows that, at the normative level, an unwilling contractor would not conclude a valid contract. In other words, the unwillingness or coercion of the contractor could be deemed a key justification for not complying or even overturning the contract. A criminal case involving the judgment of the validity of an unwillingly concluded contract which happened in 1763 in Guizhou province illustrates this point.[70] This contract concerning the sale of a wet-rice field was written in a helpless situation, where a group of people holding and threatening with sticks wanted to bargain at a low price. The result shows that the final validity of this contract has not been recognized, and the field could still be sold by the original owner according to his wishes.

In this case, since unwillingness could be the reason for not keeping the contract, it should then be regarded as a vital justification for demonstrating the valid establishment of a contract and the obligation to comply with it.

---

[67] See Liang Cong, *Qing dai Qingshuijiang xiayou cunzhai shehui de qiyue guifan yu zhixu*, 120; Chen [22].

[68] See Daniels et al. [31].

[69] For a detailed study on the willingness and the erosion of contract effectiveness when it is lacking in the Song dynasty, see Gao [44].

[70] For the record of the case, including testimonies, see Zhongguo diyi lishi dang'an guan and Zhongguo shehui kexue yuan lishi yanjiusuo [214]. A discussion of this case can be found in Lin [90].

3.2.2 Estoppel

Estoppel as a collective term originally refers to a group of legal doctrines in common law legal systems.[71] However, here the concept is borrowed to express a similar contractual principle that frequently appears in manuscripts from the Qingshui River region. Although the two uses have utterly distinctive connotations and intentions considering their different contexts,[72] their essential requirements are basically similar. Put succinctly, the term "estoppel" used here refers to the principle that my word is my bond, and so one shall not go back on it.[73]

In the text of sales contracts in the Qingshui River region, it can be seen as a common request that the contractor should declare, in the ending part of the main text after the whole process of the sale had been narrated, that no further objections against the to-be-established transaction could be raised, since the contract has been concluded (referred henceforth as the expression of estoppel). The popularity of this expression can be explained by an examination of the last one hundred contracts of sale, again as a set of random samples, in Jiang Yuanze's family collection during the Qing dynasty.[74] The result shows that 93% of the samples include the expression of estoppel.[75] In most cases, the marked words for this expression are *bude yiyan*, which literally means "shall not [raise] dissenting voices." In some contracts, a similar meaning is expressed as "shall not [raise] arguments"[76] or "shall not stir up troubles."[77] It is clear that what these statements are trying to prohibit is future opposition against what is currently being established, and the reason for this prohibition of dissenting voices is that the contractor has already made a commitment, so he or she should not go back on it.

Nonetheless, three further questions need to be answered with respect to this justification of estoppel. First, what shall the dissenting voice not be raised against? Or in other words, what exactly is the promise stated in and then protected by the

---

[71] See Kötz [80], Peel [121], Feinman [39], Henderson [58].

[72] It is broadly accepted that laying down the rules of estoppel, and especially promissory estoppel, represented a diminishment of the force of the doctrine of consideration in the theory of contract law, and that the major purpose of promissory estoppel is "a vehicle for protecting the expectation interest" as well as reliance. See Hein Kötz, *European Contract Law*, 64; Stanley D. Henderson, "Promissory Estoppel and Traditional Contract Doctrine," 379.

[73] The conclusion of an experimental study suggests that people, in general, have a preference for word keeping, and the commitment-based account for promise keeping could have a stronger explanatory power than the expectation-based account. See Vanberg [151].

[74] Chen Jinquan and Du Wanhua, *Jiang Yuanze jiacang qiyue wenshu*, 349, 350(2), 352, 353(1, 2), 354, 355(1, 2), 356, 357(1, 2), 358, 359(2), 360, 361(1, 2), 362, 363(1, 2), 364, 367, 371–374, 375(1), 376–380, 382–386, 388, 390–393, 394(1, 2), 395, 396(1, 2),397–399, 401–405, 406(2), 407, 408, 410(2), 414–415, 417, 419, 420(1), 421–422, 425(1), 426 (1), 428(2), 437(2), 438, 441, 448, 451–453, 455(1, 2), 456–457, 459(1), 460(2), 463(1, 2), 464(1, 2), 465–467, 484–485, 487, 492, 494, 497–498, 500, 503–505, 510. Since there might be more than one manuscripts on one page, the numbers in parentheses are used to indicate the corresponding contract.

[75] For exceptions, see ibid., 353(1), 408, 410(2), 426 (1), 441, 457, 463(1).

[76] See ibid., 358, 378.

[77] See ibid., 415.

contract? Generally, the sentence right before the statement of *bude yiyan* should be "since the sale of the field, the vendee can farm and manage this property at will,"[78] which means that the content of the contractor's promise is the recognition of the vendee's ownership.[79] In this case, no matter how the new proprietor of the field utilizes (farms and manages) or disposes of his property, the original proprietor, like all other people, shall not raise any dissenting voices against the new proprietor's rightful claims over the subject matter of the contract of sale.

Second, who specifically should not raise dissenting voices? In a sales contract, the subject of the sentence directly related to estoppel is generally the vendor, who should also be the establisher of the contract under most circumstances.[80] In the case that there are two vendors, then naturally both of them must be restrained by their own expression of estoppel, as it is shown in a contract of property exchange.[81] However, in some cases, apart from the vendor or direct disposer, those who made the commitment also included, according to the degree of intimacy,[82] the vendor's brothers, uncles and nephews, clansmen,[83] descendants,[84] and even outsiders who have no blood connection with the vendor's family at all.[85] Regarding the scope of the promisers, it is noteworthy that those who need to make the contract included a series of related persons other than the vendor. In other words, in considering the answer to the previous question, the vendee's property rights needed to be recognized by not only the most conspicuous contractor, the vendor, but also many other hidden contractors. In particular, the inclusion of descendants and outsiders shows that the new proprietor needs to be widely recognized both in terms of time and space—in terms of time, the recognition should exceed the limit of the current generation, and, in terms of social space, it should not be confined to the transferrer's family clan. After all, these are actually the integral components of a right *in rem*.

Finally, what if someone still raises a dissenting voice? The solution to this situation is clearly stipulated in the contract by saying that, "if there are any dissenting voices, the vendor shall be in charge of them."[86] There are two points that one must

---

[78]See, e.g., ibid., 27.

[79]It is admitted that, in the practice of traditional land laws of Qing China, ownership might not be a precise term to indicate the rights that one could have over one's property, which, in its Chinese context, was often expressed as "*ye*." Here the term "ownership" is used to refer to the free rights that one could have in utilizing one's property (such as the field). For studies on the issue of "*ye*," see Terada [147], Li [85]. In addition, it should be noted that the controversial issue of whether the true "property rights" or absolute "ownership" existed in the traditional Chinese context or not is avoided here. For a similar attitude on this debate, see Zhao and Liu [210]. In regard to this issue, see also Aihara [2].

[80]See, e.g., Chen Jinquan and Du Wanhua, *Jiang Yuanze jiacang qiyue wenshu*, 27.

[81]See, e.g., ibid., 500.

[82]For a discussion of the sequence of listing the following figures, see Qu Jian, "Qing zhonghouqi Qiandongnan Wendou zhai Miaozu dianzhi yanjiu," 203.

[83]See, e.g., Chen Jinquan and Du Wanhua, *Jiang Yuanze jiacang qiyue wenshu*, 505.

[84]See, e.g., ibid., 496.

[85]See, e.g., ibid., 503.

[86]See, e.g., ibid., 27.

pay attention to in understanding this provision. First, the assumption of the contract writer is that the dissenting voice shall not be raised by those who have been listed in the contract, which is here understood as their agreement on the issue and their consent not to take back their own words. Therefore, only those who are unlisted or, in fact, unforeseen would probably dissent against the effectiveness or rightfulness of the transaction. On this assumption, the dispute could only happen under two certain circumstances, namely when the vendor intentionally concealed the truth that there were other unmentioned rights holders of the property, or when he was unaware of it.[87] Second, if this dispute happens, the vendor should handle it properly. The emphasis of this stipulation is not laid on how the vendor should deal with possible disputes, but rather on how the vendee should ensure that the property for sale has no defects in rights.[88] In particular, the vendor must not only ensure that he and other related family members had offered their recognition of the new proprietor's ownership, but he also needs to guarantee that all other social members have previously recognized his ownership of the property for sale so that no other challenges would emerge in the future.

According to the above analysis, it can be concluded that the main reason for the existence of the expression of estoppel in the sales contract is to demonstrate the rightfulness of the new property order generated through the contract. It can even be understood that the foundation of rightfulness of the post-transaction property rights lies in the contractor's recognition of the new proprietor's ownership. Furthermore, in a broader sense, the alteration of the property order is not merely a matter between the vendor and the vendee, but rather, all people who may have claims on the property need to participate in the recognition of the transfer of the property in either an explicit or implicit way. To a certain extent, the scope of this recognition could even involve all possible members of the whole society.

3.3 Recognition and Property Order

The above textual analyses of expressions of willingness and estoppel in the sales contract of the Qingshui River region jointly present a logic of the following justification: the rightfulness of the contract lies in the fact that the contractor willingly recognizes what the contract stipulates (the transfer of the property and therefore the ownership of the new proprietor), and, for this reason, he or she should be bound by such willing and irreversible recognition.

However, the property order could not be successfully constructed solely by the recognition offered by the contractor, who, on most occasions, is also the transferrer

[87]This means that, theoretically speaking, other circumstances would not be considered as rightful, such as those who wished to retract their recognition in the contract, or an unlisted claimer who disputed the property without rightful grounds.

[88]This is similar to the device of security for defects of right in modern contract law, see Qu Jian, "Qing zhonghouqi Qiandongnan Wendou zhai Miaozu dianzhi yanjiu," 203.

of the property. The alteration of the property order through the conclusion of the contract in a village society could by no means be an entirely private issue. Therefore, this finding poses the question, what degree of recognition is needed for the establishment of the new property order in the society of the Qingshui River region?

3.3.1 Universal Recognition and its Limitations in Context

Naturally, the ultimate purpose of a property sales contract, as it is stated in the contract text itself, is to enable the vendee to rightfully acquire the rights of the property and to avoid any potential interference. Thus, true compliance with the contract requires the participation of not only the vendor but also many or all others. In this sense, the post-transaction property order seemingly needs the universal recognition of the ownership of the new proprietor.

In theoretical discussions of laws, universal recognition indeed plays a key role in the establishment of property rights. It is a basic assumption in property law that "[t]he touchstone of a property right in a thing is its universality."[89] The property rights (*ius in rem*) are often mentioned in comparison to the personal rights (*ius in personam*) or obligations, and the practical difference between the two bears on the question against whom the right can be demanded.[90] A property right means that "it can be asserted against the world at large," rather than "only against another individual such as a contracting partner."[91] Moreover, the true meaning of ownership is that, no matter how the owner possesses the property, physically or conceptually, others must not interfere; the essence of one's ownership is in this sense not to vest rights to the owner, but to impose obligations on others.[92] Hence, theoretically, one's ownership needs to be recognized by people of the whole world on account of the binding effect of recognition towards recognizers. In this sense, ownership itself can be considered a collection of recognition.

On this assumption, the ideal situation of owning one parcel of the field in Wendou Village is that people from every corner of the earth, whether the official in Beijing or the merchant in Baden-Württemberg, have all recognized the proprietary rights, and thereby do not trespass on the property unless permission has been granted by the recognized absolute owner. In reality, however, this is not the case.

Quod omnes tangit, omnibus tractari et approbari debet.[93] The rediscovery of this rule of Roman law can be used to explain the rightful grounds of the effectiveness of

---

[89]Bridge [10].

[90]See Smith [142].

[91]Michael Bridge, *Personal Property Law*, 1–2.

[92]See Zhang [192], Lawson and Rudden [81].

[93]"All those affected should be heard and agree (Mike Robert Horenstein's translation in Luhmann's article)." This was originally a rule in Roman law dealing with the situation of plural legal guardians (*tutores*) over the same single ward, and the rule is that "their joint administration could not be dissolved without the consent of all." See Berman [8], Luhmann [101]. The maxim of Roman law was later "raised to the level of a constitutional principle." See Harold J. Berman, *Law and Revolution*, 221. After showing its possibility of being "extended to maxims of legal rationality,"

issues of public concern, such as a sales contract causing the alternation of property order. Two specific elements can be cited to justify it: on the one hand, general agreements are required, while, on the other hand, only those affected shall be involved. The latter especially throws some light on the need to explore the practical boundary of the influence of a property contract as an issue of public concern.

Although ownership is an absolute right against the whole world in theory, in real life it seems that the most likely challenger to one's proprietary rights could only be members from the same community as the owner. Thus, a transaction between villagers in Wendou would not need the recognition from residents in Beijing who lived far from the place where the transaction happened at all. Accordingly, the limitation of the universal recognition in practice should be determined by the reach of the "cannons" of contract matters (e.g. the sale of property), as is the generally accepted proposal of the classical cannon-shot rule regarding territorial waters.[94] The cannon-shot rule of recognition defines the scope of necessary recognizers regarding a contract matter. For those located outside the range of the "cannon" of the property, although there could still be a theoretical connection between them and the property and a possibility, albeit low, of a real-life encounter, practically speaking it is no longer necessary to take them into consideration and to obtain their recognition of the property. On the other hand, for those who fall within the range, recognition is surely needed for they could stand in a relationship of relatively close interest with the property. In most cases, by all appearances, the interest-related group of a property contract in the Qingshui River region would not exceed the scope of the village society in which the contractor lives or where the subject matter of the contract is located.

3.3.2 Three Levels of Recognizers

In light of the cannon-shot rule of recognition, the transaction of proprietary rights (among other rights) should be recognized by all potential challengers with actual threats. According to the degree of their potential threats against the property, as well as the degree of intimacy mentioned in the expression of estoppel, members of the society can be divided into several levels, and the intensity of the recognition that societal members at each level must make is also different.

(1) The first level surely includes all direct contracting parties, i.e. all vendors and vendees in the case of a sales contract. They should explicitly offer their recognition by complying with all necessary formalities of contracting, so that especially their expression of willingness is recorded in the contract text. Among all, the most "threatening" person for the consistent success of the transaction is the vendor. Therefore, as seen in the expression of estoppel, he or she needs

---

however, people still clearly notice that "it is not possible for all those concerned (including the unborn generations) to be heard and agree." See Niklas Luhmann, "Quod Omnes Tangit," 884.

[94] For re-examinations of this rule and its origins, see Walker [152], Kent [79].

to provide the most solemn and serious recognition for the newly established property order in the contract text.

(2) People at the second level are those who, apart from the direct contracting parties, natively or previously have a direct basis for causing potential defects in the rights or completely overthrowing the foundation of the transaction. One may notice the existence of these people in the expression of estoppel in the contract text, in which their recognition must be provided along with that of the contractor. As mentioned above, these people mainly include the relatives (e.g. brothers, uncles, nephews, and clansmen) and neighbors[95] of the contractor.[96] The traditionally existed pre-emptive right that relatives and neighbors are endowed with makes it necessary to solicit their opinions for the transaction. Although the process of consultation before the formal conduct of the transaction was no longer a nationwide obligation since the middle of the Qing dynasty,[97] the legacy of the pre-emptive right could still be seen in the contract practice of Wendou Village.[98]

Normally it is the middleman's task to ask the relatives of the transferring party about their purchasing intentions; the middleman can inquire about other potential buyers only if the relatives refused to make an offer or the offered price was much lower than expected. If others bid a higher price, the middleman should ask the relative if it is possible for him or her to match the price. After several rounds of back-and-forth communication, the highest-price offer would be accepted.[99]

The importance of the recognition from relatives and neighbors can be thoroughly explained by the above-mentioned criminal case, in which a dissenting elder cousin threatened the contractor with violence in order to cancel the already completed transaction and resell the property to himself.[100] Similar cases happened repeatedly in practice.[101] An explanation of this phenomenon of relatives and neighbors' position in the transaction is that, for the former, they could be considered as potential co-owners[102] of the rights of the selling

---

[95] It should be noted that the term "neighbors" sometimes referred to those who own the property neighboring the contractor's property, rather than those who lived near the living place of the contractor. The latter situation has been discussed in the sub-section of witnessing in Chap. 3.

[96] See Wu [170], Han [50].

[97] See Shi [140].

[98] See Liang Cong, *Qing dai Qingshuijiang xiayou cunzhai shehui de qiyue guifan yu zhixu*, 81–82.

[99] A detailed description based on field investigations in southeastern Guizhou on this point can be seen in *Zhongguo shaoshu minzu shehui lishi diaocha ziliao congkan* xiuding bianji weiyuanhui [1].

[100] See Zhongguo diyi lishi dang'an guan and Zhongguo shehui kexue yuan lishi yanjiusuo, *Qing dai tudi zhanyou guanxi yu diannong kangzu douzheng*, 454–456; Lin Qian, *Tudong sancun*, 393.

[101] See Shi Jianyun, "Jindai huabei tudi maimai de jige wenti," 129.

[102] In this case, other co-owners of the selling property should be included in the transaction unless there are "several co-owners" who, distinctly rather than jointly, possess interests over the property. However, a planter of the forest would normally first ask the landlord, sometimes as one of several co-owners of the forest, about his intention of purchasing the planter's shares before selling them

property (even descendants might have a ground to claim their proportions in the future) and, for the latter, the rights of the neighboring property could be affected by the alteration of the property order. As for the neighbors, a study shows that, in Zhejiang province, the re-confirmation of the ownership of land without a contract, due to its loss during wartime, required the express recognition from the owners of neighboring properties in written form.[103] Consequently, since these people possess a solid ground for claiming their rights over the subject matter of the contract, whether considered a co-owner or one who may dispute the border, obtaining their recognition becomes essential to the new proprietor. Differently from the first level, the recognition provided by the people at the second level might not be directly expressed by themselves, but to a certain extent by the contractor and sometimes through the facilitation of the middleman.[104] Since there might be relatives who do not show up often or neighbors who are deliberately ignored, the composition of people at the second level could be complicated and not be fully defined. Thus, it is natural to ask the contractor to offer a guarantee to the representative recognition in the case that he or she has to tackle unexpected situations.

(3) Outsiders should be placed at the third level. They stand outside of the transaction for they have no legal, moral, customary, consanguineous, or any other kind of rightful grounds to claim the property. However, they are still indispensable for the completion of the transaction, since they are affected in the slightest way—they must abide, unconsciously in an overwhelming majority of cases, by the obligation not to attempt to damage the property rights that have been imposed on them. However, the scope of the outsiders should also be limited to the farthest reach of the "cannon" of the property, and, as mentioned, most of the "cannonballs" fell within the village society where the "cannon" is located.

For outsiders, there is surely a fundamental difference between the recognition they should provide and that offered by insiders. In a dispute document from Wendou Village, one of the narrator's defenses for his ownership is that "nothing unusual had happened in these years regarding the management of the property."[105] This implies that all social members have acquiescently recognized his rights over the property by taking no action[106] against his day-to-day management. From the internal point of view mirrored in the text of the document, the recognition provided by outsiders could actually be termed "passive recognition."

---

to others. See Liang Cong, *Qing dai Qingshuijiang xiayou cunzhai shehui de qiyue guifan yu zhixu*, 81–82. For the disposition of jointly-owned property in the Qingshui River region, see Qu [128].

[103]See Hu and Chen [63]. In addition to recognition from neighbors, the study suggests that it is also necessary to include the recognition of the community represented by the local leader. In other words, the practical experience has somewhat proven that land rights can be established on the basis of recognition, including that of neighbors and the community.

[104]An example can be found in Liang Cong, *Qing dai Qingshuijiang xiayou cunzhai shehui de qiyue guifan yu zhixu*, 81–82.

[105]Chen and Guo [19].

[106]Raising dissenting voices is also an action in this regard.

The distinction between active and passive recognition is that, whereas the former entails recognizing that a certain object belongs to (a) specified person(s) and ensures that the object would not be infringed by the recognizer (*viz.* as a positive recognition of negative duties), the latter only includes recognizing that the object is not the recognizer's own (giving up one's claim to the object) or that it should belong to some other ones with the proper proof presented.[107] In other words, an active recognizer needs to take active actions with respect to the establishment of the new ownership, but, for passive recognizers ("outsiders"), they do not actually need to behave actively—most of the time, giving their value-neutral and tacit consent to the result of the transaction could be more than enough.

In addition, the "utmost" outsiders should be expressly singled out as they are those in the outermost periphery of the transaction—those who are previously not a member of the society and adventitiously enter the village society from the outside world. Their respect for property rights could only be reflected in the above-mentioned passive recognition. They should, first of all, understand and recognize that they themselves cannot and will not claim the property. Furthermore, due to their unfamiliarity with the local situation,[108] they need not, and in fact cannot, offer their recognition actively concerning the owner of the property, but only need to recognize the standing property order and transaction rules of the local society.[109] To a large extent, this actually constitutes a recognition of the existing indigenous contract system in the context of the Qingshui River region.

Overall, the establishment of property rights and its order through contracts only require the recognition of those affected. The recognition should thus be offered by a limited number of interest-related persons at one of the above-explained three different levels.

3.3.3 Justifying the Post-transaction Property Order in the Contract Text

To sum up, the rightfulness of the contract in context should rest on various degrees of willingly offered recognition that come from a limited number of interests-related persons. This rightful root is embodied in the contract text in various aspects. A more

---

[107] Compared to the term "promise" that is commonly seen in contracts and contract theories, the term "recognition" is chosen because it seems to have a slightly more passive sense. In contracts of the Qingshui River region, what was originally presented is more of a negative obligation than an active promise, while, for the outsiders to a contract, they do not have to actively make any promise, but only need to recognize the effectiveness of the proof of property rights when facing it.

[108] Local knowledge is especially stressed in the land disputes; therefore, it would be technically impossible for a complete outsider to interfere in matters of local property issues. See Lin [91].

[109] An example of a foreign purchaser in the village may shed some light on this point. The non-native vendee was asked to hire a local middleman and a scribe according to the instruction of the vendor, which was obviously an expression of recognition to the property order and transaction rules of the local society. See "Appendix 2: Field Research Report," He [55].

specific analysis of the logic of justifying the post-transaction property order in the contract text may be given as follows.[110]

Firstly, the vendor needs to ensure the validity, completeness, and defect-freeness of the property rights he or she holds, as guaranteed by the contract terms of security for defects of right, before formally launching the process of sale. At this time, the property rights should be deemed already containing the universal recognition of all involved, which could be embodied in a former contract. Secondly, the contractor (vendor), as the first-level recognizer, should willingly recognize the alteration of the property rights, as stated by the expressions of willingness and estoppel, when transferring the property to the vendee. Thirdly, all those who may have some direct connections with the property, i.e. the second-level recognizers, should also collaterally provide their recognition of the change and have their declaration recorded in the contract text. Finally, outsiders at the third level of recognition do not need to specifically express their recognition concerning the change of the property rights of "others." Their attitude does not, and does not need to, change during either the pre-transaction or post-transaction stage; in their eyes, the transaction is merely an irrelevant change of ownership from John Doe to Richard Roe.

At this point, the new proprietor can therefore obtain a complete, once again universally recognized, ownership of the property. Moreover, since everyone affected has willingly recognized the new property rights stipulated, they should naturally abide by the recognition they themselves have made. Consequently, not only the contracting parties but all related societal members should honor the contract and the property order that is constructed upon it. On the other hand, as proof of the new property rights, the contract itself could be regarded as a collection of the recognition of the community. In regard to the search of basic principles mentioned at the beginning of this section, this kind of recognition forms the foundation of the rightfulness of the contract. In short, matters related to all must be recognized by all; and, once the matter has been willingly recognized by all, it should naturally be observed by all. In this sense, it is not the contract but the universal recognition embodied in the contract that must be observed.

4 Making Recognition Provable: The Publicity and Perpetuity of Contracts

It is known that, based on the previous discussion, the contract could be deemed a form of expression of a collection of recognition, but how specifically is this achieved? Since the possibility of involving all those affected has been doubted at the theoretical level,[111] how was the collection of recognition accomplished through contracts within the Qingshui River region? Moreover, since it is believed that the

---

[110] A renowned theoretical elaboration of the process of disposing property through contract can be found in Hegel [56]. A English translation can be found in Hegel [57].

[111] See Niklas Luhmann, "Quod Omnes Tangit," 884.

scope of the doctrine of *quod omnes tangit* was somewhat limited by its derivation from procedural requirements,[112] what were the potential procedural settings in this process of collection? If the recognition contained in the contract itself indicates a sufficient justification for the rightfulness of the contract, then what is the contract's role in it? In short, the following investigation of the recognition as the source of rightfulness will be guided by two questions: why did the collection of recognition need to be represented by a contract, and how is it achieved?

4.1 Indispensable Proofs: Ping *in the Contract Text*

When speaking of "deals over property, salt, marriages, or family divisions," it would appear that "memorializing an agreement in writing was seen as the essential step toward making it proper and investing it with durability as well as legitimacy."[113] In contrast to the unreliable and fleeting memories of individual people, the written form of the contract can undoubtedly be considered as a more trustworthy method to record what happened, even for "transactions involving friends and relatives."[114]

This characteristic is closely related to the justification of the rightfulness of contract. In fact, if one can distinguish them carefully, two purposes are involved in the justification argument in the contract text. On the one hand, this argument maintains why the provisions of the contract need to be observed, and, on the other hand, it explains why the contract itself, as a practical device, is needed in the whole process of ensuring the observance of contract terms. The former issue has been thoroughly discussed previously. For the latter issue of justifying the necessity of a contract, an often overlooked key term is *ping*.[115]

The term *ping* was briefly mentioned previously when tackling the issue of the third party as the middleman. Literally speaking, this word is either a verb meaning to "lean on" or "count on" something,[116] or a noun meaning a "certificate" or "proof."[117] The link between the two word classes of the character is obviously that a "certificate" or "proof" is exactly something that can be "leaned on" or "counted on." In standard contracts from the Qingshui River region, especially if a contract of land sale, this

---

[112]Harold J. Berman, *Law and Revolution*, 608.

[113]Zelin et al. [190].

[114]Zelin [188]. It is widely believed that most social and economic transactions in Qing China must have been based on written materials including contracts, see Hayes [54].

[115]For the relation of contract and *ping*, see Qu [126].

[116]An extended meaning of "lean on" or "count on" can be used in a contract with reference to the boundary of the land parcel, as this parcel of land is "leaning on" the edge of the next parcel. See, e.g., Chen Jinquan and Du Wanhua, *Jiang Yuanze jiacang qiyue wenshu*, 116.

[117]See Luo [103]. The word can also be used as a conjunction meaning "no matter (what, how, etc.)." In the context of a contract, this meaning can be used to ensure the vendee's rights over the sold property that, "no matter what" the vendee wants to do in managing the property, he or she can do so at will. See, e.g., An and Pan [4].

term mainly appears in two contexts—either when speaking of the contract itself,[118] or when speaking of the middleman.

4.1.1 *Ping* and the Contract Manuscript

The circumstance concerning the contract is relatively easy to understand. The very last sentence of the main text of a contract is usually a formulaic statement which expresses why this contract should be established, justifying the indispensability of having this piece of paper in the transaction.

Generally speaking, there are three types of reasoning regarding this issue. The first kind of reasoning for the necessity of a contract is that, for contracting parties, only verbal consent obviously cannot make them feel assured. A standard expression of this reason is as follows: "Fearing that a verbal agreement might not suffice as proof, the contract of irrevocable sale is hereby established for retention and reference."[119] The second kind is similar to the first one, though the key concern is not to avoid the original orality of the agreement, but to ensure that the reached agreement can be continuously tracked in the future. The customary expression in this case is: "Fearing that no other thing can be proof in later times, this contract of reimbursement is hereby established for retention and reference."[120] The third type concerns the clarity of the agreement: "Fearing that there might be unclearness [regarding the agreement in later times], this contract of sale is hereby established for retention and reference."[121]

In addition, there is another type of formulaic expression on this issue, which however provides no clearly specified reason for establishing the contract, such as "now the proof is wanted,"[122] or "fearing that there might be no proof."[123]

Summarizing the above four situations, the reason why one needs a written contract for a transaction is that the reached agreement or the offered recognition in the transaction requires a proof. According to the above-mentioned statements, the

118 Here it needs to be noted that, although contract is a complex term, this term is used to solely refer to the physical and normally paper-based manuscript, excluding its institutional and social implications.

119 Chen Jinquan and Du Wanhua, *Jiang Yuanze jiacang qiyue wenshu*, 27.

120 Daniels et al. [29].

121 An Zunhua and Pan Zhicheng, *Tudi qiyue wenshu jiaoshi*, vol. 1, 293.

122 Ibid., 287.

123 Ibid., 307.

proof is to be used, possibly in future disputes,[124] to avoid vagueness[125] caused by the agreement if it remains verbal and unwritten. Since it is believed that the formation of a contract is based on the intention of the parties and its declaration,[126] the contract manuscript assumes the role of declaring, and therefore honestly recording, the recognition provided during the negotiation of the transaction.

In short, a *ping*, here understood as a written contract, is needed, since the three things that the contracting parties fear—the passing of time, the untraced verbal words, and the vagueness or even denial caused by the previous two—can be adequately cured by the work of a competent scribe.

4.1.2 *Ping* and the Middleman

A written contract is absolutely necessary but far from sufficient. The middleman is frequently mentioned alongside the key character *ping*, and sometimes the *zhongren* (middleman) would even be explicitly identified as *pingzhong* or *pingzhongren*,[127] linking *ping* and the middleman together as a new term.[128]

For contracts in the Qingshui River region, the activities of middlemen are constantly associated with *ping* in almost all cases. The character *ping* appears in two places of the contract text when related to the middleman. In the main text, it means to "lean on" or "count on" the middleman, such as when the contract price is discussed and a certain amount is agreed on with the help of (*ping*) the middleman.[129] In this case, the word is often used as a verb describing the facilitation offered by the middleman to the processes of price negotiation or matchmaking.

The more intricate situation can be found in the ending part of a contract. The term *pingzhong* is often placed right before the name of the middleman to indicate the status of the following person. It is generally believed that this term is an indigenous designation for the middleman and that the two characters are understood comprehensively as a single word.[130] In this case, given the meaning of *ping* in other parts

[124]In the disputes heard by the government, judging based on the contract was the basic principle for determining the ownership of property, but there were surely some exceptions. See Wen-kai Lin, "'Ye ping qi guan'?," 1–52. Also, although it was written in the Ming dynasty, a fiction vividly described the importance of having a written contract. The judge in a loan dispute made it clear that the official only recognized contracts, and it was assumed that, where there was no contract, there was no loan. But in the underworld, officials ignored the superficies of whether one has a contract or not but focused on the conscience of the person instead. Thus, though the protagonist's prosecution failed in the upper world in the tale, it ultimately succeeded in the underworld. See Ling [92].

[125]The vagueness in a normative text also has an exceptive meaning in modern law and needs to be specially treated. For the void-for-vagueness doctrine, see Hessick [59], Goldsmith [46], Beck [7].

[126]See Jaap Hage, "What is a Legal Transaction?," 103.

[127]See, e.g., Zhang and Wang [205].

[128]Examples of *pingzhong* and *pingzhongren* can be seen in Kang [77].

[129]See An Zunhua and Pan Zhicheng, *Tudi qiyue wenshu jiaoshi*, vol. 1, 293.

[130]It is asserted that here *ping* could mean "asking" or "requesting someone's help," though no reference is provided, see Kang Caiyun, "Gudai qiyue wenshu de zhongbaoren chengwei yuci yanbian yanjiu," 33.

of the contract, if this term is to be understood as a short phrase, its meaning must be "according to the middleman" or "counting on the middleman," or, if the *ping* is taken as a noun, "taking the middleman as the proof."

It is thus clear that the indispensable proofs of a contractual fact include not only the contract manuscript but also the middleman.[131] These two components are generally mentioned at the same time in records of judicial cases, since they are both important proofs for investigating the real situation of property disputes.[132] The difference between middlemen and contract manuscripts is that the former, unlike the latter, is a "living proof"—this phrase was frequently used in litigation documents in the region.[133] In fact, many other people can provide testimony in a court but the middleman was believed to have the primary responsibility to bear witness and his or her words should be considered as more trustworthy than others.[134] Therefore, the middleman also becomes another type of *ping* besides the contract manuscript itself.

Hence, the answer to the first question that needs to be answered is clear: a contract is needed since it can offer the *ping* for the recognition of the negotiation outcome. The collection of recognition needs to be represented by a contract because its successful establishment requires a series of *ping*, comprising both the inanimate proof and the living proof.

In addition, it may be noted in this connection that the conceptual establishment of the contract is not equivalent to its material establishment: the latter depends on the writing of the manuscript, while the former needs an additional construction of the proof system, including not only material evidence but also living witnesses represented by the middleman. Thus, the establishment of the contract can no longer be understood as simple paperwork but has to be understood as a process of weaving the contractual fact into the social fabric. This signifies the completion of the transformation of the contract from being a single practical device to a complex social system.

4.2 Middlemen and the Publicity of Contracts

4.2.1 From private to Public Through the Middleman

How was the convergence of recognition in the contract possible in the Qingshui River region? As noted above, recognizers at the first and second levels are mostly directly included in the contracting events with assistance from the middleman, but those affected third-level "outsiders" are mostly absent. Thus, a practical obstacle that seems to be insurmountable is that no one might be able to practically consult

[131] It should be noted that the middleman here should be understood in a broader sense as incorporating all third parties to a contract.

[132] See Zhang [194].

[133] See, e.g., Zhang and Wang [202], Zhang and Wang [206].

[134] See Zhang Wuwei, *Weinengxin lu*, 516–517.

every single social member, still less the whole world owing to the cannon-shot rule of recognition, and thereby try to obtain their separate recognition one by one. Two theoretical approaches, in general, can help to solve this problem.

The first one involves delegation. Middlemen, and all those who are present in the contracting event, shall be seen as the "representatives of the clan and village community," and as such they would "then be given time to raise questions, object to the sale or to the price proposed or to any detail of the deed, clarify or seek clarification of points and so on."[135] Consequently, the recognition that is held by the middleman should be regarded as the recognition of the whole population that he or she represents, and the contracting event becomes a representative meeting that can justifiably make the decision concerning the interests of all, including those absent.

The second one is similar to "legal fiction," in cases in which the fact is not assumed by the law or court. This approach proposes an assumption that, if there is no seeable objection, tacit approval is implied. Any objections are expected to be raised at the contracting event, and "subsequent challenges could be argued to be spurious."[136] It is a "recognitory fiction" which assumes that the peaceful possession of the property indicates the rightful possession of the property in the society.[137]

To a large extent, these two approaches are justified. However, further analysis would argue that both the representative and the fiction of the recognition of the absent majority should be derived from the publicity created by the appearance of the middleman to the contract as the third party. More fundamentally, special attention should be paid to the possibility brought about by this publicity.[138]

In truth, the representativeness of the middleman might not come entirely from his or her special position in the society, since this cannot explain why people who are too young and do not seem to have any special social status can also become middlemen.[139] It is likely that what needs to be considered is not the special social identity that a middleman possesses, but his or her most basic identity of being a member of the local society.[140] Thus, the representativeness of the middleman

---

[135] Hase [53].

[136] Zelin [189]; Madeleine Zelin, "Merchant Dispute Mediation in Twentieth-Century Zigong, Sichuan," 253–254. Similar arguments can also be seen in Patrick H. Hase, *Custom, Land and Livelihood in Rural South China*, 151; Hansen [51].

[137] When speaking of possession, peacefulness has a strong implication of rightfulness. As the ancient doctrine of "acquisitive prescription" suggests, a continuous (uninterrupted), public, and peaceful possession can lead to ownership under certain situations. For the emphasis of peacefulness in acquisitive prescription, see Johnson [76].

[138] In a key formula raised by Habermas— "Those norms for action are valid, to which all potentially affected persons could agree as participants in a rational discourse (*Gültig sind genau die Handlungsnormen, denen alle möglicherweise Betroffenen als Teilnehmer an rationalen Diskursen zustimmen könnten*)"—the modal concept "could (*könnten*)" is specially singled out by Luhmann, signifying the importance, at least from the viewpoint of a reader, of the "possibility" in the argument of validity. See Niklas Luhmann, "Quod Omnes Tangit," 891; Habermas [47].

[139] See Qu Jian, "Qing dai Wendou zhai zhongren zhidu," 273.

[140] The local identity of a middleman was specially stressed in contracting activities. See Wen-kai Lin, "'Ye ping qi guan'?," 18–19; He Yumei, "Qing dai Minguo shiqi Qiandongnan Wendou zhai de linye jingji xisu yanjiu," 57.

concerning the recognition of the society might intuitively stem from nothing else but his or her position as a locally sourced third party to the contract.

The emergence of a local middleman in the structure of contract implies that the nature of the contract has fundamentally changed from private to public, while the direction of this change is taken toward the local society which is seen as the source of effectiveness as well as the functioning field of the contract. In other words, this act of opening and showing the private sphere to the public society actually gives members of the society a possibility to participate or even interfere in the private agreement. The rightfulness of a contract may be built precisely on its capability of offering this possibility, so that all those who are concerned in the society may seize the opportunity provided by the publicity of the contract as a chance to express their opinions about it, either personally as a voiced middleman due to the partly open system or merely as a member of the audience who can applaud and boo. This possibility is the premise of all subsequent justifications. It should be specially noted that, if the inference or "fiction" of the silent voice of the absent is conducted without the presence of this critical premise, the rightful effect of compliance that the contract intends to achieve would justifiably be greatly reduced.

This publicity and the possibility it brings underscore the basic logic of discussions following the two above-mentioned approaches. The process of collecting recognition must be procedural and so practical, and setting the procedure evidently requires a limitation of time or prescription in terms of the law. If the possibility of raising an objection has been provided but the opposite opinion has not been timely expressed, then it seems right that the subsequent challenges would not be indisputably accepted. In this case, either the contracting feast or other kinds of gatherings becomes an event of crucial importance to the final construction of the contractual relations.[141] However, the conceivable exception for this is the case wherein the relevant person has legitimate reasons for not expressing their opinions in a timely manner, such as being away from their hometown at the time of contracting. Here, he or she should not be strictly limited by the prescription and a further examination of the contractual relations might be conducted.[142]

In addition, it should be noted that publicity itself could mean rightfulness to a certain extent. An insightful observer would discover that, from the perspective of social psychology, within the region or even in the whole of China, privacy was often considered to serve some ulterior motives, so that there stood a possibility of lawlessness; on the contrary, publicity, or the act of daring to disclose, itself means one has nothing to hide, which in this sense generates rightfulness. The inscriptions on stone tablets which widely existed in the Qingshui River region illustrate

[141] As the field investigation suggests, no retraction would be allowed after the feast. See *Zhongguo shaoshu minzu shehui lishi diaocha ziliao congkan* xiuding bianji weiyuanhui, *Miaozu shehui lishi diaocha*, vol. 1, 57.

[142] A similar situation arose in a modern forestry dispute which occurred in De'an county, Jiangxi province, in which the author personally participated in mediation as the deputy director of the legislative affairs office of the local government. Some agreements were concluded when the interested parties were not in the village, and disputes certainly arose when those parties returned home.

people's recognition of the importance of publicity. Compared with paper-based contracts, texts carved on the stone are obviously more accessible to the general public and symbolize the finalization of the related issue. Among various kinds of tablet inscriptions, the purpose of some, known as "contract tablets," was to disclose the transfer process of the property to the public, thereby declaring the rightfulness of their ownership.[143] As a government proclamation, transactions of timbers in private which bypassed the involvement of recognized agency (who should also be seen as the middleman[144]) are clearly condemned, and the key to the argument of the proclamation is that these transactions were conducted privately.[145]

In sum, the middleman is the vital figure who plays a role in the transformation of contract from private to public, and it is this transformation that endows the contract with the character of publicity which the rightfulness could spring from.

4.2.2 Contracts Without Middlemen

Where there is a contract, there is a middleman. This is regarded as a basic principle in the study of contracts in the Qing dynasty.[146] The investigation of this historical reality also suggests that this principle has been followed in most cases. However, it has been noticed that the phenomenon of not having a middleman in a contract also existed in the Qingshui River region.[147] Therefore, it is necessary to briefly explain why, in a situation where the middleman seems to be of crucial importance, there still exist contracts without middlemen.

According to one statistic,[148] a middleman was not indicated in 12.11% (889/7,344) of the contracts of irrevocable sale in the Qingshui River region, although the examined period is not limited in the Qing dynasty but also includes the Republican era. 60.74% (540/889) of the contracts that do not feature middlemen are dated to the latter period. Thus, the figure for the Qing dynasty could probably be much lower.

Several reasons can help to explain this phenomenon, such as relatively low contract prices, closer relationships between the two contracting parties, and many more people involved in the transaction (for example, if there is more than one vendor) rather than just two.[149] Ultimately, the root cause of these three reasons is that it is not cost-effective. For sure it is known that inviting a middleman has a cost, no matter what form this cost would take. Thus, if the contract price is too low, not inviting a middleman would then become a choice. Similarly, if the degree of mutual

---

143 See Li [83].

144 The agency here refers to the *hanzhong* or *zhujia*, as mentioned previously in the discussion of middlemen.

145 See Pan et al. [116].

146 See Chen [15].

147 See Wang [157].

148 See Fang [171], Wu [169].

149 See Wu Fang, "Lun Qingshuijiang wenshu zhong de wu zhongren xianxiang," 4–10.

trust between the transaction parties is high,[150] or if there are quite a few people involved in the transaction,[151] then it is possible for the publicity to appear among the parties of the transaction, so that the necessity of having a middleman seems not to be significant. In these cases, by taking the transaction cost into account, the middleman might not be invited accordingly.

Another root cause for not involving a middleman in a contract could be that, for a few types of contracts, the middleman seems to be non-essential. The most notable example of this type is the loan contract. According to the cannon-shot rule of recognition, unlike the property right, the obligatory right created by the loan contract does not need universal recognition but only the recognition of the debtor. The involvement of a middleman could evidently enhance the possibility for the debtor to perform the contract.[152] However, as is shown by the field investigation,[153] it does not seem to have an essential influence on the establishment of the contract if no middleman is present in the contracting. Similarly to the loan contract, it is found that contracts of tenancy sometimes do not require a middleman.[154] Also, in the case of *hetong* (indenture), which would have several duplicates to be produced and then be preserved by respective parties, a middleman is sometimes absent.[155] The form of the *hetong* often means mutual recognition, and it is not easy to falsify because each party holds a duplicate. Therefore, the role of endorsement played by the middleman has been largely replaced. Moreover, if the introduction of public recognition is not necessary, the existence of an intermediary naturally becomes non-essential.

Admittedly, there are still some cases that shall be deemed normal deviations in contract practice of the region—there are always people who make choices that are difficult for the observer to explain for various reasons. However, this is obviously not the mainstream.

Overall, the principle of "where there is a contract, there is a middleman" is still applicable in the Qingshui River region, although there was deviation of various kinds in the application of this principle in historical practice.

---

[150] See Wang and Zhao [155].

[151] In Wendou Village there are many contracts that are organized in the form of a list of profit allocation, and some of them have no middleman. The reason for this could also be that there are already many participants in the transaction, which means that the public could know the issue since it is actually not a private relation. In many situations there can be more than ten people involved, see, e.g., Zhang and Wang [200].

[152] Middlemen would normally act as witnesses or guarantors in loan contracts, see Duara [35].

[153] See *Zhongguo shaoshu minzu shehui lishi diaocha ziliao congkan* xiuding bianji weiyuanhui, *Miaozu shehui lishi diaocha*, vol. 1, 62. Also, an investigation on villages in north China suggests that "guarantors were not usually required for rental contracts," see Prasenjit Duara, "Elites and the Structures of Authority in the Villages of North China, 1900–1949," 266.

[154] *Zhongguo shaoshu minzu shehui lishi diaocha ziliao congkan* xiuding bianji weiyuanhui, *Miaozu shehui lishi diaocha*, vol. 1, 65.

[155] See, e.g., Zhang and Wang [201].

4.3 Scribes and the Perpetuity of Contracts

The contract could be recognized through its transformation towards publicity by those concerned in the society, and the middleman plays a significant role in this regard. However, it must be understood that a complete expression of publicity should include both (socio-)spatial publicity and temporal publicity. The latter obviously depends on the work of the scribe.

4.3.1 The Power of Words: Readers in the Future

Did the contract in the region have a period of validity?[156] The answer seems to be no: even a contract that has been performed needs to be preserved for as long as possible and may play a role in the far future when necessary. When a scribe is drafting a contract, he needs to consider not only those who are present but also those who are absent, including those who have not yet been born. In order to finally reach its potential number of readers, the contract, as the material carrier, must exist long enough in time. The perpetuity of contract, which can be reflected by the frequently seen expression of "forever retention" (*yongyuan cunzhao*) in contracts,[157] suggests that it is not a temporary document but is intended to last eternally.

It is conceivable that the reason for the need for a contract to exist forever is due to concerns about possible "lawlessness" in the future.[158] Therefore, people attempt to extend the duration of the contract as much as possible, and the maximization of this effort is mirrored in the inclusion of the contract content in the tablet inscription. It is claimed in an inscription on a Qing stone tablet in Tianzhu County that the motivation of setting up the tablet was to avoid paper rot caused by age, and that the stone tablet as the material carrier of the contract content will be "immortal."[159] Obviously, a stele can improve the publicity of the contract not only in a socio-spatial sense but also in a temporal sense—the latter highlights the enhancement of the perpetuity of the contract.

The effectiveness of the contract also largely stems from its perpetuity. It is a familiar fact that, in the Chinese tradition, people including the emperor himself show great respect to historians[160]—they shall be seen as scribes within a larger background—to some extent out of fear of being recorded as performing shameful deeds. Under ideal circumstances, historians' writings on past events will circulate forever in the country, and the scribe's record of established contractual facts will continuously exist in the village too. An oft-repeated question is how a contract that seems to merely be words can counter the power of, for example, the rich. The

[156] It is believed that the middleman has almost unlimited liability in time for the transactions they participate in. See Liang [87].

[157] See, e.g., Chen Jinquan and Du Wanhua, *Jiang Qigui jiacang qiyue wenshu*, 296.

[158] See An Zunhua and Pan Zhicheng, *Tudi qiyue wenshu jiaoshi*, vol. 1, 7.

[159] See Li Bo, "Qing dai Qingshuijiang xiayou beiming zhong de shehui zhixu," 56.

[160] See Liang [88].

perpetuity of the contract could exactly be the answer—the power of the giants may change dramatically within a few generations, but, theoretically, the words that have been written down will remain forever. As Rousseau stated, albeit from a political perspective, "[t]he stronger party is never strong enough to remain the master for ever, unless he transforms his strength into right, and obedience into duty."[161] People may succumb for a while because of the suppression of someone's or some families' power,[162] but from the vantage-point of history the power which they hold could not last long, no matter how powerful it used to be. On the other hand, properly writing down the contractual fact indicates that the temporary fact has entered an eternal dimension, and that the jural relation embodied in text can be conceptually unbreakable for a much longer time compared to the lifespan of one's power.

One of the most extreme examples is that, even if the dynasties change, the effectiveness of the contract remains and the contract still needs to be faithfully executed.[163] A current case of such disputes from the Qingshui River region can offer a good illustration of this point. The case involves the boundary of a house foundation. After a long-term stand-off, the conclusive evidence leading to the final settlement of this dispute is that one party finally found out and presented a Guangxu twenty-eighth-year (1902) contract of sale concerning the foundation of the house, in which the boundaries of the foundation are stated clearly.[164] A contract, concluded over 110 years ago, has gone through the three eras of the Qing dynasty, the Republic of China, and the People's Republic of China, but it can still exert the same effect as intended when it was originally stipulated. It should be noted that similar cases are not uncommon in the local area. In the real practice of history, the perpetuity grants to the contract a relatively stable state regardless of the ups and downs of these practical forces.

---

[161] Jean-Jacques Rousseau, *Du Contrat Social; ou Principes du Droit Politique*, 7. For an English translation, see Jean-Jacques Rousseau, *Discourse on Political Economy and The Social Contract*, 48.

[162] In dispute documentation, it is an important accusation that one improperly uses his or her superiority in power or wealth to seize the property of others. An example in Wendou Village can be seen in Chen Jinquan and Guo Liang, *Yi Zunfa Jiang Qicheng deng jiacang susong wenshu*, 61.

[163] See Long [96]. An interesting, more modern, example regarding this point is the provisions in the "Joint Declaration of the Government of the United Kingdom of Great Britain and Northern Ireland and the Government of the People's Republic of China on the Question of Hong Kong." One of the three annexes and one of the eight articles of the Joint Declaration is devoted to the issue of land leases in Hong Kong. Article 6 states that "land leases in Hong Kong and other related matters will be dealt with in accordance with the provisions of Annex III to this Joint Declaration." The Annex III stipulates that "[a]ll leases of land granted or decided upon before the entry into force of the Joint Declaration and those granted thereafter in accordance with paragraph 2 or 3 of this Annex, and which extend beyond 30 June 1997, and all rights in relation to such leases shall continue to be recognised and protected under the law of the Hong Kong Special Administrative Region." At least in the legal and later judicial sense, contracts concluded long ago "shall continue to be recognised and protected." For a review of a modern case in Hong Kong but which was judged jointly by modern law and the customs of the Qing dynasty, see Jin [73]. Also, for the discussion of the phenomenon of inviting experts in legal history to the courts in Hong Kong, see Bourgon [9].

[164] See Long [98].

Therefore, as there could be a connection between the publicity of the contract and its rightfulness, the eternity of the contract throughout time is also related to the justification argument of contract. It should always be borne in mind that these contracts, as in the Hobbesian "words without sword," might seem to be vulnerable, but in truth they are tough enough to pass through the mists of time, faithfully transmitting the recognition provided by people of earlier times to its future readers. Regardless of earth-shaking changes of dynasties and societies, they can convey the rightfulness constructed at that far-off time to a multitude of future generations.

4.3.2 Renewing the Contract

A contract without a scribe is essentially an oral contract, as has been discussed previously. Further, a contract could have more than one scribe throughout the course of its history. This does not refer to the situation that a single contract was written by multiple scribes, as was mentioned in the discussion on the number of scribes, but that the same contract text might be continuously renewed by scribes of different generations.

Although contracts are in general carefully preserved for posterity, people would still worry that the time-worn paper of the contract will inevitably be damaged as time passes by. In addition to physical damages, the jural relations recorded in some contracts could also change with the development of the situation. As a precautionary measure to avoid disputes, it is therefore necessary to re-clarify the relations in response to the changes when appropriate. The above two aspects of physical and conceptual damages or alterations to the clarity of the contract over time were both extensively present in the Qingshui River region. For example, the following contract was re-established for the purpose of re-clarification.[165]

Manuscript 17: A re-established contract of profit shares (June 1, 1771)

The establisher of the contract, Jiang Youwen, [Jiang] Laoyou, [Jiang] Fanbao, Chen Qingyun, [Chen] Baodui, etc., [established this contract] because of [their] possession of an ancestral common mountain which is located in the place named Yanduiyue. Over the years, the cunninghamia trees have been sold multiple times and the price has been allocated. However, the shares of it have become quite mixed and unclear. Fortunately, there exists an old manuscript. Currently, it has been aging for a long time, and it has inevitably been subject to decay. [Thus, we] especially establish this contract in duplicate, [and each is to be] received for reference.

The shares are as follows: …

The contracts in duplicate are the proof.[166]

Qianlong, thirty-sixth year, fourth month, nineteenth day (June 1, 1771), established.

[165] Christian Daniels, Yang Yougeng, and Takeuchi Fusaji, *Kishū Myaozoku ringyō keiyaku monjo kaihen (1736–1950-nen)*, vol. 3, E-0001.

[166] This line of words was written at the junction of the edges of two sheets of paper, so only the right part was written on this manuscript.

At the outset, there was "an old manuscript" regarding this "ancestral common mountain." According to the narrative of the above contract, the joint occurrence of two things makes it necessary to renew the contract. On the one hand, the jural relations established by the old agreement have been changed due to the multiple sales and profit allocations. On the other hand, the old manuscript "has inevitably been subject to decay" after a long time. In sum, these two things resulted in the "mixed and unclear" situation of shares. Therefore, although the old manuscript still existed, the parties involved have decided to conclude a new contract or renew the existing one out of prevention.

To use a simple analogy, such terms as are found in the above contract are similar to the "merger clause" in modern contract law.[167] The merger or integration clause is mainly aimed at the long process of contract formation. Accordingly, the result of a prior negotiation process will be fixed at a certain time, after which the new agreement shall be seen as being recognized by all parties, thereby merging all previous arguments. The advantage of this approach is that it prevents parties from going back to ancient disputes in the future.

Similar practices widely existed in the contract tradition of Wendou Village,[168] and sometimes even multiple old contracts could be "merged" into a new one. For example, it is stated in a recently written contract that, although the boundaries of their own mountain have been "recorded by their respective old contract," out of worries about the long lapse of time and in order to avoid future disputes, after a general discussion it was decided to draw up a new contract. In addition, the new contract shall prevail after its conclusion—if the trees were to be sold for logging in the future, the allocation of each share shall be based on the new contract.[169] To some extent, this denoted a process of redistribution which restrictedly introduced the changing facts and updated the recognition of the contract which had been established in the former time.

It should be noted that this approach actually represents a practical need if the perspective of Qing legislators is taken into account, although there is no evidence showing that the formation of this custom in the Qingshui River region was related to the requirement of the law. In response to the general situation of people competing for the cemetery in long past years, the *Great Qing Code* stipulates that those time-worn contracts provided by the litigants shall not be allowed to be used as evidence.[170] This once again demonstrates that the practice of re-clarifying the content of the old contract and renewing it into a new contract is in truth necessary for the prevention of disputes.

[167]It is "a clause in a contract that integrates all prior agreements into the contract with any prior contradictory terms or conditions excluded from the final contract of the parties." See Tepper [146].

[168]It is noteworthy that the similar custom seems to exist widely, as it is also reported in, for example, Xiangyin, Hunan province, see Qian Nanjing guomin zhengfu sifa xingzheng bu [123].

[169]Christian Daniels, Yang Yougeng, and Takeuchi Fusaji, *Kishū Myaozoku ringyō keiyaku monjo kaihen (1736–1950-nen)*, vol. 3, E-0023.

[170]See Xue [180].

In sum, the practice of renewing the contract enables it to retain its vitality and so its effectiveness for quite a long time, which ultimately helps to preserve, update, and finally deliver the recognition collected from previous generations to guarantee their posterity.

4.4 *Provable Recognition*

As touched upon above, two types of *ping* can be found at a conceptual level: first, the middleman and the publicity (or the public) he represents; and, second, the contract manuscript written by the scribe and the perpetuity it possesses. However, before entering the concluding part of this section, it might be helpful to revisit the concept of *ping* from a sociopsychological perspective to better understand the logic behind it.

People may not be fully aware of the fact that the concept *ping* is so important in discourses of rightfulness that the wording most often found in a question that challenges the rightful grounds is *pingshenme* ("whereby/by virtue of which"), rather than *weishenme* ("why/for what reason").[171] The difference between the two may be explained in this way: in contrast with the latter, which expresses concerns about the substantive exploration of causes and the demonstration of fundamental principles, the former mostly focusses on the presentation of the proof.[172] In other words, it can be argued that presenting the proof per se is sufficient to complete the justification on many occasions. Normally, people tend not to think and ask the deeper question of why the presentation of the proof can justify, say, one's ownership over the property—it seems that this did not fall within the core scope of public discourse. In this case, the authenticity of the proof could be the only issue that one can continue to dispute after the proof had been provided. On the basis of this discovery, the importance and necessity of *ping* can be explained more clearly, and more significantly, can also help to construct an integrated discourse on the rightfulness of contracts centering on this concept. Accordingly, the normative function of the contract is to provide the proof, and jural relations that can be proven by contracts shall be deemed rightful.

At this point, an answer can be provided to the outer but crucial part of the question regarding the compliance of contract. In practice, people would not actually ask the question why or according to what (*pingshenme*) they should observe the contract.

[171] However, this does not mean that this exact vocabulary was used by people in the Qingshui River region in the Qing dynasty. However, questions with the same meaning can often be seen in related dispute documents. The often-raised question by one party against his or her opponent is that on what basis you make this claim, or, put more bluntly, whether there is evidence or not, no matter if it is a testimony of a middleman or physical evidence. See, e.g., Chen Jinquan and Guo Liang, *Yi Zunfa Jiang Qicheng deng jiacang susong wenshu*, 37, 41, 53.

[172] Sometimes the justice of nature, *tianli*, would be associated with the term *ping*, as it is shown in a Kangxi-era contract. See Shan [138]. This could also provide the major premise of a syllogistic argument of contract performance. An example of such an argument is: according to the requirements of natural justice (*ping tianli*), a debt must be paid; according to the contract as the proof, A owes B the money; therefore, the conclusion is that A should repay the money to B.

It is more often a specific question that is asked, such as “according to what is the plot yours?”, “according to what should I pay you back?”, or “according to what do get I this amount of money?”. In this case, a practical answer is directed at the basis of the claim, namely that the contract as a whole includes the contract manuscript and related persons such as the middleman. Thus, answering these questions shall be simple—because I hold such a contract. Therefore, the familiar scenario in practice may be that someone presents the contract to the challenger or send the challenger to the middleman for confirmation.

In general, the argument of contract compliance could be terminated by the presentation of the contract. However, if one insists on asking the question, which is usually the task of theoretical researchers, he would then formally enter into the core part of the argument about the rightfulness of the contract. The core concept in this part is recognition. As demonstrated above, the contract can collect all the recognition needed, and, since adhering to the offered recognition was regarded as a basic norm of rightfulness in the local society, then all related people arguably need to honor what had been stipulated in the contract. Undoubtedly, after an individual’s simple recognition has become socialized through the contract system, all challenges to the individual recognition would be essentially considered as challenges to the entire contract system and even the customary law tradition behind it. These clearly lie beyond the jurisdiction of the basic norm of rightfulness.

A conceptual expression of the above discussion in the outer and core parts is exactly the title of this section: provable recognition. For most cases, “provable” alone could constitute a sufficient reason for rightfulness. Only an in-depth investigation of what is provable will reveal the principle of rightfulness centering on the recognition. Admittedly, the issue of recognition can be examined continuously, but this study intends to stop here.[173] As mentioned at the beginning of the previous section, when formally entering the discussion of the rightfulness of the contract, it is noticed that the complex concept of contract “can be traced to and is determined by a small number of basic moral principles.”[174] The task set in this study is to investigate and clarify these basic principles, and, which is a more significant challenge, to discover and re-construct the internal logic that integrates these basic principles with the whole practice of contracts.

5 In Contract we Trust? A Blockchain-Like Trust Network

Given people’s adherence to their own recognition and the public’s requirement for the appearance of recognition in practice, contract, as a representation of provable recognition, is able to furnish a basis for the establishment of interpersonal order.

[173]This is also the most basic conceptual principle used by the contract authors at that time when conducting self-justification arguments in the contract text, whether in the expression of the willingness or estoppel.

[174]Charles Fried, *Contract as Promise*, ix.

However, it is nevertheless reliant on the premise that the contract is authentic, since "[w]ritten documentation could only be useful if its authenticity could be verified."[175]

In the context of the Qingshui River region, how could the authenticity of the contract as a carrier of recognition be guaranteed? Furthermore, how was the public convinced to believe that the content of the contract would not be easily changed once it is written, and then to trust the contract itself? Differently from the discussion on the anti-counterfeiting techniques of contract in history,[176] this section aims to reveal and explain some non-counterfeiting technical aspects regarding the construction of social trust in contracts.

5.1 *Blockchain, Non-centrality, and Trust Network*

Understood as the ultimate foundation of legitimacy,[177] trust is undoubtedly of pivotal importance in the justification of contracts. Once the contract as a whole becomes untrustworthy to the contracting parties as well as the public, it will be rightfully groundless. Therefore, theories about the construction of trust deserve special attention, and, among the many out there, the novel theory of blockchain[178]—the one underlying the Bitcoin cryptocurrency[179]—could be the most compelling and contextually applicable for the purposes of this study.

5.1.1 Blockchain as a Novel Solution

It is conceivable that, for many researchers, it sounds ill-suited to discuss the theory of blockchain in the context of the Qingshui River region. However, it should be specially emphasized that this "mismatch" is not the result of deliberately pursuing the new wave—after an in-depth investigation of the theory, the reader will soon notice a closer link between the two.

Behind the fancy and sophisticated technical design of the blockchain as "decentralized ledger technology,"[180] one will find its deeper purpose to provide "a novel

---

[175] Madeleine Zelin, "Merchant Dispute Mediation in Twentieth-Century Zigong, Sichuan," 252–253.

[176] For studies on the anti-counterfeiting technology in the writing of contracts, see Feng [42], Feng [41], Jiang [71].

[177] See Zheng [211].

[178] The blockchain is widely perceived to be a technology; however, this study uses the term *theory of blockchain* in order to emphasize the underlying theoretical logic of the technical design of blockchain. For another attempt to introduce the theory of blockchain, see Yuan and Wang [185].

[179] See Crosby et al. [28].

[180] The term *decentralized ledger technology* can illustrate and encompass the concept of blockchain well, and the key features of the blockchain can be summarized by the three-word term. Firstly, it is decentralized. Secondly, it "enables users to upload programs" and "maintains a permanent and public record (ledger) of the current and past states of every program." Thirdly, at a purely

solution to the age-old human problem of trust."[181] To put it more specifically, the "problem of trust" is about how to make the general public believe in something, such as cryptocurrency or financial institutions, as it is considered that "[a] fact in the social world can obtain because sufficiently many members of a social group believe it obtains and also believe that (sufficiently many) other members of the group have the same belief, both about this fact and about what the others believe."[182] To a large extent, this also forms the foundation of the normative order in a society.[183] Put succinctly, what the theory of blockchain ultimately tries to touch is the issue of how to construct a trust network in society.

This problem of trust is in this sense persistent throughout the history of human society, and therefore varied solutions have been presented and applied. In many cases, as stated in the white paper of Bitcoin, "[a] common solution is to introduce a trusted central authority",[184] since the establishment of trust is closely linked to the concept of authorities. The most representative example for this is the fiat currency, or nonconvertible paper money, endorsed by government credit. These government-backed papers are intrinsically valueless until the sufficient majority in the society believes that they are valuable.

Similarly, in the field of contracts and economic transactions, another example underscoring the endorsement of government authority is the establishment of a unified registration system for real estate.[185] The key steps in the process of conveyance are controlled by the registration authority, and related information shall also be collected by the registry and then preserved in its database, or cadaster. In this way, the successful operation of the whole system is built upon the trust of the public in the impartiality of the registration authority (for example, it will never tamper with the data).

However, in the traditional context (and this context needs to be emphasized), there are two almost inevitable dangers for such a trusted authority, no matter whether it is a legal authority, traditional authority, or a charismatic authority.[186] Internally,

---

technical level, it "uses public key cryptography for authentication," and the network maintains the technology that is ensured by economic incentives. See Reyes [132]. However, this study obviously does not intend to amply repeat in regard to the basic framework of blockchain that has hitherto been foregrounded too often. The fundamental idea of the groundbreaking technological innovation can be seen in the original white paper written by Bitcoin's mysterious creator, as the name presented on the paper is just an alias to hide the true identity of the person or entity, see Nakamoto [111]. In addition to novel technical and algorithmic factors, one of the main reasons why blockchain appears to be abstruse is that it does not have an authoritative text to explain all related issues, which evidently leads to difficulties in understanding due to divergent opinions. Therefore, this study selected the white paper that first proposed this concept (even though it is too concise and does not cover many subsequent developments) as the main textual basis of the blockchain theory.

[181] Werbach [166].

[182] Jaap Hage, "What is a Legal Transaction?," 105.

[183] See MacCormick [104].

[184] Satoshi Nakamoto, "Bitcoin," 2. Though this sentence specifically aims at the problem of double-spending in the context.

[185] See, both historically and today, e.g., Matsubara [107], Wang et al. [156].

[186] See Weber [163].

one cannot guarantee that the person or entity that is in charge of a certain issue will not do evil at all. Conversely, for the external aspect, no one can absolutely ensure that it (or he or she) will not be invaded and then destroyed by foreign forces (hijacked, killed, or the like in the case of a person). Taking the unified real estate registration system as an example, no one can promise that every registration officer will perform his duties completely faithfully; alternatively, in the case that the register is destroyed due to external factors, such as being stolen or burned, then it will cause a devastating blow to the operation of the entire system. In order to tackle these risks, people have come up with many institutional precautions to reduce the risks, such as the implementation of supervisory mechanisms or more comprehensive and strict information protection systems. In any case, numerous historical facts have concluded that the above two risks cannot be eliminated totally. The essential reason lies in a dilemma: an authority, such as a Leviathan,[187] needs to be given enough trust to obtain sufficient power to effectively guarantee the operation of the whole system, but, once the power has been concentrated, it will predictably lead to the risks of internal uncertainty and external vulnerability.[188] Nevertheless, it is precisely this dilemma that the blockchain theory targets to solve. For it was designed to exclude the participation of "a trusted party"[189] in transactions, and probably in many areas beyond.

The antidote given by the blockchain is decentralization. Apart from having a more powerful technological means than any traditional society could ever have, blockchain provides a seemingly ultimate solution: since all the endeavors of providing a trusted authority are centralized in nature, the key that needs to be changed is exactly the centralization.[190] The blockchain thus attempts to build a decentralized database by introducing the "distributed ledger technology (DLT)."[191] No central authority exists in this distributed system where the information provided by everyone will be stored in everyone. Therefore, for potential internal intruders, it seems that no one has enough ability to corrupt the whole system,[192] while outside intruders also lose focus—for both internal and external attackers, the only way to destroy the network is seemingly to develop the capability that can wipe out every single system member.[193] Except being decentralized and distributed, more importantly the

[187] See Werbach [165].

[188] See Kevin Werbach, "Trust, but Verify," 494.

[189] Satoshi Nakamoto, "Bitcoin," 2.

[190] In one of the few references of the Bitcoin white paper, there are two families of timestamping techniques: one with "a trusted third party," and the other which is based on "the concept of distributed trust." See Massias et al. [106].

[191] For the basic workings of the DLT, see Walport [153], Rauchs et al. [130].

[192] See Henri Massias, X Serret Avila, and J-J Quisquater, "Design of A Secure Timestamping Service with Minimal Trust Requirement," 1.

[193] In theory, a successful attacker only needs to control more than 50% of the computing power or mining hash rate of the entire network, which is still considered a mission impossible. This is called a 51% attack. The attack can be in various means, such as direct tampering or indirect manipulation. For assessments of the 51% attack, see Ye et al. [184], Sayeed and Macro-Gisbert [136].

blockchain technically promises that the recorded information is immutable.[194] One may carry out further actions that can counteract previous actions, but all moves will be faithfully recorded step-by-step and can then be traced. As for the information recording, this database follows the rule of irreversibility. On the basis of the cryptographic immutability of data,[195] which is an ingenious and powerful design,[196] the DLT "allows participants to trust the outcome of a system without trusting any individual participant."[197]

To offer an extremely concise overview, by means of the decentralized and distributed data immutability,[198] the theory of blockchain succeeds in providing an elaborate novel solution to the long-standing trust dilemma without requiring any "trusted third party."[199]

5.1.2 A Noncentral Trust Network

A similar approach was also taken in the Qingshui River region. For example, the trust mechanism for property transactions was not provided by a trusted third-party authority. Although some taxation-purposed field cadasters, known as fish-scale map registers, were found in this area,[200] and a limited number of red contracts also mirrors the influence of government authority, a trust mechanism supported by a unified authority was generally not established in this area. Thus, it seems that there was no centralized narrative in the operation of many local affairs at that time. In this sense, the region provides a historical analog of the blockchain environment.

However, in the context of the Qingshui River region, a term needs to be revised when tentatively trying to apply some key components of the theory of blockchain. There was no "decentralization" in the context. The theory of blockchain marks an endeavor of decentralization against this centralized background. For example, the promotion of Bitcoin can be deemed a decentralized effort against the centralized control of currency. However, it seems that the centralization in terms of the management of contract practice was far from established in the context of the Qingshui

[194] See Hofmann et al. [60], Williams [167].

[195] To a large extent, both the decentralized design and the DLT ultimately serve to achieve the immutability of the data. The advantage of not putting all one's eggs in one basket is that these "synchronized digital eggs" will not be easily changed, for even if one of the eggs has been attacked, there are still a large number of eggs that have not been tampered with and which are stored all over the world. This makes the modification of less than 50% of the eggs meaningless.

[196] Kevin Werbach, "Trust, but Verify," 516.

[197] Ibid., 494.

[198] It is summarily described in the white paper as "a peer-to-peer network using proof-of-work to record a public history of transactions that quickly becomes computationally impractical for an attacker to change if honest nodes control a majority of CPU power." See Satoshi Nakamoto, "Bitcoin," 8.

[199] Ibid., 1.

[200] See Chen and Long [18], Huang and Zhang [65].

River region, and therefore there might not be an imaginary target for deconstruction. The contract practice in the folk society was not centrally controlled. Thus, a better descriptive term for this state is "noncentral."

In addition, the term "trust" has to be re-defined in the context. In general, trusting in an individual or institution for whatever reason means being unreserved so that no verification is required.[201] However, this is not the original situation concerning both the blockchain and the context of the Qingshui River region. The technical mechanism is designed to convince the verifiers that it is an incorruptible construction,[202] thereby justifiably gaining the trust of participants. There is no need for a double check since the mechanism has a built-in or prepositive procedure of verification. As mentioned, the object of this trust is the "outcome of a system"[203]—since the system has been verified, there is no need to recheck its outcome. Hence, it would be more precise to re-define it as a kind of "technical trust" rather than the natural kind of interpersonal trust.

Inspired by the theory of blockchain and based on the fact that the Qing region faced a similar situation and came up with a comparable solution, it does not seem too bold to suggest that a noncentral trust network[204] of contract was actually constructed in the local society concerning related affairs, which, along with other anti-counterfeiting writing techniques, largely ensured the immutability of contracts. On this basis, three aspects of the network will be elaborated respectively through comparison with several key components of the blockchain theory in the following sections.

5.2 Broadcasting the Contract: Distributed Ledger in the Village Society

Broadcasting is an important step in the process of the DLT system to reaching its goal of producing a set of authoritative records.[205] A new transaction shall be broadcasted to all nodes in a network of timestamps.[206] The support from modern

---

[201] For a thorough study on trust construed as a mechanism for the reduction of social complexity, see Luhmann [102].Also, see Qu [127]; Kevin Werbach, "Trust, but Verify," 494.

[202] See Henri Massias, X Serret Avila, and J-J Quisquater, "Design of A Secure Timestamping Service with Minimal Trust Requirement," 1.

[203] Kevin Werbach, "Trust, but Verify," 494.

[204] Instead of using the term "architecture," this study chooses "network" on the grounds that it better presents both the dynamic and static aspects of how the trust in contracts is organized in the society. Also, it implies that there could be no specific "architect" or "designer" in the formation of this network. For the explanation of using the term "architecture" in a blockchain context, see Kevin Werbach, *The Blockchain and the New Architecture of Trust*, 25–28.

[205] See Michel Rauchs et al., *Distributed Ledger Technology Systems: A Conceptual Framework*, 24, 59–60.

[206] See Satoshi Nakamoto, "Bitcoin," 3. The "timestamp," in general, is used to identify the occurrence time of a certain event.

information technology maximizes this ability to broadcast, although theoretically "new transactions broadcasts do not necessarily need to reach all nodes."[207] In any case, broadcasting, as the very first step in the process, has been designed to play a significant role in the formation and maintenance of distributed ledgers, and thus to help keep the promise of data immutability.

In the context of a non-digital world, broadcasting as an effort in the public distribution of information[208] is also in widespread use when conducting transactions. In this case, although there are substantial differences from a technical perspective, it seems that "broadcasting" within a village society can also be of great help in forming a primitive version of the distributed ledger. This version of the broadcast is mainly reflected in the public announcement of the contract.

It is believed that, in order to avoid double spending or double selling, one needs to be aware of all transactions, and "[t]o accomplish this without a trusted party, transactions must be publicly announced."[209] For this reason, the disclosure of the transaction will lead to probably virtual distributed ledgers among the crowd that could be sufficient to play its due role of avoiding double selling or counterfeit transactions.

More specifically, the broadcast of contract includes three layers. The first layer is the announcement of the main content of the contract at the contracting ceremony. On the one hand, this manner of publication is suggested in the discussions of the contract content among the participants at the event, while, on the other hand, it is more formally reflected in the above-mentioned reading process required by contracting rituals before the final conclusion of the contract. In addition, the effect of this broadcasting lies in the natural spread of its influence in society as an event. It may be conceivable that, in a village society with a relatively small number of households, anything that can be called an event would soon get the attention of almost every villager.[210] For example, a transaction concerning the share of forest land that happened in Wendou Village was described in the subsequent litigation documentation as something which "every single person in the locality knows about."[211] Therefore, in practice, this kind of broadcasting event was able to form a "passive ledger" in the memory of its social members. Depending on the degree of one's closeness with the contracting parties, the levels of details that one would know about the facts of the contract could vary, but, in any case, these distributed memories have created great difficulties for counterfeiting related transactions in the future.

---

[207] See ibid., 4.

[208] Analogously, in the theory of blockchain, messages also "need to be delivered on a best effort basis." See ibid., 8.

[209] See ibid., 2.

[210] In the field investigation conducted by the author in Wendou Village in 2011, though as a personal and modern experience, the speed of the information transmission in the local society was extremely impressive. For a brief record of the fieldwork, see Qu Jian, "Qing zhonghouqi Qiandongnan Wendou zhai Miaozu dianzhi yanjiu," 204.

[211] See Chen Jinquan and Guo Liang, *Yi Zunfa Jiang Qicheng deng jiacang susong wenshu*, 45. A similar expression can also be seen in Pan and Wu [118].

These passive distributed memory-based ledgers often show their importance only when disputes occur. For example, when disputing the authenticity of a contract, one may ask "in what year and in which month was the contract known to whom?"[212] In another more significant case, an applicant requested the local government to issue a new special certificate since the contracts he originally owned had been damaged. The final confirmation made by the government, which stated that the applicant actually owned the properties he claimed, was based on an official investigation including the questioning of the local people, including the applicant's neighbor who provided his endorsement on the basis of his memory.[213] When an "attack" occurs, these passive distributed ledgers in memories play their role of correcting false information. Thus, by means of comparing the information recorded in most of the distributed ledgers, the effectiveness of the contract can possibly be restored even in the most extreme case that the original had been lost.

The second layer has been much discussed above when examining the publicity of the contract. Unlike other village members, the middleman, as well as the scribe who was formally present at the event, was able to record the content of the contract more accurately due to his or her knowledge and special position in the contract relationship. Therefore, as repeatedly mentioned, the middleman and the scribe also play a crucial role as *ping* in contract dispute resolution.

The third layer is the writing of the post-contract documents including the single contract copies (*chaobai*) and their collections.[214] These phenomena have been noted in Sect. 5.3.2 of Chap. 2. In a substantial and material sense, such post-contract documents can be seen as distributed ledgers of the transaction. They can be many copies in number; the content of these documents can be exactly the same as the original, or it can only retain the main information. These documents could be kept by multiple contracting parties. Their existence is primarily for the ease of the unified management and reference of the property information within a household or a clan, but in fact, though these documents cannot be deemed valid contracts, they play a role in the distributed preservation of the contract's content and therefore could serve as evidence in dispute settlements.[215]

In addition, another point to be noted is the accessibility of contracts as well as other distributed ledgers (e.g. memories and copies) after broadcasting. In most cases, in the village societies of the region, after the initial announcement, the contract would be properly preserved and therefore cannot be easily visited thereafter, including those third-layer copies.[216] However, this does not mean that these contracts would never appear again. Rather, they will only be presented when necessary, such as when there is a household division or property dispute and the owner of the property needs

[212]Chen Jinquan and Guo Liang, *Yi Zunfa Jiang Qicheng deng jiacang susong wenshu*, 49.

[213]See Wang [154].

[214]See, e.g., Zhang and Wang [208]. In some villages, there could have been an unified account book regarding the land of the village, as was certainly conducted in a much later time. See Shan Honggen, *Jinping wenshu yu Qingshuijiang linye shihua*, 103.

[215]See, e.g., Long [97].

[216]See Zhang et al. [199], Qian [122].

the proof. At this point, the first and second layers of memory-based ledgers become relatively important since they exist in the memories of villagers who can easily be asked about them. It is conceivable that, when needed, one could find out the owner of a piece of land by asking the local people, though for further confirmation of this information a paper contract is still required.

In short, contract broadcasting may not only help to restore the authentic situation when disputes arise but, more importantly, it may also significantly increase in the cost of fraud, for there are too many ledgers that need to be falsified. Especially for memory-based distributed ledgers at the first layer, one or several people may have the possibility to immorally change the testimony due to coercion and temptation, even when the falsification of the collective memory is obviously not realistic.

5.3 *Chaining the Contract: The Contextualization of a Contract*

5.3.1 The Consecutiveness of Contracts

Blockchain, as its literal meaning shows, "is composed by consecutive chained blocks, each one containing a set of transactions, a hash referencing the previous block, and a special number called *proof-of-work* (PoW)."[217] The immutability, as well as the irreversibility of the transaction data, largely lies in the consecutiveness of blocks in the chain. Analogously, a similar design can be found in the institutional design of traditional Chinese contracts—the conclusion of a contract has never been an independent event but exists as a part of a series of historical transactions regarding the specific property. In this sense, a contract containing the information of transactions shall also be deemed a "block" on the "blockchain."

In Qing China, it was conventionally the vendor's duty to pass to the vendee all former contracts related to the property, called *qianshou qi* or *shangshou qi*. The purpose of doing so was thought to be the declaration of the vendor's true ownership over the subject matter to the vendee.[218] The same custom also existed in the Qingshui

---

[217] Aniello et al. [5].

[218] In the case that there existed no former contracts, the source of the property shall be declared by the vendor in the new contract. See Yang [183], Chen [17]; Wu Dahua, *Qian fa tanyuan*, 205–206. Normally, original acquisition and derivative acquisition were the two kinds of modes of acquiring ownership; only in the case of original acquisition (reclamation or pre-empting) will there also be no contract. Sometimes a certificate was issued by the government as the proof of one's rights over his reclaimed land. For a discussion of certificate manuscripts in the Qingshui River region, see Xu [175].

River region;[219] contracts that were drawn up in different time periods but concerned the same property were generally kept together.[220]

This conventional requirement is similar to the concept of "uninterrupted series of endorsement" in the law of negotiable instruments.[221] As the negotiable instrument is rights-oriented rather than owner-oriented, the connecting point shared by the two contracts before and after also lies in the property rights recorded in the manuscripts. As such the series of contracts represents a growing record of the transaction history of the property. Therefore, the key to the issue becomes the property and its antecedents.[222] The emphasis on the antecedents of the contract's subject matter forms a narrative that is not centered on the proprietors but the property, in which the individual involved, both the vendor and the vendee, are only temporary participants in this continuously extending chain of contracts.

"The land has existed for a thousand years, of which there have appeared eight hundred landlords."[223] As this popular saying states, the protagonist in the contractual narrative is actually the property rather than the owner. Transactions concerning this property could be frequent and complex, and their specific forms include, as mentioned previously, selling, conditional selling, mortgage, redemption, exchange, and so on. Therefore, in order to clarify the rights and interests that one contract party holds, the consecutive context of the contract centering on the subject matter appears to be vital.

Similarly to a block in the blockchain, a contract also contains the information of one or several transactions and a "hash," understood as a link, which refers to the previous contract, although the "PoW" can be replaced by other verification methods. The link of the chain of contracts is the property, which means that a new contract can be added to this chain because it deals with the same property as previous contracts. In some cases, the latter contract could be physically rather than merely conceptually attached to the previous contract (using glue), and therefore formed a set of *lianqi* or consecutive contracts.[224] Sometimes there might even have been more than a dozen contracts stuck together end to end.[225]

Due to the existence of such a "contract-chain," it becomes extremely difficult for a falsified contract to emerge out of the void. An unexpected and unfounded contract cannot find its place in any of the existing "contract-chains." Thus, this context-less

---

[219] If the former contract has not been handed over on the spot, it is necessary to specify this matter in the postscript of the contract and guarantee that it will be sent out in person later. See Christian Daniels, Yang Yougeng, and Takeuchi Fusaji, *Kishū Myaozoku ringyō keiyaku monjo kaihen (1736–1950-nen)*, vol. 1, A-0234. Also, if the property was originally inherited from ancestors and thus a former contract did not exist a former contract, the situation would be specifically stated in the contract too. See Zhang Yingqiang and Wang Zongxun, *Qingshuijiang wenshu*, vol. 3 (7), 104.

[220] See Wang [160]; Wang Zongxun, *Qingshuijiang lishi wenhua tanwei*, 108.

[221] See *Zhonghua renmin gongheguo piaoju fa* [Negotiable instruments law of the People's Republic of China], Art. 31 (2004).

[222] See Terada Hiroaki, "Quanli yu yuanyi," 217–220; Xu [176].

[223] Wang and Yang [162].

[224] See ibid.; Jinping xian difangzhi bianzuan weiyuanhui [74].

[225] See Zhang [195].

contract will naturally not be accepted by all unless the counterfeiter would be willing to spend a huge cost to forge a full set of contracts and then create a false chain of contracts. Even so, one should be aware that every forged contract on this chain needs to be verified in both its temporal and spatial context. Since none of them was ever "broadcasted" in its local society previously, it seems highly impossible that they will successfully pass all verifications.

5.3.2 Correcting the Chaining Error: A Case

Judging from currently available materials, an integrated falsification of a contract and its existing context seems to be impracticable. However, this does not mean that the operation of the system was completely bug-free. Sometimes, errors might occur at the link between contracts. For example, a cunning counterfeiter would try to take advantage of some rarely seen coincidences to "hack" into the system and implant a "Trojan horse program." A case of dispute concerning contract forgery that happened in Wendou Village helpfully illustrates this error and its correction.[226]

The cause of this dispute was that, when Jiang Dengpan was negotiating with Fan Zhiwei to buy the latter's forest land named "Congjiebang," another villager named Jiang Huanqing suddenly stopped the transaction. The stopper claimed that the forest land was owned by him and presented a contract to prove his ownership. As noted previously, the argument would normally be terminated here once the proof is presented, unless the authenticity of it is questionable. According to the material in the case, it is argued that the forest land named "Congjiebang" was sold by Jiang Shichen to Fan Zhiwei in the early years, so that Fan was undoubtedly the rightful owner of the property and could sell it to whomever he chose.

The key problem, in this case, was that, in the twenty-second year of Guangxu (1896), the original owner Jiang Shichen had exchanged a parcel of forest land with Jiang Shifa for a house foundation; then Jiang Shifa later sold the forest land to the stopper Jiang Huanqing. It is interesting that, in this exchange, the forest land that Jiang Shifa received was also named "Congjiebang." In other words, Jiang Shichen, the original owner, once had two parcels of forest land, both of which were named "Congjiebang" (hereafter referred to as CjbA and CjbB). One of them (CjbA) was sold to Fan Zhiwei, and then Fan was ready to resell it to Jiang Dengpan; the other one (CjbB) was transferred to Jiang Shifa, and then conveyed to Jiang Huanqing, who stopped the transaction of the forest land CjbA. A sketch of the transaction relationship among all parties is shown in Figure 1.

A property-oriented narrative is much easier to understand. There existed two chains of contracts for two different parcels of forest land, namely CjbA and CjbB.

---

[226]There are three documents related to the case, see Pan Zhicheng and Wu Dahua, *Tudi guanxi ji qita shiwu wenshu*, vol. 1, 227–229. It must be noted that only the documents from one side of the dispute survives. According to the requirement that both sides of a dispute should be heard, it would be hard to confirm whether the statements in these documents are completely true or not. All subsequent descriptions and discussions are based on this prudent understanding. However, these documents at least shed some light on some of the facts and their expression.

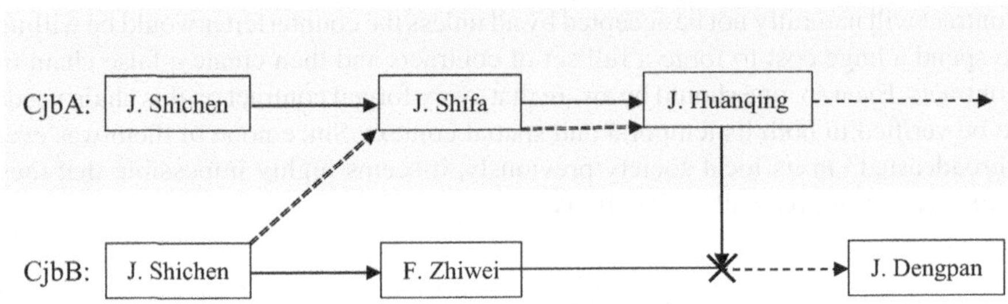

Fig. 1 A diagrammatic sketch of the case of contract forgery

These two conveying tracks were independent of each other as marked by the two background colors in the Figure. However, due to the coincidence that the names of the two properties were the same, according to the complaint from the CjbB side, Jiang Huanqing counterfeited contracts stating that he was the owner of "Congjiebang." This "Congjiebang" should be referred to CjbB rather than CjbA.[227] Although the original material does not clearly indicate this, it seems that Jiang Huanqing forged a contract stating that Jiang Shichen had transferred CjbB, instead of CjbA, to Jiang Shifa and that in the subsequent contract CjbB was transferred from Jiang Shifa to himself (as illustrated in Fig. 1 by the double dash lines).

It is conceivable that, if the key "bug" of the namesake did not exist, Jiang Huanqing, who was called a "habitual forger"[228] by the other party, would probably not counterfeit the contract and confidently prevented the CjbB from trading. Exactly due to the "error" in the key link, the accused forger thought that it was possible to connect the forged contract to the chain of authentic contracts and secretly take up the CjbB. Since Jiang Huanqing already had a real contract chain, and every contract in it had actually been verified by the "broadcasting," the seemingly minor revisions based on the naming limitation on his authentic chain appear to be not only low-cost but also not easy to discover.

Obviously, however, this attempt was not finally realized.[229] After the dispute occurred, the middleman was invited to mediate. By examining the contract manuscripts provided by both parties, the arbitrator found that the version presented by Jiang Huanqing suffered not only material problems (the paper was too new and the handwriting was inconsistent) but also lapses in the text content, since the description of the number of shares was wrong. Finally, after drawing the conclusion that one party had forged the contract, Jiang Huanqing was required to draw up a new contract of dispute resolution as proof to clarify the facts.[230]

[227] An analysis of this case can also be found in Pan [117].

[228] See Pan Zhicheng and Wu Dahua, *Tudi guanxi ji qita shiwu wenshu*, vol. 1, 227.

[229] A similar case of forgery with regard to the coincidence of the names can be found in a record of fieldwork, see Wang [161]. However, it was not the case that two places shared the same name but one place had two names, and therefore some tried to forge a contract bearing the other name of the property.

[230] See Pan Zhicheng and Wu Dahua, *Tudi guanxi ji qita shiwu wenshu*, vol. 1, 228.

In many cases, people ignore the *context* in which contracts exist. But in reality, the signing of a contract is only a short-lived part in a much larger context, which is not only socio-spatial, as the requirement of broadcasting suggests, but also temporal. Yet the contextualization of a contract also makes the cost of contract fraud rise exponentially. This is in fact the logic underlying the ambition of the blockchain theory, namely to link the recognition of individual behavior with the trust of the overall system. Thus, if one believes that the whole is difficult to be subverted, then he or she can trust the individual with confidence.

5.4 *Literacy as a Technical Barrier*

5.4.1 Literacy as a Technique

In the eyes of ordinary people, blockchain is a high-tech innovation. The reason why the blockchain is invulnerable to an attack is that the great majority of people in society are unqualified to be the attacker due to the existence of technical barriers. It is academic whether the cryptographical or algorithmic design of the blockchain is rigorous enough from the professional perspective, so long as the barriers are created with a decent level of technology for the average people who are not technical experts. The technical barriers set by the contract were largely the same. Just as an ordinary person who has no knowledge of programming or information technology can still use a smartphone perfectly, so too in the context of the Qingshui River region an illiterate villager can also enjoy the benefits of the device of contract in the society.

Given the general educational level and literacy of village people in the Qing dynasty,[231] and taking the regional factors of the Qingshui River region into account, such as the fact that they were ethnic minorities in peripheral areas,[232] the literacy rate of contract users involved in this research could not have been high.[233] Some data, which may not be completely reliable on this score, shows that, similarly for the scribe, the rate of proper holographic contracts in the Wendou Village is only 9.44%. This means that, except for "professional scribes," over ninety percent of contracts in the village society needed a scribal helper.

This suggests that most villagers were not able to produce contracts, still less to forge them. The ability concerning the contracts, including contract-related literacy

---

[231] See Rawski [131], Liu [95], Xu and van Leeuwen [179].

[232] Studies have shown that the literacy varied greatly among regions in the Qing dynasty. See Xu Yi and Bas van Leeuwen, "19 shiji Zhongguo dazhong shizilü de zai gusuan," 240–247.

[233] As noted previously, a report from a missionary living in the Miao area during the late Qing period shows that "not one in a hundred of them when he buys a piece of land is able to read the deed of sale when it is written." See Clarke [26].

and relevant contractual knowledge,[234] could vary among villagers.[235] Leaving aside those who were completely illiterate,[236] it is likely that some of the villagers were at the level of being able to use the contract; a small number of them might had the ability to draw up a contract; but only a tiny minority of people may have been proficient at this, and therefore had the potential to become a "forger."

In this sense, literacy as a technical barrier excludes the vast majority of potential counterfeiters from becoming so in practice. Therefore, one who intends to falsify a contract has only two options: either he himself is literate (or tries hard to become literate, which is not realistic), or he invites a scribe to participate in collusion.[237] In either case, the requirement of literacy greatly increased the cost of counterfeiting. Although the technical barrier of the contract is only the first line of defense for its authenticity, it may in fact be the most efficient.

5.4.2 The Fall of a Scribe: The Price of Forgery

The low-level literacy prevalent in villages also suggests that the scribal service was provided by a relatively stable small group of scribes in each community of the region,[238] for only a few of the villagers can provide the scribal service. As a result, there was likely a tension between the group of scribes and the public. On the one hand, members of the society generally relied on the help of the scribe group when applying the contract in daily life, but, on the other hand, since the scribe group included almost all people who had a possibility to engage in corruption regarding the contract system, they must have been respected, supported, or at least recognized by the village society. If a scribe was involved in the falsification of a contract (or even merely an unconfirmed "scandal"), what consequences from the scribe group or the entire village society would the scribe suffer?

Regarding the legal consequence for scribes' falsification of documents, some scholars believe that, according to several lawsuits involving forgery and the abuse of contracts in the Longquan judicial archives in the late Qing dynasty, there was basically no risk in falsifying contracts for them,[239] and that "the counterfeiters

[234]In fact, literacy was only one of many important criteria necessary to become a qualified scribe. Other abilities include relevant knowledge of contracts, understanding of local customs, and familiarity with the contractual background. The failure of the previous forged contract of the homonymous forest land was largely due to the counterfeiter's unfamiliarity with the number of shares allocation concerning the property.

[235]It is suggested that literacy can be distinguished as moderately literate, fully literate, and highly literate. See Idema [68].

[236]For a contract which especially states that the parties involved were completely illiterate, see Zhang and Wang [203].

[237]At the same time, the anti-counterfeiting technology of the contract was also a requisite for scribes. See Feng Xuewei, *Ming Qing qiyue de jiegou gongneng ji yiyi*, 109.

[238]See Zhao [209].

[239]See Du and Wu [34].

were often not punished."[240] If this was the case, it seems that, at that time, the scribes' behavior of counterfeiting would not be evaluated at the level of official justice. However, their experience in the village society seems to have been somewhat different.

As an illustration, a manuscript from Wendou Village mentions that a scribe who was rather popular in the village was involved in a dispute of forgery.[241] According to the narrative of the manuscript text, the scribe's general situation in this case was that, by some means, he obtained the opportunity to read the contract held by the accuser, after which he falsified the date from an authentic contract and forged a new one, thereby selling the property that was involved in the original. Unfortunately, the follow-up information on this case is insufficient, and it is unclear how the dispute was resolved and whether there was a "punishment" for the "counterfeiter." However, the act of falsification would undoubtedly bring corresponding negative evaluations to the village scribe, but how heavy might the costs have been? It is possible to gain an insight into this question by connecting this case with a series of related manuscripts involving the scribe.

In this case, the accused "counterfeiter" was Jiang Shaoya, who happened to be one of the most prominent scribes in Wendou Village in the Qing period. In all accessible contract manuscripts in Wendou Village, there are a total of 85 contracts written by "Jiang Shaoya."[242] Among them, only 10 were written holographically, while most were written for others by Jiang Shaoya as a scribe. In these contracts, except for one which is so stained that the date is illegible,[243] the earliest is dated to 1797[244] and the latest to 1839,[245] reaching a time-span of 43 years.

In addition, there are 47 contracts in which Jiang Shaoya participated solely as a middleman[246]; among them, except for one with an unknown date,[247] the earliest is dated to 1804[248] and the latest to 1838.[249] This time-span basically falls within the range of the era in which Jiang was practicing as a scribe.

Combining these two scales of information, there are a total of 132 contracts which survived in Wendou Village in which Jiang Shaoya was some kind of participant

---

240 See Du [33].

241 See Pan Zhicheng, Wu Dahua, and Liang Cong, *Qingjiang si an yanjiu*, vol. 3, 121.

242 One of them was only partially written by Jiang Shaoya. See Chen Jinquan and Du Wanhua, *Jiang Yuanze jiacang qiyue wenshu*, 204.

243 See ibid., 202. Regarding the time period of this contract, special attention given in a study came to the conclusion that the manuscript "should be established in the period of Jiaqing." See Lin [89].

244 See Zhang and Wang [207].

245 See Chen Jinquan and Du Wanhua, *Jiang Qigui jiacang qiyue wenshu*, 263.

246 Among the above-mentioned 85 contracts, Jiang Shaoya assumed the roles of both middleman and scribe in 36 of them; here, only those he joined solely as a middleman are counted.

247 See Chen Jinquan and Du Wanhua, *Jiang Yuanze jiacang qiyue wenshu*, 203. The conclusion of a study investigating the time of the contract is that it would be in the reign of either Jiaqing or Daoguang. See Lin Dongjie, "Qing zhi Minguo nianjian Qingshuijiang qiyue wenshu liqi shijian jiaobu," 66–67.

248 See Zhang Yingqiang and Wang Zongxun, *Qingshuijiang wenshu*, vol. 1 (12), 337.

249 See Chen Jinquan and Du Wanhua, *Jiang Yuanze jiacang qiyue wenshu*, 348.

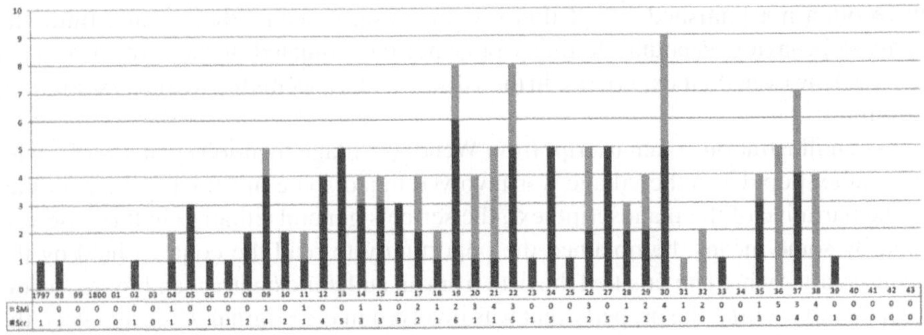

Fig. 2 Jiang Shaoya's career as a scribe and middleman in Wendou (1797–1839)

(see Fig. 2).[250] In his forty-plus-year career of contract activities, the annual average number of contracts that Jiang was involved with is ca. 3.07.[251]

According to the frequency of his appearances in contracts, it is not difficult to infer his renowned status and influence in the village contract activities. Also, from the ten contracts written holographically by Jiang himself, one can get a glimpse of his early life. Nine of them are contracts regarding the sale of his properties during the Jiaqing period (1795–1820),[252] and the reasons stated are all about a lack of living expenses, which may give a clue about his living conditions.[253] The tenth contract, which is much later than the previous nine, was a tenancy contract in the fifteenth year of Daoguang (1835), in which Jiang rented another man's forest land as a planter.[254]

However, some other documents show that, at least in a later period, Jiang became a highly respected figure in the village. For instance, in the tenth year of Daoguang (1830), Jiang had been called "the elder of the village" in the text of a contract of innocence, and the title before his name was "the head of the clan."[255] In addition, the description of his behavior in the contract is interesting: "Fortunately, the elder of the village could not bear to sit back and went straight to reprimand

250 The lighter-color parts of "Smi" in the bar chart refer to Jiang solely as a middleman, while the darker parts of "Scr" refer to Jiang as a scribe as well as when he assumed both roles.

251 For a list of thirteen contracts related to Jiang Shaoya, see Lin Dongjie, "Qing zhi Minguo nianjian Qingshuijiang qiyue wenshu liqi shijian jiaobu," 66.

252 See Zhang Yingqiang and Wang Zongxun, *Qingshuijiang wenshu*, vol. 1 (12), 43, 336; Zhang Yingqiang and Wang Zongxun, *Qingshuijiang wenshu*, vol. 3 (7), 370; Zhang and Wang [204]; Chen Jinquan and Du Wanhua, *Jiang Yuanze jiacang qiyue wenshu*, 80, 83; Chen Jinquan and Du Wanhua, *Jiang Qigui jiacang qiyue wenshu*, 33, 60, 70.

253 Two interpretations of his life's state seem possible here: on the one hand, his life was in such distress that he had to sell his properties; on the other hand, the fact of selling properties also shows that he originally owned a considerable number of properties, and they could be realized once necessary.

254 See Daniels et al. [30].

255 See Pan Zhicheng and Wu Dahua, *Tudi guanxi ji qita shiwu wenshu*, vol. 1, 221.

and mediate."[256] Differently from general situations, it seems to be abnormal for a secondary middleman to become involved directly in a dispute without an invitation from both parties. In another dispute document from the Daoguang period, Jiang was called "the middleman of the village" and was invited to arbitrate a dispute of logging.[257]

However, it was also exactly in this period that Jiang Shaoya was involved in the above-mentioned scandal of forgery. The prominent year of the above dispute document is the twentieth year of Daoguang (1840), which mentioned that Jiang Shaoya's "forgery" had happened last year, i.e. in the nineteenth year of Daoguang (1839). Coincidentally, the last contract that Jiang participated in is dated to the twenty-ninth day, second month, nineteenth year of Daoguang (April 2, 1839).[258] Prior to this, Jiang was highly active and had a record of participating in contract activities in almost every year for 35 years. Yet, once Jiang Shaoya was involved in the scandal of forgery in the nineteenth year of Daoguang, it seems that his scribal career came to an abrupt end.

Although a record of Jiang's activities after the nineteenth year of Daoguang is lacking, according to the above-mentioned dispute document, at least in the twentieth year of Daoguang he was still alive.[259] In addition, an early contract in which he participated still contained an agreement of subsequent arrangements: here Jiang agreed with the mountain owner in the fifteenth year of Daoguang (1835) that the forest should be established in the fifth year from then on, which is the twentieth year of Daoguang.[260]

Overall, due to the surprising coincidence of the above two events in time,[261] one may reasonably infer that the key reason why Jiang no longer participated in any contract activity was the result of the "forgery" incident. It is conceivable that, although the actual situation and the final ruling still remain unknown, the incident caused a strong negative evaluation on him in the village, with the result that no one was willing to invite him to write a contract on their behalf after the twentieth year of Daoguang.

The assumed fall of this once-esteemed scribe in the village indicates the price that a scribe had to pay if he was related to forgery in a village society; even if he was only involved in an unconfirmed scandal, it was enough to bury his career. This can be interpreted as a kind of social scrutiny. The career of scribes greatly relied on the public's trust, and even the slightest suspicion could be a fatal blow to it. In most

---

[256] Ibid.

[257] See Jinping xian Hekou xiang renmin zhengfu [75].

[258] See Chen Jinquan and Du Wanhua, *Jiang Qigui jiacang qiyue wenshu*, 263.

[259] Otherwise, the dispute involving him is somewhat unnecessary, and one might have expected that his death would be reflected in the dispute document.

[260] See Christian Daniels, Yang Yougeng, and Takeuchi Fusaji, *Kishū Myaozoku ringyō keiyaku monjo kaihen (1736–1950-nen)*, vol. 2, C-0050.

[261] There are still many possibilities that cannot be ruled out. It is still possible that, for example, there are relevant manuscripts that have not yet been found or survived until today, or that he could no longer act as a scribe for others due to his age or health condition.

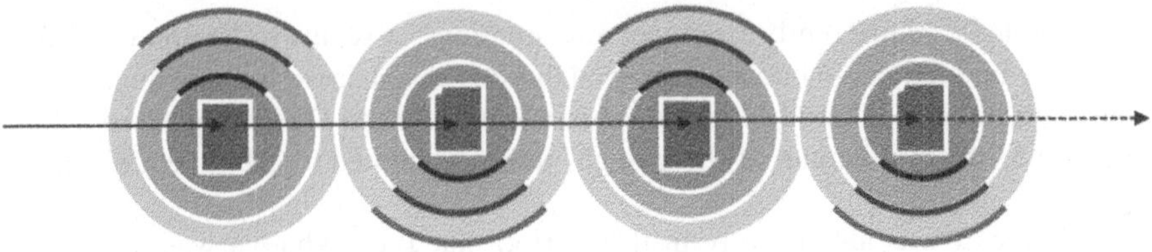

Fig. 3 A diagram of the operation of the broadcasting and chaining mechanisms of contracts

cases, both contracting parties could be illiterate and thus the scribe was the one who bore all the trust.

In sum, due to the technical barrier of the literacy rate, the possibility of engaging in corruption was limited to an extremely small crowd and, for the sake of their career, these "vital few" needed to cherish their reputation among the public. This adds another layer of protection to the authenticity of the contract beyond the broadcasting and chaining mechanism.

5.5 Authenticity and the Cconstruction of Trust Network

Among previous studies, many researchers have shown pessimism about the effect of contract mechanisms and their results of maintaining authenticity. In particular, it is claimed that "[t]rust in rural society is based not on the importance of contracts but, rather, on the dependability of people, people who are so enmeshed in customary norms that they cannot behave in any other way."[262] Specifically in the context of the Qingshui River region, it is believed that the phenomenon of counterfeiting contracts still occurred from time to time due to the shortcomings of the contract mechanism.[263]

However, throughout the previous discussion, one can find that not only was the actual effect of the contract in the region satisfactory, but its internal logic was also clear and strict.

The basic idea of the operation of the blockchain-like trust network is shown above in Fig. 3. Each one of the four contracts (the four rectangles) is broadcast (the three sound waves) and reaches its three layers of distributed ledgers (the three concentric circles), after which these four contracts need to be linked together chronologically in order to form a "contract-chain." Moreover, the operators of this system are limited by the barrier of literacy. By means of the effective operation of the broadcasting and chaining mechanism, the technical barrier of literacy, the public scrutiny of the vital few, and the anti-counterfeiting techniques in writings, the authenticity of a contract can be assured to a great extent. In this case, a perfect forgery must achieve the effect of "deceiving the dead and hiding from the living,"[264] which means that the

[262] Hamilton and Zheng [49]. For the original Chinese text, see Fei [38].

[263] See Liang Cong, *Qing dai Qingshuijiang xiayou cunzhai shehui de qiyue guifan yu zhixu*, 134.

[264] See Zhang [198].

forgery must tackle not only the distant history in the chain of contracts but also the wide social field in its own time. This was in fact extremely difficult to achieve, and the cost would be huge. But it was also the key of this network—what make it almost invulnerable were not multiple cast-iron armor, but it was rather designed to be an extremely open and tightly-woven fabric, so open that any tiny movement would trigger the alteration of the whole body and counterfeiting everything is undoubtedly costly or unpractical. Therefore, just like the blockchain system, it does not need to be completely unbreakable; it only needs to keep the cost of successful falsification above its possible benefits.

Unlike a popular belief, the surviving dispute manuscripts actually illustrate the success of the above network. The outbreaks of disputes show that these rare forgeries failed. The discovery of the forgery is deemed a built-in mechanism of error correction in the network, while a successful forgery would not be discovered.

When people in the region chose to arrange a contract in property transactions or dispute settlements, they were presenting their beliefs in the contract that it could uphold the authenticity of what had been written. Through the contract, true recognition would be preserved and protected from tampering, and thereby a systematic trust in the contract in society was well established. It should also be noted that, once the trust network of contract was constructed, its usage was not limited to the relatively private aspects of social life, such as property transactions, loans, or tenancy, but could be utilized in more public aspects too. In other words, the distinction between public and private has been transcended through the establishment of contracts.

6 Restoration of Order: Challenges from Breaches and Forgeries

What a positive argument must confront are challenges from counterexamples, which are in this case represented by the breaches and forgeries of contract that occurred in the context of the Qingshui River region. At the beginning of this chapter, the issue of the overall default rate in this context was discussed through the provision of concrete proofs, and it is believed in this study that contracts were generally honored and cases of breach and forgery did not substantively affect the overall effectiveness of the contract system in the region. Thus, while discussing counterexamples in the following parts, it shall again be borne in mind that these breaches were marginal to the whole situation.

6.1 Disputes and Excuses for Breach

The outbreak of disputes does not entail the occurrence of breaches. There are too many types of disputes and not all of them, or actually only a few of them, are related to contract breach. According to a summary of disputes that happened in Wendou Village,[265] hardly any dispute was caused directly by the nonperformance of the contracting parties. The most frequently attested causes are issues of vagueness (concerning boundaries, the number of shares, and ownership) as well as arguments over the above-discussed pre-emptive rights. Apart from these, there were also sporadic cases of "robbery" and "quarrels," such as grabbing timbers from others[266] or being noisy after drinking,[267] and these should not be considered within the scope of the contractual order.

In general, vagueness is the most prominent single reason for triggering disputes, especially in connection with contract terms. For example, one dispute arose exactly because of the vague definition of the boundary in the original contract.[268] This is also the reason why many contracts of dispute settlement were named contract of "innocence," the wording of which could literally imply the meaning of restoring the "clarity" of the situation.[269]

However, disputes caused by the vagueness of property rights could not directly be seen as a breach of "contract," for the "contract" had not been clearly declared and there was nothing firm left to be broken. More specifically, the vague situation could be the result of either objective or subjective factors—it may be caused by technical problems in writing or a confusion caused by a malicious party. In this case, vagueness can actually be used as an excuse for a contract's breach since the basis for compliance is not clear enough. This is also why all contract parties constantly pursue clarity in the contract writing, as an endeavor to avoid providing excuses for future malicious people.

Although most disputes are not directly related to the breach of contract, two typical breaches of contract in both modern and ancient times can be examined in the context of the Qingshui River region. The first one is double sales,[270] including both intentional and unintentional cases.[271] This phenomenon is known to have occurred occasionally in the region. Some sellers seem to be deliberate,[272] while others found an excuse of imprudence or unconsciousness; for example, someone's wife claimed that she did not know the property had been sold years ago by her husband who had

---

[265] For the long list of disputes, see Liang Cong, *Qing dai Qingshuijiang xiayou cunzhai shehui de qiyue guifan yu zhixu*, 131–133. See also Pan Zhicheng, *Qing dai Qingshuijiang liuyu xiangcun shehui de jiufen yu zhixu yanjiu*, Chap. 3.

[266] See Liang Cong, *Qing dai Qingshuijiang xiayou cunzhai shehui de qiyue guifan yu zhixu*, 146.

[267] See ibid., 132.

[268] See Pan [119].

[269] See Deng Jianpeng and Qiu Kai, "Cong heyi dao qiangzhi," 26–27.

[270] For the previously discussed case, see Christian Daniels, Yang Yougeng, and Takeuchi Fusaji, *Kishū Myaozoku ringyō keiyaku monjo kaihen (1736–1950-nen)*, vol. 1, A-0098.

[271] For a discussion on this point, see Pan Zhicheng, *Qing dai Qingshuijiang liuyu xiangcun shehui de jiufen yu zhixu yanjiu*, Chap. 3.

[272] See Chen Jinquan and Guo Liang, *Yi Zunfa Jiang Qicheng deng jiacang susong wenshu*, 234–235.

passed away.[273] These unintentional cases may be easy to forgive, but the former is an obvious breach of contract.

The second kind is a multiple-times unilateral denial of the contract term which stipulates the price, and which can be referred to as *zhaotie* within ancient Chinese contract practice.[274] It originally refers to the addition of supplementary payments to the original price in order to transfer the conditional sale of the property to an absolute one.[275] However, the practice shows that the original owner would repeatedly ask for supplementary payments for the property that had already been absolutely sold. Although it has largely been regarded as a trading custom in many regions in Qing China and has a solid cultural and economic background, it was still seen as a kind of breach of contract if the vendor failed to keep his promise that is stipulated in the contract. However, surprisingly, this phenomenon is rarely found in the Qingshui River region.[276] There are many speculations about the reason why such an extremely common practice, or rather custom, of breach of contract was unfamiliar in the Qingshui River region.[277] Although the root cause remains unclear, it might be possible to explain this phenomenon, even if partially, by the successful operation of the contract and the general compliance of it in the area.

Overall, most disputes which happened in the region seem not to be directly related to the performance of an original contract. However, within the fault-tolerance limit, there did occur breaches of contract, although most of them can still be accounted for with a seemingly appropriate excuse, such as the vagueness of contract terms or one's lack of awareness of previous transactions.

6.2 Forgeries: Legitimization within the Context

There was also a small proportion of disputes that were caused by contract forgeries. Their basic situation has been discussed above, but a further explanation of this phenomenon is needed in terms of order restoration. A forgery is undoubtedly an act that seriously disrupts the order of the contract, but it must be realized that, from the perspective of the counterfeiters, it is also a process of order restoration.

Firstly, it is necessary to understand that the emergence of contract forgeries underlines precisely the importance of the contract manuscript in property order and property possession in the region. As recorded in the previously cited manuscript of

[273]For a discussion of this case, see Pan Zhicheng, *Qing dai Qingshuijiang liuyu xiangcun shehui de jiufen yu zhixu yanjiu*, Chap. 3.

[274]For studies of *zhaotie*, see, e.g., Huang [64], Buoye [11], Isett [69], Fan [36].

[275]See Qu Jian, "Qing zhonghouqi Qiandongnan Wendou zhai Miaozu dianzhi yanjiu," 207–209.

[276]See Liang Cong, *Qing dai Qingshuijiang xiayou cunzhai shehui de qiyue guifan yu zhixu*, 69.

[277]See ibid., 70. Also, at a conference in Paris (October 16th to 18th, 2019) titled "New perspectives on Chinese history: The use of archives from the middle and lower course of the Yangzi River and related regions (16th century–1949)," Professor Zheng Zhenman from Xiamen University speculated about this phenomenon to the author saying that the "good nature" of the people in the region might be the reason.

forgery disputes,[278] one may be surprised by the fact that the forger directly sold the related property to the next buyer immediately through the completion of the forged contract. This seems to mean that one's possession of the real estate only needed to be conceptual possession, rather than physical—the buyer did not even need to check the land in person. The development of the contract system had also probably reached a relatively virtual stage, since a large number of transactions, especially those regarding timber shares, could be completed through paperwork. This feature marks the key position of the contract manuscript in the property order. Admittedly, it is entirely possible that the buyer was a colluder, but what is more important is that, once he had a contract, even a forged one (as he might realize as such), he could truly own the property as long as the forgery did not come to light.

Secondly, on the basis of the principle above, one would soon notice that the activity of forging the contract represented the legitimization of the fake ownership, and the legitimization through a contract, albeit a forged one, mirrors the robustness of the contract system in the region. If the operation of the contract system was not satisfactory, it is conceivable that no one would attempt or risk to forge a contract as even an authentic one would not be honored. Therefore, the interesting logic of the forgery emerges: the forger tries to justify his unjustified intention through a seemingly justified means (the contract, but a forged one), deceptively hoping to incorporate a counterfeit contract into the authentic contract system of rightfulness. This is called laundering; it only happens within a generally effective system. In addition, if a forged contract successfully remains unrevealed to the subsequent buyers of the property and later becomes a previous link in the ever-extending "contract-chain," then the effectiveness of this ancient forged contract will be extremely complicated to judge.

6.3 Restoring Order Through Contracts

The state of order requires two underpinnings, namely its formation and its maintenance. The latter specifically refers to the restoration of order once there occurs a certain level of disorder that can be caused by breaches and forgeries.

An effective dispute resolution mechanism can quickly reverse disorder to the state of order when chaos occurs.[279] The system of maintaining social order through contracts was never perfect. Disputes would occur from time to time, but they would also be solved through the multiple means of dispute resolution, and no matter what these ways were—official or customary, with force or with reasoning—the contract played an irreplaceable role in the process, serving as the grounds (the "prediction," "reason," and "justification")[280] for restoring the order and the restored order itself.

---

[278] See Pan Zhicheng, Wu Dahua, and Liang Cong, *Qingjiang si an yanjiu*, vol. 3, 121.

[279] See Liang Cong, *Qing dai Qingshuijiang xiayou cunzhai shehui de qiyue guifan yu zhixu*, 130.

[280] See H. L. A. Hart, *The Concept of Law*, 11, 84.

In addition, as noted above, middlemen and scribes were of vital importance in the dispute settlement as proofs of the truth, and middlemen further played a pivotal role in solving problems as arbitrators or peacemakers.

In sum, one would notice that the social order formed through contracts may be disrupted due to various causes, but it will also be restored again through contracts. The contract as a social system cannot guarantee that no violation of the order will occur, but the grounds of rightfulness it provides entail the establishment and reconstruction of social order.

7 Private Contracts and Public Order: Public Issues and Limitations

The dichotomy between private and public[281] in terms of contracts in the Qingshui River region has already been dissolved in previous discussions, since it has been proved that the contract was not merely a device limited to the private field, but largely a social system in which publicity played a pivotal role. However, it is still necessary to explain and give a few specific examples of how private contracts function directly in the public sphere.

7.1 Applying Contracts in Public Issues

Public issues in a village society can be divided into two kinds: on the one hand, there were issues concerning the establishment and continuation of public utilities, while, on the other hand, there were issues concerning the maintenance of public safety and order, which could be reflected in the establishment of prohibitive regulations against the public.[282] In the context of the Qingshui River region, an observer would notice the existence of the contract with regard to both kinds.

The establishment of prohibitive provisions in the form of drawing up a contract was in practice a relatively common phenomenon in village societies.[283] Remarkable evidence in this regard is the large number of stone inscriptions concerning self-made restraints which existed in the region, many of which can be seen as the enhanced public version of contracts.[284] Apart from these stone inscriptions, there were still many examples of trying to protect and improve public security through contract stipulations on paper.

[281] For a concise introduction of the dichotomy between private and public, see Chen [16].

[282] This division can also be found in the basic ideas of the important and influential "Lü's Clan's Village Pact" formulated in the Song dynasty. See Pan [115].

[283] For a study concerning the role of contract in self-governance, see Jiang Ming, *Guizhou Cengong qiyue wenshu yanjiu*, 156 ff. See also Jiang Ming et al. [72].

[284] See Qin and Li [124], An [3]. See also Cheng Zeshi, *Hudong yu gongxiang*, 318–320.

For example,[285] one contract stipulated that it was forbidden to bring sick cattle and pigs into the village; if one truly wanted to butcher pigs bought from outside, he or she must first raise them in the village for seven days to ensure that they were not sick.[286] This kind of quarantine-like regulation was obviously intended to prevent the plague from entering the village. The same regulation can also be found in the inscription of a renowned stele erected in front of the village gate.[287] This shows that the content of the paper-based contract and that of the stone-based public discourse were closely connected and interacted with each other. Moreover, it is noteworthy that, according to the narrative of the contract text, the process of concluding this contract stood in full compliance with the establishment procedure of a typical contract, except that the number of participants was much greater than a normal contract of property transaction.

In addition to the biosecurity of the village, the safety of life and property of villagers was also an object that people tried to protect through contracts.[288] In Wendou Village, people from four families once agreed in a contract to work together to maintain the order and try to arrest the thieves, with money rewards at stake for the co-operation.[289] In another contract,[290] the scope of participants included both the Upper Village and the Lower Village of Wendou—two villages that once harbored ill feelings against each other but that co-operated in the face of threats to social peace.[291] The contract of this alliance was finally drawn up after the agreement had been reached between the heads of the two villages, and it was determined that they should also be responsible for anything that went wrong according to contract terms. In the end, the two villages each kept one of the two duplicates of the trans-village contract.

An even larger exercise of cross-village participation appeared in a contract involving four villages—Wendou, Ping'ao, Yanwan, and Jiachi.[292] Their contract expresses concerns in many aspects, but the most important one was to prevent the unlawful felling of trees. Unlike a normal commercial contract, there was no personal name listed at the beginning as the establisher of the contract. Instead, the contract literally claimed that all people from the four villages were the establishers and the contract was agreed at a meeting of the public. Four names were indicated in the ending part of the contract as representatives of each village to preserve one of the four duplicates. Moreover, the witnesses were no longer invited middlemen but gods. Although this contract still follows the basic format and other requirements of a general contract, according to the above features—it claims to have obtained

[285] See Zhang Yingqiang and Wang Zongxun, *Qingshuijiang wenshu*, vol. 1 (12), 330.

[286] For an explanation of this contract, see Zhang Yingqiang, *Mucai zhi liudong*, 216–218.

[287] See Long and Fan [99].

[288] See, e.g., Li [82].

[289] See Christian Daniels, Yang Yougeng, and Takeuchi Fusaji, *Kishū Myaozoku ringyō keiyaku monjo kaihen (1736–1950-nen)*, vol. 3, F-0045.

[290] See Chen Jinquan and Du Wanhua, *Jiang Yuanze jiacang qiyue wenshu*, 549.

[291] For the relations between the two villages, see Zhang Yingqiang, *Mucai zhi liudong*, 218–245.

[292] See Zhang Yingqiang and Wang Zongxun, *Qingshuijiang wenshu*, vol. 1 (8), 205.

the consent of all members of the societies, sending representatives to participate in negotiations, and seeking justification from superman power—it was close to being a treaty or pact of inter-village cooperation on public security. This illustrates the role that even the most common business contract model can play at the most public level.

Another aspect of applying the contract in public affairs is to establish public utility through the contract. The key point in this regard is not whether any welfare services could be provided through the contract, but the possibility that a probably impersonal entity could be established through a contract,[293] similarly to the function of "trust" in the common law system. A convincing example here is a contract used for setting up a market.[294] The background story of this contract, according to its narrative, is that the location of the original market is too far away from some of the villages in which those contract participants lived, which makes it extremely inconvenient for villagers from these places to go to the market to trade. Therefore, forty-four people came together and negotiated on the issue and decided to build a jointly funded new market. In addition to terms that concern the capital allocation and the distribution of shares, the contract also specified in detail the basic regulation of market operation and the selection criteria of management personnel. This contract has in some ways become a "company charter." It highlights the possibility of establishing an impersonal and public entity through contracts. Moreover, since it was set up to be a public and open market, the contract was also setting up public rules for all potential market participants.

In sum, in addition to the repeatedly stressed publicity of the contract itself, its direct application in public issues of the village or even inter-village societies also explains how the boundary between private contract and public order was transcended.

7.2 *Facing the Super-Large-Scale Stranger Society*

Before finally concluding, it may be worthwhile to comment briefly on the possible limitations of the framework of contracts constructed in this study in terms of its specific social and historical environment.

In general, the interaction between the contract and its context provided the basis for the establishment of the contract-based social order. The greatest convenience that this rare social context has given to researchers is that it allows observers to explore the extent to which contracts played a role in society, since a large number of "disturbance terms," such as governmental/political, legal/judicial, and religious/moral authorities,

[293] The unfolding of this point can partially be seen in the contract practice in the salt industry in Zigong, see Zelin [186]. For a history of the Chinese shareholding practices, especially in late imperial times, see Zelin [187].

[294] See Zhang [197].

can be excluded. This is not saying that these factors did not exist in the context of the Qingshui River region, but that their influence was visibly relatively small.

At the same time, this does not mean that the contract structure could only be established and function in this "vacuum" environment, for even in other regions "the writ of law and mandate of the courts did not easily touch the populace,"[295]. Further detailed studies of contracts in other regions are now needed. However, to an observer, the effect might not be as obvious in the frontier area due to the existence of many more powerful and conspicuous social structures—the role of contract in society was likely replaced by other social mechanisms. In this case, to what extent was the success of the contract of the Qingshui River region attributed to the particularity of its environment?

Regarding the circumstances of Qingshui River contracts, the real challenge is not those mighty authorities but another fundamental change in the social environment when it finally enters a super-large-scale stranger society.[296] These contracts seem to depend to a large extent on a relatively small social scale, and the relatively familiar interpersonal relationships that result from it.[297] For example, on the premise of no corresponding improvement in technology, in a true super-large-scale society, the effect of contract broadcasting will be greatly reduced. Further, when transactions in society happen mostly between complete strangers, due to the custom of "double contingency,"[298] an authoritative and thus trusted third party seems to be naturally needed, as it is believed that "[a] stable social/economic practice of contract—beyond the realm of a small and closed group in which everyone knows each other—cannot exist without such a functioning and trustworthy legal infrastructure."[299] Therefore, the non-centrality of the network of contract in the pre-modern context will be dissolved. Instead it can be seen as a centralization process of a noncentral society, as history had shown time and time again.

However, the super-large-scale stranger society may only be a modern concept that cannot be properly applied in the context of late imperial China; none of the societies of even the biggest city at that time could meet its standard. On the other hand, even in large cities, it seems that people tended to live in a sub-society in which its members are more or less acquaintances and the running contract system there, including the customs concerning middlemen and scribes, did not present a fundamental difference.[300] This also partially explains the successful operation of the contract in the urban grassroots in the late imperial period.[301] Moreover, one may

[295] Buxbaum [12].

[296] For the concept of "super-large-scale stranger society" and its application in the modern Chinese context, see Pan [112–114].

[297] See, e.g., Chen [14].

[298] See Parsons [120], Luhmann [100].

[299] Radin [129].

[300] This can be noticed in the related customs survey, see, e.g., Wu [173].

[301] For a study of contracts in urban areas of Beijing during the Qing era, see Zhang [196].

still argue that all shortages of the contract system could be fixed by advanced technologies when a true super-large-scale stranger society eventually appears, probably in modern times, although that is not the concern of this study.

At any rate, the contract as both a practical device and a social system and its interaction with the social order has now been explained and theorized within the Qingshui River region. Though the understanding of the contract might not be limited to the seemingly special context of a peripheral area, its application in other fields should be aware of the limitations caused by considerable social changes.

8 Conclusion

It is now time to go back to the metaphor of the "box" which was introduced at the beginning of this chapter. In the main discussion the functioning mechanism of contracts in the given society has been expounded in detail according to such logic. Firstly, what is actually in the box is the recognition collected by the contract from related people based on the cannon-shot rule of recognition, and its rightfulness precisely lies in the fact that it is willingly offered and the norm of estoppel was widely accepted in the society. Secondly, the reason for packing the "rightful content (recognition)" into the box is because recognition needs to be provable, and the "packing process" can be achieved through the facilitation of the middleman and the scribe. And, thirdly, through the construction of the trust network of contracts, the box shall be deemed a solid one that is capable of protecting the recognition from being "attacked" from both outside and inside. Accordingly, people put their trust in the box which can actually contain more objects than private issues.

The question of why people honor the contract may also be tentatively answered through the above-presented mechanism, which guarantees the contract as a container of *tamper-resistant provable recognition*. In addition, it should be noted that the effective operation of this mechanism mobilized various elements of the entire society to the greatest extent, which formed the foundation of both its rightfulness and its implementation.

References

1. *Zhongguo shaoshu minzu shehui lishi diaocha ziliao congkan* xiuding bianji weiyuanhui, ed. 2009. *Miaozu shehui lishi diaocha* [Investigation to the society and history of the Miao people]. vol. 1, 57. Beijing: Minzu chubanshe.
2. Aihara, Yoshiyuki. 2019. Forests as commons in early modern China: An analysis of legal cases. In *Public goods provision in the early modern economy: Comparative perspectives from Japan, China, and Europe*, ed. Masayuki Tanimoto and R. Bin Wong, 278–280. Oakland, California: University of California Press.
3. An, Chengxiang, ed. 2015. *Shi shang lishi* [History on the stone]. Guiyang: Guizhou minzu chubanshe.

4. An, Zunhua, and Pan Zhicheng, eds. 2016. *Tudi qiyue wenshu jiaoshi* [Collation and annotation of land-related contract manuscripts], vol. 1, 301. Guiyang: Guizhou minzu chubanshe.
5. Aniello, Leonardo, Roberto Baldoni, and Federico Lombardi. 2018. A Blockchain-based solution for enabling log-based resolution of disputes in multi-party transactions. In *Proceedings of 5th international conference in software engineering for defence applications: SEDA 2016*, ed. Paolo Ciancarini, Stanislav Litvinov, Angelo Messina, Alberto Sillitti, and Giancarlo Succi, 55. Cham: Springer International Publishing AG.
6. Austen-Baker, Richard, and Qi Zhou. 2015. *Contract in Context*, 49–50. London and New York: Routledge.
7. Beck, Andrew. 1985. Void for vagueness: The layman's contract in court. *South African Law Journal* 102: 660–673.
8. Berman, Harold J. 1983. *Law and revolution: The formation of the western legal tradition*, 608. Cambridge, Massachusetts: Harvard University Press.
9. Bourgon, Jérôme. 2020. Historians at the court: How cultural expertise in Qing law contributes to the invention of Hong Kong 'Chinese Customary Law'. *Law and History Review* 38 (1): 85–98.
10. Bridge, Michael. 2015. *Personal property law*, 1. Oxford: Oxford University Press.
11. Buoye, Thomas. 2004. Litigation, Legitimacy, and lethal violence: Why county courts failed to prevent violent disputes over property in eighteenth-century China. In *Contract and property in early modern China*, ed. Madeleine Zelin, Jonathan K. Ocko, and Robert Gardella, 105. Stanford: Stanford University Press.
12. Buxbaum, David C. 1993. Contracts in China during the Qing dynasty: Key to the civil law. *Journal of Oriental Studies XXXI* (2): 231.
13. Calvert, Randall L. 1998. Explaining social order: Internalization, external enforcement, or equilibrium?. In *Institutions and social order*, ed. Karol Sołtan, Eric M. Uslaner, and Virginia Haufler, 131–162. Ann Arbor: The University of Michigan Press.
14. Chen, Baifeng. 2011. Shuren shehui: Cunzhuang zhixu jizhi de lixiangxing tanjiu [On the acquaintance community: An ideal-type exploration of the mechanism in the village order]. *Shehui* 31 (1): 223–241.
15. Chen, Shengqiang. 2010. Zhongren dui Qing dai tudi juemai qiyue de yingxiang jiqi jiejian yiyi [The impact of middlemen to land contracts of absolute sale in the Qing dynasty and its referential value]. *Faxue pinglun* (3): 155.
16. Chen, Xixi. 2018. Lun guanxi qiyue lilun de helixing he qianli [On the rationality and potential of the relational contract theory]. *Qinghua fazhi lunheng* 26 (2): 79–80.
17. Chen, Yu. 2018. 'Rent-in-Perpetuity' system and Xiamen title deed: A study of Sino-Anglo land transactions in China's treaty ports. In *Life in treaty port China and Japan*, ed. Donna Brunero and Stephanie Villalta Puig, 194–195. Singapore: Springer Nature Singapore Pte Ltd.
18. Chen, Hongbo, and Zejiang Long. 2014. Xin faxian Guizhou Qingshuijiang Dongzu yulin ce pingjie [A study of the newly discovered Dong's *Yulince* in Tianzhu County on the Qingshui River in Guizhou Province]. *Yunnan minzu daxue xuebao (zhexue shehui kexue ban)* 31 (4): 103–108.
19. Chen, Jinquan, and Liang Guo, eds. 2017. *Guizhou Wendouzhai Miaozu qiyue falü wenshu huibian—Yi Zunfa Jiang Qicheng deng jiacang susong wenshu* [The compilation of contractual and legal manuscripts of the Miao from Wendou Village, Guizhou—Litigation manuscripts from family collections of Yi Zunfa, Jiang Qicheng, etc.], 45. Beijing: Renmin chubanshe.
20. Chen, Jinquan, and Wanhua Du, eds. 2008. *Guizhou Wendouzhai Miaozu qiyue falü wenshu huibian—Jiang Yuanze jiacang qiyue wenshu* [The compilation of contractual and legal manuscripts of the Miao from Wendou Village, Guizhou—Manuscripts from Jiang Yuanze's family collection], 415. Beijing: Renmin chubanshe.
21. Cheng, Jinquan, and Wanhua Du, eds. 2015. *Guizhou Wendouzhai Miaozu qiyue falü wenshu huibian—Jiang Qigui jiacang qiyue wenshu* [The compilation of contractual and legal manuscripts of the Miao from Wendou Village, Guizhou—Manuscripts from Jiang Qigui's family collection], 85. Beijing: Renmin chubanshe.

22. Cheng, Zeshi. 2011. Jinping yindi fengshui qiyue wenshu yu fengshui xiguan fa [On contracts concerning gravelands and fengshui and fengshui customary laws in Jinping]. *Yuanshengtai minzu wenhua xuekan* 3 (3): 51.
23. Cheng, Zeshi. 2011. *Qingshuijiang wenshu zhi fayi chutan* [A primary legal research on the Qingshui River manuscripts], 117–123. Beijing: Zhongguo zhengfa daxue chubanshe.
24. Cheng, Zeshi. 2017. *Hudong yu gongxiang: Qing dai Miao Jiang shehui zhuanxing zhi lisong tiaoshi* [Trial adjustment and social transition in Qing Miao areas], 286. Beijing: Zhongguo fazhi chubanshe.
25. Chow, Kai-wing. 2004. *Publishing, culture, and power in early modern china*, 15–16. Stanford, California: Stanford University Press.
26. Clarke, Samuel R. 1911. *Among the tribes in South-west China*, 39. London: Morgan & Scott.
27. Cooter, Robert. 2006. The intrinsic value of obeying a law: Economic analysis of the internal viewpoint. *Fordham Law Review* 75 (3): 1281.
28. Crosby, Michael, Nachiappan, Pradan Pattanayak, Sanjeev Verma, and Vignesh Kalyanaraman. 2016. BlockChain technology: Beyond Bitcoin. *Applied Innovation Review* (2): 9.
29. Daniels, Christian, Yougeng Yang, and Fusaji Takeuchi, eds. 2001. *Kishū Myaozoku ringyō keiyaku monjo kaihen (1736–1950-nen)* [Old forestry contracts of the Miao in Guizhou, 1736–1950], vol. 1, A-0144. Tokyo: Tōkyō gaikokugo daigaku Ajia Afurika gengo bunka kenkyūjo.
30. Daniels, Christian, Yougeng Yang, and Fusaji Takeuchi, eds. 2002. *Kishū Myaozoku ringyō keiyaku monjo kaihen (1736–1950-nen)* [Old forestry contracts of the Miao in Guizhou, 1736–1950], vol. 2, C-0050. Tokyo: Tōkyō gaikokugo daigaku Ajia Afurika gengo bunka kenkyūjo.
31. Daniels, Christian, Yougeng Yang, and Fusaji Takeuchi, eds. 2003. *Kishū Myaozoku ringyō keiyaku monjo kaihen (1736–1950-nen)* [Old forestry contracts of the Miao in Guizhou, 1736–1950], vol. 3, F-0033. Tokyo: Tōkyō gaikokugo daigaku Ajia Afurika gengo bunka kenkyūjo.
32. Deng, Jianpeng, and Kai Qiu. 2013. Cong heyi dao qiangzhi: Qing zhi Minguo Qingshuijiang jiufen wenshu yanjiu [From consensus to enforcement: A study on disputes manuscripts in the Qing and Republican periods]. *Gansu zhengfa xueyuan xuebao* 126 (1): 25–35.
33. Du, Zhengzhen. 2014. Cong susong dang'an huidao qiyue huodong de xianchang—Yi wan Qing Min chu de Longquan sifa dang'an wei li [Reproduce the contracts activities through reading judicial archives: Taking the Longquan judicial archives in late Qing and early Republic of China as an example]. *Zhejiang shehui kexue* (1): 121.
34. Du, Zhengzhen, and Zhengqiang Wu. 2012. Difang susong zhong de qiyue yingyong yu qiyue guannian: Cong Longquan sifa dang'an wan Qing bufen kan guojia yu minjian de qiyue guize [Contract application and the concept of contract in local litigations: The national and civil rules of contract based on the Longquan judicial archives in the late Qing dynasty]. *Wenshi* (1): 207–225.
35. Duara, Prasenjit. 1990. Elites and the structures of authority in the villages of North China, 1900–1949. In *Chinese local elites and patterns of dominance*, ed. Joseph W. Esherick and Mary Backus Rankin, 266. Berkeley, Los Angeles, Oxford: University of California Press.
36. Fan, Yiding. 2017. *Gudai qiyue fa shi gao* [A history of ancient contract law], 252–256. Beijing: Falü chubanshe.
37. Farnsworth, E. Allan. 1970. Legal remedies for breach of contract. *Columbia Law Review* 70 (7): 1145–1216.
38. Fei, Xiaotong. 1985. *Xiangtu Zhongguo* [Rural China], reprinted ed., 6. Beijing: Shenghuo, dushu, xinzhi sanlian shudian.
39. Feinman, Jay M. 1984. Promissory estoppel and judicial method. *Harvard Law Review* 97 (3): 678–718.
40. Feinman, Jay M. 2000. Relational contract theory in context. *Northwestern University Law Review* 94 (3): 738–739.

41. Feng, Xuewei. 2013. Qiyue wenshu de weizao fangwei yu bianwei [Forgery, anti-counterfeiting, and identification of contract manuscripts]. *Fazhi yu shehui fazhan* (2): 133–140.
42. Feng, Xuewei. 2015. *Ming Qing qiyue de jiegou gongneng ji yiyi* [The structure, function, and meaning of contracts in the Ming-Qing eras], 94–109. Beijing: Falü chubanshe.
43. Fried, Charles. 2015. *Contract as promise: A theory of contractual obligation*, 2nd ed., ix. New York: Oxford University Press.
44. Gao, Lingyu. 2015. *Songdai maimai qiyue de falü xiaoli wenti yanjiu* [A study on the legal validity of contracts of sale in the Song dynasty], 126 ff. Wuhu: Anhui shifan daxue chubanshe.
45. Gilmore, Grant. 1995. *The death of contract*, 2nd ed. Columbus, Ohio: Ohio State University Press.
46. Goldsmith, Andrew E. 2003. The Void-for-Vagueness doctrine in the supreme court, revisited. *American Journal of Criminal Law* 30 (2): 279–314.
47. Habermas, Jürgen. 1992. *Faktizität und Geltung: Beiträge zur Diskurstheorie des Rechts und des demokratischen Rechtsstaats*, 138. Frankfurt am Main: Suhrkamp Verlag.
48. Hage, Jaap. 2016. What is a legal transaction?. In *Law as institutional normative order*, ed. Maksymilian Del Mar and Zenon Bankowski, 107. London and New York: Routledge.
49. Hamilton, Gary G., and Wang Zheng. 1992. *From the soil, the foundations of Chinese society: A translation of Fei Xiaotong's Xiangtu Zhongguo, with an Iitroduction and epilogue*, 43. Berkeley, Los Angeles, London: University of California Press.
50. Han, Wei. 2014. Zhongguo chuantong maimai zhidu jiqi dangdai jiazhi [Traditional institution of sale in China and its modern value]. *Yuelu faxue pinglun* 9: 206.
51. Hansen, Valerie. 1995. *Negotiating daily life in traditional China: How ordinary people used contracts, 600–1400*, 10, 28, 32, 54. New Haven and London: Yale University Press.
52. Hart, H. L. A. 2012. *The concept of law*, 3rd ed., 6. Oxford: Oxford University Press.
53. Hase, Patrick H. 2013. *Custom, land and livelihood in rural South China: The traditional land law of Hong Kong's new territories, 1750–1950*, 151. Hong Kong: Hong Kong University Press.
54. Hayes, James. 1985. Specialists and written materials in the village world. In *Popular culture in late imperial China*, ed. David Johnson, Andrew J. Nathan, and Evelyn S. Rawski, 87. Berkeley, Los Angeles, London: University of California Press.
55. He, Yumei. 2014. Qing dai Minguo shiqi Qiandongnan Wendou zhai de linye jingji xisu yanjiu [The research on the customs of forestry economy of Wendou Village in Qiandongnan during the Qing dynasty and the Republican era]. Master dissertation, Guangxi Normal University, 57.
56. Hegel, Georg Wilhelm Friedrich. 1986. *Grundlinien der Philosophie des Rechts oder Naturrecht und Staatswissenschaft im Grundrisse*, 152–157. Frankfurt am Main: Suhrkamp Verlag.
57. Hegel, Georg Wilhelm Friedrich. 2003. *Elements of the philosophy of right*. (trans. by H. B. Nisbet. 8th ed., ed. Allen W. Wood), 102–105. Cambridge: Cambridge University Press.
58. Henderson, Stanley D. 1969. Promissory estoppel and traditional contract doctrine. *The Yale Law Journal* 78 (3): 343–387.
59. Hessick, Carissa Byrne. 2016. *Johnson v. United States* and the future of the Void-for-Vagueness doctrine. *New York University Journal of Law and Liberty* 10 (1): 152–167.
60. Hofmann, Frank, Simone Wurster, Eyal Ron, and Moritz Böhmecke-Schwafert. 2017. The immutability concept of blockchains and benefits of early standardization. Paper presented at the 2017 ITU Kaleidoscope: Challenges for a data-driven society (ITU K), Nanjing, 1–8.
61. Hogg, Martin. 2013. Competing theories of contract: An emerging consensus? In *Commercial contract law: Transatlantic perspectives*, ed. Larry A. DiMatteo, Qi Zhou, Séverine Saintier, and Keith Rowley, 14–40. Cambridge: Cambridge University Press.
62. Holmes, Oliver Wendell. 1897. The path of the law. *Harvard Law Review* 10 (8): 462.
63. Hu, Tieqiu, and Siqi Chen. 2020. Yulin tuce zai diquan queren zhong de quanweixing yu kuangjiaxing—Yi *Tongzhi Lanxi yulin tuce* wei zhongxin de taolun [The authority and framework of yulin tuce in the confirmation of land rights—Discussion on 'Tongzhi Lanxi yulin tuce']. *Zhejiang shehui kexue* (1): 144–145.

64. Huang, Philip C.C. 2001. *Code, custom, and legal practice in China: The Qing and the republic compared*, 75–76. Stanford, California: Stanford University Press.
65. Huang, Jingbin, and Haiying Zhang. 2015. Chunhua yulin ce chutan [A preliminary study of the book of *Chunhua and yulin*]. *Guizhou daxue xuebao (shehui kexue ban)* 33 (2): 65–74.
66. Hume, David. 1896. *A Treatise of Human Nature*. ed. L.A. Selby-Bigge, 455–470. Oxford: The Clarendon Press.
67. Huo, Cunfu. 2008. Zhongguo gudai qiyue jingshen de neihan jiqi xiandai jiazhi—Jingwei qiyue, zunzhong qiyue yu dui qiyue de zhiduxing anpai zhi lijie [The connotation and its modern value of the contract spirits of ancient China]. *Jilin daxue shehui kexue xuebao* 48 (5): 57–64.
68. Idema, W.L. 1974. *Chinese vernacular fiction: The formative period*, L–LIII. Leiden: E. J. Brill.
69. Isett, Christopher. 2007. *State, peasant, and merchant in Qing Manchuria, 1644–1862*, 91. Standford, California: Standford University Press.
70. Jiang, Ming. 2018. *Guizhou Cengong qiyue wenshu yanjiu* [A study on contract manuscripts in Cengong, Guizhou], 171. Guiyang: Guizhou renmin chubanshe.
71. Jiang, Tiechu. 2012. Qushe zhijian: Qing dai minshi qiyue de quexian fenxi—Jiedu yipian Qing dai anyu biji [Dealing with trade-offs: An analysis of the shortcomings of the civil contract in the Qing dynasty—An interpretation of a note of judging in the Qing dynasty]. *Xibu faxue pinglun* (5): 1–6.
72. Jiang, Ming, Caimao Wu, and Chunjun Yang, eds. 2015. *Quyu shehui shi gailun* [General introduction to regional social history], 135–136. Chengdu: Xinan jiaotong daxue chubanshe.
73. Jin, Min. 2013. Mingtian shi 'haofou' haishi 'youwu'? Xianggang gaodeng fayuan 'Deng Guangyu tang an' shuping [Will tomorrow be 'good or not' or will there be tomorrow? A review of 'Tang Kwong Yu Tong case' in the High Court of the Hong Kong SAR]. *Zhongwai faxue* 25 (3): 571–582.
74. Jinping xian difangzhi bianzuan weiyuanhui, ed. 2011. *Jinping xianzhi 1991–2009* [Jinping County gazetteer 1991–2009]. vol. 2, 1263–1264. Beijing: Fangzhi chubanshe.
75. Jinping xian Hekou xiang renmin zhengfu, ed. 2010. *Hekou xiang zhi* [Hekou Sub-county gazetteer], 156. Jinping: Jinping xian Hekou xiang renmin zhengfu.
76. Johnson, D. H. N. 1950. Acquisitive prescription in international law. *British Year Book of International Law* 27: 341.
77. Kang, Caiyun. 2013. Gudai qiyue wenshu de zhongbaoren chengwei yuci yanbian yanjiu [The diachronic evolution of mediator appellation words in ancient contract documents]. Master dissertation, Shaanxi Normal University, 33–34.
78. Kato, Masanobu. 2012. *Suoyouquan de dansheng* [Birth of ownership rights]. (trans. Furong Zheng), 1–2. Beijing: Falü chubanshe.
79. Kent, H.S.K. 1954. The historical origins of the three-mile limit. *The American Journal of International Law* 48 (4): 537–553.
80. Kötz, Hein. 2017. *European contract law*. (trans. Gill Mertens and Tony Weir), 2nd ed., 57–58, 64–65. Oxford: Oxford University Press.
81. Lawson, F.H., and Bernard Rudden. 1982. *The law of property*. 2nd ed., 7. Oxford: Oxford University Press.
82. Li, Bin, ed. 2017. *Guizhou Qingshuijiang wenshu, Liping wenshu* [Guizhou Qingshui River Manuscripts, Manuscripts in Liping County], vol. 12, 93. Guiyang: Guizhou minzu chubanshe.
83. Li, Bo. 2014. Qing dai Qingshuijiang xiayou beiming zhong de shehui zhixu—Guizhou Tianzhu diqu beiming tianye diaocha [Social order reflected on the inscriptions in downstream Qingshui River areas in the Qing dynasty: A field investigation in Tianzhu County of Guizhou Proviinc]. *Yuanshengtai minzu wenhua xuekan* 6 (4): 56.
84. Li, Yongjun. 1998. Qiyue xiaoli de genyuan jiqi zhengdanghua shuoming lilun [Rationale of validity of contract and the theory of its justification]. *Bijiaofa yanjiu* (3): 225–256.
85. Li, Li. 2005. Qing dai minfa yujing zhong 'ye' de biaoda jiqi yiyi [The expression and meaning of 'ye' in Qing dynasty civil law]. *Lishi yanjiu* (4): 131–142.

86. Liang, Cong. 2008. *Qing dai Qingshuijiang xiayou cunzhai shehui de qiyue guifan yu zhixu* [Contractual norm and order in the village society of the lower reaches of Qingshui River in Qing China], 117–130. Beijing: Renmin chubanshe.
87. Liang, Zhiping. 1996. *Qing dai xiguanfa: Shehui yu guojia* [Customary law in the Qing: Society and state], 124. Beijing: Zhongguo zhengfa daxue chubanshe.
88. Liang, Qichao. [1922] 2017. *Zhongguo lishi yanjiu fa* [Research method for Chinese history], 239 ff. Nanchang: Jiangxi jiaoyu chubanshe.
89. Lin, Dongjie. 2012. Qing zhi Minguo nianjian Qingshuijiang qiyue wenshu liqi shijian jiaobu—Yi *Guizhou Wendou zhai Miaozu qiyue falü wenshu huibian: Jiang Yuanze jiacang qiyue wenshu* wei zhongxin de yanjiu [A reevaluation and making-up for the time of deed for the documents in Qingshuijiang region from the Qing dynasty to the Republic: A study of Guizhou Wendou Miao contract documents with the collected documents by Jiang Yuan-ze family as a case]. *Guizhou daxue xuebao (shehui kexue ban)* 30 (5): 65–66.
90. Lin, Qian. 2014. *Tudong sancun: Qing zhi Minguo yige Dongzu shanxiang de jingji yu shehui—Qingshuijiang Tianzhu wenshu yanjiu* [Three villages in Tudong: Economy and society of a mountain village of the Dong minority during the Qing and Republican eras—A study of Qingshui River (Tianzhu) manuscripts], 393. Chengdu: Bashu shushe.
91. Lin, Wen-kai. 2011. 'Ye ping qi guan'?: Qing dai Taiwan tudi yezhuquan yu susong wenhua de fenxi ['Deed owner, land owner?' Land property rights and litigation culture in Qing Taiwan]. *Taiwan shi yanjiu* 18 (2): 18–19.
92. Ling, Mengchu. [1632] 1992. *Er ke pai an jing qi* [Amazing tales: Second series], 199–208. Shanghai: Shanghai guji chubanshe.
93. Linzer, Peter. 1981. On the amorality of contract remedies—efficiency, equity, and the second restatement. *Columbia Law Review* 81 (1): 114–117.
94. Liu, Shigu. 2018. Qing dai neilu shuiyu yuye bulao zhixu de jianli jiqi yanbian—Yi Jiangxi Boyang huqu wei zhongxin [The establishment and evolution of the order of fishery in inland waters in the Qing dynasty—A study focused on the Boyang Lake area in Jiangxi]. *Jindaishi yanjiu* (3): 72–73.
95. Liu, Yonghua. 2017. Qing dai minzhong shizi wenti de zai renshi [Rethinking popular literacy in the Qing dynasty]. *Zhongguo shehui kexue pingjia* (2): 96–110.
96. Long, Denggao. 2012. *Diquan shichang yu ziyuan peizhi* [Land market and resource allocation], 170–176. Fuzhou: Fujian renmin chubanshe.
97. Long, Linglie. 2016. Minjian xiguan yu guanfu guifan hutong huren de fanben—Qing Guangxu shisi nian 'Peiliang shanlin tiantu guanye zhizhao' [A sample for the mutual recognition between civil customs and official regulations: A license in the fourteenth year of Guangxu]. In *Jinping wenshu: Zouxiang shijie de shaxiang jiyi* [Jinping manuscripts: The memories of Jinping County], ed. Linglie Long, 133–135. Beijing: Zhongguo wenhua chubanshe.
98. Long, Linglie. 2016. Yi zhi jiacang wenshu—Pingwei zuxian chuanyue bainian de shenghuo da zhihui [A contract from the family collection: The great wisdom of ancestors through a century]. In *Jinping wenshu: Zouxiang shijie de shaxiang jiyi* [Jinping manuscripts: The memories of Jinping County], ed. Linglie Long, 126–128. Beijing: Zhongguo wenhua chubanshe.
99. Long, Qijia, and Tongshou Fan, eds. 2003. *Guizhou sheng zhi wenwu zhi* [Guizhou province gazetteer of cultural relics], 335. Guiyang: Guizhou renmin chubanshe.
100. Luhmann, Niklas. 1991. *Soziale Systeme: Grundriß einer allgemeinen Theorie*, 4th ed., 148 ff. Frankfurt am Main: Suhrkamp.
101. Luhmann, Niklas. 1996. Quod omnes tangit: Remarks on Jürgen Habermas's legal theory. *Cardozo Law Review* 17: 883.
102. Luhmann, Niklas. 2014. *Vertrauen. Ein Mechanismus der Reduktion sozialer Komplexität*. 5th ed., 1–38. Konstanz und München: UVK Verlagsgesellschaft mbH.
103. Luo, Zhufeng, ed. 2015. *Hanyu da cidian* [Comprehensive Chinese word dictionary]. 23 vols. vol. 2(1), 290. Shanghai: Shanghai cishu chubanshe.

104. MacCormick, Neil. 2007. *Institutions of law: An essay in legal theory*, 11–74. New York: Oxford University Press.
105. Macneil, Ian Roderick. 1980. *The new social contract: An inquiry Into modern contractual relations*. New Haven and London: Yale University Press.
106. Massias, Henri, X. Serret Avila, and J.-J. Quisquater. 1999. Design of a secure timestamping service with minimal trust requirement. Paper presented at the 20th Symposium on Information Theory in the Benelux, 1.
107. Matsubara, Kentaro. 2011. Land registration and local society in Qing China: Taxation and property rights in mid-nineteenth century Guangdong. *International Journal of Asian Studies* 8 (2): 163–187.
108. Miaozu wenxueshi bianxiezu, ed. 1959. *Minjian wenxue ziliao, Qiandong Miaozu chuanshuo gushi* [Materials of folk literature, folk stories and legends of the Miao in Qiandong]. vol. 13, 150–153. Guiyang: Zhongguo zuojia xiehui Guiyang fenhui chouweihui.
109. Miaozu wenxueshi bianxiezu, ed. 1959. *Minjian wenxue ziliao, Qiandongnan Miaozu minjian gushi ji* [Materials of folk literature, a collection of folk stories of the Miao in Qiandongnan]. vol. 9, 77–80. Guiyang: Zhongguo zuojia xiehui Guiyang fenhui chouweihui.
110. Mielke, Katja, Conrad Schetter, and Andreas Wilde. 2011. Dimensions of Social Order: Empirical Fact, Analytical Framework and Boundary Concept. *ZEF Working Paper Series* (78): 4–7.
111. Nakamoto, Satoshi. 2008. Bitcoin: A peer-to-peer electronic cash system. Accessed 17 Mar 2020. https://bitcoin.org/bitcoin.pdf, 1–9.
112. Pan, Weijiang. 2018. Chaoda guimo moshengren shehui zhili: Zhongguo shehui fazhihua zhili de jiben yujing [The governance of a super-large-scale stranger society: The basic context of the governance by rule of law in Chinese society]. *Minzhu yu kexue* (2): 23–26.
113. Pan, Weijiang. 2018. Shuishi moshengren? [Who is the stranger?]. *Dushu* (8): 139–148.
114. Pan, Weijiang. 2019. Ruhe lijie Zhongguo de chaodaguimoxing [How to understand the super scale of China]. *Dushu* (5): 3–11.
115. Pan, Yi. 2017. *Rural welfare in China*, 35–36. Cham: Springer International Publishing AG.
116. Pan, Zhicheng, ed. 2014. *Qingjiang si an yanjiu* [Studies on the four cases in the Qingshui River region], vol. 3, 26. Guiyang: Guizhou minzu chubanshe.
117. Pan, Zhicheng. 2015. *Qing dai Qingshuijiang liuyu xiangcun shehui de jiufen yu zhixu yanjiu—Yi Qingshuijiang wenshu wei zhongxin* [A study on the disputes and orders of rural society in the Qingshui River Basin in the Qing dynasty—Evidence from the Qingshui River manuscripts], Chap. 5, Sect. 3. Guiyang: Law School of Guizhou Minzu University (unpublished).
118. Pan, Zhicheng, and Dahua Wu, eds. 2011. *Tudi guanxi ji qita shiwu wenshu* [Manuscripts on land relationship and other issues], vol. 1, 228. Guiyang: Guizhou minzu chubanshe.
119. Pan, Zhicheng, Dahua Wu, and Cong Liang, eds. 2012. *Linye jingying wenshu* [Manuscripts on forestry management]. vol. 2, 156–157. Guiyang: Guizhou minzu chubanshe.
120. Parsons, Talcott. 1962. Some fundamental categories of the theory of action: A general statement. In *Toward a general theory of action*, ed. Talcott Parsons and Edward A. Shils, 14–17. Cambridge, Massachusetts: Harvard University Press.
121. Peel, Edwin. 2015. *Treitel the law of contract*, 14th ed., 3-118 ff. London: Sweet & Maxwell Ltd.
122. Qian, Zongwu. 2014. Qingshuijiang wenshu yanjiu zhi huigu yu qianzhan [Recalling and prospecting the study of Qingshui River documents]. *Guizhou daxue xuebao (shehui kexue ban)* 32 (1): 89.
123. Qian Nanjing guomin zhengfu sifa xingzheng bu, ed. [1930] 2000. *Mingshi xiguan diaocha baogao lu* [Collection of reports of custom surveys on civil matters]. 2 vols. vol. 1, 357–358. Beijing: Zhongguo zhengfa daxue chubanshe.
124. Qin, Xiuqiang, and Bin Li, eds. 2016. *Qingshuijiang wenshu, Tianzhu gu beike kaoshi* [Qingshui River manuscripts, Transcription and annotation to ancient inscriptions in Tianzhu County]. 3 vols. Guiyang: Guizhou daxue chubanshe.

125. Qu, Jian. 2012. Qing zhonghouqi Qiandongnan Wendou zhai Miaozu dianzhi yanjiu [A treatise on the dian of the Miaos in Wendou Village of southeastern Guizhou in the mid and late Qing dynasty]. *Minjian fa* 11: 205.
126. Qu, Jian. 2013. Qing dai Wendou zhai zhongren zhidu [The zhongren system of Wendou Village in the Qing dynasty]. *Minjian fa* 12: 265–267.
127. Qu, Jian. 2015. Xintuo quanqiuhua: Falü xushu yu neizai lilu [The globalization of trusts: Legal narrative and its inner logic]. Master dissertation, Tsinghua University, 21–26.
128. Qu, Jian. 2018. Qingshuijiang linye qiyue zhong de caifaquan: Guifan jiqi shijian [Harvesting rights in forestry contracts of Qingshui River region: Norms and practices]. *Guizhou daxue xuebao (shehui kexue ban)* 36 (3): 53–57.
129. Radin, Margaret Jane. 2017. The deformation of contract in the information society. *Oxford Journal of Legal Studies* 37 (3): 509.
130. Rauchs, Michel, Andrew Glidden, Brian Gordon, Gina C. Pieters, Martino Recanatini, François Rostand, Kathryn Vagneur, and Bryan Zheng Zhang. 2018. *Distributed ledger technology systems: A conceptual framework*. Cambridge: Cambridge Centre for Alternative Finance, https://doi.org/10.2139/ssrn.3230013.
131. Rawski, Evelyn Sakakida. 1979. *Education and popular literacy in Ch'ing China*, 140. Ann Arbor: The University of Michigan Press.
132. Reyes, Carla L. 2016. Moving beyond bitcoin to an endogenous theory of decentralized ledger technology regulation: An initial proposal. *Villanova Law Review* 61 (1): 191.
133. Rousseau, Jean-Jacques. 1762. *Du Contrat Social; ou Principes du Droit Politique*, 9. Amsterdam: Marc—Michel Rey.
134. Rousseau, Jean-Jacques. 1999. *Discourse on political economy and the social contract*. (trans. Christopher Betts), 49. Oxford: Oxford University Press.
135. Sang, Benqian. 2004. Qiyue weihe bixu zunshou [Why contract must be kept]. *Fazhi yu shehui fazhan* 56 (2): 22–28.
136. Sayeed, Sarwar, and Hector Marco-Gisbert. 2019. Assessing blockchain consensus and security mechanisms against the 51% attack. *Applied Sciences* 9 (9): 1788–1805.
137. Schwartz, Alan, and Robert E. Scott. 2003. Contract theory and the limits of contract law. *The Yale Law Journal* 113 (3): 556 ff.
138. Shan, Honggen. 2017. *Jinping wenshu yu Qingshuijiang linye shihua* [Jinping manuscripts and the history of the forestry industry in the Qingshui River region], 107. Beijing: Zhongguo zhengfa daxue chubanshe.
139. Sharp, Malcolm P. 1941. Pacta sunt servanda. *Columbia Law Review* 41 (5): 783–798.
140. Shi, Jianyun. 2002. Jindai huabei tudi maimai de jige wenti [Several questions of the sale of land in modern northern China]. In *Xiangcun shehui wenhua yu quanli jiegou de bianqian—'Huabei xiangcun shi xueshu yantaohui' lunwenji* [Village social culture and the change of power structures—Proceedings of the conference for village history in northern China], ed. Xianming Wang and Weimin Guo, 129. Beijing: Renmin chubanshe.
141. Shi, Qigui. [1986] 2002. *Xiangxi Miaozu shidi diaocha baogao* [A report of field survey of the Miao in Xiangxi]. revised and enlarged ed., 165. Changsha: Hunan renmin chubanshe.
142. Smith, Roger J. 2015. *Property law: Cases and materials*, 6th ed., 7. Harlow: Pearson Education Limited.
143. Speidel, Richard E. 1982. The new spirit of contract. *Journal of Law and Commerce* 2 (2): 193–199.
144. Szonyi, Michael A., and Shanshan Peng. 2020. Song Yiming tan Ming dai richang zhengzhi yu 'Huanan xuepai' [Michael A. Szonyi on the everyday politics in the Ming dynasty and South China studies]. *Shanghai shuping* [Shanghai review of books]. Accessed 17 March 2020. https://www.thepaper.cn/newsDetail_forward_6068457.
145. Takeuchi, Fusaji. 2003. Narukami to nakan no aida—Shindai Kishū Myaozoku ringyō keiyaku bunsho ni miru nae zoku no shūzoku to funsō shori [Between divine judgment and lawsuit in court: Dispute resolution among the Miao people as seen in the forestry contracts in Qing Guizhou]. In *Kishū Myaozoku ringyō keiyaku monjo kaihen (1736–1950-nen)* [Old forestry contracts of the Miao in Guizhou, 1736–1950], ed. Christian Daniels, Yougeng Yang,

and Fusaji Takeuchi, 83–120. Tokyo: Tōkyō gaikokugo daigaku Ajia Afurika gengo bunka kenkyūjo.

146. Tepper, Pamela R. 2012. *The law of contracts and the uniform commercial code*, 2nd ed., 477. Delmar: Cengage Learning.
147. Terada, Hiroaki. 2012. Quanli yu yuanyi—Qing dai tingsong he minzhong de minshi fa zhixu [Rights and injustice—Civil justice and civil-law order of the Qing-dynasty people]. (trans. Yaxin Wang). In *Quanli yu yuanyi: Sitian haoming Zhongguo fashi lunji* [Rights and injustice: Hiroaki Terada's essays on Chinese legal history], ed. Hiroaki Terada, 215–220. Beijing: Qinghua daxue chubanshe.
148. Tianzhu xian minzu shiwu weiyuanhui, and Tianzhu xian wenhuaguan, eds. 1984. *Tianzhu minzu minjian wenxue* [Ethnic folk literature in Tianzhu County]. vol. 1., 38–42. Tianzhu: Tianzhu xian wenhuaguan.
149. Tuomela, Raimo. 2002. *The philosophy of social practices: A collective acceptance view*, 122 ff. Cambridge: Cambridge University Press.
150. Uchida, Takashi. 1990. *Keiyaku no saisei* [The rebirth of contract]. Tokyo: Kobundo.
151. Vanberg, Christoph. 2008. Why do people keep their promises? An experimental test of two explanations. *Econometrica* 76 (6): 1467–1480.
152. Walker, Wyndham L. 1945. Territorial waters: The cannon shot rule. *British year book of international law* 22: 210–231.
153. Walport, Mark. 2016. Distributed ledger technology: Beyond block chain. *UK Government Office for Science*. Accessed 21 April 2020. https://assets.publishing.service.gov.uk/government/uploads/system/uploads/attachment_data/file/492972/gs-16-1-distributed-ledger-technology.pdf, 1–87.
154. Wang, Kui, ed. c. 2017. *Jinping wenshu jiyi duben* [A memorial reader of Jinping manuscripts], 102–103. Jinping: Jinping County Archives.
155. Wang, Fengmei, and Yonglun Zhao. 2013. Qingshuijiang wenshu shuxie chengshi de zongzu xing tantao—Yi Tianzhu xian Gaoniang zhen Diliang cun qiyue wenshu weili [A probe into the patriarchal clans from the writing style in the Qingshui River manuscripts: Based on Diliang Village, Gaoniang Town in Tianzhu County]. *Guizhou daxue xuebao (shehui kexue ban)* 31 (4): 68.
156. Wang, Hao, Shuyan Wei, Bo-sin Tang, Junhua Chen, and Wenbin Li. 2018. A Comparative Study on Registration System of Real Estate between Hong Kong and Mainland China. *Property Management* 36 (1): 5–19.
157. Wang, Shengjun. 2014. Cong fuhaoxue kan Qingshuijiang qiyue wenshu beihou de fengsu bianqian [The changes of customs behind the Qingshui River contract manuscripts from the perspective of semiology]. In *Tansuo Qingshuijiang wenming de zongji—Qingshuijiang wenshu yu zhongguo difang shehui guoji xueshu yantaohui lunwenji* [Exploring the trace of Qingshui River civilization—Proceedings of the international symposium on the Qingshui River manuscripts and Chinese local society], ed. Xinmin Zhang, 379. Chengdu: Bashu shushe.
158. Wang, Zongxun. 2009. *Wendou: Kan de jian lishi de cunzhai* [Wendou: A village with visible history], 102. Guiyang: Guizhou renmin chubanshe.
159. Wang, Zongxun. 2013. *Qingshuijiang lishi wenhua tanwei* [Studies on the historical culture of the Qingshui River region], 211–213. Kunming: Yunnan meishu chubanshe.
160. Wang, Zongxun. 2015. Jiachi siheyuan wenshu zongshu [A summarized description on Jiachi courtyard instruments]. *Guizhou daxue xuebao (shehui kexue ban)* 33 (5): 87.
161. Wang, Zongxun. 2015. *Xunshi yiluo de jiyi: Jinping wenshu zhengji shouji* [Finding the lost memories: A diary of collecting the Jinping manuscripts], 63. Guangzhou: Shijie tushu chuban Guangdong youxian gongsi.
162. Wang, Zongxun, and Junchang Yang. 2006. Qing dai Jinping linqu tudi suoyouzhi xingshi he tudi qiyue guanxi [Land ownership form and land contract relationship in Jinping forest area in the Qing dynasty]. In *Renkou, shehui, fazhi yanjiu* [Demographic, social, and legal studies], ed. Shiyu Li, 399. Beijing: Zhongguo minzhu fazhi chubanshe.

163. Weber, Max. 1922. Die drei reinen Typen der legitimen Herrschaft. *Preussische Jahrbücher* 187 (1): 1–12.
164. Wehberg, Hans. 1959. Pacta Sunt Servanda. *The American Journal of International Law* 53 (4): 755–786.
165. Werbach, Kevin. 2018. *The Blockchain and the New Architecture of Trust*, 27. Cambridge, Massachusetts/London, England: The MIT Press.
166. Werbach, Kevin. 2018. Trust, but verify: Why the blockchain needs the law. *Berkeley Technology Law Journal* 33: 487.
167. Williams, Idongesit. 2020. *Cross-industry use of blockchain technology and opportunities for the future*, 40. Hershey, PA: IGI Global.
168. Wu, Caimao. 2014. Lijiang, mingshen yu mingguan: Minjian wenxian suo jian Ming Qing Qiandongnan jiufen jiejue jizhi de duoyuanhua yanjiu [Arbitration, proceeding to the gods, and complaint to the official: Dispute resolution from the local historical documents in Qiandongnan area in the Ming and Qing dynasties]. *Zhongguo shehui lishi pinglun* 15: 269–289.
169. Wu, Caimao. 2016. Ming dai yilai Qingshuijiang wenshu shuxie geshi de bianhua yu minzhong xiguan de bianqian [The changes of the writing forms of Qingshui River manuscripts and the transition of popular customs since the Ming dynasty]. *Xinan daxue xuebao (shehui kexue ban)* 42 (4): 185.
170. Wu, Dahua. 2013. *Qian fa tanyuan* [A study on the origin of laws in Guizhou], 215–216. Guiyang: Guizhou renmin chubanshe.
171. Wu, Fang. 2010. Lun Qingshuijiang wenshu zhong de wu zhongren xianxiang [On the phenomenon of not having middlemen in the Qingshui River manuscripts]. Bachelor dissertation, Kaili University, 1–4.
172. Wu, Shengjun. 2020. Qingshuijiang liuyu rengong yinglin jiufen jiqi jiejue jizhi—Yi Ming Qing yilai de qiyue wenshu wei zhongxin de kaocha [Dispute of artificial forest management in the Qingshui River Basin and its solution mechanism—Investigation basing on contracts since the Ming and Qing dynasties]. *Zhongyang minzu daxue xuebao (zhexue shehui kexue ban)* 47 (1): 126–134.
173. Wu, Xiangxiang, ed. [1923] 1962. *Zhongguo minshi xiguan daquan* [A compendium of Chinese popular customs]. Taipei: Wenxing shudian.
174. Xiao, Guanghui. 2016. *Falixue zhuanti yanjiu* [Research on the special issues of jurisprudence], 110–125. Shanghai: Shanghai shehui kexue chubanshe.
175. Xu, Bin. 2016. Qingshuijiang wenshu zhong de 'zhizhao' yanjiu [A study on the 'license' in the Qingshui River manuscripts]. *Guizhou daxue xuebao (shehui kexue ban)* 34 (1): 120–129.
176. Xu, Xiaoguang. 2014. *Qingshuijiang liuyu chuantong linye guize de shengtai renleixue jiedu* [An explanation of ecological anthropology on the traditional forestry rules in the Qingshui River Basin]. 183–184. Beijing: Zhishi chanquan chubanshe.
177. Xu, Xiaoguang. 2015. Qingshuijiang qiyue wenshu jiqi tezheng [Contract manuscripts in the Qingshui River region and their characteristics]. *Guangming ribao* (Beijing), October 15.
178. Xu, Xiaoguang. 2018. *Qingshuijiang liuyu chuantong maoyi guize yu shangye wenhua yanjiu* [Study of traditional trade rules and commercial culture of the Qingshui River Basin], 201. Beijing: Shehui kexue wenxian chubanshe.
179. Xu, Yi, and Bas van Leeuwen. 2013. 19 shiji Zhongguo dazhong shizilü de zai gusuan [A re-estimation of mass literacy in China in the 19th century]. *Qing shi luncong* (1): 240–247.
180. Xue, Yunsheng. 1970. *Duli cunyi chongkanben* [Doubts remaining after perusing the substatutes: A reprinted and annotated version]. ed. Jingjia Huang, 277. Taipei: Chengwen chubanshe.
181. Yan, Bao, ed. 1981. *Miaozu minjian gushi xuan* [A selection of folk stories of the Miao], 226–229. Shanghai: Shanghai wenyi chubanshe.
182. Yan, Qiyan. 2017. Qingshuijiang liuyu linye beike de xiaoli jichu [Foundation of the effectiveness of the forestry inscription in the Qingshui River Basin]. In *Jinping wenshu yu fawenhua yanjiu* [Jinping manuscripts and the studies of legal culture], ed. Qicai Gao and Kui Wang, 19. Beijing: Zhongguo zhengfa daxue chubanshe.

183. Yang, Guozhen. 2009. *Ming Qing tudi qiyue wenshu yanjiu (xiudingban)* [On land-related contracts in the Ming-Qing period]. revised ed., 17. Beijing: Zhongguo renmin daxue chubanshe.
184. Ye, Congcong, Guoqiang Li, Hongming Cai, Yonggen Gu, and Akira Fukuda. 2018. Analysis of Security in Blockchain: Case Study in 51%-Attack Detecting. Paper presented at the 2018 5th International Conference on Dependable Systems and Their Applications (DSA), Dalian, 15–24.
185. Yuan, Yong, and Feiyue Wang. 2019. *Qukuailian lilun yu fangfa* [Blockchain: Theory and method]. Beijing: Qinghua daxue chubanshe.
186. Zelin, Madeleine. 2005. *The merchants of zigong: Industrial entrepreneurship in early modern China*, 27–28. New York: Columbia University Press.
187. Zelin, Madeleine. 2019. A deep history of Chinese shareholding. *Law and History Review* 37 (2): 325–351.
188. Zelin, Madeleine. 1994. Merchant dispute mediation in twentieth-century Zigong, Sichuan. In *Civil law in Qing and Republican China*, ed. Kathryn Bernhardt and Philip C.C. Huang, 252. Stanford, Calif.: Stanford University Press.
189. Zelin, Madeleine. 2004. A critique of rights of property in prewar China. In *Contract and property in early modern China*, ed. Madeleine Zelin, Jonathan K. Ocko, and Robert Gardella, 25–26. Stanford: Stanford University Press.
190. Zelin, Madeleine, Jonathan Ocko, and Robert Gardella. 2004. Introduction. In *Contract and property in early modern China*, ed. Madeleine Zelin, Jonathan K. Ocko, and Robert Gardella, 13. Stanford: Stanford University Press.
191. Zhang, Guanghong. 2017. Mingshen yu mingguan: Qing dai Qingshuijiang liuyu minjian jiufen duoyuan jiejue jizhi shitan [Appealing to the gods or to the court: The multiple mechanisms of civil dispute settlement in the Qingshui River Basin in the Qing dynasty]. *Guizhou daxue xuebao (shehui kexue ban)* 35 (2): 25–34.
192. Zhang, Hengshan. 2002. Lun caichan suoyouquan de biyaoxing ji zhengdangxing yiju [On the justification and necessity of ownership]. *Qinghua fazhi lunheng* 2: 161–162.
193. Zhang, Honglin. 2012. *Qing dai Sichuan yanfa yanjiu* [A study on salt laws of Sichuan in the Qing dynasty], 77. Beijing: Zhongguo zhengfa daxue chubanshe.
194. Zhang, Wuwei. [1813] 2005. *Weinengxin lu* [A record on not being able to trust oneself]. Reprinted in *Lidai panli pandu* [Historical collection of judgments and judicial documents]. ed. Yifan Yang and Lizhi Xu, 516–517. Beijing: Zhongguo shehui kexue chubanshe.
195. Zhang, Honglin, ed. 2018. *Zhongguo chuantong falü wenhua* [Chinese traditional legal culture]. 145. Guangzhou: Huanan ligong daxue chubanshe.
196. Zhang, Xiaolin. 2000. *Qing dai Beijing chengqu fangqi yanjiu* [A study of real estate sale contracts in the city of Beijing in the Qing dynasty]. Beijing: Zhongguo shehui kexue chubanshe.
197. Zhang, Xinmin, ed. 2014. *Tianzhu wenshu* [Tianzhu manuscripts]. vol. 1(9), 155. Nanjing: Jiangsu renmin chubanshe.
198. Zhang, Yingqiang. 2006. *Mucai zhi liudong: Qing dai Qingshuijiang xiayou diqu de shichang, quanli yu shehui* [The wood flow: Market, power, and society in the downstream sections of Qingshui River in the Qing dynasty], 300. Beijing: Shenghuo, dushu, xinzhi sanlianshudian.
199. Zhang, Jiyuan, Xuehua Meng, and Mengyi Wang. 2013. Zuqun bianyuan didai de Qingshuijiang wenshu diaocha yu yanjiu—Yi Jinping xian Miaogeng cunluo wei kaocha duixiang [A survey of the Qingshui River manuscripts in clan margins: A case study of Miaogeng Village of Jinping County]. *Yuanshengtai minzu wenhua xuekan* 5 (1). 40.
200. Zhang, Yingqiang, and Zongxun Wang, eds. 2007. *Qingshuijiang wenshu* [Qingshui River manuscripts]. vol. 1(13), 39. Guilin: Guangxi shifan daxue chubanshe.
201. Zhang, Yingqiang, and Zongxun Wang, eds. 2007. *Qingshuijiang wenshu* [Qingshui River manuscripts]. vol. 1(12), 246. Guilin: Guangxi shifan daxue chubanshe.
202. Zhang, Yingqiang, and Zongxun Wang, eds. 2007. *Qingshuijiang wenshu* [Qingshui River manuscripts]. vol. 1(1), 104. Guilin: Guangxi shifan daxue chubanshe.

203. Zhang, Yingqiang, and Zongxun Wang, eds. 2007. *Qingshuijiang wenshu* [Qingshui River manuscripts]. vol. 1(8), 273. Guilin: Guangxi shifan daxue chubanshe.
204. Zhang, Yingqiang, and Zongxun Wang, eds. 2011. *Qingshuijiang wenshu* [Qingshui River manuscripts]. vol. 3(8), 42. Guilin: Guangxi shifan daxue chubanshe.
205. Zhang, Yingqiang, and Zongxun Wang, eds. 2011. *Qingshuijiang wenshu* [Qingshui River manuscripts]. vol. 3(7), 228. Guilin: Guangxi shifan daxue chubanshe.
206. Zhang, Yingqiang, and Zongxun Wang, eds. 2011. *Qingshuijiang wenshu* [Qingshui River manuscripts]. vol. 3(3), 456, 463, 398. Guilin: Guangxi shifan daxue chubanshe.
207. Zhang, Yingqiang, and Zongxun Wang, eds. 2011. *Qingshuijiang wenshu* [Qingshui River manuscripts]. vol. 3(9), 338. Guilin: Guangxi shifan daxue chubanshe.
208. Zhang, Yingqiang, and Zongxun Wang, eds. 2011. *Qingshuijiang wenshu* [Qingshui River manuscripts]. vol. 3(10). Guilin: Guangxi shifan daxue chubanshe.
209. Zhao, Siyuan. 2015. 19 shiji Huizhou xiangcun de tudi shichang, xinyong jizhi yu guanxi wangluo [Land market, credit mechanism, and relational network in Huizhou villages during the nineteenth century]. *Jindaishi yanjiu* (4): 95.
210. Zhao, Siyuan, and Zhiwei Liu. 2020. Zai huji fushui zhidu yu diquan shichang yunzuo zhong renshi Ming Qing tudi zhidu [Rethinking the land ownership in the Ming and Qing dynasties in the perspectives of land market and the land tax system]. *Zhongguo shehui kexue* (1): 195–196.
211. Zheng, Yefu. 2001. *Xinren lun* [On trust], 114. Beijing: Zhongguo guangbo dianshi chubanshe.
212. Zhong, Yiwei. 2018. Qing zhi Min chu Guizhou shaoshu minzu de minshi quanli yanjiu—Yi Qingshuijiang jiufen wenshu wei shijiao [The study on the civil rights of the minority nationalities in Guizhou—From the perspective of the Qingshui River dispute instruments]. Doctoral dissertation, Zhongnan University of Economics and Law.
213. Zhong, Yiwei. 2020. Zhongguo chuantong qiyue zhong de 'qiyue ziyou' yu 'zhuti pingdeng'—Yi Qingshuijiang wenshu wei shijiao ['Freedom of contract' and 'equality of subject' in Chinese traditional contracts—From the perspective of the Qingshui River instruments]. *Zhengfa luncong* (1): 39, 43.
214. Zhongguo diyi lishi dang'an guan, and Zhongguo shehui kexue yuan lishi yanjiusuo. 1988. *Qing dai tudi zhanyou guanxi yu diannong kangzu douzheng* [Landownership relations and tenant rent resistance struggles in the Qing dynasty]. 2 vols. vol. 1, 454–456. Beijing: Zhonghua shuju.
215. Zhu, Yingui. 2013. Cong Guizhou Qingshuijiang wenshu kan jindai Zhongguo de diquan zhuanyi [The transfer of land ownership in contemporary China reflected in Qingshuijiang documents in Guizhou]. *Guizhou daxue xuebao (shehui kexue ban)* 31 (6): 70–74.
216. Zhu, Liyu, and Dan Su. 2017. Qingshuijiang wenshu de qiyue jingshen jiqi chuancheng yu fazhan—Yi Jinping Huazhai cun weili [The spirit of contract of the Qingshui River manucripts and its inheritance and development: Taking Huazhai Village, Jinping County as an example]. In *Jinping wenshu yu fawenhua yanjiu* [Jinping manuscripts and the studies of legal culture], ed. Qicai Gao and Kui Wang, 393–406. Beijing: Zhongguo zhengfa daxue chubanshe.

Chapter 6
Conclusion

Having thoroughly analyzed the aspects of the contract as a practical device and as a social system, the precondition of the stories of wealth in the Qingshui River region during the Qing dynasty, including but not limited to Jiang Shichao, have been explained: the social order which provides predictability and regularity for economic prosperity in the region could be formed and maintained through contracts even in the condition of relatively weak influence on the part of governmental and legal authorities in this frontier area. In this sense, the notion of "a contract society," as tentatively proposed in response to Maine's conception, can now be used to describe and explain this specific area.

The rediscovered notion of contracts in the given context stands as the foundation of further theoretical construction and has been examined with respect to three aspects, namely materiality, formality, and substantiality. Firstly, the requirement of materiality is seen by the embodiment of the contract text in certain valid material carriers, among which paper was of course the most prevalent. Oral agreements are excluded from this aspect since their text has not been recorded physically. Moreover, only original copies were valid; duplicates or drafts, which were commonly seen, are deemed invalid versions, and thus cannot be recognized as contracts from the perspective of materiality. Secondly, the formality of a contract lies not only in its internal/textual but also its external/ritual aspects. The latter was embedded in and required by the customs of contracting and can be seen through its textual reflections in contracts. The former finds its expression particularly in the specialized language and formulaic expressions, with the noteworthy beginning formula of *li* acting as a feasible and highly efficient short-cut indicator in testing the formality of a contract. Thirdly, the substantiality of a contract was examined by determining whether its content is about to establish or confirm certain kinds of Hohfeldian jural, i.e. relating to rights and obligations, relations among parties. In addition, a connection between content and form has been shown through the implication of the character *li*: drawing up a contract substantially means to establish or confirm a jural relation, and "to establish or confirm" is exactly the meaning of *li* which is most relevant in the previously noted formula at the beginning of a contract form. Ultimately, these three aspects of a

J. Qu, *Social Order through Contracts*,
https://doi.org/10.1007/978-981-33-4947-6_6

contract have been organized by a tripartite structure of contracts, which is applicable especially in identifying those borderline cases of contracts.

After systematically explaining the various aspects of the contract as a practical device, the unfolding of the contract in its context is expounded at length over a number of chapters regarding middlemen, scribes, and its functioning mechanism. Apart from the details previously presented, a few summative points need to be specifically pointed out here.

Firstly, a decontextualized approach has been chosen for this study in analyzing the phenomena of middlemen and scribes, who are portrayed as indispensable and fundamental figures within the internal structure of contracts, and with an emphasis throughout on their contractual identities rather than social identities. Thus, their appearance in contracts should not be described as the personalization of contracts but the contractualization of persons—this underscores a transition from facts of life to institutional(ized) facts. Consequently, the results presented by this study not only highlight the institutional aspects of the contract that have been neglected for a long time but also provide a basis for the subsequent construction of the explanatory theory of the contract system. To avoid ambiguity, a contextualized study of the contract needs a decontextualized basis to determine whom the context is interacting with.

Secondly, throughout the discussion of middlemen and scribes, a constant interest is the extent of their substantial participation in the contract. Unlike its modern and Western counterparts, the contract in the Qingshui River region takes the participation of the middleman and the scribe as third parties in contract activities as constituted requisites, rather than merely having them assume the role of helpers or intermediate service providers. The investigation of the middleman reveals his surprising "power," which is sufficient to determine the contract's fundamental content. Also, while examining the activities of the long-neglected scribes, one notices that the scribe remarkably obtained the same status as the middleman in the Qingshui River region. In response to concerns over their contractual status, the institutional facts about the two contractual figures have been discussed in detail. While clarifying these details, their connection with society, as the wider context of the contractual figures, began to emerge. The interaction between the individual and social domains primarily mirrors the understanding that middlemen and scribes joined the contract as representatives of institutionalized social facts.

Thirdly, through the interaction between the contract and its social context, especially with the middleman and scribe as core links, the functioning mechanism of contracts in the society was revealed and reconstructed. The successful running of the contract as a system lies in its capability to integrate various social elements, providing a suitable field for the expression of social opinions and the competition of social forces. The reason why this field was suitable is that it was noncentral and therefore could not be controlled by any party. Consequently, no matter what the final result of the cooperation or contest was, it was necessary for every party to settle the result in a contract as proof of rightfulness. In this sense, a contract should be perceived as a platform for presentation and a database for information storage in society. A complete account of the contract requires the clarification of the platform's own mechanism as well as an analysis of the social facts it stores and presents.

Finally, after structuring and conceptualizing the findings, the explanatory theory provided in this study laid more emphases on the technical, rather than the social or cultural, aspects. When examining the functioning mechanism of contracts in the society, the notion of recognition was underscored as the most basic moral principle in the justification of the effectiveness of contracts. Nonetheless, the exploration of the functioning mechanism does not stop here, but leads to further investigation of the technical and morally irrelevant trust network of contracts. This ensures that the contract is tamper-resistant and finally connects the successful operation of contracts with their context in terms of both time and social space. Thus, as a social system, the contract offers a trustworthy rightfulness/legitimacy mechanism, persistently storing, conveying, and, when necessary, presenting the untampered recognition originally collected from various contract participants and related societal members through the facilitation of middlemen and scribes.

This complex mechanism of contract rightfulness, which re-organizes all related elements of the contract and its social context, can be simplified as well as conceptualized as rooted in the "technicalization of morality." Admittedly, a minimum and most basic moral principle regarding contract compliance did exist in the social context. But obviously, if having morality was enough for the society, no contract would be needed—the repayment of debts could be based on moral requirements in a law-free situation, but its realization would be rather difficult in the absence of a loan contract (and the publicity which the contract brings). As it is, what a contract offers was not merely a moral obligation but a technicalized or contractualized version, and the sophisticated designs of the contract as a device and a system both play a pivotal role in the process of technicalization. The explicit and persistent presentation (publicity in space and time) of undeniable facts (i.e. those which are guaranteed to be authentic and unable to be tampered with) would definitively prove the existence and greatly promote the fulfillment of moral obligations. In this sense, although it is difficult to distinguish the roles played by the morality and its technicalization in the effectiveness system, the importance of the latter needs to be particularly emphasized. Further, in the context of the Qingshui River region, those "contractual techniques" that helped in the technicalization of a contract were specifically offered by the middleman (especially introducers and arbitrators) and the scribe (literate and learned in contract knowledge). The additional question whether the technology itself will become a source of legitimacy/rightfulness is worthy of further discussion, though it is not covered within the scope of this study.

In sum, the three basic questions related to the contract, what it was and how and why it worked, have been answered at length. Put succinctly, firstly, a contract is a piece of paper (or a stone tablet, a piece of cloth, etc.) that describes the establishment or/and confirmation of rights and obligations between the parties in a certain form. Secondly, the operation of the contract in society depends on the two key figures of the middleman and the scribe. The former is a complex group in which middlemen can assume four roles (serving as introducers, witnesses, guarantors, and mediators) at two levels (the primary and secondary) in the contract. The long-ignored latter figure is placed at an equally important position as the middleman through the investigation of the degree of their substantial participation in the contract. The participation of the two does not merely facilitate contract activities but acts as the foundation for the workings of contracts in society. Thirdly, the functioning and rightfulness mechanism of contracts in the specific society were theorized by the perception that the contract acts as a method for collecting, storing, and presenting the *tamper-resistant provable recognition*. Through the operation of this mechanism, the social order, in terms of not only fields of civil and commercial matters but also public issues, could be constructed by contracts in the region. Finally, the impact of the regional characteristics, its advantages and limitations, on the theory raised by this study has also been examined.

As the first Western-language monograph that is entirely devoted to the study of the Qingshui River manuscripts, this research introduces its readers to the completely non-stereotypical socio-legal landscape in a frontier area of southwest China during late imperial times. The main concern for historians may be the historical and regional facts of the frontier villages presented and interpreted in this study, which are not yet so widely known, while, for researchers of comparative contract law, this study can provide a novel and empirical interpretation of the supposedly well-known contract device, which in actual practice can be more complex and versatile than it seems. This may also present materials with which to expand the boundaries of the notion of contracts in general. For the study of the Qingshui River manuscripts, this work has attempted to re-organize and systematize the various empirical facts concerning the contract and its social context, thereby proposing the long-noted scholarly desideratum of an integrated theoretical explanatory framework of contracts in the area.

Finally, for those people who lived in the Qingshui River region over many generations, this academic exercise offers an interpretive written account of their social and legal life in history from a devoted and well-treated "outsider" in terms of both time and space. For construction is often contained in interpretation.

Appendix
A List of the Qingshui River Manuscripts

Archives Consulted and Manuscripts Collected Through Fieldwork

Jinping County Archives, Qiandongnan Miao and Dong Autonomous Prefecture, Guizhou

The First Historical Archives of China, Beijing

National Science Library, Chinese Academy of Sciences (NSLC), Beijing

"Contract manuscripts from Fan Ermei's family collection," collected and edited by Qu Jian, March 2011, Wendou Village, Guizhou

"Manuscripts collected from Miaogeng Village," edited by Zhang Jiyuan, July–August 2011, Miaogeng Village, Guizhou

"Contract manuscripts from Jiang Tingqing's family collection," collected and edited by Qu Jian, September 2015, Wendou Village, Guizhou

"Manuscripts collected from Wendou Village (1)," collected by Prof. Xie Hui, August 2002, Wendou Village, Guizhou

"Manuscripts collected from Wendou Village (2)," collected by Prof. Chen Jinquan, Prof. Pan Zhicheng, etc., 2004, Wendou Village, Guizhou

Publications (142 Volumes)

[A.1–3] Daniels, Christian, Yang Yougeng, and Takeuchi Fusaji (eds.). 2001, 2002, 2003. *Kishū Myaozoku ringyō keiyaku monjo kaihen (1736–1950-nen)* [Old forestry

J. Qu, *Social Order through Contracts*,
https://doi.org/10.1007/978-981-33-4947-6

contracts of the Miao in Guizhou, 1736–1950] Vol. 1, 2, 3. Tokyo: Tōkyō gaikokugo daigaku Ajia Afurika gengo bunka kenkyūjo.

[B.1] Hongyang, Luo. 2004. Guizhou Jinping linqi jingxuan [A selection of forestry contracts in Jinping, Guizhou]. *Minjian fa* 3 (1): 509–572.

[B.2] Hui, Xie, and Luo Hongyang. 2005. Guizhou Jinping linqi tianqi jingxuan [A selection of forestry contracts and land contracts in Jinping, Guizhou]. *Minjian fa* 4 (1): 554–567.

[C.1–3] Zhang, Yingqiang and Wang Zongxun. (eds.). 2007, 2009, 2011. *Qingshuijiang wenshu* [Qingshui River manuscripts], vol. 1 (1–13), 2 (1–10), 3(1–10). Guilin: Guangxi shifan daxue chubanshe.

[D.1] Chen, Jinquan, and Du Wanhua (eds.). 2008. *Guizhou Wendouzhai Miaozu qiyue falü wenshu huibian—Jiang Yuanze jiacang qiyue wenshu* [The compilation of contractual and legal manuscripts of the Miao from Wendou Village, Guizhou—Manuscripts from Jiang Yuanze's family collection]. Beijing: Renmin chubanshe.

[D.2] Chen, Jinquan, and Du Wanhua (eds.). 2015. *Guizhou Wendouzhai Miaozu qiyue falü wenshu huibian—Jiang Qigui jiacang qiyue wenshu* [The compilation of contractual and legal manuscripts of the Miao from Wendou Village, Guizhou—Manuscripts from Jiang Qigui's family collection]. Beijing: Renmin chubanshe.

[D.3] Chen, Jinquan, and Guo Liang (eds.). 2017. *Guizhou Wendouzhai Miaozu qiyue falü wenshu huibian—Yi Zunfa Jiang Qicheng deng jiacang susong wenshu* [The compilation of contractual and legal manuscripts of the Miao from Wendou Village, Guizhou—Litigation manuscripts from family collections of Yi Zunfa, Jiang Qicheng, etc.]. Beijing: Renmin chubanshe.

[E.1] Pan, Zhicheng, and Wu Dahua (eds.). 2011. *Tudi guanxi ji qita shiwu wenshu* [Manuscripts on land relationship and other issues], vol. 1, ed. Wu Dahua. Qingshuijiang wenshu yanjiu congshu [Series of the study of the Qingshui River Manuscripts]. Guiyang: Guizhou minzu chubanshe.

[E.2] Pan, Zhicheng, Wu Dahua, and Liang Cong (eds.). 2012. *Linye jingying wenshu* [Manuscripts on forestry management], vol. 2, ed. Wu Dahua. Qingshuijiang wenshu yanjiu congshu [Series of the study of the Qingshui River Manuscripts] Guiyang: Guizhou minzu chubanshe.

[E.3] Pan, Zhicheng, Wu Dahua, and Liang Cong (eds.). 2014. *Qingjiang si an yanjiu* [Studies on the four cases in the Qingshui River region], vol. 3, ed. Wu Dahua. Qingshuijiang wenshu yanjiu congshu [Series of the study of the Qingshui River Manuscripts] Guiyang: Guizhou minzu chubanshe.

[F.1] Cong, Gao, and Tan Hongpei (eds.). 2013. *Guizhou Qingshuijiang liuyu Ming Qing tusi qiyue wenshu, Jiunan pian* [Tusi contract manuscripts in the Qingshui River Basin of Guizhou during the Ming-Qing eras, Jiunan volume]. Beijing: Minzu chubanshe.

[F.2] Cong, Gao, and Tan Hongpei (eds.). 2014. *Guizhou Qingshuijiang liuyu Ming Qing tusi qiyue wenshu, Liangzhai pian* [Tusi contract manuscripts in the Qingshui River Basin of Guizhou during the Ming-Qing eras, Liangzhai volume]. Beijing: Minzu chubanshe.

[G.1] Zhang, Xinmin. (ed.). 2014. *Tianzhu wenshu* [Tianzhu manuscripts], vol. 1, 1–22. Nanjing: Jiangsu renmin chubanshe.

[H.1–4] Wang, Zongxun (ed.). 2015. *Jiachi siheyuan wenshu kaoshi* [Collection and annotation of the Jiachi siheyuan manuscripts], vol. 1–4. Guiyang: Guizhou minzu chubanshe.

[I.1–2] An, Zunhua, and Zhicheng Pan. (eds.). 2016. *Tudi qiyue wenshu jiaoshi* [Collation and annotation of land-related contract manuscripts], vol. 1–2. Guiyang: Guizhou minzu chubanshe.

[J.1] Long, Zejiang, Anhui Fu, and Hongbo Chen. (eds.). 2016. *Jiuzhai Dongzu baojia tuanlian dang'an* [Baojia and tuanlian documents of the Dong people in Jiuzhai]. Guiyang: Guizhou daxue chubanshe.

[K.1–22] Li, Bin. (ed.). 2017. *Guizhou Qingshuijiang wenshu, Liping wenshu* [Guizhou Qingshui River Manuscripts, Manuscripts in Liping County], vol. 1–22. Guiyang: Guizhou minzu chubanshe.

[L.1–3] Guizhou sheng dang'an guan, Qiandongnan zhou dang'an guan, and Sansui xian dang'an guan. (eds.). 2016, 2017, 2019. *Guizhou Qingshuijiang wenshu, Sansui juan* [Qingshui River manuscripts, Jianhe County volume], vol. 1 (1–5), 2 (6–10), 3 (11–15). Guiyang: Guizhou renmin chubanshe.

[L.4–6] Guizhou sheng dang'an guan, Qiandongnan zhou dang'an guan, and Liping xian dang'an guan. (eds.). 2016, 2017, 2018. *Guizhou Qingshuijiang wenshu, Liping juan* [Qingshui River manuscripts, Liping County volume], vol. 1 (1–5), 2 (6–10), 3 (11–15). Guiyang: Guizhou renmin chubanshe.

[L.7] Guizhou sheng dang'an guan, Qiandongnan zhou dang'an guan, and Jianhe xian dang'an guan. (eds.). 2017. *Guizhou Qingshuijiang wenshu, Jianhe juan* [Qingshui River manuscripts, Jianhe County volume], vol. 1 (1–5). Guiyang: Guizhou renmin chubanshe.

[L.8] Guizhou sheng dang'an guan, Qiandongnan zhou dang'an guan, and Tianzhu xian dang'an guan (eds.). *Guizhou Qingshuijiang wenshu, Cengon juan* [Qingshui River manuscripts, Cengong County volume]. vol. 1 (1–5). Guiyang: Guizhou renmin chubanshe, 2018.

[L.9] Guizhou sheng dang'an guan, Qiandongnan zhou dang'an guan, and Tianzhu xian dang'an guan. (eds.). 2018. *Guizhou Qingshuijiang wenshu, Tianzhu juan* [Qingshui River manuscripts, Tianzhu County volume], vol. 1 (1–5). Guiyang: Guizhou renmin chubanshe.

Glossary

Terms

baiqi 白契
baozhang 保長
baozhong 保中
biyin 筆銀
bizi 筆資
bude yiyan 不得異言
chaobai 抄白
cheng'an 成案
chengli 成立
chigeshi 吃割食
chiyin 喫艮（銀）
chizhong 吃中
chong 沖
cun 村
Da Qing Huidian《大清會典》
daibi 代筆
daibiren 代筆人
daishu 代書
daishu xiansheng 代書先生
daixie minjian qizi 代寫民間契字
dian 典
dianqi 典契
dibao 地保
dongdao 東道
dongshi 董事
Dongwanggong 東王公
Duli cunyi《讀例存疑》

J. Qu, *Social Order through Contracts*,
https://doi.org/10.1007/978-981-33-4947-6

duzhong 度中
fenshan hetong 分山合同
guandaishu 官代書
guanfa qigao 官發契稿
guanqi 官契
guoge 過割
hanzhong 喊中
hetong 合同
Hetong wenyue tengqibu《合同文約謄契簿》
hongqi 紅契
huaya 花押
huazi qian 畫字錢
huoqi 活契
huotao 活套
huozhi 活質
jianliyin 見禮銀
jianzhong 見中
jiaqi 假契
jieyue 借約
jikai 計開
jingxi zizhi 敬惜字紙
jiuqi 舊契
juemai 絶賣
kongkou wupin, lizi weizheng 恐口無憑，立字為證
kunyin 梱艮（銀）
lairen 來人
li 例
li dian zhongdi hetong zai shamu zi 立佃種地合同栽杉木字
li xx zi 立某某字
li zhongdi fenhetong zai shamu zi 立種地分合同栽杉木字
lianqi 連契
lijiang 理講
ling 嶺
liqi 立契
liqiren 立契人
lishi 理師
liyue 立約
lizhong 理中
lü 律
maidiquan 買地券
maiqi 賣契
mao'er qi 貓兒契
mianzi 面子
Miao Jiang 苗疆
Muling xuzhi《牧令須知》

ping 憑
pingshenme 憑什麼
pingzhong 憑中
pingzhongren 憑中人
qi 契
qian 錢
qianshou qi 前手契
qimai 契買/契賣
qinbi 親筆
qindaibi 親代筆
qing zhong chumai yu 請中出賣與
qing zhong wendao 請中問到
qingyuan 情願
qingzhong zi 請中字
qinshen 親身
Qiquan huishi 《契券匯式》
qizhi 契紙
qizhi qigen zhifa 契紙、契根之法
quanzhong 勸中
queli 確立
ren 人
rihou qingchu, yiwei guzhi 日後清出，以為故紙
ruyou yiyan 如有異言
sanmian 三面
shangshou qi 上手契
shanke 山客
shengyuan 生員
shi 師
shouyin 受艮（銀）
shuike 水客
shuiqi 稅契
shuohe zhongren 説合中人
Shuqi bianmeng 《書契便蒙》
Shuqi chengshi 《書契程式》
siyue 私約
sizhi 四至
songshi 訟師
tianli 天理
tiaoyue 條約
tusi 土司
Wanbao quanshu 《萬寶全書》
Wanshi buqiuren 《萬事不求人》
weiyin wuyin yongdu 為因無銀用度
weishenme 為什麼
weiyue 違約

wen 文
wenqi 文契
wenyue 文約
xiangbao 鄉保
xiejia 歇家
Xieqi toushui zhangcheng "寫契投稅章程"
Xieyue buqiuren《寫約不求人》
Xiwangmu 西王母
ya 押
yafada 押發達
yangwen 樣文
yazhong 牙中
ye 業
yi mai yi liao 一買一了
yikou daibi 依口代筆
yin 銀
yinqi (Chap. 2) 印契
yinqi (Chap. 6) 陰契
yiyan daibi 依言代筆
yizhongkou 依眾口
yongyuan cunzhao 永遠存照
yuan 元
yuanqi 原契
yuanzhong 原中
yue 約
zaichang 在場
zaisi 在司
zeli 則例
zhai 寨
zhangguan si 長官司
zhaotie 找貼
zhongbaoren 中保人
zhongbi 中筆
zhongjianren 中見人
zhongren 中人
zhongzi 中資
zhujia 主家
zi 字
zi (Chap. 5) 自
ziji 自己
ziji qingyuan 自己情願
zilaigao 自來稿
ziyuan 自願
ziyue 字約

Personal Names

Baodui 保堆
Bingzhi 秉智
Chaogan 朝干
Chaoji 朝吉
Chen Jianfang 陳見芳
Chen Jianwen 陳見文
Chen Laowun 陳老五
Chen Mu'an 陳木庵
Chen Qingyun 陳慶雲
Chen Shimin 陳士敏
Chen Yutian 陳玉田
Chen Zongyu 陳宗虞
Dazhen 大振
Defang 德芳
Dehong 德宏
Dengxiang 登相
Fachun 發春
Fan Guofan 范國璠
Fan Guorui 范國瑞
Fan Shaozhao 范紹昭
Fan Xianlin 范獻琳
Fan Xingxiu 范興秀
Fan Xishou 范錫壽
Fan Zhiwei 范之偉
Fanbao 番保
Gangyi 剛毅
Guang… 廣□
Guangben 光本
Guangdian 光典
Guangwen 光文
Guangxian 光限
Guangxiu 光秀
Guangyu 光禹
Guangzhao 光照
Guangzhen 廣珍
Guangzong 光宗
Guangzu 光祖
Hailong 海瓏
Haiwen 海聞
Haizhi 海治
Huang Futing 黃輔庭
Jiang Baofu 姜保富

Jiang Baowu 姜包五
Jiang Benqing 姜本清
Jiang Benshen 姜本伸
Jiang Benwang 姜本旺
Jiang Birong 姜必榮
Jiang Bizhou 姜弼周
Jiang Chaojin 姜朝瑾
Jiang Chaowang 姜朝望
Jiang Chaoxiang 姜朝相
Jiang Chongying 姜重英
Jiang Dengcheng 姜登程
Jiang Dengpan 姜登泮
Jiang Deyu 姜得宇
Jiang Dezhong 姜得中
Jiang Faxiang 姜發祥
Jiang Fengyi 姜鳳儀
Jiang Guang… 姜光口
Jiang Guangxiu 姜光秀
Jiang Guangyu 姜光裕
Jiang Guangzong 姜光宗
Jiang Guanlüe 姜觀略
Jiang Haishun 姜海順
Jiang Han 姜翰
Jiang Hongwen 姜弘文
Jiang Huaiyi 姜懷義
Jiang Huanqing 姜煥卿
Jiang Jizhao 姜吉兆
Jiang Kaiming 姜開明
Jiang Kairang 姜開讓
Jiang Kaiyuan 姜開元
Jiang Laotuan 姜老團
Jiang Peigang 姜培剛
Jiang Qi 姜琦
Jiang Qihu 姜啓湖
Jiang Qiwei (Chap. 2) 姜啓渭
Jiang Qiwei (Chap. 4 Sect. 3) 姜啓謂
Jiang Qiwei (Chap. 4 Sect. 4) 姜起渭
Jiang Qixiang 姜啓相
Jiang Shaoya 姜紹牙
Jiang Shaoyu 姜紹虞
Jiang Shi'an 姜世安
Jiang Shichang 姜世昌
Jiang Shichen 姜世臣
Jiang Shifa 姜世法
Jiang Shihe 姜世和

Jiang Shilian (Chap. 3) 姜世連
Jiang Shilian (Chap. 4) 姜世璉
Jiang Shiyuan 姜世元
Jiang Tianxiang 姜天相
Jiang Tingjun 姜廷俊
Jiang Tingwei 姜廷偉
Jiang Tingzhou 姜廷周
Jiang Tingzuo 姜廷佐
Jiang Tongxue 姜通騰
Jiang Wei 姜偉
Jiang Xiangrong 姜相榮
Jiang Xianzong 姜先宗
Jiang Xianzu 姜顯祖
Jiang Xihao 姜熙豪
Jiang Xing 姜興
Jiang Xingyu 姜興宇
Jiang Xueguang 姜學廣
Jiang Yingbao 姜應保
Jiang Yingguang 姜映光
Jiang Yinghui 姜映輝
Jiang Yingyou 姜映友
Jiang Yongfa 姜永發
Jiang Youwen 姜有文
Jiang Yuanze 姜元澤
Jiang Yunca 姜雲彩
Jiang Zhihao 姜之豪
Jiang Zhilian 姜之璉
Jiang Zhiyuan 姜志遠
Jiang Zhongying 姜鍾英
Jiang Zhoulong 姜周隆
Jiang Zongyou 姜宗友
Jiaosheng 絞生
Jingui 金桂
Kaixiang 開相
Keqing 克清
Laolan 老蘭
Laosong 老宋
Laoyou 老有
Laozhu 老主
Li Tiancai 李天才
Liu Chaoyuan 劉朝元
Long Xiancai 龍現彩
Lu Honggui 陸宏貴
Luo Laolong 羅老龍
Luo Tiancai 羅天才

Ma Fuxiang 馬輔鄉
Peng Taihe 彭太和
Qican 啟璨
Qihua 啓華
Qiming 啓明
Ren De 任德
Shaolun 紹倫
Shaoqi 紹齊
Shaoxiang 紹襄
Shaoya 紹牙
Shen Jiaben 沈家本
Shihong 世洪
Shilian 世連
Shu Shaoji 舒紹緝
Sun Zhankui 孫占魁
Teng Haiming 滕海明
Teng Jiaxing 滕家興
Teng Wanming 滕萬明
Tianxiang 天相
Wang Chengbang 王承邦
Wang Shikui 王士魁
Wang Weicheng 王維城
Weibang 為邦
Weichen 為臣
Weiguang 為光
Weiming 為明
Weixian 為先
Wenguang 文光
Wenhao 文浩
Xiangkai 相開
Xiangkui 相魁
Xiangrong 相榮
Xingjue 興爵
Xingui 辛貴
Xinlong 辛龍
Xuanshu 宣澍
Xuezheng 學政
Yang Cheng 楊成
Yang Guang… 楊光□
Yang Guanglin 楊光林
Yang Kuai 楊快
Yang Qinchi 楊芹池
Yang Zhiyi 楊枝一
Yanhua 延華
Yao Baiwan 姚百萬

Yao Jizhou 姚繼周
Yao Tingbiao 姚廷標
Yao Yukui 姚玉魁
Yonglong 永隆
Yongwang 永旺
Yongxiang 永祥
Zeng Guangsheng 曾光生
Zhang Guofu 張國富
Zhang Guoyao 張國要
Zhang Youyuan 張有元
Zhi'an 志安
Zhongying 鍾英
Zhoucai 周才
Zhu Dacai 朱達材
Zhu Daquan 朱達泉
Zongkui 宗揆
Zuomei 作梅

Place Names

Benchu 坌處
Chongjiukuang 沖九匡
Chongjiwang 沖基王
Congjiebang 從皆榜
Dangyi 黨宜
Gangwan 岡晚
Jiachi 加池（嘉池）
Jiashitang (Chap. 2) 加十塘
Jiashitang (Chap. 3) 加什塘
Jingdu 井都
Jiuyou 九佑
Longli 龍裡
Miaosui 苗綏
Peiliang 培亮
Ping'ao 平鼇
Randi 冉抵
Sanjiang 三江
Shao'ai 韶靄
Sifang 四方
Tuge 凸格
Wuxia 烏下
Yanduiyue 眼對約
Yangbao 羊豹

Yanwan 岩灣
Yuangupo 圓古坡
Yuhe 裕和
Zhanghua 張化
Zhongyang 中仰

The manufacturer's authorised representative in the EU is Springer Nature Customer Service Centre GmbH, Europaplatz 3, 69115 Heidelberg, Germany. If you have any concerns regarding our products, please contact ProductSafety@springernature.com

Printed and bound by CPI Group (UK) Ltd, Croydon, CR0 4YY
30/09/2026
02225296-0012